SAMS
Teach Yourself

PHP, MySQL™
and Apache

in 24 Hours

Julie C. Meloni

SAMS   *201 West 103rd St., Indianapolis, Indiana, 46290 USA*

Sams Teach Yourself PHP, MySQL™ and Apache in 24 Hours

Copyright © 2003 by Sams Publishing

International Standard Book Number: 0-6723-2489-X

Library of Congress Catalog Card Number: 2002115016

Printed in the United States of America

First Printing: December 2002

05   04   03   02   4   3   2

Trademarks

Warning and Disclaimer

ACQUISITIONS EDITOR
Shelley Johnston

DEVELOPMENT EDITOR
Chris Newman

MANAGING EDITOR
Charlotte Clapp

PROJECT EDITOR
Tricia Liebig

COPY EDITORS
Chip Gardner
Mike Henry
Chuck Hutchinson
Matt Wynalda

INDEXER
Sharon Shock

PROOFREADER
Wendy Ott

TECHNICAL EDITOR
Chris Newman

TEAM COORDINATOR
Lynne Williams

MULTIMEDIA DEVELOPER
Dan Scherf

INTERIOR DESIGNER
Gary Adair

COVER DESIGNER
Alan Clements

PAGE LAYOUT
Point 'n Click Publishing, LLC.

GRAPHICS
Tammy Graham

Contents at a Glance

Introduction   1

Part I Getting Up and Running   5

Hour 1   Installing and Configuring MySQL   7

2   Installing and Configuring Apache   25

3   Installing and Configuring PHP   47

Part II Basic Language Elements   63

Hour 4   The Building Blocks of PHP   65

5   Flow Control Functions in PHP   85

6   Working with Functions   107

7   Learning Basic SQL Commands   131

8   Interacting with MySQL Using PHP   157

Part III Getting Involved with the Code   169

Hour 9   Working with Forms   171

10   Working with Files   193

11   Working with Dates and Times   217

12   Creating a Simple Calendar   237

13   Working with Strings   253

14   Creating a Simple Discussion Forum   285

15   Restricting Access to Your Applications   311

16   Working with User Sessions   333

17   Logging and Monitoring Server Activity   343

Part IV Simple Projects   359

Hour 18   Managing a Simple Mailing List   361

19   Creating an Online Address Book   373

20   Creating an Online Storefront   397

21   Creating a Shopping Cart Mechanism   409

Part V Administration and Fine-Tuning   423

Hour 22   Apache Performance Tuning and Virtual Hosting   425

   23   Setting Up a Secure Web Server   441

   24   Optimizing and Tuning MySQL   455

      Index   471

Contents

Introduction   **1**

Who Should Read This Book? 1

How This Book Is Organized 1

Conventions Used in This Book 3

Part I Getting Up and Running   **5**

Hour 1 Installing and Configuring MySQL   **7**

How to Get MySQL 7

Installing MySQL on Linux/Unix 8

Installing MySQL on Windows 9

Troubleshooting Your Installation 14

Basic Security Guidelines 15

    Starting MySQL 15

    Securing Your MySQL Connection 16

Introducing the MySQL Privilege System 17

    The Two-Step Authentication Process 17

Working with User Privileges 18

    Adding Users 19

    Removing Privileges 21

Summary 21

Q&A 22

Workshop 22

    Quiz 22

    Answers 22

    Activities 23

Hour 2 Installing and Configuring Apache   **25**

Choosing the Appropriate Installation Method 25

    Building from Source 26

    Installing a Binary 26

Installing Apache on Linux/Unix 26

    Downloading the Apache Source Code 27

    Uncompressing the Source Code 27

    Preparing to Build Apache 27

    Building and Installing Apache 29

Installing Apache on Windows 29

Apache Configuration File Structure 32

    Directives 32

    Containers 34

Conditional Evaluation 35

ServerRoot 36

Per-Directory Configuration Files 36

Apache Log Files 37

access_log 37

error_log 38

Additional Files 38

Apache-Related Commands 38

Apache Server Binary 38

Apache Control Script 40

Starting Apache for the First Time 40

Check Your Configuration File 40

Starting Apache 41

Troubleshooting 42

Already an Existing Web Server 42

No Permission to Bind to Port 42

Access Denied 43

Wrong Group Settings 43

Summary 43

Q&A 43

Workshop 44

Quiz 44

Answers 44

Activities 45

HOUR 3 Installing and Configuring PHP   **47**

Building PHP on Linux/Unix with Apache 47

Additional Configuration Options 49

Integrating PHP with Apache on Linux/Unix 50

Installing PHP Files on Windows 51

Integrating PHP with Apache on Windows 51

php.ini Basics 52

Testing Your Installation 53

Getting Installation Help 54

The Basics of PHP Scripts 55

Beginning and Ending a Block of PHP Statements 56

The print() Function 58

Combining HTML and PHP 58

Adding Comments to PHP Code 60

Summary 60

Q&A 61

Workshop 61

Quiz 61

Answers 62

Activities 62

Part II Basic Language Elements   63

HOUR 4 The Building Blocks of PHP   65

Variables 66

Data Types 67

Changing Type with settype() 69

Changing Type by Casting 71

Why Test Type? 72

Operators and Expressions 73

The Assignment Operator 74

Arithmetic Operators 74

The Concatenation Operator 74

Combined Assignment Operators 75

Automatically Incrementing and Decrementing an Integer Variable 75

Comparison Operators 77

Creating More Complex Test Expressions with the Logical Operators 77

Operator Precedence 78

Constants 80

Predefined Constants 81

Summary 81

Q&A 82

Workshop 82

Quiz 82

Answers 83

Activities 83

HOUR 5 Flow Control Functions in PHP   85

Switching Flow 86

The if Statement 86

Using the else Clause with the if Statement 87

Using the elseif Clause with the if Statement 88

The switch Statement 89

Using the ? Operator 91

Loops 92

The while Statement 92

The do...while Statement 93

The for Statement 95

Breaking Out of Loops with the break Statement 96

Skipping an Iteration with the continue Statement 98

Nesting Loops 100

Code Blocks and Browser Output 101

Summary 103

Q&A 104

Workshop 104

    Quiz 104

    Answers 105

    Activity 105

HOUR 6 Working with Functions   **107**

What Is a Function? 108

Calling Functions 108

Defining a Function 110

Returning Values from User-Defined Functions 112

Dynamic Function Calls 113

Variable Scope 114

    Accessing Variables with the global Statement 115

Saving State Between Function Calls with the static Statement 118

More About Arguments 120

    Setting Default Values for Arguments 120

    Passing Variable References to Functions 122

Creating Anonymous Functions 124

Testing for the Existence of a Function 125

Summary 127

Q&A 128

Workshop 128

    Quiz 128

    Answers 129

    Activity 129

HOUR 7 Learning Basic SQL Commands   **131**

Learning the MySQL Data Types 132

    Numeric Data Types 132

    Date and Time Types 133

    String Types 134

Learning the Table Creation Syntax 135

Using the INSERT Command 136

    A Closer Look at INSERT 137

Using the SELECT Command 138

    Ordering SELECT Results 139

    Limiting Your Results 140

Using WHERE in Your Queries 141

    Using Operators in WHERE Clauses 142

    String Comparison Using LIKE 143

Selecting from Multiple Tables 143

Using JOIN 145

Using the UPDATE Command to Modify Records 148

 Conditional UPDATEs 149

 Using Existing Column Values with UPDATE 150

Using the REPLACE Command 150

Using the DELETE Command 151

 Conditional DELETE 152

Summary 153

Q&A 154

Workshop 155

 Quiz 155

 Answers 155

 Activity 155

HOUR 8 Interacting with MySQL Using PHP   157

Connecting to MySQL with PHP 157

 Using mysql_connect() 158

 Executing Queries 159

 Retrieving Error Messages 161

Working with MySQL Data 161

 Inserting Data with PHP 162

 Retrieving Data with PHP 165

 Additional MySQL Functions in PHP 167

Summary 167

Workshop 168

 Quiz 168

 Answers 168

 Activity 168

Part III Getting Involved with the Code   169

HOUR 9 Working with Forms   171

Predefined Variables 172

Creating a Simple Input Form 174

Accessing Form Input with User-Defined Arrays 175

Combining HTML and PHP Code on a Single Page 178

Using Hidden Fields to Save State 180

Redirecting the User 182

Sending Mail on Form Submission 183

 System Configuration for the mail() Function 184

Creating the Form 185

Creating the Script to Send the Mail 186

Working with File Uploads 188
    Creating the File Upload Form 188
    Creating the File Upload Script 189
Summary 191
Workshop 192
    Quiz 192
    Answers 192
    Activities 192

Hour 10 Working with Files   **193**

Including Files with include() 193
    Returning a Value from an Included Document 195
    Using include() Within Control Structures 196
include_once() 197
    The include_path Directive 198
Testing Files 198
    Checking for Existence with file_exists() 198
    A File or a Directory? 199
    Checking the Status of a File 199
    Determining File Size with filesize() 199
    Getting Date Information About a File 200
    Creating a Function That Performs Multiple File Tests 200
Creating and Deleting Files 202
Opening a File for Writing, Reading, or Appending 203
Reading from Files 204
    Reading Lines from a File with fgets() and feof() 204
    Reading Arbitrary Amounts of Data from a File with fread() 205
    Reading Characters from a File with fgetc() 207
Writing or Appending to a File 208
    Writing to a File with fwrite() or fputs() 209
    Locking Files with flock() 210
Working with Directories 211
    Creating Directories with mkdir() 211
    Removing a Directory with rmdir() 211
    Opening a Directory for Reading with opendir() 211
    Reading the Contents of a Directory with readdir() 212
Summary 214
Q&A 214
Workshop 214
    Quiz 214
    Answers 215
    Activities 215

HOUR 11 Working with Dates and Times   **217**

Using Date and Time Functions in PHP 218

Getting the Date with time() 218

Converting a Timestamp with getdate() 218

Converting a Timestamp with date() 220

Creating Timestamps with mktime() 222

Testing a Date with checkdate() 223

Using Date and Time Functions in MySQL 223

Working with Days 223

Working with Months and Years 226

Working with Weeks 227

Working with Hours, Minutes, and Seconds 228

Formatting Dates and Times with MySQL 229

Performing Date Arithmetic with MySQL 232

Special Functions and Conversion Features 234

Summary 235

Workshop 236

Quiz 236

Answers 236

Activity 236

HOUR 12 Creating a Simple Calendar   **237**

Building a Simple Display Calendar 237

Checking User Input 238

Building the HTML Form 239

Creating the Calendar Table 241

Creating a Calendar library 244

Summary 250

Q&A 251

Workshop 251

Quiz 251

Answers 251

Activity 251

HOUR 13 Working with Strings   **253**

Formatting Strings with PHP 254

Working with printf() 254

Specifying a Field Width 257

Argument Swapping 260

Storing a Formatted String 261

Investigating Strings in PHP 262

A Note About Indexing Strings 262

Finding the Length of a String with strlen() 262

Finding a Substring Within a String with strstr() 263

Finding the Position of a Substring with strpos() 263
Extracting Part of a String with substr() 264
Tokenizing a String with strtok() 264
Manipulating Strings with PHP 266
Cleaning Up a String with trim() and strip_tags() 266
Replacing a Portion of a String Using substr_replace() 267
Replacing Substrings Using str_replace 268
Converting Case 268
Wrapping Text with wordwrap() and nl2br() 269
Breaking Strings into Arrays with explode() 271
Frequently Used String Functions in MySQL 271
Length and Concatenation Functions 271
Trimming and Padding Functions 274
Location and Position Functions 276
Substring Functions 277
String Modification Functions 277
Obscure String Functions 279
Summary 281
Q&A 282
Workshop 283
Quiz 283
Answers 284
Activities 284

Hour 14 Creating a Simple Discussion Forum   285

Types of Table Relationships 286
One-to-One Relationships 286
One-to-Many Relationships 287
Many-to-Many Relationships 288
Understanding Normalization 290
Problems with the Flat Table 290
First Normal Form 291
Second Normal Form 291
Third Normal Form 292
Following the Design Process 293
Creating a Discussion Forum 294
Designing the Database Tables 294
Creating the Input Forms and Scripts 295
Displaying the Topic List 298
Displaying the Posts in a Topic 302
Adding Posts to a Topic 305
Summary 308

Q&A 309

Workshop 309

    Quiz 309

    Answers 309

    Activity 309

HOUR 15 Restricting Access to Your Applications   **311**

Authentication Overview 311

    Client Authentication 312

Apache Authentication Module Functionality 313

    File-Based Authentication 315

    Database File-Based Access Control 316

Using Apache for Access Control 318

    Implementing Access Rules 318

    Evaluating Access Rules 319

Combining Apache Access Methods 320

Limiting Access Based on HTTP Methods 321

Introducing Cookies 322

    The Anatomy of a Cookie 322

Setting a Cookie with PHP 323

    Deleting a Cookie 325

Restricting Access Based on Cookie Values 325

    Creating the Authorized Users Table 325

    Creating the Login Form and Script 326

    Testing for the auth Cookie 329

Summary 330

Q&A 331

Workshop 331

    Quiz 331

    Answers 332

    Activity 332

HOUR 16 Working with User Sessions   **333**

Session Function Overview 334

Starting a Session 334

Working with Session Variables 335

Passing Session IDs in the Query String 340

Destroying Sessions and Unsetting Variables 340

Summary 341

Q&A 342

Workshop 342

    Quiz 342

    Answers 342

    Activity 342

HOUR 17 Logging and Monitoring Server Activity   **343**

Standard Apache Access Logging 343
   Deciding What to Log 344
   Logging Accesses to Files 348
   Logging Accesses to a Program 348
Standard Apache Error Logging 349
   Logging Errors to a File 349
   Logging Errors to a Program 350
   The syslog Daemon Argument 350
   The LogLevel Directive 350
Managing Apache Logs 351
   Resolving Hostnames 351
   Log Rotation 351
   Merging and Splitting Logs 352
   Log Analysis 353
   Monitoring Error Logs 353
Logging Custom Information to a Database 353
   Creating the Database Table 354
   Creating the PHP Code Snippet 354
   Creating Sample Reports 355
Summary 357
Q&A 358
Workshop 358
   Quiz 358
   Answers 358

Part IV Simple Projects   **359**

HOUR 18 Managing a Simple Mailing List   **361**

Developing the Subscription Mechanism 362
   Creating the subscribers Table 362
   Creating the Subscription Form 362
Developing the Mailing Mechanism 368
Summary 371
Q&A 371
Workshop 371
   Quiz 371
   Answers 371

HOUR 19 Creating an Online Address Book   **373**

Planning and Creating the Database Tables 373
Creating a Menu 376
Creating the Record Addition Mechanism 377

Viewing Records 382

Creating the Record Deletion Mechanism 387

Adding Subentries to a Record 389

Summary 395

Workshop 395

    Quiz 395

    Answers 396

    Activities 396

HOUR 20 Creating an Online Storefront   **397**

Planning and Creating the Database Tables 398

    Inserting Records into the store_categories Table 400

    Inserting Records into the store_items Table 400

    Inserting Records into the store_item_size Table 401

    Inserting Records into the store_item_color Table 401

Displaying Categories of Items 402

Displaying Items 405

Summary 408

Workshop 408

    Quiz 408

    Answers 408

HOUR 21 Creating a Shopping Cart Mechanism   **409**

Planning and Creating the Database Tables 410

Integrating the Cart with Your Storefront 412

    Adding Items to Your Cart 414

    Viewing the Cart 416

    Removing Items from Your Cart 419

Payment Methods and the Checkout Sequence 420

    Creating the Checkout Form 420

    Performing the Checkout Actions 421

Summary 422

Workshop 422

    Quiz 422

    Answers 422

Part V Administration and Fine-Tuning   **423**

HOUR 22 Apache Performance Tuning and Virtual Hosting   **425**

Scalability Issues 426

    Operating System Limits 426

    Performance-Related Apache Settings 427

Load Testing with ApacheBench 429

Proactive Performance Tuning 431

Mapping Files to Memory 431
Distributing the Load 431
Caching 432
Reduce Transmitted Data 432
Network Settings 432
Preventing Abuse 433
Robots 433
Implementing Virtual Hosting 434
IP-Based Virtual Hosting 434
Name-Based Virtual Hosts 435
Mass Virtual Hosting 437
Summary 438
Q&A 439
Quiz 440
Answers 440

HOUR 23 Setting Up a Secure Web Server   441

The Need for Security 441
Confidentiality 442
Integrity 442
Authentication 442
The SSL Protocol 442
Addressing the Need for Confidentiality 443
Addressing the Need for Integrity 444
Addressing the Need for Authentication 445
Installing SSL 447
OpenSSL 447
mod_ssl 448
Managing Certificates 449
Creating a Key Pair 449
Creating a Certificate Signing Request 450
Creating a Self-Signed Certificate 451
SSL Configuration 452
Starting the Server 452
Summary 453
Q&A 453
Quiz 454
Answers 454

HOUR 24 Optimizing and Tuning MySQL   455

Building an Optimized Platform 456
Using the benchmark() Function 456

MySQL Startup Options 457
    Key Startup Parameters 458
Optimizing Your Table Structure 459
Optimizing Your Queries 460
Using the FLUSH Command 461
Using the SHOW Command 462
    Retrieving Information about Databases and Tables 463
    Retrieving Table Structure Information 464
    Retrieving System Status 466
Summary 468
Q&A 468
Workshop 469
    Quiz 469
    Answers 469
    Activities 469

Index   471

Lead Author

Julie C. Meloni is the technical director for i2i Interactive (www.i2ii.com), a multimedia company located in Los Altos, California. She's been developing Web-based applications since the Web first saw the light of day and remembers the excitement surrounding the first GUI Web browser. She has authored several books and articles on Web-based programming languages and database topics, and you can find translations of her work in several languages, including Chinese, Italian, Portuguese, Polish, and even Serbian!

Contributing Authors

Daniel López Ridruejo is a senior developer with Covalent Technologies, Inc., which provides Apache software, support, and services for the enterprise. He is the author of several popular Apache and Linux guides and of Comanche, a GUI configuration tool for Apache. Daniel is a regular speaker at open source conferences such as LinuxWorld, ApacheCon, and the O'Reilly Open Source Convention. He holds a Master of Science degree in telecommunications from the Escuela Superior de Ingenieros de Sevilla and Danmarks Tekniske Universitet. Daniel is a member of the Apache Software Foundation.

Matt Zandstra (matt@corrosive.co.uk) is a technical consultant. With his business partner, Max Guglielmino, he runs Corrosive Web Design (http://www.corrosive.co.uk), a company specializing in information design, usablity, and the creation of dynamic environments. Before this book took over his life once again, Matt was writing an XML/ Java-based scripting language and interpreter for extracting content from Web pages. He is currently keen on design patterns, unit tests, extreme programming, and space operas. Matt is fatter than he was, but is still an urban cyclist. He says he is working on a novel, but he has been saying that for a long time. He lives by the sea in Brighton, Great Britain, with his partner, Louise McDougall, and their daughter, Holly.

Acknowledgments

The Apache Foundation, the PHP Group, and MySQL AB deserve much more recognition than they ever get for creating these super products that drive a great portion of the Web.

Daniel Lopez (author of *Sams Teach Yourself Apache 2 in 24 Hours*) and Matt Zandstra (author of *Sams Teach Yourself PHP in 24 Hours*) wrote super books, which form a significant portion of this book. Obviously, this book would not exist without them!

Great thanks especially to all the editors and layout folks at Sams who were involved with this book, for their hard work in seeing this through!

Thanks as always to everyone at i2i Interactive for their never-ending support and encouragement.

We Want to Hear from You!

As the reader of this book, *you* are our most important critic and commentator. We value your opinion and want to know what we're doing right, what we could do better, what areas you'd like to see us publish in, and any other words of wisdom you're willing to pass our way.

You can email or write me directly to let me know what you did or didn't like about this book—as well as what we can do to make our books stronger.

Please note that I cannot help you with technical problems related to the topic of this book, and that due to the high volume of mail I receive, I might not be able to reply to every message.

When you write, please be sure to include this book's title and author as well as your name and phone number or email address. I will carefully review your comments and share them with the author and editors who worked on the book.

Email: opensource@samspublishing.com

Mail: Mark Taber
            Associate Publisher
            Sams Publishing
            201 West 103rd Street
            Indianapolis, IN 46290 USA

Reader Services

For more information about this book or others from Sams Publishing, visit our Web site at www.samspublishing.com. Type the ISBN (excluding hyphens) or the title of the book in the Search box to find the book you're looking for.

Introduction

Welcome to *Sams Teach Yourself PHP, MySQL, and Apache in 24 Hours*! This book combines the hours found in *Sams Teach Yourself PHP in 24 Hours*, *Sams Teach Yourself MySQL in 24 Hours,* and *Sams Teach Yourself Apache in 24 Hours*, to provide you with a solid and painless introduction to the world of developing Web-based applications using these three technologies.

Through a series of 24 easy hours, you'll learn the basics of programming in PHP, the methods for using and administering the MySQL relational database system, and the concepts necessary for configuring and managing Apache. The overall goal of the book is to provide you with the foundation you need to understand how seamlessly these technologies integrate with one another, and to give you practical knowledge of how to integrate them.

Who Should Read This Book?

This book is geared toward individuals who possess a general understanding of the concepts of working in a Web-based development environment, be it Linux/Unix or Windows. Installation and configuration lessons assume that you have familiarity with your operating system and the basic methods of building (on Linux/Unix systems) or installing (on Windows systems) software.

The lessons that delve into programming with PHP assume no previous knowledge of the language, but if you have experience with other programming languages such as C or Perl, you will find the going much easier. Similarly, if you have worked with other databases before, such as Oracle or Microsoft SQL Server, you will have a good foundation for working through the MySQL-related lessons.

The only real requirement is that you understand static Web content creation with HTML. If you are just starting out in the world of Web development, you will still be able to use this book, though you should consider working through an HTML tutorial. If you are comfortable creating basic documents and can build a basic HTML table, you will be fine.

How This Book Is Organized

This book is divided into five parts, corresponding to particular topics. The lessons within each part are designed to be read one right after another, with each lesson essentially building on the information found in those before it:

- Part I, "Getting Up and Running," will walk you through the installation and configuration of PHP, MySLQ, and Apache. You'll need to complete the lessons in Part I before moving on to the remaining lessons, unless you already have access to a working installation of these technologies. Even if you don't need to install and configure PHP, MySQL, and Apache in your environment, you should still skim these lessons so that you understand the basics.

- Part II, "Basic Language Elements," is predominantly devoted to teaching you the basics of the PHP language, and will get you in the habit of writing code, uploading it to your server, and testing the results. One of the lessons offers a basic SQL primer, and this part wraps up with an hour devoted to the integration of PHP and MySQL.

- Part III, "Getting Involved with the Code," consists of lessons that cover intermediate-level application development topics, including working with forms and files, access restriction, and other small projects designed to introduce a specific concept.

- Part IV, "Simple Projects," contains lessons devoted to performing a particular task. These lessons consist of projects that integrate all the knowledge you have gained so far, and walk you through the process of building and testing the elements you will create.

- Part V, "Administration and Fine-Tuning," is devoted to administering and tuning MySQL and Apache, and also includes information on virtual hosting and setting up a secure Web server.

If you find that you are already familiar with a topic, you can skip ahead to the next lesson. However, in some instances, lessons will refer to specific concepts learned in previous hours, so be aware that you may have to skim through a skipped lesson so that your development environment remains consistent with the book.

At the end of each hour, there are a few quiz questions that will test how well you've learned the material. Additional activities provide another way to apply the information learned in the lesson and guide you toward using this newfound knowledge in the next hour.

Conventions Used in This Book

This book uses different typefaces to differentiate between code and plain English and also to help you identify important concepts. Throughout the lessons, code, commands, and text you type or see onscreen appear in a `computer typeface`. New terms appear in *italics* at the point in the text where they are defined. Additionally, icons accompany special blocks of information:

 A Note presents an interesting piece of information related to the current topic.

 A Tip offers advice or teaches an easier method for performing a task.

 A Caution warns you about potential pitfalls and explains how to avoid them.

 A new term icon will appear next to text introducing terms to the reader for the first time.

PART I
Getting Up and Running

Hour

1   Installing and Configuring MySQL

2   Installing and Configuring Apache

3   Installing and Configuring PHP

HOUR 1

Installing and Configuring MySQL

Welcome to the first hour of *Sams Teach Yourself PHP, MySQL, and Apache in 24 Hours*. This is the first of three "installation" hours, in which you will learn how to set up your development environment. We'll tackle the MySQL installation first, because the PHP installation is much simpler when MySQL is already installed.

In this hour, you will learn

- How to install MySQL
- Basic security guidelines for running MySQL
- How to work with the MySQL user privilege system

How to Get MySQL

The method you'll use to get MySQL depends on which distribution you want. Methods range from downloading a large file (or several large files) to buying an off-the-shelf product.

- MySQL AB distributes the open source version of MySQL on their Web site: http://www.mysql.com/. There is no shrink-wrapped product; what you get is what you download from the site, which includes binary distributions for Windows and Linux/Unix, as well as RPMs and source distributions.

- NuSphere Corporation sells a variety of products including the NuSphere Technology Platform, which includes a version of MySQL with NuSphere-specific enhancements, such as the Gemini table type. NuSphere's products are available for purchase from their Web site: http://www.nusphere.com/.

- AbriaSoft distributes MySQL as part of their Merlin Server (a Web development platform), which is available for download and purchase at their Web site: http://www.abriasoft.com/.

- Linux distribution CDs usually contain some version or another of the open source MySQL distribution, although it's usually a bit out-of-date.

The installation instructions in this hour are based on the official MySQL-Pro 4.0 distributions from MySQL AB. The process of installing the 3.23 version of MySQL is virtually identical, but if you choose to install that version, read the instructions that ship with the distribution just to be on the safe side. Any functional differences between versions 3.23 and 4.0 will be noted in later hours.

Installing MySQL on Linux/Unix

The process of installing MySQL on Linux/Unix is straightforward, whether you use RPMs or install the binaries. If you choose to install from RPMs, there are several that make up a full distribution. For a minimal installation you need

- `MySQL-VERSION.i386.rpm`—The MySQL server
- `MySQL-client-VERSION.i386.rpm`—The standard MySQL client programs

To perform the minimal installation, type the following at the prompt:

```
#> rpm -i MySQL-VERSION.i386.rpm MySQL-client-VERSION.i386.rpm
```

Replace VERSION in the filename with the actual version you downloaded. For example, the current MySQL-Pro 4.0 server RPM is called MySQL-4.0.4-0.i386.rpm.

Another painless installation method is to install MySQL from a binary distribution. This method requires gunzip and tar to uncompress and unpack the distribution and also requires the ability to create groups and users on the system. The first series of commands in the binary distribution installation process has you adding a group and a user and unpacking the distribution, as follows:

```
#> groupadd mysql
#> useradd -g mysql mysql
#> cd /usr/local
#> gunzip < /path/to/mysql-VERSION-OS.tar.gz | tar xvf -
```

Next, the instructions tell you to create a link with a shorter name:

```
#> ln -s mysql-VERSION-OS mysql
#> cd mysql
```

Once unpacked, the README and INSTALL files will walk you through the remainder of the installation process for the version of MySQL you've chosen. In general, the following series of commands will be used:

```
#> scripts/mysql_install_db
#> chown -R root  /usr/local/mysql
#> chown -R mysql /usr/local/mysql/data
#> chgrp -R mysql /usr/local/mysql
#> chown -R root /usr/local/mysql/bin
```

You're now ready to start the MySQL server.

Installing MySQL on Windows

The MySQL installation process on Windows is also quite simple—the developers from MySQL AB have packaged up everything you need in one zip file with a setup program! Once you download the zip file, extract its contents into a temporary directory and run the setup.exe application. After the setup.exe application installs the MySQL server and client programs, you're ready to start the MySQL server.

The following steps detail the installation of MySQL 4.0 from MySQL AB on Windows, and show you what you can expect if you install MySQL in a Windows 95/98/NT/2000/XP environment for testing and development. Many users install MySQL on personal Windows machines, to get a feel for working with the database before deploying MySQL in a production environment.

1. Visit the MySQL-Pro 4.0 download page at
   http://www.mysql.com/downloads/mysql-pro-4.0.html and find the Windows
   section. You want to download the file under the "Installation files (zip)" heading
   rather than the one under the "Cygwin downloads (tar.bz2)" heading.

If you have the tools and skills to compile your own Windows binary files, select the Cygwin source download and follow the instructions contained in the source distribution.

2. Clicking the Download link will take you to a page of mirror sites. Select the mirror site closest to you, and download the file. It is a large file, so you may be waiting awhile, depending on your connection speed.

3. Once the zip file is on your hard drive, extract its contents to a temporary directory.

4. From the temporary directory, find the setup.exe file and double-click it to start the installation. You will see the first screen of the installation wizard, as shown in Figure 1.1. Click Next to continue.

FIGURE 1.1

The first step of the MySQL installation wizard.

5. The second screen in the installation process contains valuable information regarding the installation location (see Figure 1.2). The default installation location is C:\mysql. If you plan to install MySQL in a different location, this screen shows you a few changes that you will have to make on your own. The information on this screen is also important for Windows NT users who wish to start MySQL as a service. Read the information and note anything relevant to your situation, then click Next to continue.

6. The third screen in the installation process has you select the installation location (see Figure 1.3). If you want to install MySQL in the default location, click Next to continue. Otherwise, click Browse and navigate to the location of your choice, then click Next to continue.

FIGURE 1.2

Step 2 of the MySQL installation wizard. Note any relevant information before continuing.

FIGURE 1.3

Step 3 of the MySQL installation wizard. Select an installation location.

7. The fourth screen asks you to select the installation method—Typical, Compact, or Custom (see Figure 1.4). The Custom option allows you to select elements of MySQL to install, such as documentation and help files. Select Typical as the installation method, and click Next to continue.

FIGURE 1.4

Step 4 of the MySQL installation wizard. Select an installation type.

8. The installation process will now take over and install files in their proper locations. When the process is finished, you will see a confirmation of completion, as in Figure 1.5. Click Finish to complete the setup process.

FIGURE 1.5

MySQL has been installed.

There are no fancy shortcuts installed in your Windows Start menu after an installation of MySQL from MySQL AB, so now you must start the process yourself. If you navigate to the MySQL applications directory (usually `C:\mysql\bin\` unless you changed your installation path), you will find numerous applications ready for action (see Figure 1.6).

FIGURE 1.6

A directory listing of MySQL applications.

The `winmysqladmin.exe` application is a great friend to Windows users who are just getting started with MySQL. If you double-click this file, it will start the MySQL server and place a stoplight icon in your taskbar.

When you start WinMySQLadmin for the first time, you will be prompted for a username and password (see Figure 1.7). The application will create the initial MySQL user account on a Windows system.

FIGURE **1.7**
Creating the initial MySQL account.

When you are finished creating the account, or whenever you right-click the stoplight icon in your taskbar, the graphical user interface will launch. This interface, shown in Figure 1.8, provides an easy way to maintain and monitor your new server.

FIGURE **1.8**
WinMySQLadmin started and ready for action.

WinMySQLadmin will automatically interpret environment information, such as IP address and machine name. The tabs across the top allow you to view system information and edit MySQL configuration options.

For example, if you select the Variables tab, as shown in Figure 1.9, you can also view server configuration information. This information is similar to the output of the MySQL SHOW VARIABLES command.

FIGURE 1.9

Server configuration
information.

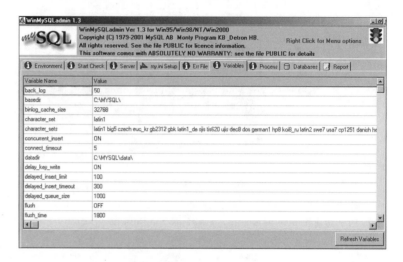

To shut down the MySQL server and/or the WinMySQLadmin tool, right-click again on
the stoplight icon in your taskbar and select the appropriate option (stop or start). As long
as the MySQL server is running, you can run additional applications through a console
window, such as the MySQL monitor.

Troubleshooting Your Installation

If you have any problems during the installation of MySQL, the first place you should
look is the "Problems and Common Errors" chapter of the MySQL manual, which is
located at http://www.mysql.com/doc/P/r/Problems.html.

The following are some common problems:

- On Linux/Unix, Incorrect permissions do not allow you to start the MySQL daemon. If this is the case, be sure you have changed owners and groups to match
  those indicated in the installation instructions.

- If you see the message "Access denied" when connecting to MySQL, be sure you
  are using the correct username and password.

- If you see the message "Can't connect to server", make sure the MySQL daemon
  is running.

- When defining tables, if you specify a length for a field whose type does not
  require a length, the table will not be created. For example, you should not specify
  a length when defining a field as TEXT (as opposed to CHAR or VARCHAR).

If you still have trouble after reading the manual, sending e-mail to the MySQL mailing list (see http://www.mysql.com/documentation/lists.html for more information) will likely produce results. You can also purchase support contracts from MySQL AB for a very low fee. If you have purchased a version of MySQL other than the one distributed by MySQL AB, you should turn to the documentation and support options for that product. The companies that sell other versions of MySQL usually have additional support contracts that you can purchase.

Basic Security Guidelines

Regardless of whether you are running MySQL on Windows or Linux/Unix, and no matter whether you administer your own server or use a system provided by your Internet service provider, every developer needs to understand basic security guidelines. If you are accessing MySQL through your Internet service provider, there are several aspects of server security that you, as a non-root user, should not be able to modify or circumvent. Unfortunately, many Internet service providers pay no mind to security guidelines, leaving their clients exposed—and for the most part, unaware of the risk.

Starting MySQL

Securing MySQL begins with the server startup procedure. If you are not the administrator of the server, you won't be able to change this, but you can certainly check it out and report vulnerabilities to your Internet service provider.

If your MySQL installation is on Linux/Unix, your primary concern should be the owner of the MySQL daemon—it should not be root. Running the daemon as a non-root user such as mysql or database will limit the ability of malicious individuals to gain access to the server and overwrite files.

You can verify the owner of the process using the ps (process status) command on your Linux/Unix system. The following output shows MySQL running as a non-root user (see the first entry on the second line):

```
#> ps auxw | grep mysqld
mysql 153  0.0  0.6 12068 2624 ? S Nov16  0:00
/usr/local/bin/mysql/bin/mysqld
--defaults-extra-file=/usr/local/bin/mysql/data/my.cnf
--basedir=/usr/local/bin/mysql --datadir=/usr/local/bin/mysql/data
--user=mysql --pid-file=/usr/local/bin/mysql/data/mike.pid --skip-locking
```

The following output shows MySQL running as the root user (see the first entry on the second line):

```
#> ps auxw | grep mysqld
root 21107  0.0  1.1 11176  1444  ?  S  Nov 27 0:00
/usr/local/mysql/bin/mysqld
--basedir=/usr/local/mysql --datadir=/usr/local/mysql/data --skip-locking
```

If you see that MySQL is running as root on your system, immediately contact your Internet service provider and complain. If you are the server administrator, you should start the MySQL process as a non-root user or specify the username in the startup command line:

```
mysqld --user=non_root_user_name
```

For example, if you want to run MySQL as user mysql, use

```
mysqld --user=mysql
```

Securing Your MySQL Connection

You can connect to the MySQL monitor or other MySQL applications in several different ways, each of which has its own security risks. If your MySQL installation is on your own workstation, you have less to worry about than users who have to use a network connection to reach their server.

If MySQL is installed on your workstation, your biggest security concern is leaving your workstation unattended with your MySQL monitor or MySQL GUI administration tool up and running. In this type of situation, anyone can walk over and delete data, insert bogus data, or shut down the server. Utilize a screen saver or lock screen mechanism with a password if you must leave your workstation unattended in a public area.

If MySQL is installed on a server outside your network, the security of the connection should be of some concern. As with any transmission of data over the Internet, it can be intercepted. If the transmission is unencrypted, the person who intercepted it can piece it together and use the information. Suppose the unencrypted transmission is your MySQL login information—a rogue individual now has access to your database, masquerading as you.

One way to prevent this from happening is to connect to MySQL through a secure connection. Instead of using Telnet to reach the remote machine, use SSH. SSH looks and acts like Telnet, but all transmissions to and from the remote machine are encrypted. Similarly, if you use a Web-based administration interface, such as phpMyAdmin (see http://phpmyadmin.sourceforge.net for more information) or another tool used by your Internet service provider, access that tool over a secure HTTP connection.

In the next section, you'll learn about the MySQL privilege system, which helps secure your database even further.

Introducing the MySQL Privilege System

The MySQL privilege system is always "on." The first time you try to connect and for each subsequent action, MySQL checks the following three things:

- Where you are accessing from (your host)
- Who you say you are (your username and password)
- What you're allowed to do (your command privileges)

All this information is stored in the database called mysql, which is automatically created when MySQL is installed. There are several tables in the mysql database:

- columns_priv—Defines user privileges for specific fields within a table.
- db—Defines the permissions for all databases on the server.
- func—Defines user-created functions.
- host—Defines the acceptable hosts that can connect to a specific database.
- tables_priv—Defines user privileges for specific tables within a database.
- user—Defines the command privileges for a specific user.

These tables will become more important to you later in this hour as you add a few sample users to MySQL. For now, just remember that these tables exist and must have relevant data in them in order for users to complete actions.

The Two-Step Authentication Process

As you've learned, MySQL checks three things during the authentication process. The actions associated with these three things are performed in two steps:

1. MySQL looks at the host you are connecting from and the username and password pair that you are using. If your host is allowed to connect, your password is correct for your username, and the username matches one assigned to the host, MySQL moves to the second step.
2. For whichever SQL command you are attempting to use, MySQL verifies that you have the ability to perform that action for that database, table, and field.

If step 1 fails, you'll see an error about it and you won't be able to continue on to step 2. For example, suppose you are connecting to MySQL with a username of joe and a password of abc123 and you want to access a database called myDB. You will receive an error message if any of those connection variables are incorrect for any of the following reasons:

- Your password is incorrect.

- Username joe doesn't exist.

- User joe can't connect from localhost.

- User joe can connect from localhost but cannot use the myDB database.

You may see an error like the following:

```
#> /usr/local/bin/mysql/bin/mysql -h localhost -u joe -pabc123 test
Error 1045: Access denied for user: 'joe@localhost' (Using password: YES)
```

If user joe with a password of abc123 is allowed to connect from localhost to the myDB database, MySQL will check the actions that joe can perform in step 2 of the process. For our purposes, suppose that joe is allowed to select data but is not allowed to insert data. The sequence of events and errors would look like the following:

```
#> /usr/local/bin/mysql/bin/mysql -h localhost -u joe -pabc123 test
Reading table information for completion of table and column names
You can turn off this feature to get a quicker startup with -A

Welcome to the MySQL monitor.  Commands end with ; or \g.
Your MySQL connection id is 61198 to server version: 4.0.2-alpha-log
Type 'help;' or '\h' for help. Type '\c' to clear the buffer.

mysql> select * from test_table;
+----+------------+
| id | test_field |
+----+------------+
|  1 | blah       |
|  2 | blah blah  |
+----+------------+
2 rows in set (0.0 sec)

mysql> insert into test_table values ('', 'my text');
Error 1044: Access denied for user: 'joe@localhost' (Using password: YES)
```

Action-based permissions are common in applications with several levels of administration. For example, if you have created an application containing personal financial data, you might grant only SELECT privileges to entry-level staff members, but INSERT and DELETE privileges to executive-level staff with security clearances.

Working with User Privileges

In most cases when you are accessing MySQL through an Internet service provider, you will have only one user and one database available to you. By default, that one user will have access to all tables in that database and will be allowed to perform all commands.

In this case, the responsibility is yours as the developer to create a secure application through your programming.

If you are the administrator of your own server or have the ability to add as many databases and users as you want, as well as modify the access privileges of your users, these next few sections will take you through the processes of doing so.

Adding Users

Administering your server through a third-party application may afford you a simple method for adding users, using a wizard-like process or a graphical interface. However, adding users through the MySQL monitor is not difficult, especially if you understand the security checkpoints used by MySQL, which you just learned.

The simplest method for adding new users is the GRANT command. By connecting to MySQL as the root user, you can issue one command to set up a new user. The other method is to issue INSERT statements into all the relevant tables in the mysql database, which requires you to know all the fields in the tables used to store permissions. This method works just as well but is more complicated than the simple GRANT command.

The simple syntax of the GRANT command is

```
GRANT privileges
ON databasename.tablename
TO username@host
IDENTIFIED BY "password";
```

The privileges you can grant are

- ALL—Gives the user all of the following privileges
- ALTER—User can alter (modify) tables, columns, and indexes
- CREATE—User can create databases and tables
- DELETE—User can delete records from tables
- DROP—User can drop (delete) tables and databases
- FILE—User can read and write files; this is used to import or dump data
- INDEX—User can add or delete indexes
- INSERT—User can add records to tables
- PROCESS—User can view and stop system processes; only trusted users should be able to do this
- REFERENCES—Not currently used by MySQL, but a column for REFERENCES privileges exists in the user table

- RELOAD—User can issue FLUSH statements; only trusted users should be able to do this
- SELECT—User can select records from tables
- SHUTDOWN—User can shut down the MySQL server; only trusted users should be able to do this
- UPDATE—User can update (modify) records in tables
- USAGE—User can connect to MySQL but has no privileges

If, for instance, you want to create a user called john with a password of 99hjc, with SELECT and INSERT privileges on all tables in the database called myDB, and you want this user to be able to connect from any host, use

```
GRANT SELECT, INSERT
ON myDB.*
TO john@"%"
IDENTIFIED BY "99hjc";
```

Note the use of two wildcards: * and %. These wildcards are used to replace values. In this example, * replaces the entire list of tables, and % replaces a list of all hosts in the known world—a very long list indeed.

Here's another example of adding a user using the GRANT command, this time to add a user called jane with a password of 45sdg11, with ALL privileges on a table called employees in the database called myCompany. This new user can connect only from a specific host:

```
GRANT ALL
ON myCompany.employees
TO jane@janescomputer.company.com
IDENTIFIED BY "45sdg11";
```

If you know that janescomputer.company.com has an IP address of 63.124.45.2, you can substitute that address in the hostname portion of the command, as follows:

```
GRANT ALL
ON myCompany.employees
TO jane@'63.124.45.2'
IDENTIFIED BY "45sdg11";
```

One note about adding users: Always use a password and make sure that the password is a good one! MySQL allows you to create users without a password, but that leaves the door wide open should someone with bad intentions guess the name of one of your users with full privileges granted to them!

If you use the GRANT command to add users, the changes will immediately take effect. To make absolutely sure of this, you can issue the FLUSH PRIVILEGES command in the MySQL monitor to reload the privilege tables.

1

Removing Privileges

Removing privileges is as simple as adding them; instead of a GRANT command, you use REVOKE. The REVOKE command syntax is

```
REVOKE privileges
ON databasename.tablename
FROM username@hostname;
```

In the same way that you can grant permissions using INSERT commands, you can also revoke permissions by issuing DELETE commands to remove records from tables in the mysql database. However, this requires that you be familiar with the fields and tables, and it's just much easier and safer to use REVOKE.

To revoke the ability for user john to INSERT items in the myCompany database, you would issue this REVOKE statement:

```
REVOKE INSERT
ON myDB.*
FROM john@"%";
```

Changes made to the data in the privilege tables happen immediately, but in order for the server to be aware of your changes, issue the FLUSH PRIVILEGES command in the MySQL monitor.

Summary

Installing MySQL on Windows is a very simple process due to a wizard-based installation method. MySQL AB provides a GUI-based administration tool for Windows users, called WinMySQLadmin. Linux/Unix users do not have a wizard-based installation process, but it's not difficult to follow a simple set of commands to unpack the MySQL client and server. Linux/Unix users can also use RPMs for installation.

Security is always a priority, and there are several steps you can take to ensure a safe and secure installation of MySQL. Even if you are not the administrator of the server, you should be able to recognize breaches and raise a ruckus with the server administrator!

The MySQL server should not run as the root user. Additionally, named users within MySQL should always have a password, and their access privileges should be well defined.

MySQL uses the privilege tables in a two-step process for each request that is made. MySQL needs to know who you are and where you are connecting from, and each of these pieces of information must match an entry in its privilege tables. Also, the user whose identity you are using must have specific permission to perform the type of request you are making.

You can add user privileges using the GRANT command, which uses a simple syntax to add entries to the user table in the mysql database. The REVOKE command, which is equally simple, is used to remove those privileges.

Q&A

Q How do I completely remove a user? The REVOKE command just eliminates the privileges.

A To completely remove a user from the privilege table, you have to issue a specific DELETE command from the user table in the mysql database.

Q What if I tell my Internet service provider to stop running MySQL as root, and they won't?

A Switch providers. If your Internet service provider doesn't recognize the risks of running something as important as your database as the root user, and doesn't listen to your request, find another provider. There are providers with plans as low as $9.95/month that don't run important processes as root!

Workshop

The workshop is designed to help you anticipate possible questions, review what you've learned, and begin learning how to put your knowledge into practice.

Quiz

1. True or False: Telnet is a perfectly acceptable method to securely connect to MySQL from a remote host.

2. Which three pieces of information does MySQL check each time a request is made?

3. What command would you use to grant SELECT, INSERT, and UPDATE privileges to a user named bill on localhost to all tables on the BillDB database? Also, what piece of information is missing from this statement that is recommended for security purposes?

Answers

1. False. The key word is "secure," and Telnet does not encrypt data between hosts. Instead, use SSH to connect to your server.

2. Who you are, where you are accessing from, and what actions you're allowed to perform.

3. The command is
```
GRANT SELECT, INSERT, UPDATE
ON BillDB.*
TO bill@localhost;
```

The important missing piece is a password for the user!

Activities

1. Think of situations in which you might want to restrict command access at the table level. For example, you wouldn't want the intern-level administrator to have shutdown privileges for the corporate database.

2. If you have administrative privileges in MySQL, issue several GRANT commands to create dummy users. It doesn't matter whether the tables and databases you name are actually present.

3. Use REVOKE to remove some of the privileges of the users you created in activity 2.

HOUR 2

Installing and Configuring Apache

In this second of three "installation" hours, you will install the Apache Web server and familiarize yourself with its main components, including log and configuration files. In this hour, you will learn

- How to install the Apache server on Linux/Unix
- How to install the Apache server on Windows
- How to make configuration changes to Apache
- Where Apache log and configuration files are stored

Choosing the Appropriate Installation Method

You have several options when it comes to getting a basic Apache installation in place. Apache is open source, meaning that you can have access to the full source code of the software, which in turn enables you to build your own custom server. Additionally, pre-built Apache binary distributions are available for most modern Unix platforms. Finally, Apache comes already bundled with a variety of Linux distributions, and you can purchase commercial versions from software vendors such as Covalent Technologies and IBM. The examples in this hour will teach you how to build Apache from source if you are using Linux/Unix, and how to use the installer if you plan to run Apache on a Windows system.

Building from Source

Building from source gives you the greatest flexibility, as it enables you to build a custom server, remove modules you do not need, and extend the server with third-party modules. Building Apache from source code enables you to easily upgrade to the latest versions and quickly apply security patches, whereas updated versions from vendors can take days or weeks to appear.

The process of building Apache from the source code is not especially difficult for simple installations, but can grow in complexity when third-party modules and libraries are involved.

Installing a Binary

Linux/Unix binary installations are available from vendors and can also be downloaded from the Apache Software Foundation Web site. They provide a convenient way to install Apache for users with limited system administration knowledge, or with no special configuration needs. Third-party commercial vendors provide prepackaged Apache installations together with an application server, additional modules, support, and so on.

The Apache Software Foundation provides an installer for Windows systems—a platform where a compiler is not as commonly available as in Linux/Unix systems.

Installing Apache on Linux/Unix

This section explains how to install a fresh build of Apache 2.0 on Linux/Unix. The steps necessary to successfully install Apache from source are

1. Downloading the software
2. Running the configuration script
3. Compiling the code and installing it

The following sections describe these steps in detail.

Downloading the Apache Source Code

The official Apache download site is located at http://www.apache.org/dist/httpd. You can find several Apache versions, packaged with different compression methods. The distribution files are first packed with the tar utility and then compressed either with the gzip tool or the compress utility. Download the .tar.gz version if you have the gunzip utility installed in your system. This utility comes installed by default in open source operating systems such as FreeBSD and Linux. Download the tar.Z file if gunzip is not present in your system. (It isn't included in the default installation of many commercial Unix operating systems.)

The file you want to download will be named something similar to httpd-2.0. version.tar.Z or httpd-2.0.version.tar.gz, where version is the most recent release version of Apache. For example, Apache version 2.0.43 is downloaded as a file named httpd-2.0.43.tar.gz. Keep the downloaded file in a directory reserved for source files, such as /usr/src/ or /usr/local/src/.

Uncompressing the Source Code

If you downloaded the tarball compressed with gzip (it will have a tar.gz suffix), you can uncompress it using the gunzip utility (part of the gzip distribution).

> *Tarball* is a commonly used nickname for software packed using the tar utility.

You can uncompress and unpack the software by typing the following command:

```
#> gunzip < httpd-2.0*.tar.gz | tar xvf -
```

If you downloaded the tarball compressed with compress (tar.Z suffix), you can issue the following command:

```
#> cat httpd-2.0*.tar.Z | uncompress | tar xvf -
```

Uncompressing the tarball creates a structure of directories, with the top-level directory named httpd-2.0_version. Change your current directory to this top-level directory to prepare for configuring the software.

Preparing to Build Apache

You can specify which features the resulting binary will have by using the configure script in the top-level distribution directory. By default, Apache will be compiled with a

set of standard modules compiled statically and will be installed in the
/usr/local/apache2 directory. If you are happy with these settings, you can issue the
following command to configure Apache:

```
#> ./configure
```

However, in preparation for the PHP installation in Hour 3, you will need to make sure
that mod_so is compiled into Apache. This module, named for the Unix shared object
(*.so) format, enables the use of dynamic modules such as PHP with Apache. To configure Apache to install itself in a specific location (in this case /usr/local/apache2/) and
to enable the use of mod_so, issue the following command:

```
#> ./configure --prefix=/usr/local/apache2 --enable-module=so
```

The purpose of the configure script is to figure out everything related to finding
libraries, compile-time options, platform-specific differences, and so on, and to create a
set of special files called *makefiles*. Makefiles contain instructions to perform different
tasks, called *targets*, such as building Apache. These files will be read by the make utility,
which will carry out those tasks. If everything goes well, after executing configure, you
will see a set of messages related to the different checks just performed, and will be
returned to the prompt:

```
...
creating test/Makefile
config.status: creating docs/conf/httpd-std.conf
config.status: creating include/ap_config_layout.h
config.status: creating support/apxs
config.status: creating support/apachectl
config.status: creating support/dbmmanage
config.status: creating support/envvars-std
config.status: creating support/log_server_status
config.status: creating support/logresolve.pl
config.status: creating support/phf_abuse_log.cgi
config.status: creating support/split-logfile
config.status: creating build/rules.mk
config.status: creating include/ap_config_auto.h
config.status: executing default commands
#>
```

If the configure script fails, warnings will appear, alerting you to track down additional
software that must be installed, such as compilers or libraries. After you install any missing software, you can try the configure command again, after deleting the config.log
and config.status files from the top-level directory.

Building and Installing Apache

The make utility reads the information stored in the makefiles and builds the server and modules. Type make at the command line to build Apache. You will see several messages indicating the progress of the compilation, and you will end up back at the prompt. After compilation is finished, you can install Apache by typing make install at the prompt. The makefiles will install files and directories, and return you to the prompt:

```
...
Installing header files
Installing man pages and online manual
mkdir /usr/local/apache2/man
mkdir /usr/local/apache2/man/man1
mkdir /usr/local/apache2/man/man8
mkdir /usr/local/apache2/manual
Installing build system files
make[1]: Leaving directory '/usr/local/src/httpd-2.0.43'
#>
```

The Apache distribution files should now be in the /usr/local/apache2 directory, as specified by the --prefix switch in the configure command. To test that the httpd binary has been correctly built, type the following at the prompt:

#> /usr/local/apache2/bin/httpd -v

You should see the following output (your version and build date will be different):

```
Server version: Apache/2.0.43
Server built:   Sep  1 2002 09:20:47
```

Unless you want to learn how to install Apache on Windows, skip ahead to the "Apache Configuration File Structure" section to learn about the Apache configuration file.

Installing Apache on Windows

Apache 2.0 runs on most Windows platforms and offers increased performance and stability over the 1.3 versions for Windows. You can build Apache from source, but because not many Windows users have compilers, this section deals with the binary installer.

Before installing Apache, you'll probably want to make sure that you are not currently running a Web server (for instance, a previous version of Apache, Microsoft Internet Information Server, or Microsoft Personal Web Server) in your machine. You might want to uninstall or otherwise disable existing servers. You can run several Web servers, but they will need to run in different address and port combinations.

You can download an installer from
`http://www.apache.org/dist/httpd/binaries/win32`.

After you download the installer, double-click on the file to start the installation process. You will get a welcome screen, as shown in Figure 2.1. Select Next to continue the installation process, and you will be prompted to accept the Apache license. Basically the license says that you can do whatever you want with the software—including making proprietary modifications—except claim that you wrote it, but be sure to read the license so that you fully understand the terms.

FIGURE 2.1

The Windows installer welcome screen.

After you accept the license, the installer presents you with a brief introduction to Apache. Following that, it asks you to provide basic information about your computer, as shown in Figure 2.2. This includes the full network address for the server (for instance, `mycomputer.mydomain.com`) and the administrator's email address. The server name will be the name that your clients will use to access your server, and the administrator email address will be added to error messages so that visitors know how to contact you when something goes wrong.

> If your machine does not have a full network address, use localhost or
> `127.0.0.1` as the `ServerName`.

In the next step, you can install Apache as a service or require it to be started manually. Installing Apache as a service will cause it to run every time Windows is started, and you can control it through the usual Windows service administration tools. Choose this option if you plan to run Apache in a production environment or otherwise require Apache to run continuously. Installing Apache for the current user will require you to start Apache manually and set the default port on which Apache listens to requests to 8080. Choose this option if you use Apache for testing or if you already have a Web server running on port 80.

FIGURE 2.2
The basic information screen.

The next screen enables you to choose the type of installation, as shown in Figure 2.3. *Typical* installation means that Apache binaries and documentation will be installed, but headers and libraries will not. This is the best option to choose unless you plan to compile your own modules.

FIGURE 2.3
The installation type selection screen.

A *custom* installation enables you to choose whether to install header files or documentation. After selecting the target installation directory, which defaults to c:\Program Files\Apache Group, the program will proceed with the installation process. If everything goes well, it will present you with the final screen shown in Figure 2.4.

FIGURE 2.4

*The successful instal-
lation screen.*

In the next section, you'll learn about the Apache configuration file, and eventually start
up your new server.

Apache Configuration File Structure

Apache keeps all of its configuration information in text files. The main file is called
`httpd.conf`. This file contains *directives* and *containers*, which enable you to customize
your Apache installation. Directives configure specific settings of Apache, such as authorization, performance, and network parameters. Containers specify the context to which
those settings refer. For example, authorization configuration can refer to the server as a
whole, a directory, or a single file.

Directives

The following rules apply for Apache directive syntax:

- The directive arguments follow the directive name.
- Directive arguments are separated by spaces.
- The number and type of arguments vary from directive to directive; some have no
  arguments.
- A directive occupies a single line, but you can continue it on a different line by
  ending the previous line with a backslash character (\).
- The pound sign (#) should precede the directive, and must appear on its own line.

In the Apache server documentation, found online at `http://httpd.apache.org/
docs-2.0/`, you can browse the directives in alphabetical order or by the module to
which they belong. You'll soon learn about some of the basic directives, but you should
supplement your knowledge using the online documentation.

Figure 2.5 shows an entry from the documentation for the ServerName directive description. You can read this description in the online documentation at http://httpd.apache.org/docs-2.0/mod/core.html#servername.

FIGURE 2.5
Directive description example.

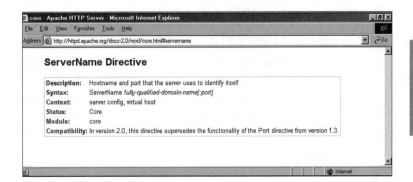

The schema, as detailed in the documentation at http://httpd.apache.org/docs-2.0/mod/directive-dict.html, is the same for all directives:

- **Syntax**—This entry explains the format of the directive options. Compulsory parameters appear in italics, optional parameters appear in italics and brackets.
- **Default**—If the directive has a default value, it will appear here.
- **Context**—This entry details the containers or sections in which the directive can appear. Containers are explained in the next section. The possible values are server config, virtual host, directory, and .htaccess.
- **Status**—This entry indicates whether the directive is built in Apache (core), belongs to one of the bundled modules (base or extension, depending on whether they are compiled by default), is part of a Multi-Processing Module (MPM), or is bundled with Apache but not ready for use in a production server (experimental).
- **Module**—This entry indicates the module to which the directive belongs.
- **Compatibility**—This entry contains information about which versions of Apache support the directive.
- **Override**—Apache directives belong to different categories. The override field is used to specify which directive categories can appear in .htaccess per-directory configuration files.

A brief explanation of the directive follows these entries in the documentation, and a reference to related directives or documentation may appear at the end.

Containers

Directive containers, also called *sections*, limit the scope for which directives apply. If directives are not inside a container, they belong to the default server scope (server config) and apply to the server as a whole.

These are the default Apache directive containers:

- <VirtualHost>—A VirtualHost directive specifies a virtual server. Apache enables you to host different Web sites with a single Apache installation. Directives inside this container apply to a particular Web site. This directive accepts a domain name or IP address and an optional port as arguments. You will learn more about virtual hosts in Hour 22, "Apache Performance Tuning and Virtual Hosting."

- <Directory>, <DirectoryMatch>—These containers allow directives to apply to a certain directory or group of directories in the file system. Directory containers take a directory or directory pattern argument. Enclosed directives apply to the specified directories and their subdirectories. The DirectoryMatch container allows regular expression patterns to be specified as an argument. For example, the following allows a match of all subdirectories of the www directory that are made up of four numbers, such as a directory named after a year and month (0902 for September 2002):

  ```
  <DirectoryMatch "^/www/.*/[0-9]{4}">
  ```

- <Location>, <LocationMatch>—These containers allow directives to apply to certain requested URLs or URL patterns. They are similar to their Directory counterparts. LocationMatch takes a regular expression as an argument. For example, the following matches directories containing either "/my/data" or "/your/data":

  ```
  <LocationMatch "/(my|your)/data">
  ```

- <Files>, <FilesMatch>—Similar to Directory and Location containers, Files sections allow directives to apply to certain files or file patterns.

Containers surround directives, as shown in Listing 2.1.

LISTING 2.1 Sample Container Directives

```
 1: <Directory "/some/directory">
 2: SomeDirective1
 3: SomeDirective2
 4: </Directory>
 5: <Location "/downloads/*.html">
 6: SomeDirective3
 7: </Location>
 8: <Files "\.(gif|jpg)">
 9: SomeDirective4
10: </Files>
```

Sample directives *SomeDirective1* and *SomeDirective2* will apply to the directory /www/docs and its subdirectories. *SomeDirective3* will apply to URLs referring to pages with the .html extension under the /download/ URL. *SomeDirective4* will apply to all files with .gif or .jpg extensions.

Conditional Evaluation

Apache provides support for conditional containers. Directives enclosed in these containers will be processed only if certain conditions are met.

- <IfDefine>—Directives in this container will be processed if a specific command-line switch is passed to the Apache executable. The directive in Listing 2.2 will be processed only if the -DMyModule switch was passed to the Apache binary being executed. You can pass this directly or by modifying the apachectl script, as described in the "Apache-Related Commands" section later in this hour.

  IfDefine containers allow the argument to be negated. That is, directives inside a <IfDefine !MyModule> section will be processed only if no -DMyModule parameter was passed as a command-line argument. For example, if -DSSL is not passed, listening on the SSL port (usually 443) will not occur.

- <IfModule>—Directives in an IfModule section will be processed only if the module passed as an argument is present in the Web server. For example, Apache ships with a default httpd.conf configuration file that provides support for different MPMs. Only the configuration belonging to the MPM compiled in will be processed, as you can see in Listing 2.3. The purpose of the example is to illustrate that only one of the directive groups will be evaluated.

LISTING 2.2 IfDefine Example

```
1: <IfDefine MyModule>
2: LoadModule my_module modules/libmymodule.so
3: </IfDefine>
```

LISTING 2.3 IfModule Example

```
1: <IfModule prefork.c>
2: StartServers          5
3: MinSpareServers       5
4: MaxSpareServers      10
5: MaxClients           20
6: MaxRequestsPerChild   0
7: </IfModule>
8:
```

LISTING 2.3   continued

```
 9: <IfModule worker.c>
10:  StartServers          3
11:  MaxClients            8
12:  MinSpareThreads       5
13:  MaxSpareThreads      10
14:  ThreadsPerChild      25
15:  MaxRequestsPerChild   0
16: </IfModule>
```

ServerRoot

The ServerRoot directive takes a single argument: a directory path pointing to the directory where the server lives. All relative path references in other directives are relative to the value of ServerRoot. If you compiled Apache from source on Linux/Unix, as described earlier in this hour, the default value of ServerRoot is /usr/local/apache2. If you used the Windows installer, the ServerRoot is c:\Program Files\Apache Group.

Per-Directory Configuration Files

Apache uses per-directory configuration files to allow directives to exist outside the main configuration file httpd.conf. These special files can be placed in the file system. Apache will process the content of these files if a document is requested in a directory containing one of these files or any subdirectories under it. The contents of all the applicable per-directory configuration files are merged and processed. For example, if Apache receives a request for the /usr/local/apache2/htdocs/index.html file, it will look for per-directory configuration files in the /, /usr, /usr/local, /usr/local/apache2, and /usr/local/apache2/htdocs directories, in that order.

Enabling per-directory configuration files has a performance penalty. Apache must perform expensive disk operations looking for these files in every request, even if the files do not exist.

Per-directory configuration files are called .htaccess by default. This is for historical reasons; they were originally used to protect access to directories containing HTML files.

The directive AccessFileName enables you to change the name of the per-directory configuration files from .htaccess to something else. It accepts a list of filenames that Apache will use when looking for per-directory configuration files.

To determine whether a directive can be overridden in the per-directory configuration file, check whether the Context: field of the directive syntax definition contains .htaccess.

Apache directives belong to different groups, specified in the `Override:` field in the directive syntax description. Possible values are

- `AuthConfig`—Authorization directives
- `FileInfo`—Directives controlling document types
- `Indexes`—Directives controlling directory indexing
- `Limit`—Directives controlling host access
- `Options`—Directives controlling specific directory features

You can control which of these directive groups can appear in per-directory configuration files by using the `AllowOverride` directive. `AllowOverride` can also take an `All` or a `None` argument. `All` means that directives belonging to all groups can appear in the configuration file. `None` disables per-directory files in a directory and any of its subdirectories. Listing 2.4 shows how to disable per-directory configuration files for the server as a whole. This improves performance and is the default Apache configuration.

LISTING 2.4   Disabling Per-Directory Configuration Files

```
1: <Directory />
2: AllowOverride none
3: </Directory>
```

Apache Log Files

Apache includes two log files by default. The `access_log` file is used to track client requests. The `error_log` is used to record important events, such as errors or server restarts. These files don't exist until you start Apache for the first time. The files are named `access.log` and `error.log` in Windows platforms.

access_log

When a client requests a file from the server, Apache records several parameters associated with the request, including the IP address of the client, the document requested, the HTTP status code, and the current time. Listing 2.5 shows sample log file entries. Hour 17, "Logging and Monitoring Server Activity," will show you how to modify which parameters are logged.

LISTING 2.5 Sample access_log Entries

```
1: 127.0.0.1 - - [01/Sep/2002:09:43:37 -0700] "GET / HTTP/1.1" 200 1494
2: 127.0.0.1 - - [01/Sep/2002:09:43:40 -0700] "GET /manual/ HTTP/1.1" 200 10383
```

error_log

This file includes error messages, startup messages, and any other significant events in the life cycle of the server. This is the first place to look when you have a problem with Apache. Listing 2.6 shows sample error_log entries.

LISTING 2.6 Sample error_log Entries

```
1: [Sun Sep 01 09:42:59 2002] [notice] Parent: Created child process -2245
2: [Sun Sep 01 09:42:59 2002] [notice] Child -2242: Child process is running
3: [Sun Sep 01 09:42:59 2002] [notice] Child -2242: Acquired the start mutex.
4: [Sun Sep 01 09:42:59 2002] [notice] Child -2242: Starting 250 worker threads.
```

Additional Files

The httpd.pid file contains the process ID of the running Apache server. You can use this number to send signals to Apache manually, as described in the next section.

The scoreboard file, present on Linux/Unix Apache, is used by the process-based MPMs to communicate with their children.

In general, you do not need to worry about these files.

Apache-Related Commands

The Apache distribution includes several executables. This section covers only the server binary and related scripts. Hour 15, "Restricting Access to Your Applications," and Hour 22, "Apache Performance Tuning and Virtual Hosting," cover additional utilities included with the Apache distribution.

Apache Server Binary

The Apache executable is named httpd in Linux/Unix and apache.exe in Windows. It accepts several command-line options, which are described in Table 2.1. You can get a complete listing of options by typing /usr/local/apache2/bin/httpd -h on Linux/Unix, or by typing apache.exe -h from a command prompt on Windows.

TABLE 2.1 httpd Options

Option	Meaning
-D	Allows you to pass a parameter that can be used for \<IfDefine\> section processing
-l	Lists compiled-in modules
-v	Shows version number and server compilation time
-f	Allows you to pass the location of httpd.conf if it is different from the compile-time default

After Apache is running, you can use the kill command on Linux/Unix to send signals to the parent Apache process. Signals provide a mechanism to send commands to a process. To send a signal, execute the following command:

```
#> kill -SIGNAL pid
```

where *pid* is the process ID and *SIGNAL* is one of the following:

- HUP—Stop the server
- USR1 or WINCH—Graceful restart; which signal to use depends on the underlying operating system
- SIGHUP—Restart

If you make some changes to the configuration files and you want them to take effect, you must signal Apache that the configuration has changed. You can do this by stopping and starting the server or by sending a restart signal. This tells Apache to reread its configuration.

A normal restart can result in a momentary pause in service. A graceful restart takes a different approach. Each thread or process serving a client will keep processing the current request, but when it is finished, it will be killed and replaced by a new thread or process with the new configuration. This allows seamless operation of the Web server with no downtime.

On Windows, you can signal Apache using the apache.exe executable:

- apache.exe -k restart—Tells Apache to restart
- apache.exe -k graceful—Tells Apache to do a graceful restart
- apache.exe -k stop—Tells Apache to stop

You can access shortcuts to these commands in the Start menu entries that the Apache installer created. If you installed Apache as a service, you can start or stop Apache by using the Windows service interface: In Control Panel, select Administrative Tasks and then click on the Services icon.

Apache Control Script

Although it is possible to control Apache on Linux/Unix using the httpd binary, it is recommended that you use the apachectl tool. The apachectl support program wraps common functionality in an easy-to-use script. To use apachectl, type

```
#> ./apachectl command
```

where command is stop, start, restart, or graceful. You can also edit the contents of the apachectl script to add extra command-line options.

Some OS distributions provide you with additional scripts to control Apache; please check the documentation included with your distribution.

Starting Apache for the First Time

Before you start Apache, you should verify that the minimal set of information is present in the Apache configuration file, httpd.conf. The following sections describe the basic information needed to configure Apache, and how to start the server.

Check Your Configuration File

You can edit the Apache httpd.conf file with your favorite text editor. In Linux/Unix, this probably means vi or emacs. In Windows, you can use Notepad or WordPad. You must remember to save the configuration file in plain text, which is the only format Apache will understand.

There are only two parameters that you might need to change to enable you to start Apache for the first time: the name of the server and the address and port to which it is listening. The name of the server is the one Apache will use when it needs to refer to itself (for example, when redirecting requests).

Apache can usually figure out its server name from the IP address of the machine, but this is not always the case. If the server does not have a valid DNS entry, you might need to specify one of the IP addresses of the machine. If the server is not connected to a network (you might want to test Apache on a standalone machine), you can use the value 127.0.0.1, which is the loopback address. The default port value is 80. You might need to change this value if there is already a server running in the machine at port 80, or if you do not have administrator permissions—on Linux/Unix systems, only the `root` user can bind to privileged ports (those with port numbers lower than 1024).

You can change both the listening address and the port values with the `Listen` directive. The `Listen` directive takes either a port number or an IP address and a port, separated by a semicolon. If only the port is specified, Apache will listen on that port at all available IP addresses in the machine. If an additional IP address is provided, Apache will listen at only that address and port combination. For example, `Listen 80` tells Apache to listen for requests at all IP addresses on port 80. `Listen 10.0.0.1:443` tells Apache to listen only at 10.0.0.1 on port 443.

The `ServerName` directive enables you to define the name the server will report in any self-referencing URLs. The directive accepts a DNS name and an optional port, separated by a colon. Make sure that `ServerName` has a valid value. Otherwise, the server will not function properly; for example, it will issue incorrect redirects.

On Linux/Unix platforms, you can use the `User` and `Group` directives to specify which user and group IDs the server will run as. The `nobody` user is a good choice for most platforms. However, there are problems in the HP-UX platform with this user ID, so you must create and use a different user ID, such as `www`.

Starting Apache

To start Apache on Linux/Unix, change to the directory containing the `apachectl` script and execute the following command:

```
#> ./apachectl start
```

To start Apache on Windows, click on the Start Apache link in the Control Apache section in the Start menu. If you installed Apache as a service, you must start the Apache service instead.

If everything goes well, you can access Apache using a browser. The default installation page will be displayed, as shown in Figure 2.6. If you cannot start the Web server or an error page appears instead, please consult the "Troubleshooting" section that follows. Make sure that you are accessing Apache in one of the ports specified in the `Listen` directive—usually 80 or 8080.

FIGURE 2.6

FIGURE 2.6

Apache default instal-
lation page.

Troubleshooting

The following subsections describe several common problems that you might encounter the first time you start Apache.

Already an Existing Web Server

If there is already a server running in the machine and listening to the same IP address and port combination, Apache will not be able to start successfully. You will get an entry in the error log file indicating that Apache cannot bind to the port:

```
[crit] (48)Address already in use: make_sock: could not bind to
➥address 10.0.0.2:80
[alert] no listening sockets available, shutting down
```

To solve this problem, you need to stop the running server or change the Apache configuration to listen on a different port.

No Permission to Bind to Port

You will get an error if you do not have administrator permissions and you try to bind to a privileged port (between 0 and 1024):

```
[crit] (13)Permission denied: make_sock: could not bind to address 10.0.0.2:80
[alert] no listening sockets available, shutting down
```

To solve this problem, you must either log on as the administrator before starting Apache or change the port number (8080 is a commonly used nonprivileged port).

Access Denied

You might not be able to start Apache if you do not have permission to read the configuration files or to write to the log files. You will get an error similar to the following:

```
(13)Permission denied: httpd: could not open error log file
 ➥ /usr/local/apache2/logs/error_log.
```

This problem can arise if Apache was built and installed by a different user than the one trying to run it.

Wrong Group Settings

You can configure Apache to run under a certain username and group. Apache has default values for the running server username and group. Sometimes the default value is not valid, and you will get an error containing setgid: unable to set group id.

To solve this problem on Linux/Unix, you must change the value of the Group directive in the configuration file to a valid value. Check the /etc/groups file for existing groups.

Summary

This hour explained different ways of getting an Apache 2.0 server installed on your Linux/Unix or Windows machine. It covered both binary and source installation and explained the basic build-time options. Additionally, you learned the location of the server configuration files, and the syntax of the commands used to modify your Apache configuration. You learned about the two main log files—access_log and error_log. Finally, you saw how to start and stop the server using the Apache control scripts or the Apache server binary on Linux/Unix and Windows platforms.

Q&A

Q How can I start a clean build?

A If you need to build a new Apache from source and do not want the result of earlier builds to affect the new one, it is always a good idea to run the make clean command. That will take care of cleaning up any existing binaries, intermediate object files, and so on.

Q Why are per-directory configuration files useful?

A Although per-directory configuration files have an impact on server performance, they can be useful for delegated administration. Because per-directory configuration files are read every time a request is made, there is no need to restart the server when a change is made to the configuration.

You can allow users of your Web site to make configuration changes on their own without granting them administrator privileges. In this way, they can password-protect sections of their home pages, for example.

Q What do you mean by a valid `ServerName` directive?

A The DNS system is used to associate IP addresses with domain names. The value of `ServerName` is returned when the server generates a URL. If you are using a certain domain name, you must make sure that it is included in your DNS system and will be available to clients visiting your site.

Workshop

The workshop is designed to help you anticipate possible questions, review what you've learned, and begin putting your knowledge into practice.

Quiz

1. How can you specify the location where you want to install Apache?
2. What is the main difference between `<Location>` and `<Directory>` sections?
3. What is the difference between a restart and a graceful restart?

Answers

1. Linux/Unix users can use the `--prefix` option of the `configure` script. If an existing installation is present at that location, the configuration files will be preserved but the binaries will be replaced. On Windows, this location is set in the installation wizard.
2. Directory sections refer to file system objects; Location sections refer to elements in the address bar of the Web page (also called the URI).
3. During a normal restart, the server is stopped and then started, causing some requests to be lost. A graceful restart allows Apache children to continue to serve their current requests until they can be replaced with children running the new configuration.

Activities

1. Practice the various types of server shutdown and restart procedures.
2. Make some configuration changes such as different port assignments and `ServerName` changes.

2

Hour 3

Installing and Configuring PHP

In the last of the three "installation" hours, you will acquire, install, and configure PHP and make some basic changes to your Apache installation. In this hour, you will learn

- How to install PHP with Apache on Linux/Unix
- How to install PHP with Apache server on Windows
- How to test your PHP installation
- How to find help when things go wrong
- The basics of the PHP language

Building PHP on Linux/Unix with Apache

In this section, we will look at one way of installing PHP with Apache on Linux/Unix. The process is more or less the same for any Unix operating system. While you might be able to find pre-built versions of PHP for your system, compiling PHP from the source gives you greater control over the features built into your binary.

To download the PHP distribution files, go to the home of PHP, `http://www.php.net/`, and follow the link to the Downloads section. Grab the latest version of the source code—for this example, we are using 4.2.3. Your distribution will be named something similar to `php-version.tar.gz`, where *version* is the most recent release number. This archive will be a compressed tar file, so you will need to unpack it:

```
#> tar -xvzf php-version.tar.gz
```

Keep the downloaded file in a directory reserved for source files, such as `/usr/src/` or `/usr/local/src/`. After your distribution is unpacked, you should move to the PHP distribution directory:

```
#> cd php-version
```

Within your distribution directory you will find a script called `configure`. This script accepts additional information that is provided when the `configure` script is run from the command line. These "command-line arguments" will control the features that PHP will support. For this example, we will include the basic options you need to use to install PHP with Apache and MySQL support. We will discuss some of the available `configure` options later in the hour.

```
#> ./configure  --prefix=/usr/local/php \
--with-mysql=/usr/local/bin/mysql \
--with-apxs2=/usr/local/apache2/bin/apxs
```

Once the `configure` script has run, you will be returned to the prompt after receiving several informational notes from the PHP Group:

```
+-------------------------------------------------------------------+
|                          *** WARNING ***                          |
|                                                                   |
| Apache 2 Support is EXPERIMENTAL and should NOT be used in        |
| production environment. Before submitting bug reports, try the    |
| latest CVS snapshot from http://snaps.php.net                     |
+-------------------------------------------------------------------+
| License:                                                          |
| This software is subject to the PHP License, available in this    |
| distribution in the file LICENSE.  By continuing this installation|
| process, you are bound by the terms of this license agreement.    |
| If you do not agree with the terms of this license, you must abort|
| the installation process at this point.                           |
+-------------------------------------------------------------------+
|                           *** NOTE ***                            |
|             The default for register_globals is now OFF!          |
|                                                                   |
```

```
| If your application relies on register_globals being ON, you      |
| should explicitly set it to on in your php.ini file.              |
| Note that you are strongly encouraged to read                     |
| http://www.php.net/manual/en/security.registerglobals.php         |
| about the implications of having register_globals set to on, and  |
| avoid using it if possible.                                       |
+-------------------------------------------------------------------+
#>
```

 Depending on the PHP version you install, you may or may not receive the warning regarding the status of Apache 2 support. As of this writing, Apache 2 and PHP work splendidly together for all functionality in this book. However, you should run your own tests to determine whether you wish to use these versions in production.

Next, issue the make command, followed by the make install command. These commands should end the process of PHP compilation and installation and return you to your prompt.

You will need to ensure that two very important files are copied to their correct locations. First, issue the following command to copy the distributed version of php.ini to its default location. You will learn more about php.ini later in this hour.

```
#> cp php.ini-dist /usr/local/php/lib/php.ini
```

Next, copy the PHP shared object file to its proper place in the Apache installation directory, if it has not already been placed there by the installation process:

```
#> cp libs/libphp4.so /usr/local/apache2/modules/
```

You should now be able to configure and run Apache, but let's cover some additional configuration options before heading on to the "Integrating PHP with Apache on Linux/Unix" section.

Additional Configuration Options

When we ran the configure script, we included some command-line arguments that determined some features that the PHP engine will include. The configure script itself gives you a list of available options, including the ones we used. From the PHP distribution directory, type the following:

```
#> ./configure --help
```

This produces a long list, so you might want to add it to a file and read it at your leisure:

```
#> ./configure --help > configoptions.txt
```

If you discover additional functionality you wish to add to PHP after it has been installed, simply run the configuration and build process again. Doing so will create a new version of libphp4.so and place it in the Apache directory structure. All you have to do is restart Apache in order for the new file to be loaded.

Integrating PHP with Apache on Linux/Unix

To ensure that PHP and Apache get along with one another, you need to check for—and potentially add—a few items to the httpd.conf configuration file. First, look for a line like the following:

```
LoadModule php4_module          modules/libphp4.so
```

If this line is not present, or only appears with a pound sign (#) at the beginning of the line, you must add the line or remove the #. This line tells Apache to use the PHP shared object file that was created by the PHP build process (libphp4.so).

Next, look for this section:

```
#
# AddType allows you to add to or override the MIME configuration
# file mime.types for specific file types.
#
```

Add the following lines:

```
AddType application/x-httpd-php .php .phtml .html
AddType application/x-httpd-php-source .phps
```

This ensures that the PHP engine will parse files that end with the .php, .phtml, and .html extensions. Your selection of filenames may differ, and you may wish to add .php3 as an extension, for backwards compatibility with any very old scripts you may have.

Any files with the .phps extension will be output as PHP source (that is, the source code will be converted to HTML and color-coded). This can be useful for debugging your scripts.

Save this file, and then restart Apache. When you look in your error_log, you should see something like the following line:

```
[Sun Sep 29 10:42:47 2002] [notice] Apache/2.0.43 (Unix) PHP/4.2.3 configured
```

PHP is now part of the Apache Web server. If you want to learn how to install PHP on a Windows platform, keep reading. Otherwise, you can skip ahead to the "Testing Your Installation" section.

Installing PHP Files on Windows

Unlike building and installing PHP on Linux/Unix, installing PHP on Windows requires nothing more than downloading the distribution and moving a few files around. To download the PHP distribution files, go to the home of PHP, http://www.php.net/, and follow the link to the Downloads section. Grab the latest version of the zip package from the Windows Binaries section—for this example we are using 4.2.3. Your distribution will be named something similar to php-version.zip, where version is the most recent release number.

Once the file is downloaded to your system, double-click on it to launch your unzipper. The distribution is packed up with pathnames already in place, so if you extract the files to the root of your drive, it will create a directory called php-version-Win32, and place all the files and subdirectories under that new directory.

Now that you have all the basic PHP distribution files, you just need to move a few of them around:

1. In the PHP installation directory, find the php.ini-dist file and rename it php.ini.
2. Move the php.ini file to C:\WINDOWS\ or wherever you usually put your *.ini files.
3. Move the php4ts.dll file to C:\WINDOWS\SYSTEM\ or wherever you usually put your *.dll files.

To get a basic version of PHP working with Apache, you'll need to make a few minor modifications to the Apache configuration file.

Integrating PHP with Apache on Windows

To ensure that PHP and Apache get along with one another, you need to add a few items to the httpd.conf configuration file. First, find a section that looks like this:

```
# Example:
# LoadModule foo_module modules/mod_foo.so
#
LoadModule access_module modules/mod_access.so
LoadModule actions_module modules/mod_actions.so
LoadModule alias_module modules/mod_alias.so
LoadModule asis_module modules/mod_asis.so
LoadModule auth_module modules/mod_auth.so
#LoadModule auth_anon_module modules/mod_auth_anon.so
#LoadModule auth_dbm_module modules/mod_auth_dbm.so
#LoadModule auth_digest_module modules/mod_auth_digest.so
LoadModule autoindex_module modules/mod_autoindex.so
```

3

```
#LoadModule cern_meta_module modules/mod_cern_meta.so
LoadModule cgi_module modules/mod_cgi.so
#LoadModule dav_module modules/mod_dav.so
#LoadModule dav_fs_module modules/mod_dav_fs.so
LoadModule dir_module modules/mod_dir.so
LoadModule env_module modules/mod_env.so
#LoadModule expires_module modules/mod_expires.so
#LoadModule file_cache_module modules/mod_file_cache.so
#LoadModule headers_module modules/mod_headers.so
```

At the end of this section, add the following:

```
LoadModule php4_module c:/php-version/sapi/php4apache2.dll
```

Next, look for this section:

```
#
# AddType allows you to add to or override the MIME configuration
# file mime.types for specific file types.
#
```

Add the following lines:

```
AddType application/x-httpd-php .php .phtml .html
AddType application/x-httpd-php-source .phps
```

This ensures that the PHP engine will parse files that end with the `.php`, `.phtml`, and `.html` extensions. Your selection of filenames may differ, and you may wish to add `.php3` as an extension, for backwards compatibility with any very old scripts you may have.

Any files with the `.phps` extension will be output as PHP source. That is, the source code will be converted to HTML and color-coded. This can be useful for debugging your scripts.

Save this file, and then restart Apache. If the server starts, PHP is now part of the Apache Web server.

php.ini Basics

After you have compiled or installed PHP, you can still change its behavior with the `php.ini` file. On Unix systems, the default location for this file is `/usr/local/php/lib`, or the `lib` subdirectory of the PHP installation location you used at configuration time. On a Windows system, this file should be in the Windows directory.

Directives in the php.ini file come in two forms: values and flags. Value directives take the form of a directive name and a value separated by an equals sign. Possible values vary from directive to directive. Flag directives take the form of a directive name and a positive or negative term separated by an equals sign. Positive terms include 1, On, Yes, and True. Negative terms include 0, Off, No, and False. Whitespace is ignored.

You can change your php.ini settings at any time, but after you do, you'll need to restart the server for the changes to take effect. At some point, take time to read through the php.ini file on your own, to see the types of things that can be configured.

Testing Your Installation

The simplest way to test your PHP installation is to create a small test script utilizing the phpinfo() function. This function will produce a long list of configuration information. Open a text editor and type the following line:

```
<? phpinfo(); ?>
```

Save this file as phpinfo.php and place it in the document root of your Web server—the htdocs subdirectory of your Apache installation. Access this file via your Web browser and you should see something like Figure 3.1 or Figure 3.2.

FIGURE 3.1

The results of phpinfo() on a Linux/Unix system.

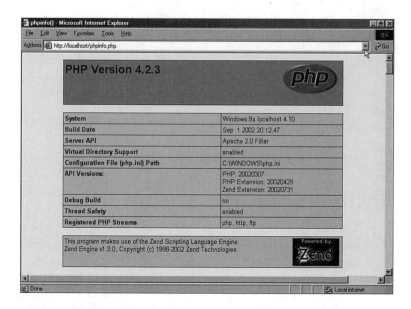

FIGURE 3.2

The results of phpinfo() on a Windows system.

Getting Installation Help

Help is always at hand on the Internet, particularly for problems concerning open source software. Wait a moment before you click the send button, however. No matter how intractable your installation, configuration, or programming problem might seem, chances are you are not alone. Someone has probably already answered your question.

When you hit a brick wall, your first recourse should be to the official PHP site at http://www.php.net/ (particularly the annotated manual at http://www.php.net/manual/).

If you still can't find your answer, don't forget that the PHP site is searchable. The advice you are seeking may be lurking in a press release or a Frequently Asked Questions file. You can also search the mailing list archives at http://www.php.net/search.php. These archives represent a huge information resource with contributions from many of the great minds in the PHP community. Spend some time trying out a few keyword combinations.

If you are still convinced that your problem has not been addressed, you may well be doing the PHP community a service by exposing it. You can join the PHP mailing lists at http://www.php.net/support.php. Although these lists often have high volume, you can learn a lot from them. If you are serious about PHP scripting, you should certainly subscribe to at least a digest list. Once you've subscribed to the list that matches your concerns, you might consider posting your problem.

When you post a question, it is a good idea to include as much information as possible (without writing a novel). The following items are often pertinent:

- Your operating system
- The version of PHP you are running or installing
- The configuration options you chose
- Any output from the `configure` or `make` commands that preceded an installation failure
- A reasonably complete example of the code that is causing problems

Why all these cautions about posting a question to a mailing list? First, developing research skills will stand you in good stead. A good researcher can generally solve a problem quickly and efficiently. Posting a naive question to a technical list often results in a wait rewarded only by a message or two referring you to the archives where you should have begun your search for answers in the first place.

Second, remember that a mailing list is not analogous to a technical support call center. No one is paid to answer your questions. Despite this, you have access to an impressive pool of talent and knowledge, including that of some of the creators of PHP itself. A good question and its answer will be archived to help other coders. Asking a question that has been answered several times just adds more noise.

Having said this, don't be afraid to post a problem to the list. PHP developers are a civilized and helpful breed, and by bringing a problem to the attention of the community, you might be helping others to solve the same problem.

The Basics of PHP Scripts

Let's jump straight in with a PHP script. To begin, open your favorite text editor. Like HTML documents, PHP files are made up of plain text. You can create them with any text editor, such as Notepad on Windows, Simple Text and BBEdit on Mac OS, or vi and Emacs on Unix operating systems. Most popular HTML editors provide at least some support for PHP.

Keith Edmunds maintains a handy list of PHP-friendly editors at
`http://www.itworks.demon.co.uk/phpeditors.htm`.

Type in the example in Listing 3.1 and save the file, calling it something like `first.php`.

LISTING 3.1 A Simple PHP Script

```
1: <?php
2:     print "Hello Web!";
3: ?>
```

If you are not working directly on the machine that will be serving your PHP script, you will probably need to use an FTP client such as WS-FTP for Windows or Fetch for Mac OS to upload your saved document to the server.

Once the document is in place, you should be able to access it via your browser. If all has gone well, you should see the script's output. Figure 3.3 shows the output from the first.php script.

FIGURE 3.3

Success: the output from Listing 3.1.

Beginning and Ending a Block of PHP Statements

When writing PHP, you need to inform the PHP engine that you want it to execute your commands. If you don't do this, the code you write will be mistaken for HTML and will be output to the browser. You can designate your code as PHP with special tags that mark the beginning and end of PHP code blocks. Table 3.1 shows four such PHP delimiter tags.

TABLE 3.1 PHP Start and End Tags

Tag Style	Start Tag	End Tag
Standard tags	`<?php`	`?>`
Short tags	`<?`	`?>`
ASP tags	`<%`	`%>`
Script tags	`<SCRIPT LANGUAGE="php">`	`</SCRIPT>`

Of the tags in Table 3.1, only the standard and script tags are guaranteed to work on any configuration. The short and ASP style tags must be explicitly enabled in your php.ini.

To activate recognition for short tags, you must make sure that the short_open_tag switch is set to On in php.ini:

```
short_open_tag  =  On;
```

Short tags are enabled by default, so you only need to edit php.ini if you want to disable them.

To activate recognition for the ASP style tags, you must enable the asp_tags setting:

```
asp_tags = On;
```

After you have edited php.ini, you should be able to use any of the four styles in your scripts. This is largely a matter of preference, although if you intend to include XML in your script, you should disable the short tags (<? ?>) and work with the standard tags (<?php ?>).

The character sequence <? tells an XML parser to expect a processing instruction and is therefore frequently included in XML documents. If you include XML in your script and have short tags enabled, the PHP engine is likely to confuse XML processing instructions and PHP start tags. Disable short tags if you intend to incorporate XML in your document.

Let's run through some of the ways in which you can legally write the code in Listing 3.1. You can use any of the four PHP start and end tags that you have seen:

```
<?
print("Hello Web!");
?>

<?php
print("Hello Web!");
?>

<%
print("Hello Web!");
%>

<SCRIPT LANGUAGE="php">
print("Hello Web!");
</SCRIPT>
```

You can also put single lines of code in PHP on the same line as the PHP start and end tags:

```
<? print("Hello Web!"); ?>
```

Now that you know how to define a block of PHP code, let's take a closer look at the code in Listing 3.1 itself.

The `print()` Function

`print()` is a function that outputs data. In most cases, anything output by `print()` ends up in the browser window. A *function* is a command that performs an action, usually modified in some way by data provided for it. Data sent to a function is almost always placed in parentheses after the function name. In this case, you sent the `print()` function a collection of characters, or a *string*. Strings must always be enclosed in quotation marks, either single or double.

 Function calls generally require parentheses after their names regardless of whether or not they demand that data be passed to them. `print()` is an exception—enclosing the data you want to print to the browser in parentheses is optional. `print` is a more common syntax than `print()`, so we will usually omit the parentheses in our examples.

The only line of code in Listing 3.1 ended with a semicolon. The semicolon informs the PHP engine that you have completed a statement.

A *statement* represents an instruction to the PHP engine. Broadly, it is to PHP what a sentence is to written or spoken English. A sentence should end with a period; a statement should usually end with a semicolon. Exceptions to this include statements that enclose other statements, and statements that end a block of code. In most cases, however, failure to end a statement with a semicolon will confuse the PHP engine and result in an error.

Combining HTML and PHP

The script in Listing 3.1 is pure PHP. You can incorporate this into an HTML document by simply adding HTML outside the PHP start and end tags, as shown in Listing 3.2.

LISTING 3.2   A PHP Script Incorporated into HTML

```
 1: <html>
 2: <head>
 3: <title>Listing 3.2 A PHP script including HTML</title>
 4: </head>
 5: <body>
 6: <b>
 7: <?php
 8:     print "hello world";
 9: ?>
10: </b>
11: </body>
12: </html>
```

As you can see, incorporating PHP code into a predominantly HTML document is simply a matter of typing in the code. The PHP engine ignores everything outside the PHP open and close tags. If you were to view Listing 3.2 with a browser, as shown in Figure 3.4, you would see the string "hello world" in bold. If you were to view the document source, as shown in Figure 3.5, the listing would look exactly like a normal HTML document.

FIGURE 3.4

The output of Listing 3.2 as viewed in a browser.

FIGURE 3.5

The output of Listing 3.2 as HTML source code.

You can include as many blocks of PHP code as you need in a single document, interspersing them with HTML as required. Although you can have multiple blocks of code in a single document, they combine to form a single script. Any variables defined in the first block will usually be available to subsequent blocks.

Adding Comments to PHP Code

Code that seems clear at the time of writing can seem like a hopeless tangle when you try to amend it six months later. Adding comments to your code as you write can save you time later on and make it easier for other programmers to work with your code.

A *comment* is text in a script that is ignored by the PHP engine. Comments can be used to make code more readable, or to annotate a script.

Single-line comments begin with two forward slashes (//) or a single hash sign (#). The PHP engine ignores all text between these marks and either the end of the line or the PHP close tag:

```
// this is a comment
#  this is another comment
```

Multiline comments begin with a forward slash followed by an asterisk (/*) and end with an asterisk followed by a forward slash (*/):

```
/*
this is a comment
none of this will
be parsed by the
PHP engine
*/
```

Summary

In this hour, you learned how to install and configure PHP for use with Apache on either Linux/Unix or Windows. You learned that various `configure` options in the Linux/Unix build script can change the features that are supported. You learned about `php.ini` and how to change the values of its directives. Using the `phpinfo()` function, you tested your installation and produced a list of its configuration values. You created a simple PHP script using a text editor. You examined four sets of tags that you can use to begin and end blocks of PHP code. Finally, you learned how to use the `print()` function to send data to the browser, and you brought HTML and PHP together into the same script. In the next hour, you will use these skills to test some of the fundamental building blocks of the PHP language, including variables, data types, and operators.

Q&A

Q **You have covered an installation for Linux/Unix or Windows, and the Apache Web server. Does this mean that the material presented in this book will not apply to my server and operating system?**

A No, one of PHP's great strengths is that it runs on multiple platforms. You can find installation instructions for different Web servers and configuration directives for database support in the PHP Manual. While the examples throughout this book are specifically geared toward the combination of PHP, MySQL, and Apache, only slight modifications would be needed to work with the examples using different Web servers or databases.

Q **Which are the best start and end tags to use?**

A It is largely a matter of preference. For the sake of portability, the standard tags (`<?php ?>`) are probably the safest bet. Short tags are enabled by default and have the virtue of brevity, but with the increasing popularity of XML, it is safest to avoid them.

Q **What editors should I avoid when creating PHP code?**

A Do not use word processors that format text for printing (such as Word, for example). Even if you save files created using this type of editor in plain text format, hidden characters are likely to creep into your code.

Q **When should I comment my code?**

A Once again, this is a matter of preference. Some short scripts will be self-explanatory, even after a long interval. For scripts of any length or complexity, you should comment your code. This often saves you time and frustration in the long run.

3

Workshop

The workshop is designed to help you anticipate possible questions, review what you've learned, and begin putting your knowledge into practice.

Quiz

1. From a Linux/Unix operating system, how would you get help on configuration options (the options that you pass to the `configure` script in your PHP distribution)?

2. What line should you add to the Apache configuration file to ensure that the `.php` extension is recognized?

3. What is PHP's configuration file called?

4. Can a user read the source code of PHP script you have successfully installed?

Answers

1. You can get help on configuration options by calling the `configure` script in the PHP distribution folder and passing it the `--help` argument:

   ```
   ./configure --help
   ```

2. The line

   ```
   AddType application/x-httpd-php .php
   ```

   ensures that Apache will treat files ending with the `.php` extension as PHP scripts.

3. PHP's configuration file is called `php.ini`.

4. No, the user will only see the output of your script. The exception to this is if you have explicitly created a copy of the script with a `.phps` extension, which will show the color-coded source.

Activities

1. Install PHP on your system. If it is already in place, review your `php.ini` file and check your configuration.

2. Familiarize yourself with the process of creating, uploading, and running PHP scripts. In particular, create your own "hello world" script. Add HTML code to it, and additional blocks of PHP. Experiment with the different PHP delimiter tags. Which ones are enabled in your configuration? Take a look at your `php.ini` file to confirm your findings. Don't forget to add some comments to your code.

PART II
Basic Language Elements

Hour

4   The Building Blocks of PHP

5   Flow Control Functions in PHP

6   Working with Functions

7   Learning Basic SQL Commands

8   Interacting with MySQL Using PHP

Hour 4

The Building Blocks of PHP

In this hour, you will get your hands dirty with some of the nuts and bolts of the PHP scripting language. Those of you new to programming may feel overwhelmed at times, but don't worry—you can always refer back to this hour later on. Concentrate on understanding the concepts rather than memorizing the features covered.

If you're already an experienced programmer, you should at least skim this hour's lesson, as it covers a few PHP-specific features.

In this hour, you will learn

- About variables—what they are, why you need to use them, and how to use them
- How to define and access variables
- About data types
- About some of the more commonly used operators
- How to use operators to create expressions
- How to define and use constants

Variables

A variable is a special container that you can define to "hold" a value. Variables are fundamental to programming. Without variables, we would be forced to hard-code all the values in our scripts. By adding two numbers together and printing the result, you can achieve something useful:

```
print (2 + 4);
```

This script will only be useful for people who want to know the sum of 2 and 4, however. To get past this, you could write a script for finding the sum of another set of numbers, say 3 and 5. However, this approach to programming is clearly absurd, and this is where variables come into play.

Variables allow us to create templates for operations (adding two numbers, for example), without worrying about what values the variables contain. Values will be given to the variables when the script is run, possibly through user input, or through a database query.

You should use a variable whenever the data that you are subjecting to an operation in your script is liable to change from one script execution to another, or even within the lifetime of the script itself.

A variable consists of a name of your choosing, preceded by a dollar sign ($). Variable names can include letters, numbers, and the underscore character (_). They cannot include spaces. They must begin with a letter or an underscore. The following code defines some legal variables:

```
$a;
$a_longish_variable_name;
$2453;
$sleepyZZZZ;
```

Your variable names should be meaningful as well as consistent in style. For example, if your script deals with name and password values, don't create a variable called $n for the name and $p for the password—those are not meaningful names. If you pick up that script weeks later, you might think that $n is the variable for "number" rather than "name" and that $p stands for "page" rather than "password."

A semicolon (;)—also known as the *instruction terminator*—is used to end a PHP statement. The semicolons in the previous fragment of code are not part of the variable names.

A *variable* is a holder for a type of data. It can hold numbers, strings of characters, objects, arrays, or Booleans. The contents of a variable can be changed at any time.

As you can see, you have plenty of choices when naming variables. To declare a variable, you need only include it in your script. When you declare a variable, you usually assign a value to it in the same statement, as shown here:

```
$num1 = 8;
$num2 = 23;
```

The preceding lines declare two variables, using the assignment operator (=) to give them values. You will learn about assignment in more detail in the "Operators and Expressions" section later in this hour. After you give your variables values, you can treat them exactly as if they were the values themselves. In other words

```
print $num1;
```

is equivalent to

```
print 8;
```

as long as $num1 contains 8.

Data Types

Different types of data take up different amounts of memory and may be treated differently when they are manipulated in a script. Some programming languages therefore demand that the programmer declare in advance which type of data a variable will contain. By contrast, PHP is loosely typed, meaning that it will calculate data types as data is assigned to each variable. This is a mixed blessing. On the one hand, it means that variables can be used flexibly, holding a string at one point and an integer at another. On the other hand, this can lead to problems in larger scripts if you expect a variable to hold one data type when in fact it holds something completely different. For example, suppose you have created code that is designed to work with an array variable. If the variable in question instead contains a number value, errors might occur when the code attempts to perform array-specific operations on the variable.

Table 4.1 shows the six standard data types available in PHP.

TABLE 4.1   Standard Data Types

Type	Example	Description
Integer	5	A whole number
Double	3.234	A floating-point number
String	"hello"	A collection of characters
Boolean	true	One of the special values true or false
Object		An instance of a class
Array		An ordered set of keys and values

PHP also provides two special data types, listed in Table 4.2.

TABLE 4.2   Special Data Types

Type	Description
Resource	Reference to a third-party resource (a database, for example)
NULL	An uninitialized variable

Resource types are often returned by functions that deal with external applications or files. The type NULL is reserved for variables that have not been initialized (that is, variables that have not yet had a value assigned to them).

You can use PHP's built-in function gettype() to test the type of any variable. If you place a variable between the parentheses of the function call, gettype() returns a string representing the relevant type. Listing 4.1 assigns five different data types to a single variable, testing it with gettype() each time.

> You can read more about calling functions in Hour 6, "Working with Functions."

LISTING 4.1   Testing the Type of a Variable

```
1: <html>
2: <head>
3: <title>Listing 4.1 Testing the type of a variable</title>
4: </head>
5: <body>
6: <?php
7: $testing; // declare without assigning
```

LISTING 4.1 continued

```
 8: print gettype( $testing ); // null
 9: print "<br>";
10: $testing = 5;
11: print gettype( $testing ); // integer
12: print "<br>";
13: $testing = "five";
14: print gettype( $testing ); // string
15: print("<br>");
16: $testing = 5.0;
17: print gettype( $testing ); // double
18: print("<br>");
19: $testing = true;
20: print gettype( $testing ); // boolean
21: print "<br>";
22: ?>
23: </body>
24: </html>
```

Put these lines into a text file called gettype.php, and place this file in your Web server document root. When you access this script through your Web browser, it produces the following:

```
NULL
integer
string
double
boolean
```

When we declare the $testing variable in line 7, we do not assign a value to it, so when we first use the gettype() function to test the variable in line 8, we get the string NULL. After this, we assign values to $testing by using the = sign before passing it to gettype(). An integer, assigned to the $testing variable in line 10, is a whole or real number. In simple terms, you can think of it as a number without a decimal point. A string, assigned to the $testing variable in line 13, is a collection of characters. When you work with strings in your scripts, they should always be surrounded by double or single quotation marks (" or '). A double, assigned to the $testing variable in line 16, is a floating-point number (that is, a number that includes a decimal point). A Boolean, assigned to the $testing variable in line 19, can have one of two special values, true or false.

Changing Type with settype()

PHP provides the function settype() to change the type of a variable. To use settype(), you must place the variable to change and the type to change it to between the parentheses and separate them with a comma. Listing 4.2 converts the value 3.14 (a double) to each of the four types that we are focusing on in this hour.

LISTING 4.2   Changing the Type of a Variable with `settype()`

```
 1: <html>
 2: <head>
 3: <title>Listing 4.2 Changing the type of a variable with settype()</title>
 4: </head>
 5: <body>
 6: <?php
 7: $undecided = 3.14;
 8: print gettype( $undecided ); // double
 9: print " is $undecided<br>";  // 3.14
10: settype( $undecided, 'string' );
11: print gettype( $undecided ); // string
12: print " is $undecided<br>";  // 3.14
13: settype( $undecided, 'integer' );
14: print gettype( $undecided ); // integer
15: print " is $undecided<br>";  // 3
16: settype( $undecided, 'double' );
17: print gettype( $undecided ); // double
18: print " is $undecided<br>";  // 3.0
19: settype( $undecided, 'boolean' );
20: print gettype( $undecided ); // boolean
21: print " is $undecided<br>";  // 1
22: ?>
23: </body>
24: </html>
```

In each case, we use `gettype()` to confirm that the type change worked and then print the value of the variable `$undecided` to the browser. When we convert the string `"3.14"` to an integer in line 13, any information beyond the decimal point is lost forever. That's why `$undecided` contains `3.0` after we change it back to a double in line 16. Finally, in line 19, we convert `$undecided` to a Boolean. Any number other than `0` becomes `true` when converted to a Boolean. When printing a Boolean in PHP, `true` is represented as `1` and `false` is represented as an empty string, so in line 21, `$undecided` is printed as `1`.

Put these lines into a text file called `settype.php`, and place this file in your Web server document root. When you access this script through your Web browser, it produces the following:

```
double is 3.14
string is 3.14
integer is 3
double is 3
boolean is 1
```

Changing Type by Casting

By placing the name of a data type in parentheses in front of a variable, you create a copy of that variable's value converted to the data type specified.

The principal difference between a settype() and a cast is the fact that casting produces a copy, leaving the original variable untouched. Listing 4.3 illustrates this.

LISTING 4.3 Casting a Variable

```
 1: <html>
 2: <head>
 3: <title>Listing 4.3 Casting a variable</title>
 4: </head>
 5: <body>
 6: <?php
 7: $undecided = 3.14;
 8: $holder = ( double ) $undecided;
 9: print gettype( $holder ) ; // double
10: print " is $holder<br>";   // 3.14
11: $holder = ( string ) $undecided;
12: print gettype( $holder ); // string
13: print " is $holder<br>";   // 3.14
14: $holder = ( integer ) $undecided;
15: print gettype( $holder ); // integer
16: print " is $holder<br>";   // 3
17: $holder = ( double ) $undecided;
18: print gettype( $holder ); // double
19: print " is $holder<br>";   // 3.14
20: $holder = ( boolean ) $undecided;
21: print gettype( $holder ); // boolean
22: print " is $holder<br>";   // 1
23: print "<hr>";
24: print "original variable type: ";
25: print gettype( $undecided ); // double
26: ?>
27: </body>
28: </html>
```

4

We never actually change the type of $undecided, which remains a double throughout. This is illustrated on line 25, where we use the gettype() function to output the type of $undecided.

In fact, by casting $undecided, we create a copy that is then converted to the type we specify. This new value is stored in the variable $holder, first in line 8, and also in lines 11, 14, 17, and 20. Because we are working with a copy of $undecided, we never discard any information from it as we did in lines 13 and 19 of Listing 4.2.

Put these lines into a text file called `testcast.php`, and place this file in your Web server document root. When you access this script through your Web browser, it produces the following:

```
double is 3.14
string is 3.14
integer is 3
double is 3.14
boolean is 1
original variable type: double
```

Now that we can change the contents of a variable from one type to another, using either `settype()` or a cast, we should consider why this might be useful. It is certainly not a procedure that you will use often because PHP will automatically cast for you when the context requires. However, an automatic cast is temporary, and you might wish to make a variable persistently hold a particular data type.

Numbers that a user types into an HTML form will be made available to your script as a string. If you try to add two strings containing numbers, PHP will helpfully convert the strings into numbers while the addition is taking place. So

```
"30cm" + "40cm"
```

will give the integer 70. In casting the strings, PHP will ignore the non-numeric characters. However, you might want to clean up the user input yourself. Imagine that the user has been asked to submit a number. We can simulate this by declaring a variable and assigning to it:

```
$test = "30cm";
```

As you can see, the user has added units to the number. We can make sure that the user input is clean by casting it to an integer:

```
$test = (integer)$test;
print "Your imaginary box has a width of $test centimeters";
```

Why Test Type?

Why might it be useful to know the type of a variable? There are often circumstances in programming in which data is passed to you from another source. In Hour 6, for example, you will learn how to create functions in your scripts. Functions can accept information from calling code in the form of arguments. For the function to work with the data it is given, it is often a good idea to first verify that it has been given values of the correct data type. A function that is expecting a resource, for example, will not work well when passed a string.

Operators and Expressions

With what you have learned so far, you can assign data to variables. You can even investigate and change the data type of a variable. A programming language isn't very useful, though, unless you can manipulate the data you can store. Operators are symbols that make it possible to use one or more values to produce a new value. A value that is operated on by an operator is referred to as an operand.

> An *operator* is a symbol or series of symbols that, when used in conjunction with values, performs an action and usually produces a new value.
>
> An *operand* is a value used in conjunction with an operator. There are usually two operands to one operator.

Let's combine two operands with an operator to produce a new value:

`4 + 5`

4 and 5 are operands. They are operated on by the addition operator (+) to produce 9. Operators almost always sit between two operands, though you will see a few exceptions later in this hour.

The combination of operands with an operator to produce a result is called an *expression*. Although most operators form the basis of expressions, an expression need not contain an operator. In fact, in PHP, an expression is defined as anything that can be used as a value. This includes integer constants such as 654, variables such as $user, and function calls such as gettype(). (4 + 5), for example, is an expression that consists of two further expressions and an operator. When an expression produces a value, it is often said to "resolve to" that value. That is, when all subexpressions are taken into account, the expression can be treated as if it were a code for the value itself.

> An *expression* is any combination of functions, values, and operators that resolve to a value. As a rule of thumb, if you can use it as if it were a value, it is an expression.

Now that we have the principles out of the way, it's time to take a tour of PHP's more common operators.

4

The Assignment Operator

You have seen the assignment operator each time we have initialized a variable. It consists of the single character =. The assignment operator takes the value of its right-hand operand and assigns it to its left-hand operand:

```
$name = "matt";
```

The variable $name now contains the string "matt". Interestingly, this construct is an expression. It might appear at first glance that the assignment operator simply changes the variable $name without producing a value, but in fact, a statement that uses the assignment operator always resolves to a copy of the value of the right operand. Thus

```
print ( $name = "matt" );
```

prints the string "matt" to the browser in addition to assigning "matt" to $name.

Arithmetic Operators

The arithmetic operators do exactly what you would expect—they perform arithmetic operations. Table 4.3 lists these operators. The addition operator adds the right operand to the left operand. The subtraction operator subtracts the right-hand operand from the left. The division operator divides the left-hand operand by the right. The multiplication operator multiplies the left-hand operand by the right. The modulus operator returns the remainder of the left operand divided by the right.

TABLE 4.3   Arithmetic Operators

Operator	Name	Example	Example Result
+	Addition	10+3	13
-	Subtraction	10-3	7
/	Division	10/3	3.3333333333333
*	Multiplication	10*3	30
%	Modulus	10%3	1

The Concatenation Operator

The concatenation operator is represented by a single period. Treating both operands as strings, it appends the right-hand operand to the left. So

```
"hello"." world"
```

returns

```
"hello world"
```

Regardless of the data types of the operands, they are treated as strings, and the result is always a string. We will encounter concatenation frequently throughout this book when we need to combine the results of an expression of some kind with a string.

```
$centimeters = 212;
print "the width is ".($centimeters/100)." meters";
```

Combined Assignment Operators

Although there is really only one assignment operator, PHP provides a number of combination operators that transform the left-hand operand and return a result. As a rule, operators use their operands without changing their values. Assignment operators break this rule. A combined assignment operator consists of a standard operator symbol followed by an equals sign. Combination assignment operators save you the trouble of using two operators yourself. For example

```
$x = 4;
$x = $x + 4; // $x now equals 8
```

may instead be written as

```
$x = 4;
$x += 4; // $x now equals 8
```

There is an assignment operator for each of the arithmetic operators and one for the concatenation operator. Table 4.4 lists some of the most common.

TABLE 4.4 Some Combined Assignment Operators

Operator	Example	Equivalent To
+=	$x += 5	$x = $x + 5
-=	$x -= 5	$x = $x - 5
/=	$x /= 5	$x = $x / 5
*=	$x *= 5	$x = $x * 5
%=	$x %= 5	$x = $x % 5
.=	$x .= " test"	$x = $x." test"

Each of the examples in Table 4.4 transforms the value of $x using the value of the right-hand operand.

Automatically Incrementing and Decrementing an Integer Variable

When coding in PHP, you will often find it necessary to increment or decrement an integer variable. You will usually need to do this when you are counting the iterations of a loop. You have already learned two ways of doing this. We can increment the integer contained by $x with the addition operator

```
$x = $x + 1; // $x is incremented
```

or with a combined assignment operator

```
$x += 1; // $x is incremented
```

In both cases, the resultant integer is assigned to $x. Because expressions of this kind are so common, PHP provides some special operators that allow you to add or subtract the integer constant 1 from an integer variable, assigning the result to the variable itself. These are known as the post-increment and post-decrement operators. The post-increment operator consists of two plus symbols appended to a variable name:

```
$x++; // $x is incremented
```

This expression increments the variable $x by one. Using two minus symbols in the same way decrements the variable:

```
$x-; // $x is decremented
```

If you use the post-increment or post-decrement operators in conjunction with a conditional operator, the operand will only be modified after the test has been completed:

```
$x = 3;
$x++ < 4; // true
```

In the previous example, $x contains 3 when it is tested against 4 with the less than operator, so the test expression returns true. After this test is complete, $x is incremented.

In some circumstances, you might want to increment or decrement a variable in a test expression before the test is carried out. PHP provides the pre-increment and pre-decrement operators for this purpose. These operators behave in exactly the same way as the post-increment and post-decrement operators, but they are written with the plus or minus symbols preceding the variable:

```
++$x; // $x is incremented
-$x; // $x is decremented
```

If these operators are used as part of a test expression, the incrementation occurs before the test is carried out.

```
$x = 3;
++$x < 4; // false
```

In the previous fragment, $x is incremented before it is tested against 4. The test expression returns false because 4 is not smaller than 4.

Comparison Operators

Comparison operators perform tests on their operands. They return the Boolean value true if the test is successful, or false otherwise. This type of expression is useful in control structures, such as if and while statements. We will cover these in Hour 5, "Flow Control Functions in PHP."

To test whether the value contained in $x is smaller than 5, for example, you can use the less-than operator:

```
$x < 5
```

If $x contains the value 3, this expression has the value true. If $x contains 7, the expression resolves to false.

Table 4.5 lists the comparison operators.

TABLE 4.5 Comparison Operators

Operator	Name	Returns True If...	Example ($x is 4)	Result
==	Equivalence	Left is equivalent to right	$x == 5	false
!=	Non-equivalence	Left is not equivalent to right	$x != 5	true
===	Identical	Left is equivalent to right and they are the same type	$x === "7"	false
>	Greater than	Left is greater than right	$x > 4	false
>=	Greater than or equal to	Left is greater than or equal to right	$x >= 4	true
<	Less than	Left is less than right	$x < 4	false
<=	Less than or equal to	Left is less than or equal to right	$x <= 4	true

4

These operators are most commonly used with integers or doubles, although the equivalence operator is also used to compare strings. Be very sure you understand the difference between the == and = operators. The == operator tests equivalence, while the = operator assigns value.

Creating More Complex Test Expressions with the Logical Operators

The logical operators test combinations of Booleans. For example, the or operator, which is indicated by two pipe characters (||) or simply the word or, returns true if either the left or the right operand is true:

```
true || false
```

This expression returns `true`.

The and operator, which is indicated by two ampersand characters (&&) or simply the word and, only returns `true` if both the left and right operands are true:

```
true && false
```

This expression returns `false`. It's unlikely that you will use a logical operator to test Boolean constants, however. It makes more sense to test two or more expressions that resolve to a Boolean. For example

```
( $x > 2 ) && ( $x < 15 )
```

returns `true` if $x contains a value that is greater than 2 and smaller than 15. We include the parentheses to make the code easier to read. Table 4.6 lists the logical operators.

TABLE 4.6   Logical Operators

Operator	Name	Returns True If...	Example	Result
`||`	Or	Left or right is true	`true || false`	`true`
`or`	Or	Left or right is true	`true or false`	`true`
`xor`	Xor	Left or right is true but not both	`true xor true`	`false`
`&&`	And	Left and right are true	`true && false`	`false`
`and`	And	Left and right are true	`true and false`	`false`
`!`	Not	The single operand is not true	`! true`	`false`

Why are there two versions of both the or and the and operators? The answer lies in operator precedence, which we will look at later in this section.

Operator Precedence

When you use an operator, the PHP engine usually reads your expression from left to right. For complex expressions that use more than one operator, though, the waters can become a little murky. First, consider a simple case:

```
4 + 5
```

There's no room for confusion here. PHP simply adds 4 to 5. But what about the following fragment?

```
4 + 5 * 2
```

This presents a problem. Does it mean the sum of 4 and 5, multiplied by 2, giving the result 18? Or does it mean 4 plus the result of 5 multiplied by 2, resolving to 14? If you were to simply read from left to right, the former would be true. However, PHP attaches different precedence to operators. Because the multiplication operator has higher precedence than the addition operator does, the second solution to the problem is the correct one.

You can use parentheses to force PHP to execute the addition expression before the multiplication expression:

```
( 4 + 5 ) * 2
```

Whatever the precedence of the operators in a complex expression, it is a good idea to use parentheses to make your code clearer and to save you from obscure bugs. The following is a list of the operators covered in this hour in precedence order (those with highest precedence are listed first):

```
++, -, (cast)
/, *, %
+, -
<, <=, =>, >
==, ===, !=
&&
||
=, +=, -=, /=, *=, %=, .=
and
xor
or
```

As you can see, or has a lower precedence than || and and has a lower precedence than &&, so you can use the lower-precedence logical operators to change the way a complex test expression is read. This is not necessarily a good idea. The following two expressions are equivalent, but the second is much easier to read:

```
$x and $y || $z
$x && ($y || $z)
```

Taking it one step further, the following example is easier still:

```
$x and ($y or $z)
```

The three examples are all equivalent.

The order of precedence is the only reason that both && and and are present in PHP. The same is true of || and or. In most, if not all circumstances, however, use of parentheses will make for clearer code and fewer bugs than code that takes advantage of the difference in precedence of these operators. Throughout this book, we will tend to use the more common || and && operators.

Constants

Variables offer a flexible way of storing data. You can change their values and the type of data they store at any time. If, however, you want to work with a value that you do not want to alter throughout your script's execution, you can define a constant. You must use PHP's built-in define() function to create a constant. After you have done this, the constant cannot be changed. To use the define() function, you must place the name of the constant and the value you want to give it within the call's parentheses. These values must be separated by a comma:

```
define( "CONSTANT_NAME", 42 );
```

The value you want to set can be a number, a string, or a Boolean. By convention, the name of the constant should be in capital letters. Constants are accessed with the constant name only; no dollar symbol is required. Listing 4.4 defines and accesses a constant.

LISTING 4.4   Defining a Constant

```
 1: <html>
 2: <head>
 3: <title>Listing 4.4 Defining a constant</title>
 4: </head>
 5: <body>
 6: <?php
 7: define( "USER", "Gerald" );
 8: print "Welcome ".USER;
 9: ?>
10: </body>
11: </html>
```

Notice that in line 8 we used the concatenation operator to append the value held by our constant to the string "Welcome". This is because the PHP engine has no way of distinguishing between a constant and a string within quotation marks.

Put these lines into a text file called `constants.php`, and place this file in your Web server document root. When you access this script through your Web browser, it produces the following:

```
Welcome Gerald
```

The `define()` function can accept a third Boolean argument that determines whether or not the constant name should be case-independent. By default, constants are case-dependent. However, by passing `true` to the `define()` function, we can change this behavior, so if we were to set up our `USER` constant as

```
define( "USER", "Gerald", true );
```

we could access its value without worrying about case:

```
print User;
print usEr;
print USER;
```

These expressions are all equivalent. This feature can make scripts a little friendlier for programmers who work with our code, in that they will not need to consider case when accessing a constant that we have defined. On the other hand, given the fact that other constants *are* case-sensitive, this might make for more rather than less confusion as programmers forget which constants to treat in which way. Unless you have a compelling reason to do otherwise, the safest course is probably to keep your constants case-sensitive and define them using uppercase characters, which is an easy-to-remember convention.

Predefined Constants

PHP automatically provides some built-in constants for you. `__FILE__`, for example, returns the name of the file that the PHP engine is currently reading. `__LINE__` returns the line number of the file. These constants are useful for generating error messages. You can also find out which version of PHP is interpreting the script with `PHP_VERSION`. This can be useful if you need version information included in script output when sending a bug report.

Summary

In this hour, you covered some of the basic features of the PHP language. You learned about variables and how to assign to them using the assignment operator. You got an introduction to operators and learned how to combine some of the most common of these into expressions. Finally, you learned how to define and access constants.

4

Now that you have mastered some of the fundamentals of PHP, the next hour will really put you in the driver's seat. You will learn how to make scripts that can make decisions and repeat tasks, with help from variables, expressions, and operators.

Q&A

Q Why is it useful to know the type of data a variable holds?

A Often the data type of a variable constrains what you can do with it. You may want to make sure that a variable contains an integer or a double before using it in a mathematical calculation, for example.

Q Should I obey any conventions when naming variables?

A Your goal should always be to make your code easy to read and understand. A variable such as $ab123245 tells you nothing about its role in your script and invites typos. Keep your variable names short and descriptive.

A variable named $f is unlikely to mean much to you when you return to your code after a month or so. A variable named $filename, on the other hand, should make more sense.

Q Should I learn the operator precedence table?

A There is no reason that you shouldn't, but I would save the effort for more useful tasks. By using parentheses in your expressions, you can make your code easy to read while defining your own order of precedence.

Workshop

The workshop is designed to help you anticipate possible questions, review what you've learned, and begin putting your knowledge into practice.

Quiz

1. Which of the following variable names is not valid?

```
$a_value_submitted_by_a_user
$666666xyz
$xyz666666
$__counter__
$the first
$file-name
```

2. What will the following code fragment output?

```
$num = 33;
(boolean) $num;
print $num;
```

3. What will the following statement output?

```
print gettype("4");
```

4. What will be the output from the following code fragment?

```
$test_val = 5.5466;
settype( $test_val, "integer" );
print $test_val;
```

5. Which of the following statements does not contain an expression?

```
4;
gettype(44);
5/12;
```

6. Which of the statements in question 5 contains an operator?

7. What value will the following expression return?

```
5 < 2
```

What data type will the returned value be?

Answers

1. The variable name $666666xyz is not valid because it does not begin with a letter or an underscore character. The variable name $the first is not valid because it contains a space. $file-name is also invalid because it contains a non-alphanumeric character.

2. The fragment will print the integer 33. The cast to Boolean produces a converted copy of the value stored in $num. It does not alter the value actually stored there.

3. The statement will output the string "string".

4. The code will output the value 5. When a double is converted to an integer, any information beyond the decimal point is lost.

5. They are all expressions because they all resolve to values.

6. The statement 5/12; contains a division operator.

7. The expression will resolve to false, which is a Boolean value.

Activities

1. Create a script that contains at least five different variables. Populate them with values of different data types and use the gettype() function to print each type to the browser.

2. Assign values to two variables. Use comparison operators to test whether the first value is

- The same as the second
- Less than the second
- Greater than the second
- Less than or equal to the second

Print the result of each test to the browser.

Change the values assigned to your test variables and run the script again.

HOUR 5

Flow Control Functions in PHP

The scripts created in the last hour flow only in a single direction. The same statements are executed in the same order every time a script is run. This does not allow for much flexibility.

You will now look at some structures that enable your scripts to adapt to circumstances. In this hour, you will learn

- How to use the `if` statement to execute code if a test expression evaluates to `true`
- How to execute alternative blocks of code when the test expression of an `if` statement evaluates to `false`
- How to use the `switch` statement to execute code based on the value returned by a test expression
- How to repeat execution of code using a `while` statement
- How to use `for` statements to make neater loops
- How to break out of loops

- How to nest one loop within another
- How to use PHP start and end tags within control structures

Switching Flow

Most scripts evaluate conditions and change their behavior accordingly. The capability to make decisions makes your PHP pages dynamic, able to change their output according to circumstances. Like most programming languages, PHP allows you to do this with an `if` statement.

The `if` Statement

An `if` statement is a way of controlling the execution of a statement that follows it (that is, a single statement or a block of code inside braces). The `if` statement evaluates an expression between parentheses. If this expression results in a `true` value, the statement is executed. Otherwise, the statement is skipped entirely. This enables scripts to make decisions based on any number of factors:

```
if ( expression ) {
    // code to execute if the expression evaluates to true
}
```

Listing 5.1 executes a block of code only if a variable contains the string `"happy"`.

LISTING 5.1   An if Statement

```
 1: <html>
 2: <head>
 3: <title>Listing 5.1</title>
 4: </head>
 5: <body>
 6: <?php
 7: $mood = "happy";
 8: if ( $mood == "happy" ) {
 9:     print "Hooray, I'm in a good mood";
10: }
11: ?>
12: </body>
13: </html>
```

You use the comparison operator == to compare the variable $mood with the string "happy". If they match, the expression evaluates to `true`, and the code block below the `if` statement is executed.

Put these lines into a text file called `testif.php`, and place this file in your Web server document root. When you access this script through your Web browser, it produces the following:

```
Hooray, I'm in a good mood
```

If you change the value of $mood to "sad" and run the script, the expression in the `if` statement evaluates to `false`, and the code block is skipped. The script remains silent.

Using the `else` Clause with the `if` Statement

When working with the `if` statement, you will often want to define an alternative block of code that should be executed if the expression you are testing evaluates to `false`. You can do this by adding `else` to the `if` statement followed by a further block of code:

```
if ( expression ) {
    // code to execute if the expression evaluates to true
} else {
    // code to execute in all other cases
}
```

Listing 5.2 amends the example in Listing 5.1 so that a default block of code is executed if $mood is not equivalent to "happy".

LISTING 5.2   An `if` Statement That Uses `else`

```
 1: <html>
 2: <head>
 3: <title>Listing 5.2</title>
 4: </head>
 5: <body>
 6: <?php
 7: $mood = "sad";
 8: if ( $mood == "happy" ) {
 9:     print "Hooray, I'm in a good mood";
10: } else {
11:     print "Not happy but $mood";
12: }
13: ?>
14: </body>
15: </html>
```

Put these lines into a text file called `testifelse.php`, and place this file in your Web server document root. When you access this script through your Web browser, it produces the following:

```
Not happy but sad
```

Notice in line 7 that $mood contains the string "sad", which is not equal to "happy", so the expression in the if statement in line 8 evaluates to false. This means that the first block of code (line 9) is skipped. The block of code after else is executed, and the message "Not happy but sad" is printed to the browser.

Using the else clause with the if statement allows scripts to make sophisticated decisions, but your options are currently limited to an either-or branch. PHP allows you to evaluate multiple expressions one after another.

Using the elseif Clause with the if Statement

You can use an if...elseif...else construct to test multiple expressions before offering a default block of code:

```
if ( expression ) {
    // code to execute if the expression evaluates to true
} elseif ( another expression ) {
    // code to execute if the previous expression failed
    // and this one evaluates to true
} else {
    // code to execute in all other cases
}
```

If the first expression does not evaluate to true, the first block of code is ignored. The elseif clause then causes another expression to be evaluated. Once again, if this expression evaluates to true, the second block of code is executed. Otherwise, the block of code associated with the else clause is executed. You can include as many elseif clauses as you want, and if you don't need a default action, you can omit the else clause.

The elseif clause can also be written as two separate words (else if). The syntax you employ is a matter of taste.

Listing 5.3 adds an elseif clause to the previous example.

LISTING 5.3   An if Statement That Uses else and elseif

```
1: <html>
2: <head>
3: <title>Listing 5.3</title>
4: </head>
5: <body>
```

LISTING 5.3   continued

```
 6: <?php
 7: $mood = "sad";
 8: if ( $mood == "happy" ) {
 9:     print "Hooray, I'm in a good mood";
10: } elseif ( $mood == "sad" ) {
11:     print "Awww. Don't be down!";
12: } else {
13:     print "Neither happy nor sad but $mood";
14: }
15: ?>
16: </body>
17: </html>
```

Once again, $mood holds a string, "sad", in line 7. This is not equal to "happy", so the first block in line 9 is ignored. The elseif clause in line 10 tests for equivalence between the contents of $mood and the value "sad", which evaluates to true. This block of code is therefore executed. In lines 12, 13, and 14, we provide default behavior. If none of the test conditions have been fulfilled, we simply print out a message including the actual value of the $mood variable.

Put these lines into a text file called testifelseif.php, and place this file in your Web server document root. When you access this script through your Web browser, it produces the following:

```
Awww. Don't be down!
```

Change the value of $mood to "unknown" and run the script, and it will produce the following:

```
Neither happy nor sad but unknown
```

The switch Statement

The switch statement is an alternative way of changing program flow according to the evaluation of an expression. There are some key differences between the switch and if statements. Using the if statement in conjunction with elseif, you can evaluate multiple expressions. The switch statement evaluates only one expression, executing different code according to the result of that expression, as long as the expression evaluates to a simple type (a number, a string, or a Boolean). The result of an expression evaluated as part of an if statement is read as either true or false. The expression of a switch statement yields a result that is tested against any number of values:

```
switch ( expression ) {
    case result1:
```

```
        // execute this if expression results in result1
        break;
    case result2:
        // execute this if expression results in result2
        break;
    default:
        // execute this if no break statement
        // has been encountered hitherto
}
```

The `switch` statement's expression is often simply a variable. Within the `switch` state-ment's block of code, you find a number of `case` statements. Each of these tests a value against the result of the `switch` statement's expression. If these are equivalent, the code after the `case` statement is executed. The `break` statement ends execution of the `switch` statement altogether. If this is left out, the next `case` statement's expression is evaluated. If the optional `default` statement is reached, its code is executed.

Don't forget to include a `break` statement at the end of any code that will be executed as part of a `case` statement. Without `break`, the program flow will continue to the next `case` statement and ultimately to the `default` statement. In most cases, this will not be the behavior that you are expecting.

Listing 5.4 re-creates the functionality of the `if` statement example, using the `switch` statement.

LISTING 5.4   A switch Statement

```
 1: <html>
 2: <head>
 3: <title>Listing 5.4</title>
 4: </head>
 5: <body>
 6: <?php
 7: $mood = "sad";
 8: switch ( $mood ) {
 9:     case "happy":
10:         print "Hooray, I'm in a good mood";
11:         break;
12:     case "sad":
13:         print "Awww. Don't be down!";
14:         break;
15:     default:
16:         print "Neither happy nor sad but $mood";
17: }
18: ?>
19: </body>
20: </html>
```

Once again, in line 7 the $mood variable is initialized to "sad". The switch statement in line 8 uses this variable as its expression. The first case statement in line 9 tests for equivalence between "happy" and the value of $mood. There is no match, so script execution moves on to the second case statement in line 12. The string "sad" is equivalent to the value of $mood, so this block of code is executed. The break statement in line 14 ends the process.

Put these lines into a text file called testswitch.php, and place this file in your Web server document root. When you access this script through your Web browser, it produces the following:

Awww. Don't be down!

Change the value of $mood to "happy" and run the script, and it will produce the following:

Hooray, I'm in a good mood

To emphasize the caution regarding the importance of the break statement, try running this script with the second break statement commented out. Your output will be

Awww. Don't be down!Neither happy nor sad but sad

This is definitely not the desired output, so be sure to include break statements where appropriate.

Using the ? Operator

The ? or ternary operator is similar to the if statement but returns a value derived from one of two expressions separated by a colon. This construct will provide you with three parts of the whole, hence the name "ternary." Which expression is used to generate the value returned depends on the result of a test expression:

```
( expression )?returned_if_expression_is_true:returned_if_expression_is_false;
```

If the test expression evaluates to true, the result of the second expression is returned; otherwise, the value of the third expression is returned. Listing 5.5 uses the ternary operator to set the value of a variable according to the value of $mood.

LISTING 5.5   Using the ? Operator

```
1: <html>
2: <head>
3: <title>Listing 5.5</title>
4: </head>
5: <body>
```

5

LISTING 5.5   continued

```
 6: <?php
 7: $mood = "sad";
 8: $text = ($mood=="happy") ? "I'm in a good mood" : "Not happy but $mood";
 9: print "$text";
10: ?>
11: </body>
12: </html>
```

In line 7, $mood is set to "sad". In line 8, $mood is tested for equivalence to the string "happy". Because this test returns false, the result of the third of the three expressions is returned.

Put these lines into a text file called testtern.php, and place this file in your Web server document root. When you access this script through your Web browser, it produces the following:

```
Not happy but sad
```

The ternary operator can be difficult to read but is useful if you are dealing with only two alternatives and like to write compact code.

Loops

So far we've looked at decisions that a script can make about what code to execute. Scripts can also decide how many times to execute a block of code. Loop statements are designed to enable you to achieve repetitive tasks. Almost without exception, a loop continues to operate until a condition is achieved, or you explicitly choose to exit the loop.

The while Statement

The while statement looks similar in structure to a basic if statement:

```
while ( expression ) {
     // do something
}
```

As long as a while statement's expression evaluates to true, the code block is executed over and over again. Each execution of the code block in a loop is called an *iteration*. Within the block, you usually change something that affects the while statement's expression; otherwise, your loop continues indefinitely. Listing 5.6 creates a while loop that calculates and prints multiples of 2 up to 24.

LISTING 5.6 A while Statement

```
 1: <html>
 2: <head>
 3: <title>Listing 5.6</title>
 4: </head>
 5: <body>
 6: <?php
 7: $counter = 1;
 8: while ( $counter <= 12 ) {
 9:     print "$counter times 2 is ".($counter*2)."<br>";
10:     $counter++;
11: }
12: ?>
13: </body>
14: </html>
```

In this example, we initialize a variable $counter in line 7. The while statement in line 8 tests the $counter variable. As long as the integer that $counter contains is less than or equal to 12, the loop continues to run. Within the while statement's code block, the value contained by $counter is multiplied by two, and the result is printed to the browser. Then line 10 increments $counter. This last stage is extremely important. If you were to forget to change $counter, the while expression would never resolve to false, and the loop would never end.

Put these lines into a text file called testwhile.php, and place this file in your Web server document root. When you access this script through your Web browser, it produces the following:

```
1 times 2 is 2
2 times 2 is 4
3 times 2 is 6
4 times 2 is 8
5 times 2 is 10
6 times 2 is 12
7 times 2 is 14
8 times 2 is 16
9 times 2 is 18
10 times 2 is 20
11 times 2 is 22
12 times 2 is 24
```

5

The do...while Statement

A do...while statement looks a little like a while statement turned on its head. The essential difference between the two is that the code block is executed before the truth test and not after it:

```
do   {
    // code to be executed
} while ( expression );
```

 The test expression of a do...while statement should always end with a semicolon.

This statement might be useful if you want the code block to be executed at least once even if the while expression evaluates to false. Listing 5.7 creates a do...while statement. The code block is executed a minimum of one time.

LISTING 5.7   The do...while Statement

```
 1: <html>
 2: <head>
 3: <title>Listing 5.7</title>
 4: </head>
 5: <body>
 6: <?php
 7: $num = 1;
 8: do {
 9:     print "Execution number: $num<br>\n";
10:     $num++;
11: } while ( $num > 200 && $num < 400 );
12: ?>
13: </body>
14: </html>
```

The do...while statement tests whether the variable $num contains a value that is greater than 200 and less than 400. In line 7, we have initialized $num to 1, so this expression returns false. Nonetheless, the code block is executed before the expression is evaluated, so the statement will print a single line to the browser.

Put these lines into a text file called testdowhile.php, and place this file in your Web server document root. When you access this script through your Web browser, it produces the following:

```
Execution number: 1
```

The for Statement

You cannot achieve anything with a for statement that you cannot do with a while statement. On the other hand, the for statement is often a neater and safer way of achieving the same effect. Earlier, Listing 5.6 initialized a variable outside the while statement. The while statement then tested the variable in its expression. The variable was incremented within the code block. The for statement allows you to achieve this on a single line. This allows for more compact code and makes it less likely that you will forget to increment a counter variable, thereby creating an infinite loop:

```
for ( initialization expression; test expression; modification expression ) {
    // code to be executed
}
```

 Infinite loops are, as the name suggests, loops that run without bounds. If your loop is running infinitely, your script is running for an infinite amount of time. This is very stressful on your Web server, and renders the Web page in question unusable.

The expressions within the parentheses of the for statement are separated by semicolons. Usually, the first expression initializes a counter variable, the second expression is the test condition for the loop, and the third expression increments the counter. Listing 5.8 shows a for statement that re-creates the example in Listing 5.6, which multiplies 12 numbers by 2.

5

LISTING 5.8   Using the for Statement

```
 1: <html>
 2: <head>
 3: <title>Listing 5.8</title>
 4: </head>
 5: <body>
 6: <?php
 7: for ( $counter=1; $counter<=12; $counter++ ) {
 8:     print "$counter times 2 is ".($counter*2)."<br>";
 9: }
10: ?>
11: </body>
12: </html>
```

Put these lines into a text file called `testfor.php`, and place this file in your Web server document root. When you access this script through your Web browser, it produces the following:

```
1 times 2 is 2
2 times 2 is 4
3 times 2 is 6
4 times 2 is 8
5 times 2 is 10
6 times 2 is 12
7 times 2 is 14
8 times 2 is 16
9 times 2 is 18
10 times 2 is 20
11 times 2 is 22
12 times 2 is 24
```

The results of Listings 5.6 and 5.8 are exactly the same. The `for` statement, though, makes the code more compact. Because `$counter` is initialized and incremented at the top of the statement, the logic of the loop is clear at a glance. In line 7, within the `for` statement's parentheses, the first expression initializes the `$counter` variable and sets it to 1. The test expression verifies that `$counter` contains a value that is less than or equal to 12. The final expression increments the `$counter` variable.

When program flow reaches the `for` loop, the `$counter` variable is initialized, and the test expression is evaluated. If the expression evaluates to `true`, the code block is executed. The `$counter` variable is then incremented and the test expression is evaluated again. This process continues until the test expression evaluates to `false`.

Breaking Out of Loops with the `break` Statement

Both `while` and `for` statements incorporate a built-in test expression with which you can end a loop. The `break` statement, though, enables you to break out of a loop based on the results of additional tests. This can provide a safeguard against error. Listing 5.9 creates a simple `for` statement that divides a large number by a variable that is incremented, printing the result to the screen.

LISTING 5.9   A `for` Loop That Divides 4000 by 10 Incremental Numbers

```
1: <html>
2: <head>
3: <title>Listing 5.9</title>
4: </head>
5: <body>
6: <?php
7: for ( $counter=1; $counter <= 10; $counter++ ) {
```

LISTING 5.9 continued

```
 8:     $temp = 4000/$counter;
 9:     print "4000 divided by $counter is... $temp<br>";
10: }
11: ?>
12: </body>
13: </html>
```

In line 7, this example initializes the variable $counter to 1. The for statement's test expression verifies that $counter is less than or equal to 10. Within the code block, 4000 is divided by $counter, printing the result to the browser.

Put these lines into a text file called testfor2.php, and place this file in your Web server document root. When you access this script through your Web browser, it produces the following:

```
4000 divided by 1 is... 4000
4000 divided by 2 is... 2000
4000 divided by 3 is... 1333.33333333
4000 divided by 4 is... 1000
4000 divided by 5 is... 800
4000 divided by 6 is... 666.666666667
4000 divided by 7 is... 571.428571429
4000 divided by 8 is... 500
4000 divided by 9 is... 444.444444444
4000 divided by 10 is... 400
```

This seems straightforward enough. But what if the value you place in $counter comes from user input? The value could be a negative number, or even a string. Let's take the first instance. Changing the initial value of $counter from 1 to -4 causes 4000 to be divided by 0 when the code block is executed for the fifth time. It is generally not a good idea for your code to divide by zero, and Listing 5.10 guards against this by breaking out of the loop if the $counter variable equals zero.

LISTING 5.10 Using the break Statement

```
1: <html>
2: <head>
3: <title>Listing 5.10</title>
4: </head>
5: <body>
6: <?php
7: $counter = -4;
8: for ( ; $counter <= 10; $counter++ ) {
9:     if ( $counter == 0 )
```

LISTING 5.10   continued

```
10:          break;
11:      $temp = 4000/$counter;
12:      print "4000 divided by $counter is... $temp<br>";
13: }
14: ?>
15: </body>
16: </html>
```

> Dividing a number by zero does not cause a fatal error in PHP. Instead, PHP generates a warning and execution continues.

We use an `if` statement, shown in line 9, to test the value of $counter. If it is equal to zero, the `break` statement immediately halts execution of the code block, and program flow continues after the `for` statement.

Put these lines into a text file called `testfor3.php`, and place this file in your Web server document root. When you access this script through your Web browser, it produces the following:

```
4000 divided by -4 is... -1000
4000 divided by -3 is... -1333.33333333
4000 divided by -2 is... -2000
4000 divided by -1 is... -4000
```

Notice that we initialize the $counter variable in line 7, outside the `for` statement's parentheses, to simulate a situation in which the value of $counter is set according to form input or a database lookup.

> You can omit any of the expressions from a `for` statement, but you must remember to retain the semicolons.

Skipping an Iteration with the `continue` Statement

The `continue` statement ends execution of the current iteration but doesn't cause the loop as a whole to end. Instead, the next iteration begins immediately. Using the `break` statement as we did in Listing 5.10 is a little drastic. With the `continue` statement in Listing 5.11, you can avoid a divide by zero error without ending the loop completely.

LISTING 5.11 Using the `continue` Statement

```
 1: <html>
 2: <head>
 3: <title>Listing 5.11</title>
 4: </head>
 5: <body>
 6: <?php
 7: $counter = -4;
 8: for ( ;  $counter <= 10; $counter++ ) {
 9:     if ( $counter == 0 ) {
10:         continue;
11:     }
12:     $temp = 4000/$counter;
13:     print "4000 divided by $counter is... $temp<br>";
14: }
15: ?>
16: </body>
17: </html>
```

In line 10, we have swapped the `break` statement for a `continue` statement. If the `$counter` variable is equivalent to zero, the iteration is skipped, and the next one starts immediately.

Put these lines into a text file called `testcontinue.php`, and place this file in your Web server document root. When you access this script through your Web browser, it produces the following:

```
4000 divided by -4 is... -1000
4000 divided by -3 is... -1333.33333333
4000 divided by -2 is... -2000
4000 divided by -1 is... -4000
4000 divided by 1 is... 4000
4000 divided by 2 is... 2000
4000 divided by 3 is... 1333.33333333
4000 divided by 4 is... 1000
4000 divided by 5 is... 800
4000 divided by 6 is... 666.666666667
4000 divided by 7 is... 571.428571429
4000 divided by 8 is... 500
4000 divided by 9 is... 444.444444444
```

The `break` and `continue` statements can make code more difficult to read. Because they often add layers of complexity to the logic of the loop statements that contain them, you should use them with care.

5

Nesting Loops

Loop statements can contain other loop statements. The combination of such statements is particularly useful when working with dynamically created HTML tables. Listing 5.12 uses two for statements to print a multiplication table to the browser.

LISTING 5.12   Nesting Two for Loops

```
 1: <html>
 2: <head>
 3: <title>Listing 5.12</title>
 4: </head>
 5: <body>
 6: <?php
 7: print "<table border=\"1\">\n";
 8: for ( $y=1; $y<=12; $y++ ) {
 9:     print "<tr>\n";
10:     for ( $x=1; $x<=12; $x++ ) {
11:         print "\t<td>";
12:         print ($x*$y);
13:         print "</td>\n";
14:     }
15:     print "</tr>\n";
16: }
17: print "</table>";
18: ?>
19: </body>
20: </html>
```

Before we examine the for loops, let's take a closer look at line 7 in Listing 5.12:

```
print "<table border=\"1\">\n";
```

Notice that we have used the backslash character (\) before each of the quotation marks within the string. This is necessary in order to tell the PHP engine that we wish to use the quotation mark character, rather than interpret it as the beginning or end of a string. If we did not do this, the statement would not make sense to the engine, which would read it as a string followed by a number followed by another string. This would generate an error. In this listing, we use \n to represent a newline character, and \t to represent a tab character.

The outer for statement (line 8) initializes a variable called $y, setting its starting value to 1. It defines an expression that verifies that $y is less than or equal to 12 and defines the increment for $y. For each iteration, the code block prints a tr (table row) HTML element (line 9) and defines another for statement (line 10). This inner loop initializes a variable called $x and defines expressions along the same lines as for the outer loop. For each iteration, the inner loop prints a td (table cell) element to the browser (line 11), as well as the result of $x multiplied by $y (line 12). In line 13, we close the table cell. After the inner loop has finished, we fall back through to the outer loop, where we close the table row on line 15, ready for the process to begin again. When the outer loop has finished, the result is a neatly formatted multiplication table. We wrap things up by closing the table on line 17.

Put these lines into a text file called testnestfor.php, and place this file in your Web server document root. When you access this script through your Web browser, it should look like Figure 5.1.

FIGURE 5.1
Output of Listing 5.12.

5

Code Blocks and Browser Output

In Hour 3, "Installing and Configuring PHP," you learned that you can slip in and out of HTML mode at will, using the PHP start and end tags. In this hour, you have discovered that you can present distinct output to the user according to a decision-making process that we can control with if and switch statements. In this section, we will combine these two techniques.

Imagine a script that outputs a table of values only when a variable is set to the Boolean value true. Listing 5.13 shows a simplified HTML table constructed with the code block of an if statement.

LISTING 5.13   A Code Block Containing Multiple `print()` Statements

```
 1: <html>
 2: <head>
 3: <title>Listing 5.13</title>
 4: </head>
 5: <body>
 6: <?php
 7: $display_prices = true;
 8: if ( $display_prices ) {
 9:     print "<table border=\"1\">";
10:     print "<tr><td colspan=\"3\">";
11:     print "today's prices in dollars";
12:     print "</td></tr>";
13:     print "<tr><td>14</td><td>32</td><td>71</td></tr>";
14:     print "</table>";
15: }
16: ?>
17: </body>
18: </html>
```

If `$display_prices` is set to `true` in line 7, the table is printed. For the sake of readability, we split the output into multiple `print()` statements, and once again escape any quotation marks.

Put these lines into a text file called `testmultiprint.php`, and place this file in your Web server document root. When you access this script through your Web browser, it should look like Figure 5.2.

FIGURE 5.2

Output of Listing 5.13.

There's nothing wrong with the way this is coded, but we can save ourselves some typing by simply slipping back into HTML mode within the code block. In Listing 5.14 we do just that.

LISTING 5.14   Returning to HTML Mode Within a Code Block

```
 1: <html>
 2: <head>
 3: <title>Listing 5.14</title>
 4: </head>
 5: <body>
 6: <?php
 7: $display_prices = true;
 8: if ( $display_prices ) {
 9: ?>
10:     <table border="1">
11:     <tr><td colspan="3">today's prices in dollars</td></tr>
12:     <tr><td>14</td><td>32</td><td>71</td>
13:     </table>
14: <?php
15: }
16: ?>
17: </body>
18: </html>
```

The important thing to note here is that the shift to HTML mode on line 9 only occurs if the condition of the if statement is fulfilled. This can save us the bother of escaping quotation marks and wrapping our output in print() statements. It might, however, affect the readability of our code in the long run, especially as our script grows larger.

Summary

In this hour, you learned about control structures and the ways in which they can help to make your scripts flexible and dynamic. Most of these structures will reappear regularly throughout the rest of the book.

You learned how to define an if statement and how to provide for alternative actions with the elseif and else clauses. You learned how to use the switch statement to change flow according to multiple equivalence tests on the result of an expression. You learned about loops—in particular, the while and for statements—and you learned how to use break and continue to prematurely end the execution of a loop or to skip an iteration. You learned how to nest one loop within another and saw a typical use for this structure. Finally, you looked at a technique for using PHP start and end tags in conjunction with conditional code blocks.

5

You should now have enough information to write scripts of your own. These scripts can make decisions and perform repetitive tasks. In the next hour, we will be looking at a way of adding even more power to your applications. You will learn how functions enable you to organize your code, preventing duplication and improving reusability.

Q&A

Q Must a control structure's test expression result in a Boolean value?

A Ultimately, yes, but in the context of a test expression, zero, an undefined variable, or an empty string will be converted to `false`. All other values will evaluate to `true`.

Q Must I always surround a code block in a control statement with brackets?

A If the code you want executed as part of a control structure consists of only a single line, you can omit the brackets.

Workshop

The workshop is designed to help you anticipate possible questions, review what you've learned, and begin putting your knowledge into practice.

Quiz

1. How would you use an `if` statement to print the string `"Youth message"` to the browser if an integer variable, `$age`, is between 18 and 35? If `$age` contains any other value, the string `"Generic message"` should be printed to the browser.

2. How would you extend your code in question 1 to print the string `"Child message"` if the `$age` variable is between 1 and 17?

3. How would you create a `while` statement that increments through and prints every odd number between 1 and 49?

4. How would you convert the `while` statement you created in question 3 into a `for` statement?

Answers

1.

```php
$age = 22;

if ( $age >= 18 && $age <= 35 ) {
    print "Youth message<BR>\n";
} else {
    print "Generic message<BR>\n";
}
```

2.

```php
$age = 12;

if ( $age >= 18 && $age <= 35 ) {
    print "Youth message<BR>\n";
} elseif ( $age >= 1 && $age <= 17 ) {
    print "Child message<BR>\n";
} else {
    print "Generic message<BR>\n";
}
```

3.

```php
$num = 1;

while ( $num <= 49 ) {
    print "$num<BR>\n";
    $num += 2;
}
```

4.

```php
for ( $num = 1; $num <= 49; $num += 2 ) {
    print "$num<BR>\n";
}
```

5

Activity

Review the syntax for control structures. Think about how the techniques you've learned will help you in your scripting. Perhaps some of the script ideas you develop will be able to behave in different ways according to user input, or will loop to display an HTML table. Start to build the control structures you will be using. Use temporary variables to mimic user input or database queries for the time being.

HOUR 6

Working with Functions

Functions are at the heart of a well-organized script, making code easy to read and reuse. No large project would be manageable without them. Throughout this hour, we will investigate functions and demonstrate some of the ways in which they can save you from repetitive work. In this hour, you will learn

- How to define and call functions
- How to pass values to functions and receive values in return
- How to call a function dynamically using a string stored in a variable
- How to access global variables from within a function
- How to give a function a "memory"
- How to pass data to functions by reference
- How to create anonymous functions
- How to verify that a function exists before calling it

What Is a Function?

You can think of a function as a machine. A machine takes the raw materials you feed it and works with them to achieve a purpose or to produce a product. A function accepts values from you, processes them, and then performs an action (printing to the browser, for example), returns a new value, or both.

If you needed to bake a single cake, you would probably do it yourself. If you needed to bake thousands of cakes, you would probably build or acquire a cake-baking machine. Similarly, when deciding whether to create a function, the most important factor to consider is the extent to which it can save you from repetition.

A function is a self-contained block of code that can be called by your scripts. When called, the function's code is executed. You can pass values to functions, which will then work with them. When finished, a function can pass a value back to the calling code.

Calling Functions

Functions come in two flavors—those built in to the language and those you define yourself. PHP has hundreds of built-in functions. The very first script in this book, which appears in Hour 3, "Installing and Configuring PHP," consists of a single function call:

```
print "Hello Web!";
```

In this example, we call the print() function, passing it the string "Hello Web!". The function then goes about the business of writing the string. A function call consists of the function name (print in this case) followed by parentheses. If you want to pass information to the function, you place it between these parentheses. A piece of information passed to a function in this way is called an argument. Some functions require that more than one argument be passed to them. Arguments in such cases must be separated by commas:

```
some_function( $an_argument, $another_argument );
```

print() is typical in that it returns a value. Most functions give you some information back when they've completed their task—they usually at least tell whether their mission was successful. print() returns a Boolean.

The abs() function, for example, requires a signed numeric value and returns the absolute value of that number. Let's try it out in Listing 6.1.

> print() is not a typical function in that it does not require parentheses in order to run successfully:
>
> ```
> print("Hello Web!");
> ```
>
> and
>
> ```
> print "Hello Web!";
> ```
>
> are equally valid. This is an exception. All other functions require parentheses, whether or not they accept arguments.

LISTING 6.1 Calling the Built-in abs() Function

```
 1: <html>
 2: <head>
 3: <title>Listing 6.1</title>
 4: </head>
 5: <body>
 6: <?php
 7: $num = -321;
 8: $newnum = abs( $num );
 9: print $newnum;
10: // prints "321"
11: ?>
12: </body>
13: </html>
```

In this example, we assign the value -321 to a variable $num. We then pass that variable to the abs() function, which makes the necessary calculation and returns a new value. We assign this to the variable $newnum and print the result.

Put these lines into a text file called abs.php, and place this file in your Web server document root. When you access this script through your Web browser, it produces the following:

321

In fact, we could have dispensed with temporary variables altogether, passing our number straight to abs(), and directly printing the result:

```
print( abs( -321 ) );
```

We used the temporary variables $num and $newnum, though, to make each step of the process as clear as possible. Sometimes you can make your code more readable by breaking it up into a greater number of simple expressions.

6

You can call user-defined functions in exactly the same way that we have been calling built-in functions.

Defining a Function

You can define a function using the `function` statement:

```
function some_function( $argument1, $argument2 ) {
    // function code here
}
```

The name of the function follows the `function` statement and precedes a set of parentheses. If your function requires arguments, you must place comma-separated variable names within the parentheses. These variables will be filled by the values passed to your function. Even if your function doesn't require arguments, you must nevertheless supply the parentheses.

 The naming rules for functions are similar to the naming rules for variables, which you learned in Hour 4, "The Building Blocks of PHP." Names cannot include spaces, and they must begin with a letter or an underscore.

Listing 6.2 declares a function.

LISTING 6.2   Declaring a Function

```
 1: <html>
 2: <head>
 3: <title>Listing 6.2</title>
 4: </head>
 5: <body>
 6: <?php
 7: function bighello() {
 8:     print "<h1>HELLO!</h1>";
 9: }
10: bighello();
11: ?>
12: </body>
13: </html>
```

The script in Listing 6.2 simply outputs the string "HELLO" wrapped in an HTML <h1> element.

Put these lines into a text file called `bighello.php`, and place this file in your Web server document root. When you access this script through your Web browser, it should look like Figure 6.1.

FIGURE 6.1

Output of Listing 6.2.

We declare a function `bighello()` that requires no arguments. Because of this, we leave the parentheses empty. `bighello()` is a working function but is not terribly useful. Listing 6.3 creates a function that requires an argument and actually does something helpful with it.

LISTING 6.3   Declaring a Function That Requires Arguments

```
 1: <html>
 2: <head>
 3: <title>Listing 6.3</title>
 4: </head>
 5: <body>
 6: <?php
 7: function printBR( $txt ) {
 8:     print ("$txt<br>\n");
 9: }
10: printBR("This is a line");
11: printBR("This is a new line");
12: printBR("This is yet another line");
13: ?>
14: </body>
15: </html>
```

6

Put these lines into a text file called `printbr.php`, and place this file in your Web server document root. When you access this script through your Web browser, it should look like Figure 6.2.

FIGURE 6.2

A function that prints a string with an appended <br> tag.

In line 7, the `printBR()` function expects a string, so we place the variable name `$txt` between the parentheses when we declare the function. Whatever is passed to `printBR()` will be stored in `$txt`. Within the body of the function, in line 8, we print the `$txt` variable, appending a `<br>` element and a newline character to it.

When we want to write a line to the browser, such as in line 10, 11, or 12, we can call `printBR()` instead of the built-in `print()`, saving us the bother of typing the `<br>` element.

Returning Values from User-Defined Functions

In the previous example, we output an amended string to the browser within the `printBR()` function. Sometimes, however, you will want a function to provide you with a value that you can work with yourself. If your function has transformed a string that you have provided, you may wish to get the amended string back so that you can pass it to other functions. A function can return a value using the `return` statement in conjunction with a value. The `return` statement stops the execution of the function and sends the value back to the calling code.

Listing 6.4 creates a function that returns the sum of two numbers.

LISTING 6.4   A Function That Returns a Value

```
1: <html>
2: <head>
3: <title>Listing 6.4</title>
4: </head>
5: <body>
6: <?php
7: function addNums( $firstnum, $secondnum ) {
```

LISTING 6.4 continued

```
 8:     $result = $firstnum + $secondnum;
 9:     return $result;
10: }
11: print addNums(3,5);
12: // will print "8"
13: ?>
14: </body>
15: </html>
```

Put these lines into a text file called addnums.php, and place this file in your Web server document root. When you access this script through your Web browser, it produces the following:

8

Notice in line 7 that addNums() should be called with two numeric arguments (line 11 shows those to be 3 and 5 in this case). These are stored in the variables $firstnum and $secondnum. Predictably, addNums() adds the numbers contained in these variables together and stores the result in a variable called $result.

The return statement can return a value or nothing at all. How we arrive at a value passed by return can vary. The value can be hard-coded:

```
return 4;
```

It can be the result of an expression:

```
return ( $a/$b );
```

It can be the value returned by yet another function call:

```
return ( another_function( $an_argument ) );
```

Dynamic Function Calls

6

It is possible to assign function names as strings to variables and then treat these variables exactly as you would the function names themselves. Listing 6.5 shows a simple example of this.

LISTING 6.5 Calling a Function Dynamically

```
1: <html>
2: <head>
3: <title>Listing 6.5</title>
```

LISTING 6.5   continued

```
 4: </head>
 5: <body>
 6: <?php
 7: function sayHello() {
 8:     print "hello<br>";
 9: }
10: $function_holder = "sayHello";
11: $function_holder();
12: ?>
13: </body>
14: </html>
```

A string identical to the name of the sayHello() function is assigned to the $function_holder variable on line 10. Once this is done, we can use this variable in conjunction with parentheses to call the sayHello() function. We do this on line 11.

Put these lines into a text file called sayhello.php, and place this file in your Web server document root. When you access this script through your Web browser, it produces the following:

```
hello
```

Why would we want to do this? In the example, we simply make more work for ourselves by assigning the string "sayHello" to $function_holder. Dynamic function calls are useful when you want to alter program flow according to changing circumstances. We might want our script to behave differently according to a parameter set in a URL's query string, for example. We can extract the value of this parameter and use it to call one of a number of functions.

Variable Scope

A variable declared within a function remains local to that function. In other words, it will not be available outside the function or within other functions. In larger projects, this can save you from accidentally overwriting the contents of a variable when you declare two variables with the same name in separate functions.

Listing 6.6 creates a variable within a function and then attempts to print it outside the function.

LISTING 6.6   Variable Scope: A Variable Declared Within a Function Is Unavailable
Outside the Function

```
 1: <html>
 2: <head>
 3: <title>Listing 6.6</title>
 4: </head>
 5: <body>
 6: <?php
 7: function test() {
 8:     $testvariable = "this is a test variable";
 9: }
10: print "test variable: $testvariable<br>";
11: ?>
12: </body>
13: </html>
```

Put these lines into a text file called scopetest.php, and place this file in your Web
server document root. When you access this script through your Web browser, it should
look like Figure 6.3.

FIGURE 6.3

Output of Listing 6.6.

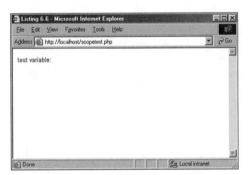

The value of the variable $testvariable is not printed. This is because no such variable
exists outside the test() function. Note that the attempt in line 10 to access a nonexistent variable does not cause an error.

Similarly, a variable declared outside a function will not automatically be available
within it.

Accessing Variables with the `global` Statement

From within a function, it is not possible by default to access a variable that has been
defined elsewhere. If you attempt to use a variable with the same name, you will only set
or access a local variable. Let's put this to the test in Listing 6.7.

6

LISTING 6.7 Variables Defined Outside Functions Are Inaccessible from Within a Function by Default

```
 1: <html>
 2: <head>
 3: <title>Listing 6.7</title>
 4: </head>
 5: <body>
 6: <?php
 7: $life = 42;
 8: function meaningOfLife() {
 9:     print "The meaning of life is $life<br>";
10: }
11: meaningOfLife();
12: ?>
13: </body>
14: </html>
```

Put these lines into a text file called scopetest2.php, and place this file in your Web server document root. When you access this script through your Web browser, it should look like Figure 6.4.

FIGURE 6.4

Attempting to reference a variable from outside the scope of a function.

As you might expect, the meaningOfLife() function does not have access to the $life variable in line 7; $life is empty when the function attempts to print it. On the whole, this is a good thing; it saves us from potential clashes between identically named variables, and a function can always demand an argument if it needs information about the outside world. Occasionally, however, you may want to access an important global variable from within a function without passing it in as an argument. This is where the global statement comes into its own. Listing 6.8 uses global to restore order to the universe.

LISTING 6.8 Accessing Global Variables with the `global` Statement

```
 1: <html>
 2: <head>
 3: <title>Listing 6.8</title>
 4: </head>
 5: <body>
 6: <?php
 7: $life=42;
 8: function meaningOfLife() {
 9:     global $life;
10:     print "The meaning of life is $life<br>";
11: }
12: meaningOfLife();
13: ?>
14: </body>
15: </html>
```

Put these lines into a text file called `scopetest3.php`, and place this file in your Web server document root. When you access this script through your Web browser, it should look like Figure 6.5.

FIGURE 6.5

Successfully accessing a global variable from within a function using the `global` *keyword.*

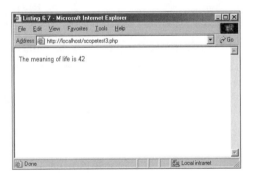

By placing `global` in front of the `$life` variable when we declare it in the `meaningOfLife()` function (line 9), we make it refer to the `global $life` variable declared outside the function (line 7).

You will need to use the `global` statement for every function that you want to access for a particular global variable.

Be careful, though. If we manipulate the contents of the variable within the function, `$life` will be changed for the script as a whole.

6

You can declare more than one variable at a time with the `global` statement by simply separating each of the variables you wish to access with commas.

```
global $var1, $var2, $var3;
```

> Usually, an argument is a copy of whatever value is passed by the calling code; changing it in a function has no effect beyond the function block. Changing a global variable within a function, on the other hand, changes the original and not a copy. Use the `global` statement sparingly.

Saving State Between Function Calls with the `static` Statement

Variables within functions have a short but happy life on the whole. They come into being when the function is called and die when execution is finished. Once again, this is as it should be. It is usually best to build a script as a series of self-contained blocks, each with as little knowledge of others as possible. Occasionally, however, you may want to give a function a rudimentary memory.

Let's assume that we want a function to keep track of the number of times it has been called. Why? In our examples, the function is designed to create numbered headings in a script that dynamically builds online documentation.

We could, of course, use the `global` statement to do this. We have a crack at this in Listing 6.9.

LISTING 6.9   Using the `global` Statement to Remember the Value of a Variable Between Function Calls

```
 1: <html>
 2: <head>
 3: <title>Listing 6.9</title>
 4: </head>
 5: <body>
 6: <?php
 7: $num_of_calls = 0;
 8: function numberedHeading( $txt ) {
 9:     global $num_of_calls;
10:     $num_of_calls++;
11:     print "<h1>$num_of_calls. $txt</h1>";
12: }
```

LISTING 6.9 continued

```
13: numberedHeading("Widgets");
14: print("We build a fine range of widgets<p>");
15: numberedHeading("Doodads");
16: print("Finest in the world<p>");
17: ?>
18: </body>
19: </html>
```

Put these lines into a text file called numberedheading.php, and place this file in your Web server document root. When you access this script through your Web browser, it should look like Figure 6.6.

FIGURE 6.6

Using the global *statement to keep track of the number of times a function has been called.*

This does the job. We declare a variable, $num_of_calls, in line 7, outside the function numberedHeading(). We make this variable available to the function using the global statement in line 9.

Every time numberedHeading() is called, $num_of_calls is incremented (line 10). We can then print out a heading complete with a heading number.

This is not the most elegant solution, however. Functions that use the global statement cannot be read as standalone blocks of code. In reading or reusing them, we need to look out for the global variables that they manipulate.

This is where the static statement can be useful. If you declare a variable within a function in conjunction with the static statement, the variable remains local to the function, and the function "remembers" the value of the variable from execution to execution. Listing 6.10 adapts the code from Listing 6.9 to use the static statement.

6

LISTING 6.10 Using the `static` Statement to Remember the Value of a Variable Between Function Calls

```
1: <html>
2: <head>
3: <title>Listing 6.10</title>
4: </head>
5: <body>
6: <?php
7: function numberedHeading( $txt ) {
8:      static $num_of_calls = 0;
9:      $num_of_calls++;
10:     print "<h1>$num_of_calls. $txt</h1>";
11: }
12: numberedHeading("Widgets");
13: print("We build a fine range of widgets<p>");
14: numberedHeading("Doodads");
15: print("Finest in the world<p>");
16: ?>
17: </body>
18: </html>
```

numberedHeading() has become entirely self-contained. When we declare the $num_of_calls variable on line 8, we assign an initial value to it. This assignment is made when the function is first called on line 12. This initial assignment is ignored when the function is called a second time on line 14. Instead, the code remembers the previous value of $num_of_calls. We can now paste the numberedHeading() function into other scripts without worrying about global variables. Although the output of Listing 6.10 is exactly the same as that of Listing 6.9 (try it and see!), we have made the code more elegant.

More About Arguments

You've already seen how to pass arguments to functions, but there's more to cover yet. In this section, you'll look at a technique for giving your arguments default values and explore a method of passing variables by reference rather than by value. This means that the function is given an "alias" of the original value rather than a copy of it.

Setting Default Values for Arguments

PHP gives you a nifty feature to help build flexible functions. Until now, we've said that some functions "demand" one or more arguments. By making some arguments optional, you can render your functions a little less autocratic.

Listing 6.11 creates a useful little function that wraps a string in an HTML font element. We want to give the user of the function the chance to change the font element's size attribute, so we demand a $size argument in addition to the string (line 7).

LISTING 6.11 A Function Requiring Two Arguments

```
 1: <html>
 2: <head>
 3: <title>Listing 6.11</title>
 4: </head>
 5: <body>
 6: <?php
 7: function fontWrap( $txt, $size ) {
 8:     print "<font size=\"$size\"
 9:         face=\"Helvetica,Arial,Sans-Serif\">
10:         $txt</font>";
11: }
12: fontWrap("A heading<br>",5);
13: fontWrap("some body text<br>",3);
14: fontWrap("some more body text<BR>",3);
15: fontWrap("yet more body text<BR>",3);
16: ?>
17: </body>
18: </html>
```

Put these lines into a text file called fontwrap.php, and place this file in your Web server document root. When you access this script through your Web browser, it should look like Figure 6.7.

FIGURE 6.7

A function that formats and outputs strings.

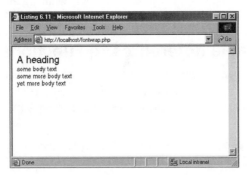

Useful though this function is, we really only need to change the font size occasionally. Most of the time we use the default value of 3. By assigning a value to an argument variable within the function definition's parentheses, we can make the $size argument optional. If the function call doesn't define an argument for this, the value we have assigned to the argument is used instead. Listing 6.12 uses this technique to make the $size argument optional.

LISTING 6.12   A Function with an Optional Argument

```
 1: <html>
 2: <head>
 3: <title>Listing 6.12</title>
 4: </head>
 5: <body>
 6: <?php
 7: function fontWrap( $txt, $size=3 ) {
 8:     print "<font size=\"$size\"
 9:         face=\"Helvetica,Arial,Sans-Serif\">
10:         $txt</font>";
11: }
12: fontWrap("A heading<br>",5);
13: fontWrap("some body text<br>");
14: fontWrap("some more body text<br>");
15: fontWrap("yet more body text<br>");
16: ?>
17: </body>
18: </html>
```

When the fontWrap() function is called with a second argument, as in line 12, this value is used to set the size attribute of the font element. When we omit this argument, as in lines 13, 14, and 15, the default value of 3 is used instead. You can create as many optional arguments as you want, but when you've given an argument a default value, all subsequent arguments should also be given defaults.

Passing Variable References to Functions

When you pass arguments to functions, they are stored as copies in parameter variables. Any changes made to these variables in the body of the function are local to that function and are not reflected beyond it. This is illustrated in Listing 6.13.

LISTING 6.13   Passing an Argument to a Function by Value

```
 1: <html>
 2: <head>
 3: <title>Listing 6.13</title>
 4: </head>
 5: <body>
 6: <?php
```

LISTING 6.13   continued

```
 7: function addFive( $num ) {
 8:      $num += 5;
 9: }
10: $orignum = 10;
11: addFive( &$orignum );
12: print( $orignum );
13: ?>
14: </body>
15: </html>
```

Put these lines into a text file called `addfive.php`, and place this file in your Web server document root. When you access this script through your Web browser, it produces the following:

```
10
```

The `addFive()` function accepts a single numeric value and adds 5 to it. It returns nothing. We assign a value to a variable $orignum in line 10, and then pass this variable to `addFive()` in line 11. A copy of the contents of $orignum is stored in the variable $num. Although we increment $num by 5, this has no effect on the value of $orignum. When we print $orignum, we find that its value is still 10. By default, variables passed to functions are passed by value. In other words, local copies of the values of the variables are made.

We can change this behavior by creating a reference to our original variable. You can think of a reference as a signpost that points to a variable. In working with the reference, you are manipulating the value to which it points.

Listing 6.14 shows this technique in action. When you pass an argument to a function by reference, as in line 11, the contents of the variable you pass ($orignum) are accessed by the argument variable and manipulated within the function, rather than just a copy of the variable's value (10). Any changes made to an argument in these cases will change the value of the original variable. You can pass an argument by reference by adding an ampersand to the argument name in the function definition, as shown in line 7.

6

LISTING 6.14   Using a Function Definition to Pass an Argument to a Function by Reference

```
1: <html>
2: <head>
3: <title>Listing 6.14</title>
4: </head>
5: <body>
6: <?php
```

LISTING 6.14   continued

```
 7: function addFive( &$num ) {
 8:      $num += 5;
 9: }
10: $orignum = 10;
11: addFive( $orignum );
12: print( $orignum );
13: ?>
14: </body>
15: </html>
```

Put these lines into a text file called `addfive2.php`, and place this file in your Web server document root. When you access this script through your Web browser, it produces the following:

```
15
```

Creating Anonymous Functions

It is possible to create functions on the fly during script execution. Because such functions are not themselves given a name, but are stored in variables or passed to other functions, they are known as anonymous functions. PHP provides the `create_function()` function for creating anonymous functions. `create_function()` requires two string arguments. The first argument should contain a comma-delimited list of argument variables, exactly the same as the argument variables you would include in a standard function declaration. The second argument should contain the function body.

Listing 6.15 creates a simple anonymous function to add two numbers together.

LISTING 6.15   A Simple Anonymous Function

```
 1: <html>
 2: <head>
 3: <title>Listing 6.15</title>
 4: </head>
 5: <body>
 6: <?php
 7: $my_anon = create_function( '$a, $b', 'return $a+$b;' );
 8: print $my_anon( 3, 9 );
 9: // prints 12
10: ?>
11: </body>
12: </html>
```

As of this writing, the use of anonymous functions will cause a segmentation fault when running the Zend Optimizer.

Put these lines into a text file called anon.php, and place this file in your Web server document root. When you access this script through your Web browser, it produces the following:

12

Note that we use single quotes when passing arguments to create_function(). That saves us from having to escape the variable names within the arguments. We could have used double quotes, but the function call would have been a little more involved:

```
$my_anon = create_function( "\$a, \$b", "return \$a+\$b;" );
```

So what is the use of anonymous functions? In practical terms, you will probably only use them when you need to pass callback functions to built-in functions. A callback function is generally written by the user and is designed to be invoked (usually repeatedly) by the function to which it is passed.

The second argument to create_function() is the function body. Don't forget to end the last statement in this string with a semicolon. The interpreter will complain and your anonymous function will not be executed if you omit it.

Testing for the Existence of a Function

You have seen that we do not always know that a function exists before we try to invoke it. If our code were to work with a function name stored in a variable, for example, it would be useful to be able to test whether or not the function exists before we attempt to call it. Furthermore, different builds of the PHP engine may include different functionality. If you are writing a script that may be run on multiple servers, you might want to verify that key features are available. You might write code that will use MySQL if MySQL-related functions are available, but simply log data to a text file otherwise.

You can use function_exists() to check for the availability of a function. function_exists() requires a string representing a function name. It will return true if the function can be located and false otherwise.

6

Listing 6.16 shows `function_exists()` in action, and illustrates some of the other topics we have covered in this hour.

LISTING 6.16   Testing for a Function's Existence

```
 1: <html>
 2: <head>
 3: <title>Listing 6.16</title>
 4: </head>
 5: <body>
 6: <?php
 7:
 8: function tagWrap( $tag, $txt, $func="" ) {
 9:     if ( ! empty( $txt ) && function_exists( $func ) ) {
10:         $txt = $func( $txt );
11:         return "<$tag>$txt</$tag>\n";
12:     }
13: }
14:
15: function underline( $txt ) {
16:     return "<u>$txt</u>";
17: }
18:
19: print tagWrap('b', 'make me bold');
20: // <b>make me bold</b>
21:
22: print tagWrap('i', 'underline me too', "underline");
23: // <i><u>underline me too</u></i>
24:
25: print tagWrap('i', 'make me italic and quote me',
26:     create_function('$txt', 'return "&quot;$txt&quot;";'));
27: // <i>&quot;make me italic and quote me&quot;</i>
28:
29: ?>
30: </body>
31: </html>
```

We define two functions, `tagWrap()` (line 8) and `underline()` (line 15). The `tagWrap()` function accepts three strings: a tag, the text to be formatted, and an optional function name. It returns a formatted string. `underline()` requires a single argument—the text to be formatted—and returns the text wrapped in <u> tags.

When we first call `tagWrap()` on line 19, we pass it the character b and the string make me bold. Because we haven't passed a value for the function argument, the default value (an empty string) is used. On line 9, we check whether the $func variable contains characters and, if it is not empty, we call `function_exists()` to check for a function by that name. Of course, the $func variable is empty, so we wrap the $txt variable in <b> tags on line 11 and return the result.

We call tagWrap() on line 22 with the string 'i', some text, and a third argument: "underline". function_exists() finds a function called underline() (line 15), so it calls this function and passes the $txt argument variable to it before any further formatting is done. The result is an italicized, underlined string.

Finally, on line 25, we call tagWrap(), which wraps text in quotation entities. Of course, it would be quicker to simply add the entities to the text to be transformed ourselves, but this illustrates the point that function_exists() works as well on anonymous functions as it does on strings representing function names.

Put these lines into a text file called exists.php, and place this file in your Web server document root. When you access this script through your Web browser, it should look like Figure 6.8.

FIGURE 6.8
Output of Listing 6.16.

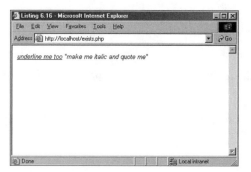

Summary

This hour taught you about functions and how to deploy them. You learned how to define and pass arguments to a function, how to use the global and static statements, how to pass references to functions, and how to create default values for function arguments. Finally, you learned how to create anonymous functions and test for the existence of functions.

6

Q&A

Q Can you include a function call within a double- or single-quoted string, as you can with a variable?

A No. You must call functions outside quotation marks. However, you can break the string apart and place the function call between the parts of the string, using the concatenation operator to tie them together. For example:

```
$newstring = "I purchased".numPurchase($somenum)." items.";
```

Workshop

The workshop is designed to help you anticipate possible questions, review what you've learned, and begin putting your knowledge into practice.

Quiz

1. True or false: If a function doesn't require an argument, you can omit the parentheses in the function call.

2. How do you return a value from a function?

3. What would the following code fragment print to the browser?

```
$number = 50;

function tenTimes() {
    $number = $number * 10;
}

tenTimes();
print $number;
```

4. What would the following code fragment print to the browser?

```
$number = 50;

function tenTimes() {
    global $number;
    $number = $number * 10;
}

tenTimes();
print $number;
```

5. What would the following code fragment print to the browser?

```
$number = 50;

function tenTimes( &$n ) {
    $n = $n * 10;
}

tenTimes( $number );
print $number;
```

Answers

1. The statement is false. You must always include the parentheses in your function calls, whether you are passing arguments to the function or not.

2. You must use the `return` keyword.

3. It would print 50. The `tenTimes()` function has no access to the global $number variable. When it is called, it will manipulate its own local $number variable.

4. It would print 500. We have used the `global` statement, which gives the `tenTimes()` function access to the $number variable.

5. It would print 500. By adding the ampersand to the parameter variable $n, we ensure that this argument is passed by reference. $n and $number point to the same value, so any changes to $n will be reflected when you access $number.

Activity

Create a function that accepts four string variables and returns a string that contains an HTML table element, enclosing each of the variables in its own cell.

6

Hour 7

Learning Basic SQL Commands

This hour takes a break from all that PHP you've been learning and provides a primer on SQL syntax, which you will use to create and manipulate your MySQL database tables. This is a very hands-on hour, and it assumes that you are able to issue queries through the MySQL monitor on Windows or Linux/Unix. Alternatively, if you use a GUI to MySQL, this hour assumes you know the methods for issuing queries through those interfaces.

In this hour, you will learn

- The basic MySQL data types
- How to use the CREATE TABLE command to create a table
- How to use the INSERT command to enter records
- How to use the SELECT command to retrieve records
- How to use basic functions, the WHERE clause, and the GROUP BY clause in SELECT expressions
- How to select from multiple tables, using JOIN

- How to use the UPDATE and REPLACE commands to modify existing records
- How to use the DELETE command to remove records

Learning the MySQL Data Types

Properly defining the fields in a table is important to the overall optimization of your database. You should use only the type and size of field you really need to use. These types of fields (or columns) are also referred to as *data types* because it's the type of data you will be storing in those fields.

MySQL uses many different data types, which are broken into three categories: numeric, date and time, and string types. Pay close attention because defining the data type is more important than any other part of the table creation process.

Numeric Data Types

MySQL uses all the standard ANSI SQL numeric data types, so if you're coming to MySQL from a different database system, these definitions will look familiar to you. The following list shows the common numeric data types and their descriptions.

> The terms *signed* and *unsigned* will be used in the list of numeric data types. If you remember your basic algebra, you'll recall that a signed integer is a positive or negative integer, whereas an unsigned integer is a non-negative integer.

- INT—A normal-sized integer that can be signed or unsigned. If signed, the allowable range is from –2147483648 to 2147483647. If unsigned, the allowable range is from 0 to 4294967295. You can specify a width of up to 11 digits.

> INT and INTEGER are synonymous. If it helps you to remember the data type by using INTEGER instead of INT, go for it.

- TINYINT—A very small integer that can be signed or unsigned. If signed, the allowable range is from –128 to 127. If unsigned, the allowable range is from 0 to 255. You can specify a width of up to 4 digits.

- SMALLINT—A small integer that can be signed or unsigned. If signed, the allowable range is from –32768 to 32767. If unsigned, the allowable range is from 0 to 65535. You can specify a width of up to 5 digits.

- MEDIUMINT—A medium-sized integer that can be signed or unsigned. If signed, the allowable range is from –8388608 to 8388607. If unsigned, the allowable range is from 0 to 16777215. You can specify a width of up to 9 digits.

- BIGINT—A large integer that can be signed or unsigned. If signed, the allowable range is from –9223372036854775808 to 9223372036854775807. If unsigned, the allowable range is from 0 to 18446744073709551615. You can specify a width of up to 11 digits.

- FLOAT(M,D)—A floating-point number that cannot be unsigned. You can define the display length (M) and the number of decimals (D). This is not required and will default to 10,2, where 2 is the number of decimals and 10 is the total number of digits (including decimals). Decimal precision can go to 24 places for a FLOAT.

- DOUBLE(M,D)—A double precision floating-point number that cannot be unsigned. You can define the display length (M) and the number of decimals (D). This is not required and will default to 16,4, where 4 is the number of decimals. Decimal precision can go to 53 places for a DOUBLE. REAL is a synonym for DOUBLE.

- DECIMAL(M,D)—An unpacked floating-point number that cannot be unsigned. In unpacked decimals, each decimal corresponds to one byte. Defining the display length (M) and the number of decimals (D) is required. NUMERIC is a synonym for DECIMAL.

Of all the MySQL numeric data types, you will likely use INT most often. You can run into problems if you define your fields to be smaller than you actually need; for example, if you define an id field as an unsigned TINYINT, you won't be able to successfully insert that 256th record if ID is a primary key (and thus required).

Date and Time Types

MySQL has several data types available for storing dates and times, and these data types are flexible in their input. In other words, you can enter dates that are not really days, such as February 30—February has only 28 or 29 days, never 30. Also, you can store dates with missing information. If you know that someone was born sometime in November of 1980, you can use 1980-11-00, where "00" would have been for the day, if you knew it.

The flexibility of MySQL's date and time types also means that the responsibility for date checking falls on the application developer. MySQL checks only two elements for validity: that the month is between 0 and 12 and the day is between 0 and 31. MySQL

7

does not automatically verify that the 30th day of the second month (February 30th) is a valid date.

The MySQL date and time data types are

- DATE—A date in YYYY-MM-DD format, between 1000-01-01 and 9999-12-31. For example, December 30th, 1973 would be stored as 1973-12-30.

- DATETIME—A date and time combination in YYYY-MM-DD HH:MM:SS format, between 1000-01-01 00:00:00 and 9999-12-31 23:59:59. For example, 3:30 in the afternoon on December 30th, 1973 would be stored as 1973-12-30 15:30:00.

- TIMESTAMP—A timestamp between midnight, January 1, 1970 and sometime in 2037. You can define multiple lengths to the TIMESTAMP field, which directly corre- lates to what is stored in it. The default length for TIMESTAMP is 14, which stores YYYYMMDDHHMMSS. This looks like the previous DATETIME format, only without the hyphens between numbers; 3:30 in the afternoon on December 30th, 1973 would be stored as 19731230153000. Other definitions of TIMESTAMP are 12 (YYMMDDHHMMSS), 8 (YYYYMMDD), and 6 (YYMMDD).

- TIME—Stores the time in HH:MM:SS format.

- YEAR(M)—Stores a year in 2 digit or 4 digit format. If the length is specified as 2 (for example, YEAR(2)), YEAR can be 1970 to 2069 (70 to 69). If the length is speci- fied as 4, YEAR can be 1901 to 2155. The default length is 4.

You will likely use DATETIME or DATE more often than any other date- or time-related data type.

String Types

Although numeric and data types are fun, most data you'll store will be in string format. This list describes the common string data types in MySQL.

- CHAR(M)—A fixed-length string between 1 and 255 characters in length (for exam- ple, CHAR(5)), right-padded with spaces to the specified length when stored. Defining a length is not required, but the default is 1.

- VARCHAR(M)—A variable-length string between 1 and 255 characters in length, for example, VARCHAR(25). You must define a length when creating a VARCHAR field.

- BLOB or TEXT—A field with a maximum length of 65535 characters. BLOBs are "Binary Large Objects" and are used to store large amounts of binary data, such as images or other types of files. Fields defined as TEXT also hold large amounts of data; the difference between the two is that sorts and comparisons on stored data are case sensitive on BLOBs and are not case sensitive in TEXT fields. You do not specify a length with BLOB or TEXT.

- TINYBLOB or TINYTEXT—A BLOB or TEXT column with a maximum length of 255 characters. You do not specify a length with TINYBLOB or TINYTEXT.

- MEDIUMBLOB or MEDIUMTEXT—A BLOB or TEXT column with a maximum length of 16777215 characters. You do not specify a length with MEDIUMBLOB or MEDIUMTEXT.

- LONGBLOB or LONGTEXT—A BLOB or TEXT column with a maximum length of 4294967295 characters. You do not specify a length with LONGBLOB or LONGTEXT.

- ENUM—An enumeration, which is a fancy term for "list." When defining an ENUM, you are creating a list of items from which the value must be selected (or it can be NULL). For example, if you wanted your field to contain either "A" or "B" or "C", you would define your ENUM as ENUM ('A', 'B', 'C') and only those values (or NULL) could ever populate that field. ENUMs can have 65535 different values.

> The SET type is similar to ENUM in that it is defined as a list. However, the SET type is stored as a full value rather than an index of a value, as with ENUMs.

You will probably use VARCHAR and TEXT fields more often than other field types, and ENUMs are useful as well.

Learning the Table Creation Syntax

The table creation command requires

- Name of the table
- Names of fields
- Definitions for each field

The generic table creation syntax is

```
CREATE TABLE table_name (column_name column_type);
```

The table name is up to you of course, but should be a name that reflects the usage of the table. For example, if you have a table that holds the inventory of a grocery store, you wouldn't name the table s. You would probably name it something like grocery_inventory. Similarly, the field names you select should be as concise as possible and relevant to the function they serve and data they hold. For example, you might call a field holding the name of an item item_name, not n.

7

This example creates a generic `grocery_inventory` table with fields for ID, name, description, price, and quantity:

```
mysql> CREATE TABLE grocery_inventory (
    -> id int not null primary key auto_increment,
    -> item_name varchar (50) not null,
    -> item_desc text,
    -> item_price float not null,
    -> curr_qty int not null
    -> );
Query OK, 0 rows affected (0.02 sec)
```

> The `id` field is defined as a primary key. You will learn more about keys in later hours, in the context of creating specific tables as parts of sample applications. By using `auto_increment` as an attribute of the field, you are telling MySQL to go ahead and add the next available number to the `id` field for you.

The MySQL server will respond with `Query OK` each time a query, regardless of type, is successful. Otherwise, an error message will be displayed.

Using the INSERT Command

After you have created some tables, you'll use the SQL command `INSERT` for adding new records to these tables. The basic syntax of `INSERT` is

```
INSERT INTO table_name (column list) VALUES (column values);
```

Within the parenthetical list of values, you must enclose strings within quotation marks. The SQL standard is single quotes, but MySQL enables the usage of either single or double quotes. Remember to escape the type of quotation mark used, if it's within the string itself.

> Integers do not require quotation marks around them.

Here is an example of a string where escaping is necessary:

```
O'Connor said "Boo"
```

If you enclose your strings in double quotes, the INSERT statement would look like this:

```
INSERT INTO table_name (column_name) VALUES ("O'Connor said \"Boo\"");
```

If you enclose your strings in single quotes instead, the INSERT statement would look like this:

```
INSERT INTO table_name (column_name) VALUES ('O\'Connor said "Boo"');
```

A Closer Look at INSERT

Besides the table name, there are two main parts of the INSERT statement—the column list and the value list. Only the value list is actually required, but if you omit the column list, you must specifically name each column in your values list in order.

Using the grocery_inventory table as an example, you have five fields: id, item_name, item_desc, item_price, and curr_qty. To insert a complete record, you could use either of these statements:

1. A statement with all columns named:
    ```
    insert into grocery_inventory (id, item_name, item_desc, item_price,
    curr_qty) values ('1', 'Apples', 'Beautiful, ripe apples.', '0.25', 1000);
    ```
2. A statement that uses all columns but does not explicitly name them:
    ```
    insert into grocery_inventory values ('2', 'Bunches of Grapes',
    'Seedless grapes.', '2.99', 500);
    ```

Give both of them a try and see what happens. You should get results like this:

```
mysql> insert into grocery_inventory
    -> (id, item_name, item_desc, item_price, curr_qty)
    -> values
    -> (1, 'Apples', 'Medium-sized Granny Smith apples.', 0.25, 1000);
Query OK, 1 row affected (0.01 sec)

mysql> insert into grocery_inventory values (2, 'Bunches of Grapes',
    -> 'Seedless grapes.', 2.99, 500);
Query OK, 1 row affected (0.01 sec)
```

Now for some more interesting methods of using INSERT. Because id is an auto-incrementing integer, you don't have to put it in your values list. However, if there's a value you specifically don't want to list (such as id), you then must list the remaining columns in use. For example, the following statement does not list the columns and also does not give a value for id, and it will produce an error:

```
mysql> insert into grocery_inventory values
    -> ('Bottled Water (6-pack)', '500ml spring water.', 2.29, 250);
ERROR 1136: Column count doesn't match value count at row 1
```

7

Because you didn't list any columns, MySQL expects all of them to be in the value list, causing an error on the previous statement. If the goal was to let MySQL do the work for you by auto-incrementing the `id` field, you could use either of these statements:

1. A statement with all columns named except `id`:

```
insert into grocery_inventory (item_name, item_desc, item_price, curr_qty)
values ('Bottled Water (6-pack)', '500ml spring water.', '2.29', 250);
```

2. A statement that uses all columns, but does not explicitly name them and indicates a NULL entry for `id` (so one is filled in for you):

```
insert into grocery_inventory values ('NULL', 'Bottled Water (6-pack)',
'500ml spring water.', 2.29, 250);
```

Go ahead and pick one to use so that your `grocery_inventory` table has three records in total. It makes no different to MySQL, but as with everything that is a preference, be consistent in your application development. Consistent structures will be easier for you to debug later because you'll know what to expect.

Using the SELECT Command

SELECT is the SQL command used to retrieve records. This command syntax can be totally simplistic or very complicated. As you become more comfortable with database programming, you will learn to enhance your SELECT statements, ultimately making your database do as much work as possible and not overworking your programming language of choice.

The most basic SELECT syntax looks like this:

```
SELECT expressions_and_columns FROM table_name
[WHERE some_condition_is_true]
[ORDER BY some_column [ASC | DESC]]
[LIMIT offset, rows]
```

Start with the first line:

```
SELECT expressions_and_columns FROM table_name
```

One handy expression is the * symbol, which stands for "everything." So, to select "everything" (all rows, all columns) from the `grocery_inventory` table, your SQL statement would be

```
SELECT * FROM grocery_inventory;
```

Depending on how much data you inserted into the `grocery_inventory` table during the previous hour, your results will vary, but it might look something like this:

```
mysql> select * from grocery_inventory;
+---+-----------------------+-----------------------+----------+---------+
| id| item_name             | item_desc             | item_price| curr_qty|
+---+-----------------------+-----------------------+----------+---------+
| 1| Apples                | Beautiful, ripe apples.|    0.25|    1000|
| 2| Bunches of Grapes      | Seedless grapes.      |    2.99|     500|
| 3| Bottled Water (6-pack)| 500ml spring water.   |    2.29|     250|
+---+-----------------------+-----------------------+----------+---------+
3 rows in set (0.00 sec)
```

As you can see, MySQL creates a lovely table with the names of the columns along the first row as part of the result set. If you only want to select specific columns, replace the * with the names of the columns, separated by commas. The following statement selects just the `id`, `item_name`, and `curr_qty` fields from the `grocery_inventory` table.

```
mysql> select id, item_name, curr_qty from grocery_inventory;
+----+-----------------------+----------+
| id | item_name             | curr_qty |
+----+-----------------------+----------+
| 1 | Apples                |    1000 |
| 2 | Bunches of Grapes      |     500 |
| 3 | Bottled Water (6-pack) |     250 |
+----+-----------------------+----------+
3 rows in set (0.00 sec)
```

Ordering SELECT Results

By default, results of SELECT queries are ordered as they were inserted into the table, and shouldn't be relied upon as a meaningful ordering system. If you want to order results a specific way, such as by date, ID, name, and so on, specify your requirements using the ORDER BY clause. In the following statement, results are ordered by `item_name`:

```
mysql> select id, item_name, curr_qty from grocery_inventory
    -> order by item_name;
+----+-----------------------+----------+
| id | item_name             | curr_qty |
+----+-----------------------+----------+
| 1 | Apples                |    1000 |
| 3 | Bottled Water (6-pack) |     250 |
| 2 | Bunches of Grapes      |     500 |
+----+-----------------------+----------+
3 rows in set (0.04 sec)
```

7

When selecting results from a table without specifying a sort order, the results may or may not be ordered by their key value. This occurs because MySQL reuses the space taken up by previously deleted rows. In other words, if you add records with ID values of 1 through 5, delete the record with ID number 4, then add another record (ID number 6), the records might appear in the table in this order: 1, 2, 3, 6, 5.

The default sorting of ORDER BY results is ascending (ASC); strings sort from A to Z, integers start at 0, dates sort from oldest to newest. You can also specify a descending sort, using DESC:

```
mysql> select id, item_name, curr_qty from grocery_inventory
    -> order by item_name desc;
+----+-----------------------+----------+
| id | item_name             | curr_qty |
+----+-----------------------+----------+
|  2 | Bunches of Grapes     |      500 |
|  3 | Bottled Water (6-pack)|      250 |
|  1 | Apples                |     1000 |
+----+-----------------------+----------+
3 rows in set (0.00 sec)
```

You're not limited to sorting by just one field—you can specify as many fields as you want, separated by a comma. The sorting priority is the order in which you list the fields.

Limiting Your Results

You can use the LIMIT clause to return only a certain number of records in your SELECT query result. There are two requirements when using the LIMIT clause: offset and number of rows. The offset is the starting position, and the number of rows should be self-explanatory.

For the most part, counting while programming always starts at 0, not 1. For example: 0, 1, 2, 3 instead of 1, 2, 3, 4.

Suppose you had more than 2 or 3 records in the grocery_inventory table, and you wanted to select the id, name, and quantity of the first 3, ordered by curr_qty. In other words, you want to select the 3 items with the least inventory, the following single-parameter limit will start at the 0 position and go to the third record:

```
mysql> select id, item_name, curr_qty from grocery_inventory
    -> order by curr_qty limit 3;
+----+-----------------------+----------+
| id | item_name             | curr_qty |
+----+-----------------------+----------+
|  4 | Bananas               |      150 |
|  3 | Bottled Water (6-pack) |     250 |
|  2 | Bunches of Grapes     |      500 |
+----+-----------------------+----------+
3 rows in set (0.00 sec)
```

The LIMIT clause can be quite useful in an actual application. For example, you can use the LIMIT clause within a series of SELECT statements to essentially page through results in steps:

1. SELECT * FROM grocery_inventory ORDER BY curr_qty LIMIT 0, 3;

2. SELECT * FROM grocery_inventory ORDER BY curr_qty LIMIT 3, 3;

3. SELECT * FROM grocery_inventory ORDER BY curr_qty LIMIT 6, 3;

If you specify an offset and number of rows in your query and no results are found, you won't see an error—just an empty result set. For example, if the grocery_inventory table contains only 6 records, a query with a LIMIT offset of 6 will produce no results:

```
mysql> select id, item_name, curr_qty from grocery_inventory
    -> order by curr_qty limit 6, 3;
Empty set (0.00 sec)
```

In Web-based applications, when lists of data are displayed with links such as "previous 10" and "next 10," it's a safe bet that a LIMIT clause is at work.

Using WHERE in Your Queries

You have learned numerous ways to retrieve particular columns from your tables, but not specific rows. This is when the WHERE clause comes in to play. From the basic SELECT syntax, you see that WHERE is used to specify a particular condition:

```
SELECT expressions_and_columns FROM table_name
[WHERE some_condition_is_true]
```

An example would be to retrieve all the records for items with a quantity of 500:

```
mysql> select * from grocery_inventory where curr_qty = 500;
+----+-------------------+-----------------------+------------+----------+
| id | item_name         | item_desc             | item_price | curr_qty |
+----+-------------------+-----------------------+------------+----------+
|  2 | Bunches of Grapes | Seedless grapes.      |       2.99 |      500 |
|  5 | Pears             | Anjou, nice and sweet.|        0.5 |      500 |
+----+-------------------+-----------------------+------------+----------+
2 rows in set (0.00 sec)
```

7

As shown previously, if you use an integer as the WHERE clause comes in to play. From part of your WHERE clause, quotation marks are not required. Quotation marks are required around strings, and the same rules apply with regard to escaping characters, as you learned in the section on INSERT.

Using Operators in WHERE Clauses

You've used the equal sign (=) in your WHERE clauses to determine the truth of a condition—is one thing equal to another. You can use many types of operators, with comparison operators and logical operators being the most popular types.

Comparison operators, shown in Table 7.1, should look familiar to you if you think about the first day of algebra class.

TABLE 7.1 Basic Comparison Operators and Their Meanings

Operator	Meaning
=	Equal to
!=	Not equal to
<=	Less than or equal to
<	Less than
>=	Greater than or equal to
>	Greater than

There's also a handy operator called BETWEEN, which is useful with integer or data comparisons because it searches for results between a minimum and maximum value. For example

```
mysql> select * from grocery_inventory where item_price
    -> between 1.50 and 3.00;
+----+---------------------+---------------------+------------+----------+
| id | item_name           | item_desc           | item_price | curr_qty |
+----+---------------------+---------------------+------------+----------+
|  2 | Bunches of Grapes   | Seedless grapes.    |       2.99 |      500 |
|  3 | Bottled Water (6-pack) | 500ml spring water. |       2.29 |      250 |
|  4 | Bananas             | Bunches, green.     |       1.99 |      150 |
+----+---------------------+---------------------+------------+----------+
3 rows in set (0.00 sec)
```

Other operators include logical operators, which enable you to use multiple comparisons within your WHERE clause. The basic logical operators are AND and OR. When using AND, all comparisons in the clause must be true to the WHERE clause comes in to play. From retrieve results, whereas using OR allows a minimum of one comparison to be true.

String Comparison Using LIKE

You were introduced to matching strings within a WHERE clause by using = or !=, but there's another useful operator for the WHERE clause comes in to play. From string comparisons: LIKE. This operator uses two characters as wildcards in pattern matching.

- %—Matches multiple characters
- _—Matches exactly one character

If you want to find records in the grocery_inventory table where the first name of the item starts with the letter "A", use

```
mysql> select * from grocery_inventory where item_name like 'A%';
+----+-----------+-----------------------+------------+----------+
| id | item_name | item_desc             | item_price | curr_qty |
+----+-----------+-----------------------+------------+----------+
|  1 | Apples    | Beautiful, ripe apples. |     0.25 |     1000 |
|  6 | Avocado   | Large Haas variety.    |      0.99 |      750 |
+----+-----------+-----------------------+------------+----------+
```

Unless performing a LIKE comparison on a binary string, the comparison is not case sensitive.

Selecting from Multiple Tables

You're not limited to selecting only one table at a time. That would certainly make application programming a long and tedious task! When you select from more than one table in one SELECT statement, you are said to be joining the tables together.

Suppose you have two tables, fruit and color. You can select all rows from each of the two tables, using two separate SELECT statements:

```
mysql> select * from fruit;
+----+-----------+
| id | fruitname |
+----+-----------+
|  1 | apple     |
|  2 | orange    |
|  3 | grape     |
|  4 | banana    |
+----+-----------+
4 rows in set (0.00 sec)
```

7

```
mysql> select * from color;
+----+-----------+
| id | colorname |
+----+-----------+
|  1 | red       |
|  2 | orange    |
|  3 | purple    |
|  4 | yellow    |
+----+-----------+
4 rows in set (0.00 sec)
```

When you want to select from both tables at once, there are a few differences in the syntax of the SELECT statement. First, you must ensure that all the tables you're using in your query appear in the FROM clause of the SELECT statement. Using the fruit and color example, if you simply want to select all columns and rows from both tables, you might think you would use the following SELECT statement:

```
mysql> select * from fruit, color;
+----+-----------+----+-----------+
| id | fruitname | id | colorname |
+----+-----------+----+-----------+
|  1 | apple     |  1 | red       |
|  2 | orange    |  1 | red       |
|  3 | grape     |  1 | red       |
|  4 | banana    |  1 | red       |
|  1 | apple     |  2 | orange    |
|  2 | orange    |  2 | orange    |
|  3 | grape     |  2 | orange    |
|  4 | banana    |  2 | orange    |
|  1 | apple     |  3 | purple    |
|  2 | orange    |  3 | purple    |
|  3 | grape     |  3 | purple    |
|  4 | banana    |  3 | purple    |
|  1 | apple     |  4 | yellow    |
|  2 | orange    |  4 | yellow    |
|  3 | grape     |  4 | yellow    |
|  4 | banana    |  4 | yellow    |
+----+-----------+----+-----------+
16 rows in set (0.00 sec)
```

Sixteen rows of repeated information is probably not what you were going for! What this query did is literally join a row in the color table to each row in the fruit table. Because there are four records in the fruit table and four entries in the color table, that's 16 records returned to you.

When you select from multiple tables, you must build proper WHERE clauses to ensure you really get what you want. In the case of the fruit and color tables, what you really want is to see the fruitname and colorname records from these two tables where the IDs of each match up. This brings us to the next nuance of the query—how to indicate exactly which field you want when the fields are named the same in both tables!

Simply, you append the table name to the field name, like this:

```
tablename.fieldname
```

So, the query for selecting `fruitname` and `colorname` from both tables where the IDs match would be

```
mysql> select fruitname, colorname from fruit, color where fruit.id = color.id;
+-----------+-----------+
| fruitname | colorname |
+-----------+-----------+
| apple     | red       |
| orange    | orange    |
| grape     | purple    |
| banana    | yellow    |
+-----------+-----------+
4 rows in set (0.00 sec)
```

However, if you attempt to select a column that appears in both tables with the same name, you will get an ambiguity error:

```
mysql> select id, fruitname, colorname from fruit, color
    -> where fruit.id = color.id;
ERROR 1052: Column: 'id' in field list is ambiguous
```

If you mean to select the `id` from the fruit table, you would use

```
mysql> select fruit.id, fruitname, colorname from fruit,
    -> color where fruit.id = color.id;
+------+-----------+-----------+
| id   | fruitname | colorname |
+------+-----------+-----------+
|    1 | apple     | red       |
|    2 | orange    | orange    |
|    3 | grape     | purple    |
|    4 | banana    | yellow    |
+------+-----------+-----------+
4 rows in set (0.00 sec)
```

This was a basic example of joining two tables together for use in a single SELECT query. The JOIN keyword is an actual part of SQL, which enables you to build more complex queries.

Using JOIN

Several types of JOINs can be used in MySQL, all of which refer to the order in which the tables are put together and the results are displayed. The type of JOIN used with the fruit and color tables is called an INNER JOIN, although it wasn't written explicitly as such. To rewrite the SQL statement using the proper INNER JOIN syntax, you would use

7

```
mysql> select fruitname, colorname from fruit inner join color
    -> on fruit.id = color.id;
+-----------+-----------+
| fruitname | colorname |
+-----------+-----------+
| apple     | red       |
| orange    | orange    |
| grape     | purple    |
| banana    | yellow    |
+-----------+-----------+
4 rows in set (0.00 sec)
```

The ON clause replaced the WHERE clause, in this instance telling MySQL to join together the rows in the tables where the IDs match each other. When joining tables using ON clauses, you can use any conditions that you would use in a WHERE clause, including all the various logical and arithmetic operators.

Another common type of JOIN is the LEFT JOIN. When joining two tables with LEFT JOIN, all rows from the first table will be returned, no matter if there are matches in the second table or not. Suppose you have two tables in an address book, one called master_name, containing basic records, and one called email, containing email records. Any records in the email table would be tied to a particular id of a record in the master_name table. For example

```
mysql> select name_id, firstname, lastname from master_name;
+---------+-----------+----------+
| name_id | firstname | lastname |
+---------+-----------+----------+
|       1 | John      | Smith    |
|       2 | Jane      | Smith    |
|       3 | Jimbo     | Jones    |
|       4 | Andy      | Smith    |
|       7 | Chris     | Jones    |
|      45 | Anna      | Bell     |
|      44 | Jimmy     | Carr     |
|      43 | Albert    | Smith    |
|      42 | John      | Doe      |
+---------+-----------+----------+
9 rows in set (0.00 sec)
mysql> select name_id, email from email;
+---------+------------------+
| name_id | email            |
+---------+------------------+
|      42 | jdoe@yahoo.com   |
|      45 | annabell@aol.com |
+---------+------------------+
2 rows in set (0.00 sec)
```

Using LEFT JOIN on these two tables, you can see that if a value from the email table doesn't exist, NULL will appear in place of an email address:

```
mysql> select firstname, lastname, email fom master_name left join email
    -> on master_name.name_id = email.name_id;
+-----------+----------+------------------+
| firstname | lastname | email            |
+-----------+----------+------------------+
| John      | Smith    | NULL             |
| Jane      | Smith    | NULL             |
| Jimbo     | Jones    | NULL             |
| Andy      | Smith    | NULL             |
| Chris     | Jones    | NULL             |
| Anna      | Bell     | annabell@aol.com |
| Jimmy     | Carr     | NULL             |
| Albert    | Smith    | NULL             |
| John      | Doe      | jdoe@yahoo.com   |
+-----------+----------+------------------+
9 rows in set (0.01 sec)
```

A RIGHT JOIN works like LEFT JOIN, but with the table order reversed. In other words, when using a RIGHT JOIN, all rows from the second table will be returned, no matter whether there are matches in the first table or not. However, in the case of the master_name and email tables, there are only two rows in the email table, whereas there are nine rows in the master_name table. This means that only two of the nine rows will be returned:

```
mysql> select firstname, lastname, email from master_name right join email
    -> on master_name.name_id = email.name_id;
+-----------+----------+------------------+
| firstname | lastname | email            |
+-----------+----------+------------------+
| John      | Doe      | jdoe@yahoo.com   |
| Anna      | Bell     | annabell@aol.com |
+-----------+----------+------------------+
2 rows in set (0.00 sec)
```

Several different types of JOINs are available in MySQL, and you've learned about the most common types. To learn more about JOINs such as CROSS JOIN, STRAIGHT JOIN and NATURAL JOIN, please visit the MySQL Manual at http://www.mysql.com/doc/J/O/JOIN.html.

7

Using the UPDATE Command to Modify Records

UPDATE is the SQL command used to modify the contents of one or more columns in an existing record. The most basic UPDATE syntax looks like this:

```
UPDATE table_name
SET column1='new value',
column2='new value2'
[WHERE some_condition_is_true]
```

The guidelines for updating a record are similar to those used when inserting a record—the data you're entering must be appropriate to the data type of the field, and you must enclose your strings in single or double quotes, escaping where necessary.

For example, assume you have a table called fruit containing an ID, a fruit name, and the status of the fruit (ripe or rotten):

```
mysql> SELECT * FROM fruit;
+----+------------+--------+
| id | fruit_name | status |
+----+------------+--------+
|  1 | apple      | ripe   |
|  2 | pear       | rotten |
|  3 | banana     | ripe   |
|  4 | grape      | rotten |
+----+------------+--------+
4 rows in set (0.00 sec)
```

To update the status of the fruit to "ripe", use

```
mysql> update fruit set status = 'ripe';
Query OK, 2 rows affected (0.00 sec)
Rows matched: 4  Changed: 2  Warnings: 0
```

Take a look at the result of the query. It was successful, as you can tell from the Query OK message. Also note that only 2 rows were affected—if you try to set the value of a column to the value it already is, the update won't occur for that column.

The second line of the response shows that 4 rows were matched, and only 2 were changed. If you're wondering "matched what?" the answer is simple—because you did not specify a particular condition for matching, the match would be "all rows".

You must be very careful and use a condition when updating a table, unless you really intend to change all the columns for all records to the same value. For the sake of argument, assume that "grape" is spelled incorrectly in the table, and you want to use UPDATE to correct this mistake. This query would have horrible results:

```
mysql> update fruit set fruit_name = 'grape';
Query OK, 4 rows affected (0.00 sec)
Rows matched: 4  Changed: 4  Warnings: 0
```

When you read the result, you should be filled with dread: 4 of 4 records were changed, meaning your fruit table now looks like this:

```
mysql> SELECT * FROM fruit;
+----+------------+--------+
| id | fruit_name | status |
+----+------------+--------+
|  1 | grape      | ripe   |
|  2 | grape      | ripe   |
|  3 | grape      | ripe   |
|  4 | grape      | ripe   |
+----+------------+--------+
4 rows in set (0.00 sec)
```

All your fruit records are now grapes. Through attempting to correct the spelling of one field, all fields were changed because no condition was specified! When doling out UPDATE privileges to your users, think about the responsibility you're giving to some-one—one wrong move and your entire table could be grapes.

Conditional UPDATEs

Making a conditional UPDATE means that you are using WHERE clauses to match specific records. Using a WHERE clause in an UPDATE statement is just like using a WHERE clause in a SELECT statement. All the same comparison and logical operators can be used, such as "equal to", "greater than", "OR", "AND"—the whole nine yards.

Assume your fruit table has not been completely filled with grapes, but instead contains four records, one with a spelling mistake ("grappe" instead of "grape"). The UPDATE statement to fix the spelling mistake would be

```
mysql> update fruit set fruit_name = 'grape' where fruit_name = 'grappe';
Query OK, 1 row affected (0.00 sec)
Rows matched: 1  Changed: 1  Warnings: 0
```

In this case, only one row was matched and one row was changed. Your fruit table should be intact, and all fruit names should be spelled properly:

```
mysql> select * from fruit;
+----+------------+--------+
| id | fruit_name | status |
+----+------------+--------+
|  1 | apple      | ripe   |
|  2 | pear       | ripe   |
|  3 | banana     | ripe   |
|  4 | grape      | ripe   |
+----+------------+--------+
4 rows in set (0.00 sec)
```

7

Using Existing Column Values with UPDATE

Another feature of UPDATE is the capability to use the current value in the record as the base value. For example, go back to the grocery_inventory table used earlier in this hour:

```
mysql> select * from grocery_inventory;
+----+---------------------+-----------------------+------------+----------+
| id | item_name           | item_desc             | item_price | curr_qty |
+----+---------------------+-----------------------+------------+----------+
|  1 | Apples              | Beautiful, ripe apples.|      0.25 |     1000 |
|  2 | Bunches of Grapes   | Seedless grapes.      |       2.99 |      500 |
|  3 | Bottled Water (6-pack)| 500ml spring water.   |      2.29 |      250 |
|  4 | Bananas             | Bunches, green.       |       1.99 |      150 |
|  5 | Pears               | Anjou, nice and sweet.|        0.5 |      500 |
|  6 | Avocado             | Large Haas variety.   |       0.99 |      750 |
+----+---------------------+-----------------------+------------+----------+
6 rows in set (0.00 sec)
```

When someone purchases an apple, the inventory table should be updated accordingly. However, you won't know exactly what number to enter in the curr_qty column, just that you sold one. In this case, use the current value of the column and subtract one:

```
mysql> update grocery_inventory set curr_qty = curr_qty - 1 where id = 1;
Query OK, 1 row affected (0.00 sec)
Rows matched: 1  Changed: 1  Warnings: 0
```

This should give you a new value of 999 in the curr_qty column, and indeed it does:

```
mysql> select * from grocery_inventory;
+----+---------------------+-----------------------+------------+----------+
| id | item_name           | item_desc             | item_price | curr_qty |
+----+---------------------+-----------------------+------------+----------+
|  1 | Apples              | Beautiful, ripe apples.|      0.25 |      999 |
|  2 | Bunches of Grapes   | Seedless grapes.      |       2.99 |      500 |
|  3 | Bottled Water (6-pack)| 500ml spring water.   |      2.29 |      250 |
|  4 | Bananas             | Bunches, green.       |       1.99 |      150 |
|  5 | Pears               | Anjou, nice and sweet.|        0.5 |      500 |
|  6 | Avocado             | Large Haas variety.   |       0.99 |      750 |
+----+---------------------+-----------------------+------------+----------+
6 rows in set (0.00 sec)
```

Using the REPLACE Command

Another method for modifying records is to use the REPLACE command, which is remarkably similar to the INSERT command.

```
REPLACE INTO table_name (column list) VALUES (column values);
```

The REPLACE statement works like this: if the record you are inserting into the table contains a primary key value that matches a record already in the table, the record in the table will be deleted and the new record inserted in its place.

> The REPLACE command is a MySQL-specific extension to ANSI SQL. This command mimics the action of a DELETE and re-INSERT of a particular record. In other words, you get two commands for the price of one.

Using the grocery_inventory table, the following command will replace the entry for Apples:

```
mysql> replace into grocery_inventory values
    -> (1, 'Granny Smith Apples', 'Sweet!', '0.50', 1000);
Query OK, 2 rows affected (0.00 sec)
```

In the query result, notice that the result states, "2 rows affected". In this case, because id is a primary key that had a matching value in the grocery_inventory table, the original row was deleted and the new row inserted—2 rows affected.

Select the records to verify that the entry is correct, which it is

```
mysql> select * from grocery_inventory;
+----+---------------------+-----------------------+------------+----------+
| id | item_name           | item_desc             | item_price | curr_qty |
+----+---------------------+-----------------------+------------+----------+
|  1 | Granny Smith Apples | Sweet!                |        0.5 |     1000 |
|  2 | Bunches of Grapes   | Seedless grapes.      |       2.99 |      500 |
|  3 | Bottled Water (6-pack)| 500ml spring water.  |       2.29 |      250 |
|  4 | Bananas             | Bunches, green.       |       1.99 |      150 |
|  5 | Pears               | Anjou, nice and sweet.|        0.5 |      500 |
|  6 | Avocado             | Large Haas variety.   |       0.99 |      750 |
+----+---------------------+-----------------------+------------+----------+
6 rows in set (0.00 sec)
```

If you use a REPLACE statement, and the value of the primary key in the new record does not match a value for a primary key already in the table, the record would simply be inserted and only one row would be affected.

Using the DELETE Command

7

The basic DELETE syntax is

```
DELETE FROM table_name
[WHERE some_condition_is_true]
[LIMIT rows]
```

Notice there is no column specification in the delete command—when you use DELETE, the entire record is removed. You might recall the fiasco earlier in this hour, regarding grapes in the fruit table, when updating a table without specifying a condition caused all records to be updated. You must be similarly careful when using DELETE.

Assuming the structure and data in a table called fruit:

```
mysql> select * from fruit;
+----+------------+--------+
| id | fruit_name | status |
+----+------------+--------+
|  1 | apple      | ripe   |
|  2 | pear       | rotten |
|  3 | banana     | ripe   |
|  4 | grape      | rotten |
+----+------------+--------+
4 rows in set (0.00 sec)
```

This statement will remove all records in the table:

```
mysql> delete from fruit;
Query OK, 0 rows affected (0.00 sec)
```

You can always verify the deletion by attempting to SELECT data from the table:

```
mysql> select * from fruit;
Empty set (0.00 sec)
```

All your fruit is gone.

Conditional DELETE

A conditional DELETE statement, just like a conditional SELECT or UPDATE statement, means you are using WHERE clauses to match specific records. You have the full range of comparison and logical operators available to you, so you can pick and choose which records you want to delete.

A prime example would be to remove all records for rotten fruit from the fruit table:

```
mysql> delete from fruit where status = 'rotten';
Query OK, 2 rows affected (0.00 sec)
```

Two records were deleted, and only ripe fruit remains:

```
mysql> select * from fruit;
+----+------------+--------+
| id | fruit_name | status |
+----+------------+--------+
|  1 | apple      | ripe   |
|  3 | banana     | ripe   |
+----+------------+--------+
2 rows in set (0.00 sec)
```

For users of MySQL 4.0 (or later), you can also use ORDER BY clauses in your DELETE statements. Take a look at the basic DELETE syntax with the ORDER BY clause added to its structure:

```
DELETE FROM table_name
[WHERE some_condition_is_true]
[ORDER BY some_column [ASC | DESC]]
[LIMIT rows]
```

At first glance, you might wonder, "Why does it matter in what order I delete records?" The ORDER BY clause isn't for the deletion order, it's for the sorting order of records.

In this example, a table called access_log shows access time and username:

```
mysql> select * from access_log;
+----+---------------------+----------+
| id | date_accessed       | username |
+----+---------------------+----------+
|  1 | 2001-11-06 06:09:13 | johndoe  |
|  2 | 2001-11-06 06:09:22 | janedoe  |
|  3 | 2001-11-06 06:09:39 | jsmith   |
|  4 | 2001-11-06 06:09:44 | mikew    |
+----+---------------------+----------+
4 rows in set (0.00 sec)
```

To remove the oldest record, first use ORDER BY to sort the results appropriately, then use LIMIT to remove just one record:

```
mysql> delete from access_log order by date_accessed desc limit 1;
Query OK, 1 row affected (0.01 sec)
```

Select the record from access_log and verify that only three records exist:

```
mysql> select * from access_log;
+----+---------------------+----------+
| id | date_accessed       | username |
+----+---------------------+----------+
|  2 | 2001-11-06 06:09:22 | janedoe  |
|  3 | 2001-11-06 06:09:39 | jsmith   |
|  4 | 2001-11-06 06:09:44 | mikew    |
+----+---------------------+----------+
3 rows in set (0.00 sec)
```

Summary

In this hour, you learned the basics of SQL, from table creation to manipulating records. The table creation command requires three important pieces of information—the table name, the field name, and the field definitions. Field definitions are important because a well-designed table will help speed along your database. MySQL has three different categories of data types: numeric, date and time, and string.

7

The INSERT command, used to add records to a table, names the table and columns you want to populate, and then defines the values. When placing values in the INSERT statement, strings must be enclosed with single or double quotes. The SELECT SQL command is used to retrieve records from specific tables. The * character enables you to easily select all fields for all records in a table, but you can also specify particular column names. If the result set is too long, the LIMIT clause provides a simple method for extracting slices of results if you indicate a starting position and the number of records to return. To order the results, use the ORDER BY clause to select the columns to sort. Sorts can be performed on integers, dates, and strings, in either ascending or descending order. The default order is ascending. Without specifying an order, results are displayed in the order they appear in the table.

You can pick and choose which records you want to return using WHERE clauses to test for the validity of conditions. Comparison or logical operators are used in WHERE clauses, and sometimes both types are used for compound statements. Selecting records from multiple tables within one statement is as advanced as it gets, as these types of statements—called JOIN—require forethought and planning to produce correct results. Common types of JOIN are INNER JOIN, LEFT JOIN, and RIGHT JOIN, although MySQL supports many different kinds of JOIN.

The UPDATE and REPLACE commands are used to modify existing data in your MySQL tables. UPDATE is good for changing values in specific columns or to change values in multiple records based on specific conditions. REPLACE is a variation of INSERT that deletes, and then reinserts a record with a matching primary key. Be very careful when using UPDATE to change values in a column because failure to add a condition will result in the given column being updated throughout all records in the table.

The DELETE command is a simple one—it simply removes whole records from tables. This also makes it very dangerous, so be sure you give DELETE privileges only to users who can handle the responsibility. You can specify conditions when using DELETE so that records are removed only if a particular expression in a WHERE clause is true. Also, you can delete smaller portions of the records in your table using a LIMIT clause. If you have an exceptionally large table, deleting portions is less resource-intensive than deleting each record in a huge table.

Q&A

Q What characters can I use to name my tables and fields, and what is the character limit?

A The maximum length of database, table, or field names is 64 characters. Any character that you can use in a directory or filename, you can use in database and table names—except (/) and (.). These limitations are in place because MySQL creates directories and files in your file system, which correspond to database and table names. There are no character limitations (besides length) in field names.

Workshop

The Workshop is designed to help you anticipate possible questions, review what you've learned, and begin learning how to put your knowledge into practice.

Quiz

1. The integer 56678685 could be which data type(s)?

2. How would you define a field that could only contain the following strings: apple, pear, banana, cherry?

3. What would be the LIMIT clauses for selecting the first 25 records of a table? Then the next 25?

4. How would you formulate a string comparison using LIKE to match first names of "John" or "Joseph"?

5. How would you explicitly refer to a field called id in a table called table1?

6. Write an SQL statement that joins two tables, orders, and items_ordered, with a primary key in each of order_id. From the orders table, select the following fields: order_name and order_date. From the items_ordered table, select the item_description field.

Answers

1. MEDIUMINT, INT, or BIGINT.

2. ENUM ('apple', 'pear', 'banana', 'cherry') or SET ('apple', 'pear', 'banana', 'cherry')

3. LIMIT 0, 25 and LIMIT 26, 25

4. LIKE 'Jo%'

5. Use table1.id instead of id in your query.

6. SELECT orders.order_name, orders.order_date, items_ordered.item_description FROM orders LEFT JOIN items_ordered ON orders.order_id = items_ordered.id.

Activity

Take the time to create some sample tables, and practice using basic INSERT and SELECT commands.

7

HOUR 8

Interacting with MySQL Using PHP

Now that you've learned about PHP and MySQL, you're ready to make the two interact. Think of PHP as a conduit to MySQL—the commands you learned in the previous hour are the same commands that you will send to MySQL in this hour, only this time you'll send them with PHP. In this hour, you will learn

- How to connect to MySQL using PHP
- How to insert and select data through PHP scripts

Connecting to MySQL with PHP

To successfully use the PHP functions to talk to MySQL, you must have MySQL running at a location to which your Web server can connect (not necessarily the same machine as your Web server). You also must have created a user (with a password), and you must know the name of the database to which you want to connect. If you followed the instructions in Hour 1,

"Installing and Configuring MySQL," and Hour 3, "Installing and Configuring PHP," you should already have taken care of this.

In all sample scripts in this hour, the sample database name is testDB, the sample user is joeuser, and the sample password is somepass. Substitute your own information when you use these scripts.

> You can find the section of the PHP Manual that covers all MySQL-related functions at http://www.php.net/manual/en/ref.mysql.php. Use it!

Using mysql_connect()

The mysql_connect() function is the first function you must call when utilizing a PHP script to connect to MySQL—without an open connection to MySQL, you won't get very far! The basic syntax for the connection is

```
mysql_connect("hostname", "username", "password");
```

Using actual sample values, the connection function looks like this:

```
mysql_connect("localhost", "joeuser", "somepass");
```

This function returns a connection index if the connection is successful or returns false if the connection fails. Listing 8.1 is a working example of a connection script. It assigns the value of the connection index to a variable called $conn, then prints the value of $conn as proof of a connection.

LISTING 8.1 A Simple Connection Script

```
1: <?php
2: $conn = mysql_connect("localhost", "joeuser", "somepass");
3: echo "$conn";
4: ?>
```

Save this script as mysqlconnect.php and place it in the document area of your Web server. Access the script with your Web browser and you will see something like the following in your Web browser:

```
Resource id #1
```

Connecting to MySQL using the mysql_connect() function is pretty straightforward. The connection closes when the script finishes its execution, but if you would like to explicitly close the connection, simply add the mysql_close() function at the end of the script, as in Listing 8.2.

LISTING 8.2 The Modified Simple Connection Script

```
1: <?php
2: $conn = mysql_connect("localhost", "joeuser", "somepass");
3: echo "$conn";
4: mysql_close($conn);
5: ?>
```

That's all there is to it. The next section will cover the query execution functions, which are far more interesting than simply opening a connection and letting it sit there!

Executing Queries

Half the battle in executing MySQL queries using PHP is knowing how to write the SQL. The mysql_query() function in PHP is used to send your SQL query to MySQL. If it does so successfully, a result index is returned. If a failure occurs, the function returns false.

When you use the mysql_query() function, you'll notice that one piece of the puzzle is missing: picking the database to use. When you connect to MySQL through the command-line interface, the database is specified in the connection string or changed manually after you log in. With PHP, this is done via a separate function called mysql_select_db() with the following syntax:

```
mysql_select_db(database name, connection index);
```

To connect to a database named testDB, first use mysql_connect(), then use mysql_select_db(), as shown in Listing 8.3.

LISTING 8.3 Connecting and Selecting a Database

```
1: <?php
2: $conn = mysql_connect("localhost", "joeuser", "somepass");
3: mysql_select_db("testDB",$conn);
4: ?>
```

You now have two important pieces of information: the connection index ($conn) and the knowledge that PHP will use testDB as the database throughout the life of this particular script. The connection index is used in mysql_query() syntax:

```
mysql_query(query, connection index);
```

In your script, first make the connection, and then execute a query. The script in Listing 8.4 creates a simple table called testTable.

LISTING 8.4   A Script to Create a Table

```
 1: <?php
 2: // open the connection
 3: $conn = mysql_connect("localhost", "joeuser", "somepass");
 4: // pick the database to use
 5: mysql_select_db("testDB",$conn);
 6: // create the SQL statement
 7: $sql = "CREATE TABLE testTable (id int not null primary key auto_increment,
 8: testField varchar (75))";
 9: // execute the SQL statement
10: $result = mysql_query($sql, $conn);
11: // echo the result identifier
12: echo $result;
13: ?>
```

> When issuing queries using mysql_query(), the semicolon at the end of the SQL statement is not required. The only semicolon in that line should be at the end of the PHP command.

Because the mysql_query function only returns a true or false result, the boring output of this script is

1

The 1 equals true, and indicates that the query was successfully executed. A 0 would have indicated failure. Access MySQL through the command-line interface to verify the creation of the testTable table:

```
mysql> describe testTable;
+-----------+-------------+------+-----+---------+----------------+
| Field     | Type        | Null | Key | Default | Extra          |
+-----------+-------------+------+-----+---------+----------------+
| id        | int(11)     |      | PRI | NULL    | auto_increment |
| testField | varchar(75) | YES  |     | NULL    |                |
+-----------+-------------+------+-----+---------+----------------+
2 rows in set (0.00 sec)
```

8

Congratulations—you have successfully created a table in your MySQL database using PHP!

Retrieving Error Messages

Take some time to familiarize yourself with the mysql_error() function, as it will become your friend. When used in conjunction with the PHP die() function, which simply exits the script at the point at which it appears, the mysql_error() function will return a helpful error message when you make a mistake.

For example, now that you have created a table called testTable, you won't be able to execute that script again without an error. Let's try to execute the script again, but modify it first to utilize the mysql_error() function (see Listing 8.5).

LISTING 8.5   The Script to Create a Table, with Error Messages

```
 1: <?php
 2: // open the connection
 3: $conn = mysql_connect("localhost", "joeuser", "somepass");
 4: // pick the database to use
 5: mysql_select_db("testDB",$conn);
 6: // create the SQL statement
 7: $sql = "CREATE TABLE testTable (id int not null primary key auto_increment,
 8: testField varchar (75))";
 9: // execute the SQL statement
10: $result = mysql_query($sql, $conn) or die(mysql_error());
11: // echo the result identifier
12: echo $result;
13: ?>
```

When you execute the script, you should see something like the following in your Web browser:

```
Table 'testTable' already exists
```

How exciting! Move on to the next section to start inserting data into your table, and soon you'll be retrieving and formatting it via PHP.

Working with MySQL Data

Inserting, updating, deleting, and retrieving data all revolve around the use of the mysql_query() function to execute the basic SQL queries. For INSERT, UPDATE, and DELETE, no additional scripting is required after the query has been executed because you're not displaying any results (unless you want to). For SELECT, you have a few options for displaying the data retrieved by your query. Let's start with the basics and insert some data, so you'll have something to retrieve later on.

Inserting Data with PHP

The easiest method for inserting data is to simply hard-code the INSERT statement, as shown in Listing 8.6.

LISTING 8.6   A Script to Insert a Record

```
 1: <?php
 2: // open the connection
 3: $conn = mysql_connect("localhost", "joeuser", "somepass");
 4: // pick the database to use
 5: mysql_select_db("testDB",$conn);
 6: // create the SQL statement
 7: $sql = "INSERT INTO testTable values ('', 'some value')";
 8: // execute the SQL statement
 9: $result = mysql_query($sql, $conn) or die(mysql_error());
10: // echo the result identifier
11: echo $result;
12: ?>
```

You might wonder why you need to echo the result identifier if you're just inserting data. Well, you don't have to; it's just there for kicks. You can clean this script up a bit by replacing the query execution line so that it simply executes and prints a relevant statement if successful, as shown in Listing 8.7.

LISTING 8.7   The Modified Insert Script

```
 1: <?php
 2: // open the connection
 3: $conn = mysql_connect("localhost", "joeuser", "somepass");
 4: // pick the database to use
 5: mysql_select_db("testDB",$conn);
 6: // create the SQL statement
 7: $sql = "INSERT INTO testTable values ('', 'some value')";
 8: // execute the SQL statement
 9: if (mysql_query($sql, $conn)) {
10:     echo "record added!";
11: } else {
12:     echo "something went wrong";
13: }
14: ?>
```

8

Running this script will result in the addition of a row to the testTable table. To enter more records than just the one shown in the script, you can either make a long list of hard-coded SQL statements and use mysql_query() multiple times to execute these statements, or you can create a form-based interface to the record addition script.

To create the form for this script, you really only need one field because the id field can automatically increment. The action of the form is the name of the record-addition script; let's call it insert.php. Your HTML form might look something like Listing 8.8.

LISTING 8.8   An Insert Form

```
 1: <HTML>
 2: <HEAD>
 3: <TITLE>Insert Form</TITLE>
 4: </HEAD>
 5: <BODY>
 6: <FORM ACTION="insert.php" METHOD=POST>
 7: <P>Text to add:<br>
 8: <input type=text name="testField" size=30>
 9: <p><input type=submit name="submit" value="Insert Record"></p>
10: </FORM>
11: </BODY>
12: </HTML>
```

Save this file as insert_form.html, and put it in the document root of your Web server. Next, create the insert.php script shown in Listing 8.9. The value entered in the form will replace the hard-coded values in the SQL query with a variable called $_POST[testField].

LISTING 8.9   An Insert Script Used with the Form

```
 1: <?php
 2: // open the connection
 3: $conn = mysql_connect("localhost", "joeuser", "somepass");
 4: // pick the database to use
 5: mysql_select_db("testDB",$conn);
 6: // create the SQL statement
 7: $sql = "INSERT INTO testTable values ('', '$_POST[testField]')";
 8: // execute the SQL statement
 9: if (mysql_query($sql, $conn)) {
10:     echo "record added!";
11: } else {
12:     echo "something went wrong";
13: }
14: ?>
```

Save the script as `insert.php`, and put it in the document root of your Web server. In your Web browser, access the HTML form that you created. It should look something like Figure 8.1.

FIGURE 8.1
The HTML form for adding a record.

Enter a string in the "Text to add" field, as shown in Figure 8.2.

FIGURE 8.2
Text typed in the form field.

Finally, press the Insert Record button to execute the `insert.php` script and insert the record. If successful, you will see results similar to Figure 8.3.

To verify your work, you can use the MySQL command-line interface to view the records in the table:

```
mysql> select * from testTable;
+----+------------------+
| id | testField        |
+----+------------------+
|  1 | some value       |
|  2 | this is some text! |
+----+------------------+
2 rows in set (0.00 sec)
```

FIGURE 8.3

*The record has been
successfully added.*

Next, you'll learn how to retrieve and format results with PHP.

Retrieving Data with PHP

Because you have a few rows in your testTable table, you can write a PHP script to
retrieve that data. Starting with the basics, write a script that issues a SELECT query but
doesn't overwhelm you with result data; let's just get the number of rows. To do this, use
the mysql_num_rows() function. This function requires a result, so when you execute the
query, put the result index in $result (see Listing 8.10).

LISTING 8.10 A Script to Retrieve Data

```
1: <?php
2: // open the connection
3: $conn = mysql_connect("localhost", "joeuser", "somepass");
4: // pick the database to use
5: mysql_select_db("testDB",$conn);
6: // create the SQL statement
7: $sql = "SELECT * FROM testTable";
8: // execute the SQL statement
9: $result = mysql_query($sql, $conn) or die(mysql_error());
10: //get the number of rows in the result set
11: $number_of_rows = mysql_num_rows($result);
12: echo "The number of rows is $number_of_rows";
13: ?>
```

Save this script as count.php, place it in your Web server document directory, and access
it through your Web browser. You should see a message like this:

```
The number of rows is 2
```

The number should be equal to the number of records you inserted during testing. Now that you know there are some records in the table, you can get fancy and fetch the actual contents of those records. You can do this in a few ways, but the easiest method is to retrieve each row as an array.

What you'll be doing is using a `while` statement to go through each record in the result-set, place the values of each field into a specific variable, then display the results onscreen. The syntax of `mysql_fetch_array()` is

```
$newArray = mysql_fetch_array($result);
```

Follow along using the sample script in Listing 8.11.

LISTING 8.11   A Script to Retrieve Data and Display Results

```
 1: <?php
 2: // open the connection
 3: $conn = mysql_connect("localhost", "joeuser", "somepass");
 4: // pick the database to use
 5: mysql_select_db("testDB",$conn);
 6: // create the SQL statement
 7: $sql = "SELECT * FROM testTable";
 8: // execute the SQL statement
 9: $result = mysql_query($sql, $conn) or die(mysql_error());
10: //go through each row in the result set and display data
11: while ($newArray = mysql_fetch_array($result)) {
12:     // give a name to the fields
13:     $id  = $newArray['id'];
14:     $testField = $newArray['testField'];
15:     //echo the results onscreen
16:     echo "The ID is $id and the text is $testField <br>";
17: }
18: ?>
```

Save this script as `select.php`, place it in your Web server document directory, and access it through your Web browser. You should see a message for each record entered into `testTable`, as shown in Figure 8.4.

Essentially, you can create an entire database-driven application using just four or five MySQL functions. This hour has barely scratched the surface of using PHP with MySQL; there are many more MySQL functions in PHP, as you'll learn in the next section.

FIGURE 8.4

Selecting records from MySQL.

Additional MySQL Functions in PHP

There are approximately 40 MySQL-specific functions in PHP. Most of these functions are simply alternate methods of retrieving data or are used to gather information about the table structure in question.

For a complete list of functions, with practical examples, visit the MySQL section of the PHP Manual at `http://www.php.net/manual/en/ref.mysql.php`.

Summary

Using PHP and MySQL to create dynamic, database-driven Web sites is a breeze. Just remember that the PHP functions are essentially a gateway to the database server; anything you'd enter using the MySQL command-line interface, you can use with `mysql_query()`.

To connect to MySQL with PHP, you need to know your MySQL username, password, and database name. Using `mysql_connect()` and `mysql_select_db()`, you can connect to and select a database to use throughout the life of the script.

Once connected, you can issue standard SQL commands with the `mysql_query()` function. If you have issued a SELECT command, you can use `mysql_numrows()` to count the records returned in the resultset. If you want to display the data found, you can use `mysql_fetch_array()` to get all the results during a loop and display them onscreen.

Workshop

The workshop is designed to help you anticipate possible questions, review what you've learned, and begin to put your knowledge into practice.

Quiz

1. What is the primary function used to make the connection between PHP and MySQL, and what information is necessary?
2. Which PHP function retrieves a MySQL error message?
3. Which PHP function is used to count the number of records in a resultset?

Answers

1. The `mysql_connect()` function creates a connection to MySQL and requires the hostname, username, and password.
2. The `mysql_error()` function returns a MySQL error message.
3. The `mysql_numrows()` function counts the number of records in a resultset.

Activity

Create a PHP script that displays the contents of the `grocery_inventory` table that was used in the previous hour.

PART III

Getting Involved with the Code

Hour

9   Working with Forms

10   Working with Files

11   Working with Dates and Times

12   Creating a Simple Calendar

13   Working with Strings

14   Creating a Simple Discussion Forum

15   Restricting Access to Your Applications

16   Working with User Sessions

17   Logging and Monitoring Server Activity

HOUR 9

Working with Forms

Until now, the PHP examples in this book have been missing a crucial dimension. Sure, you know the basics, can set variables and arrays, create and call functions, and connect to MySQL to do great things with a database. But that's all meaningless if users can't reach into a language's environment to offer it information. In this hour, you look at strategies for acquiring and working with user input. On the World Wide Web, HTML forms are the principal means by which substantial amounts of information pass from the user to the server.

In this hour, you will learn

- How to access information from form fields
- How to work with form elements that allow multiple selections
- How to create a single document that contains both an HTML form and the PHP code that handles its submission
- How to save state with hidden fields
- How to redirect the user to a new page
- How to build HTML forms and PHP code that send mail
- How to build HTML forms that upload files and how to write the PHP code to handle them

Predefined Variables

Before you actually build a form and use it to acquire data, you must make a small detour and look again at global variables. You first met global variables in Hour 6, "Working with Functions." To refresh your memory, a *global variable* is any variable declared at the top level of a script—that is, declared outside of any function. All functions are made available in a built-in associative array named $GLOBALS. This is useful in Listing 9.1 because we can take a peek at all of our script's global variables with a single loop.

LISTING 9.1 Looping Through the $GLOBALS Array

```
 1: <html>
 2: <head>
 3: <title>Listing 9.1 Looping through the $GLOBALS array</title>
 4: </head>
 5: <body>
 6: <?php
 7: $user1 = "Bob";
 8: $user2 = "Harry";
 9: $user3 = "Mary";
10: foreach ($GLOBALS as $key=>$value) {
11:     print "\$GLOBALS[\"$key\"] == $value<br>";
12: }
13: ?>
14: </body>
15: </html>
```

Put these lines into a text file named listing9.1.php, and place that file in your Web server document root. When you access this script through your Web browser, it should look something like Figure 9.1 (with your own values, of course).

In this listing, we declare three variables (lines 7–9) and then loop through the built-in $GLOBALS associative array (lines 10 and 11), writing both array keys and values to the browser. In the output, we can locate the variables we defined (look toward the bottom of your screen), but we also see an awful lot more in addition to our variables. PHP automatically defines global variables that describe both the server and client environments. The availability of these variables varies according to your system, server, and configuration, but they can be immensely useful.

PHP has several predefined variables called *superglobals*, which essentially means that they're always present and available in your scripts. Each of the following superglobals is actually an array of other variables:

- $_GET contains any variables provided to a script through the GET method.

- $_POST contains any variables provided to a script through the POST method.

- $_COOKIE contains any variables provided to a script through a cookie.

- $_FILES contains any variables provided to a script through file uploads.

- $_ENV contains any variables provided to a script as part of the server environment.

- $_REQUEST contains any variables provided to a script via any user input mechanism.

- $_SESSION contains any variables that are currently registered in a session.

FIGURE 9.1

Output of Listing 9.1.

If you're using a version of PHP earlier than 4.1.x and cannot upgrade to a newer version, you must adjust the names of the variables when you're following the scripts in this book. The old names are $HTTP_GET_VARS (for $_GET), $HTTP_POST_VARS (for $_POST), $HTTP_COOKIE_VARS (for $_COOKIE), $HTTP_POST_FILES (for $_FILES), $HTTP_ENV_VARS (for $_ENV), and $HTTP_SESSION_VARS (for $_SESSION). These are not superglobals, however, so you must declare them as such, or pass them as parameters, when using functions.

Creating a Simple Input Form

For now, let's keep our HTML separate from our PHP code. Listing 9.2 builds a simple HTML form.

LISTING 9.2   A Simple HTML Form

```
 1: <html>
 2: <head>
 3: <title>Listing 9.2 A simple HTML form</title>
 4: </head>
 5: <body>
 6: <form action="listing9.3.php" method="POST">
 7: Name: <br>
 8: <input type="text" name="user">
 9: <br>
10: Address: <br>
11: <textarea name="address" rows="5" cols="40"></textarea>
12: <br>
13: <input type="submit" value="hit it!">
14: </form>
15: </body>
16: </html>
```

Put these lines into a text file called `listing9.2.php`, and place that file in your Web server document root. This listing defines a form that contains a text field with the name `"user"` on line 8, a text area with the name `"address"` on line 11, and a submit button on line 13. The FORM element's ACTION argument points to a file called `listing9.3.php`, which processes the form information. The method of this form is POST, so the variables are stored in the `$_POST` superglobal.

Listing 9.3 creates the code that receives our users' input.

LISTING 9.3   Reading Input from the Form in Listing 9.2

```
 1: <html>
 2: <head>
 3: <title>Listing 9.3 Reading input from the form in Listing 9.2</title>
 4: </head>
 5: <body>
 6: <?php
 7: print "Welcome <b>$_POST[user]</b><P>\n\n";
 8: print "Your address is:<P>\n\n<b>$_POST[address]</b>";
 9: ?>
10: </body>
11: </html>
```

Put these lines into a text file called listing9.3.php, and place that file in your Web server document root. Now access the form itself with your Web browser, and you should see something like Figure 9.2.

FIGURE 9.2
Form created in Listing 9.2.

The script in Listing 9.3 is the first script in this book that isn't designed to be called by clicking a link or typing directly into the browser's location field. Instead, this file is called when a user submits the form defined in Listing 9.2.

In the code, we access two variables: $_POST[user] and $_POST[address]. These are references to the variables in the $_POST superglobal, which contain the values that the user added to the "user" text field and the "address" text area. Forms in PHP really are as simple as that.

Enter some information in the form fields, and click the Hit It! button. You should see your input echoed to the screen.

Accessing Form Input with User-Defined Arrays

The examples so far enable us to gather information from HTML elements that submit a single value per element name. This leaves us with a problem when working with SELECT elements. These elements make it possible for the user to choose multiple items. If we name the SELECT element with a plain name, like so

```
<select name="products" multiple>
```

the script that receives this data has access to only a single value corresponding to this name. We can change this behavior by renaming an element of this kind so that its name ends with an empty set of square brackets. We do this in Listing 9.4.

LISTING 9.4   An HTML Form Including a SELECT Element

```
 1: <html>
 2: <head>
 3: <title>Listing 9.4 An HTML form including a SELECT element</title>
 4: </head>
 5: <body>
 6: <form action="listing9.5.php" method="POST">
 7: Name: <br>
 8: <input type="text" name="user">
 9: <br>
10: Address: <br>
11: <textarea name="address" rows="5" cols="40"></textarea>
12: <br>
13: Pick Products: <br>
14: <select name="products[]" multiple>
15: <option>Sonic Screwdriver</option>
16: <option>Tricorder</option>
17: <option>ORAC AI</option>
18: <option>HAL 2000</option>
19: </select>
20: <br><br>
21: <input type="submit" value="hit it!">
22: </form>
23: </body>
24: </html>
```

Put these lines into a text file called listing9.4.php, and place that file in your Web server document root. Next, in the script that processes the form input, we find that input from the "products[]" form element created on line 14 is available in an array called $_POST[products]. Because products[] is a SELECT element, we offer the user multiple choices using the option elements on lines 15 through 18. We demonstrate that the user's choices are made available in an array in Listing 9.5.

LISTING 9.5   Reading Input from the Form in Listing 9.4

```
 1: <html>
 2: <head>
 3: <title>Listing 9.5 Reading input from the form in Listing 9.4</title>
 4: </head>
 5: <body>
 6: <?php
 7: print "Welcome <b>$_POST[user]</b><p>\n\n";
 8: print "Your address is:<p>\n\n<b>$_POST[address]</b><p>\n\n";
 9: print "Your product choices are:<p>\n\n";
10: if (!empty($_POST[products])) {
11:     print "<ul>\n\n";
12:     foreach ($_POST[products] as $value) {
13:         print "<li>$value\n";
```

LISTING 9.5 continued

```
14:     }
15:     print "</ul>";
16: }
17: ?>
18: </body>
19: </html>
```

9

Put these lines into a text file called `listing9.5.php`, and place that file in your Web server document root. Now access the form in Listing 9.4 with your Web browser and fill out the fields. Figure 9.3 shows an example.

FIGURE 9.3

Form created in Listing 9.4.

On line 7 of the script in Listing 9.5, we access the `$_POST[user]` variable, which is derived from the `user` form element. On line 10, we test for the `$_POST[products]` variable. If `$_POST[products]` is present, we loop through it on line 12, and output each choice to the browser on line 13.

Submit the form and you might see something like that shown in Figure 9.4.

FIGURE 9.4

Sample output of Listing 9.5.

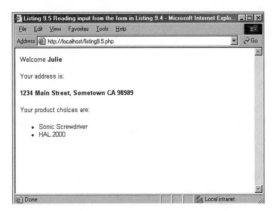

Although the looping technique is particularly useful with the SELECT element, it works with every form element. For example, by giving a number of check boxes the same name, you can enable a user to choose many values within a single field name. As long as the name you choose ends with empty square brackets, PHP compiles the user input for this field into an array. We can replace the SELECT elements from lines 15–18 in Listing 9.4 with a series of check boxes to achieve the same effect:

```
<input type="checkbox" name="products[]" value="Sonic
        Screwdriver">Sonic Screwdriver<br>
<input type="checkbox" name="products[]" value="Tricorder">Tricorder<br>
<input type="checkbox" name="products[]" value="ORAC AI">ORAC AI<br>
<input type="checkbox" name="products[]" value="HAL 2000">HAL 2000<br>
```

Combining HTML and PHP Code on a Single Page

In some circumstances, you might want to include form-parsing code on the same page as a hard-coded HTML form. Such a combination can be useful if you need to present the same form to the user more than once. You would have more flexibility if you were to write the entire page dynamically, of course, but you would miss out on one of the great strengths of PHP. The more standard HTML you can leave in your pages, the easier they are for designers and page builders to amend without reference to you. You should avoid scattering substantial chunks of PHP code throughout your documents, however. Doing so makes them hard to read and maintain. Where possible, you should create functions that can be called from within your HTML code and can be reused in other projects.

For the following examples, imagine that we're creating a site that teaches basic math to preschool children, and have been asked to create a script that takes a number from form input and tells the user whether it's larger or smaller than a predefined integer.

Listing 9.6 creates the HTML. For this example, we need only a single text field, but even so, we'll include a little PHP.

LISTING 9.6   An HTML Form That Calls Itself

```
1: <html>
2: <head>
3: <title>Listing 9.6 An HTML form that calls itself</title>
4: </head>
5: <body>
6: <form action="<?php print $_SERVER[PHP_SELF] ?>" method="POST">
7: Type your guess here: <input type="text" name="guess">
8: </form>
```

LISTING 9.6 continued

```
 9: </body>
10: </html>
```

The action of this script is $_SERVER[PHP_SELF]. This variable is the equivalent of the name of the current script. In other words, the action tells the script to reload itself.

The script in Listing 9.6 doesn't produce any output. In Listing 9.7, we begin to build up the PHP element of the page. First, we must define the number that the user guesses. In a fully working version, we'd probably randomly generate this number, but for now, we keep it simple. We assign 42 to the $num_to_guess variable on line 2. Next, we must determine whether the form has been submitted; otherwise, we'd attempt to assess variables that aren't yet made available. We can test for submission by testing for the existence of the variable $_POST[guess], which is made available if your script has been sent a "guess" parameter. If $_POST[guess] isn't present, we can safely assume that the user arrived at the page without submitting a form. If the value *is* present, we can test the value it contains. The test for the presence of the $_POST[guess] variable takes place on line 4.

LISTING 9.7 A PHP Number-Guessing Script

```
 1: <?php
 2: $num_to_guess = 42;
 3: $message = "";
 4: if (!isset($_POST[guess])) {
 5:    $message = "Welcome to the guessing machine!";
 6: } elseif ($_POST[guess] > $num_to_guess) {
 7:    $message = "$_POST[guess] is too big! Try a smaller number";
 8: } elseif ($_POST[guess] < $num_to_guess) {
 9:    $message = "$_POST[guess] is too small! Try a larger number";
10: } else { // must be equivalent
11:    $message = "Well done!";
12: }
13: ?>
14: <html>
15: <head>
16: <title>Listing 9.7 A PHP number guessing script</title>
17: </head>
18: <body>
19: <h1>
20: <?php print $message ?>
21: </h1>
22: <form action="<?php print $_SERVER[PHP_SELF] ?>" method="POST">
23: Type your guess here: <input type="text" name="guess">
24: </form>
25: </body>
26: </html>
```

Put these lines into a text file called `listing9.7.php`, and place this file in your Web server document root. Now access the script with your Web browser, and you should see something like Figure 9.5.

FIGURE 9.5

Form created in Listing 9.7.

The bulk of this script consists of an `if` statement that determines which string to assign to the variable `$message`. If the `$_POST[guess]` variable hasn't been set, we assume that the user has arrived for the first time and assign a welcome string to the `$message` variable on line 5.

Otherwise, we test the `$_POST[guess]` variable against the number we stored in `$num_to_guess`, and assign advice to `$message` accordingly. We test whether `$_POST[guess]` is larger than `$num_to_guess` on line 6, and whether it's smaller than `$num_to_guess` on line 8. If `$_POST[guess]` is neither larger nor smaller than `$num_to_guess`, we can assume that it's equivalent and assign a congratulations message to the variable (line 11). Now all we must do is print the `$message` variable within the body of the HTML.

There are still a few more additions, but you can probably see how easy it would be to hand this page over to a designer. He can make it beautiful without having to disturb the programming in any way.

Using Hidden Fields to Save State

The script in Listing 9.7 has no way of knowing how many guesses a user has made, but we can use a hidden field to keep track of this. A hidden field behaves exactly the same as a text field, except that the user cannot see it unless he views the HTML source of the document that contains it. Listing 9.8 adds a hidden field to the number-guessing script and some PHP to work with it.

LISTING 9.8   Saving State with a Hidden Field

```
 1: <?php
 2: $num_to_guess = 42;
 3: $num_tries = (isset($_POST[num_tries])) ? $num_tries  + 1 : 0;
 4: $message = "";
 5: if (!isset($_POST[guess])) {
 6:    $message = "Welcome to the guessing machine!";
 7: } elseif ($_POST[guess] > $num_to_guess ) {
 8:    $message = "$_POST[guess] is too big! Try a smaller number";
 9: } elseif ($_POST[guess] < $num_to_guess ) {
10:    $message = "$_POST[guess] is too small! Try a larger number";
11: } else { // must be equivalent
12:    $message = "Well done!";
13: }
14: $guess = $_POST[guess];
15: ?>
16: <html>
17: <head>
18: <title>Listing 9.8 Saving state with a hidden field</title>
19: </head>
20: <body>
21: <h1>
22: <?php print $message ?>
23: </h1>
24: Guess number: <?php print $num_tries?>
25: <form action="<?php print $_SERVER[PHP_SELF] ?>" method="POST">
26: Type your guess here:
27: <input type="text" name="guess" value="<?php print $guess?>">
28: <input type="hidden" name="num_tries" value="<?php print $num_tries?>">
29: </form>
30: </body>
31: </html>
```

The hidden field on line 28 is given the name "num_tries". We also use PHP to write its value. While we're at it, we do the same for the "guess" field on line 27 so that the user can always see his last guess. This technique is useful for scripts that parse user input. If we reject a form submission for some reason, we can at least allow our user to edit his previous query.

Within the main PHP code, we use a ternary operator to increment the $num_tries variable. If the $num_tries variable is set, we add one to it and reassign this incremented value; otherwise, we initialize $num_tries to 0. Within the body of the HTML, we can now report to the user how many guesses he's made.

Put these lines into a text file called listing9.8.php, and place that file in your Web server document root. Access the form a few times with your Web browser, and try to guess the number (pretend you don't already know it).

Redirecting the User

Our simple script still has one major drawback. The form is rewritten whether or not the user guesses correctly. The fact that the HTML is hard-coded makes it difficult to avoid writing the entire page. We can, however, redirect the user to a congratulations page, thereby sidestepping the issue altogether.

When a server script communicates with a client, it must first send some headers that provide information about the document to follow. PHP usually handles this for you automatically, but you can choose to send your own header lines with PHP's header() function.

To call the header() function, you must be sure that absolutely no output has been sent to the browser. The first time content is sent to the browser, PHP sends out headers and it's too late for you to send your own. Any output from your document, even a line break or a space outside of your script tags, causes headers to be sent. If you intend to use the header() function in a script, you must make certain that nothing precedes the PHP code that contains the function call. You should also check any libraries that you might be using.

Listing 9.9 shows typical headers sent to the browser by PHP, beginning with line 3, in response to the request in line 1.

LISTING 9.9   Typical Server Headers Sent from a PHP Script

```
1: HEAD /listing9.9.php HTTP/1.0
2:
3: HTTP/1.1 200 OK
4: Date: Sun, 15 Sep 2002 12:32:28 GMT
5: Server: Apache/2.0.43 (Unix) PHP/4.2.3 mod_ssl/2.8.9 OpenSSL/0.9.6
6: X-Powered-By: PHP/4.2.3
7: Connection: close
8: Content-Type: text/html
```

By sending a "Location" header instead of PHP's default, you can cause the browser to be redirected to a new page:

```
header( "Location: http://www.samspublishing.com" );
```

Assuming that we've created a suitably upbeat page called "congrats.html", we can amend our number-guessing script to redirect the user if she guesses correctly, as shown in Listing 9.10.

LISTING 9.10 Using header() to Send Raw Headers

```php
 1: <?php
 2: $num_to_guess = 42;
 3: $num_tries = (isset($_POST[num_tries])) ? $num_tries + 1: 0;
 4: $message = "";
 5: if (!isset($_POST[guess])) {
 6:     $message = "Welcome to the guessing machine!";
 7: } elseif ($_POST[guess] > $num_to_guess ) {
 8:     $message = "$_POST[guess] is too big! Try a smaller number";
 9: } elseif ($_POST[guess] < $num_to_guess ) {
10:     $message = "$_POST[guess] is too small! Try a larger number";
11: } else { // must be equivalent
12:     header("Location: congrats.html");
13:     exit;
14: }
15: $guess = $_POST[guess];
16: ?>
17: <html>
18: <head>
19: <title>Listing 9.10 Saving state with a hidden field</title>
20: </head>
21: <body>
22: <h1>
23: <?php print $message ?>
24: </h1>
25: Guess number: <?php print $num_tries?>
26: <form action="<?php print $_SERVER[PHP_SELF] ?>" method="POST">
27: Type your guess here:
28: <input type="text" name="guess" value="<?php print $guess?>">
29: <input type="hidden" name="num_tries" value="<?php print $num_tries?>">
30: </form>
31: </body>
32: </html>
```

The else clause of our if statement on line 11 now causes the browser to request congrats.html. We ensure that all output from the current page is aborted with the exit statement on line 13, which immediately ends execution and output, whether HTML or PHP.

Sending Mail on Form Submission

You've already seen how to take form responses and print the results to the screen. You're only one step away from sending those responses in an email message, as you'll soon see. Before learning about sending mail, however, read through the next section to make sure that your system is properly configured.

9

System Configuration for the `mail()` Function

Before you can use the `mail()` function to send mail, a few directives must be set up in the `php.ini` file so that the function works properly. Open `php.ini` with a text editor and look for these lines:

```
[mail function]
; For Win32 only.
SMTP = localhost

; For Win32 only.
sendmail_from = me@localhost.com

; For Unix only.  You may supply arguments as well (default: "sendmail -t -i").
;sendmail_path =
```

If you're using Windows as your Web server platform, the first two directives apply to you. For the `mail()` function to send mail, it must be able to access a valid outgoing mail server. If you plan to use the outgoing mail server of your ISP (in the following example, we use EarthLink), the entry in `php.ini` should look like this:

```
SMTP = mail.earthlink.net
```

The second configuration directive is `sendmail_from`, which is the email address used in the `From` header of the outgoing email. It can be overwritten in the mail script itself, but normally operates as the default value. For example:

```
sendmail_from = youraddress@yourdomain.com
```

A good rule of thumb for Windows users is that whatever outgoing mail server you've set up in your email client on that machine, you should also use as the value of SMTP in `php.ini`.

If your Web server is running on a Linux/Unix platform, you use the `sendmail` functionality of that particular machine. In this case, only the last directive applies to you: `sendmail_path`. The default is `sendmail -t -i`, but if `sendmail` is in an odd place or if you need to specify different arguments, feel free to do so, as in the following example:

```
sendmail_path = /opt/sendmail -odd -arguments
```

After making any changes to `php.ini` on any platform, you must restart the Web server process for the changes to take effect.

Creating the Form

In Listing 9.11, you see the basic HTML for creating a simple feedback form. This form has an action of listing9.12.php, which we create in the next section. The fields are very simple: Line 7 contains a name field, line 8 contains the return email address field, and line 10 contains the text area for the user's message.

LISTING 9.11 Creating a Simple Feedback Form

```
 1: <HTML>
 2: <HEAD>
 3: <TITLE>E-Mail Form</TITLE>
 4: </HEAD>
 5: <BODY>
 6: <FORM action="listing9.12.php" method="POST">
 7: Your Name: <INPUT type="text" name="name"><br><br>
 8: Your E-Mail Address: <INPUT type="text" name="email"><br><br>
 9: Message:<br>
10: <textarea name="message" cols=30 rows=5></textarea><br><br>
11: <INPUT type="submit" value="Send Form">
12: </FORM>
13: </BODY>
14: </HTML>
```

Put these lines into a text file called listing9.11.php, and place this file in your Web server document root. Now access the script with your Web browser, and you should see something like Figure 9.6.

FIGURE 9.6

Form created in Listing 9.11.

In the next section, you create the script that sends this form to a recipient.

Creating the Script to Send the Mail

This script is only slightly different in concept than the script in Listing 9.5, which simply printed form responses to the screen. In this script, in addition to printing the responses to the screen, you send them to an email address as well.

LISTING 9.12   Sending the Simple Feedback Form

```
 1: <html>
 2: <head>
 3: <title>Listing 9.12 Sending mail from the form in Listing 9.11</title>
 4: </head>
 5: <body>
 6: <?php
 7: print "Thank you, <b>$_POST[name]</b>, for your message!<br><br>\n\n";
 8: print "Your e-mail address is: <b>$_POST[email]</b><br><br>\n\n";
 9: print "Your message was:<br><br>\n\n";
10: print "$_POST[message] <br><br>";
11: //start building the mail string
12: $msg = "Name:     $_POST[name]\n";
13: $msg .= "E-Mail:   $_POST[email]\n";
14: $msg .= "Message:  $_POST[message]\n";
15: //set up the mail
16: $recipient = "you@yourdomain.com";
17: $subject = "Form Submission Results";
18: $mailheaders = "From: My Web Site <defaultaddress@yourdomain.com> \n";
19: $mailheaders .= "Reply-To: $_POST[email]";
20: //send the mail
21: mail($recipient, $subject, $msg, $mailheaders);
22: ?>
23: </body>
24: </html>
```

The variables you use in lines 7–9 are $_POST[name], $_POST[email], and $_POST[message]—the names of the fields in the form, as part of the $_POST superglobal. That's all well and good for printing the information to the screen, but in this script, you also want to create a string that's sent in email. For this task, you essentially build the email by concatenating strings to form one long message string, using the newline (\n) character to add line breaks where appropriate.

Lines 12 through 14 create the $msg string, which contains the values typed by the user in the form fields. This string is the one sent in the email. Note the use of the concatenation operator (.=) when adding to the variable $msg, in lines 13 and 14.

Lines 16 and 17 are hard-coded variables for the email recipient and the subject of the email message. Replace you@yourdomain.com with your own email address, obviously. If you want to change the subject, feel free!

Lines 18 and 19 set up some mail headers, namely From: and Reply-to: headers. You could put any value in the From: header; this is the information that displays in the From or Sender column of your email application when you receive this mail.

The mail() function takes four parameters: the recipient, the subject, the message, and any additional mail headers. The order of these parameters is shown in line 21, and your script is complete after you close up your PHP block and your HTML elements in lines 22–24.

Put these lines into a text file called listing9.12.php, and place that file in your Web server document root. Use your Web browser and go back to the form, enter some information, and press the submission button. You should see something like Figure 9.7 in your browser.

FIGURE 9.7
Sample results from Listing 9.12.

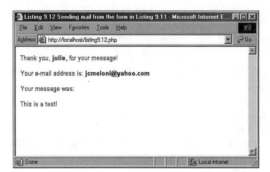

If you then check your email, you should have a message waiting for you. It might look something like Figure 9.8.

FIGURE 9.8
Email sent from Listing 9.12.

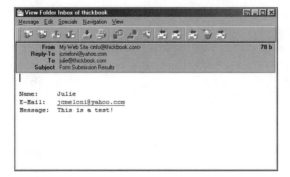

9

Working with File Uploads

So far, we've looked at simple form input. However, all popular Web browsers support file uploads, and so, of course, does PHP. In this section, you examine the features that PHP makes available to deal with this kind of input.

Information about the uploaded file becomes available to you in the $_FILES super-global, which is indexed by the name of the upload field (or fields) in the form. The corresponding value for each of these keys is an associative array. These fields are described in Table 9.2, using `fileupload` as the name of the form field used for the upload.

TABLE 9.2 File Upload Global Variables

Element	Contains	Example
$_FILES['fileupload']['name']	Original name of uploaded file	test.gif
$_FILES['fileupload']['tmp_name']	Path to temporary file	/tmp/phprDfZvN
$_FILES['fileupload']['size']	Size (in bytes) of uploaded file	6835
$_FILES['fileupload']['type']	MIME type of uploaded file (where given by client)	image/gif

Keep these elements in the back of your mind for a moment, while we create the upload form in the next section.

Creating the File Upload Form

First, we must create the HTML form to handle the upload. HTML forms that include file upload fields must include an ENCTYPE argument:

```
ENCTYPE="multipart/form-data"
```

PHP also works with an optional hidden field that can be inserted before the file upload field. This field must be called MAX_FILE_SIZE and should have a value representing the maximum size in bytes of the file that you're willing to accept. This size cannot override the maximum size set in the upload_max_filesize field in your php.ini file that defaults to 2MB. The MAX_FILE_SIZE field is obeyed at the browser's discretion, so you should rely on the php.ini setting to cap unreasonable uploads. After the MAX_FILE_SIZE field has been entered, you're ready to add the upload field itself. This is simply an INPUT element with a TYPE argument of "file". You can give it any name you want. Listing 9.13 brings all this together into an HTML upload form.

LISTING 9.13   A Simple File Upload Form

```
1: <html>
2: <head>
3: <title>Listing 9.13 A simple file upload form</title>
4: </head>
5: <body>
6: <form action="listing9.14.php" enctype="multipart/form-data" method="POST">
7: <input type="hidden" name="MAX_FILE_SIZE" value="51200">
8: File to Upload: <input type="file" name="fileupload"><br><br>
9: <input type="submit" value="upload!">
10: </form>
11: </body>
12: </html>
```

As you can see, file uploads are limited to 50KB on line 7, and the name of the file upload field is `fileupload`, as shown on line 8. Save this listing in a text file called `listing9.13.php`, and place that file in your Web server document root. Use your Web browser to access this form and you should see something like Figure 9.9.

FIGURE 9.9

Form created by Listing 9.13.

This form calls the `listing9.14.php` script, which we create next.

Creating the File Upload Script

If you remember the information regarding the `$_FILES` superglobal, you have all the information you need to write a simple file upload script. This script is the backend for the form created in Listing 9.13.

LISTING 9.14   A File Upload Script

```
 1: <html>
 2: <head>
 3: <title>Listing 9.14 A file upload script</title>
 4: </head>
 5: <body>
 6: <h1>File Upload Results</h1>
 7: <?php
 8: $file_dir = "/path/to/upload/directory";
 9:
10: foreach($_FILES as $file_name => $file_array) {
11:     print "path: ".$file_array['tmp_name']."<br>\n";
12:     print "name: ".$file_array['name']."<br>\n";
13:     print "type: ".$file_array['type']."<br>\n";
14:     print "size: ".$file_array['size']."<br>\n";
15:
16:     if (is_uploaded_file($file_array['tmp_name'])) {
17:         move_uploaded_file($file_array['tmp_name'],
18:             "$file_dir/$file_array[name]") or die ("Couldn't copy");
19:         print "file was moved!<br><br>";
20:     }
21: }
22: ?>
23: </body>
24: </html>
```

In Listing 9.14, we first create the $file_dir variable on line 8 to store path information. This path should be one that exists on your system, and you must have write permissions for it.

The path used in line 8 is a Linux/Unix path. Windows users would use backslashes, such as \My Documents\.

Line 10 begins a foreach statement that loops through every element in the $_FILES array. A loop is used rather than an if statement to make our script capable of scaling to deal with multiple uploads on the same page. The foreach loop on line 10 stores the upload file's name in the $file_name variable and the file information in the $file_array variable. We can then output the information we have about the upload.

Before moving the uploaded file from its temporary position to the location specified in line 8, first check that it exists. We do so on line 16, using the is_uploaded_file() function. This function accepts a path to an uploaded file and returns true only if the file in question is a valid upload file. This function therefore enhances the security of your scripts.

Assuming that all is well, the file is copied from its temporary home to a new directory on lines 17 and 18. We use another function, `move_uploaded_file()`, for this purpose. This function copies a file from one place to another, first performing the same security checks as those performed by `is_uploaded_file()`. The `move_uploaded_file()` function requires a path to the source file and a path to the destination. It returns true if the move is successful and false if the file isn't a valid upload file or if the file couldn't be found.

Beware of the names of uploaded files. Operating systems such as Mac OS and Windows are pretty relaxed when it comes to file naming, so expect uploaded files to come complete with spaces, quotation marks, and all manner of other unexpected characters. Therefore, it's a good idea to filter filenames. You can learn more about techniques for testing and checking strings in Hour 13, "Working with Strings."

Put these lines into a text file called `listing9.14.php`, and place that file in your Web server document root. Use your Web browser to go back to the form, and try to upload a file. If successful, you should see something like Figure 9.10 in your browser.

FIGURE 9.10

Sample results from Listing 9.14.

Summary

Things are really getting exciting now! You have the tools to create truly sophisticated and interactive environments. A few things are still missing, of course. Now that you can get information from the user, it would be nice to be able to do something with it. Write it to a file, perhaps. That's the subject of the next hour.

Throughout this hour, you learned how to work with various superglobals and form input. You also learned how to send raw headers to the client to redirect a browser. You learned how to acquire list information from form submissions and how to pass information from script call to script call using hidden fields. Finally, you learned how to send your form results in email, and also how to upload files through your Web browser via a PHP script.

Workshop

The workshop is designed to help you anticipate possible questions, review what you've learned, and begin putting your knowledge into practice.

Quiz

1. Which predefined variable do you use to find the name of the script?
2. Which built-in associative array contains all values submitted as part of a POST request?
3. Which built-in associative array contains all values submitted as part of a file upload?
4. What function do you use to redirect the browser to a new page?
5. What are the four arguments used by the mail() function?
6. How do you limit the size of a file that a user can submit via a particular upload form?

Answers

1. The variable $_SERVER['PHP_SELF'] holds the name of the script.
2. The $_POST superglobal.
3. The $_FILES superglobal.
4. The header() function.
5. The recipient, the subject, the message string, and additional headers.
6. Use a hidden field called MAX_FILE_SIZE in your form.

Activities

1. Create a calculator script that enables the user to submit two numbers and choose an operation (addition, multiplication, division, or subtraction) to perform on them.
2. Use hidden fields with the script you created in activity 1 to store and display the number of requests that the user submitted.

Hour 10

Working with Files

Testing, reading, and writing to files are staple activities for any full-featured programming language. PHP is no exception, providing you with functions that make the process straightforward. In this hour, you will learn

- How to include files in your documents
- How to test files and directories
- How to open a file before working with it
- How to read data from files
- How to write or append to a file
- How to lock a file
- How to work with directories

Including Files with `include()`

The `include()` statement enables you to incorporate files into your PHP documents. PHP code in these files can be executed as if it were part of the main document. This can be useful for including library code in multiple pages.

Having created a killer function, your only option until now would have been to paste it into every document that needs to use it. Of course, if you discover a bug or want to add a feature, you would have to find every page that uses the function to make the change. The include() statement can save you from this chore. You can add the function to a single document and, at runtime, read it into any page that needs it. The include() statement requires a single argument: a relative path to the file to be included. Listing 10.1 creates a simple PHP script that uses include() to incorporate and output the contents of a file.

LISTING 10.1   Using include()

```
 1: <html>
 2: <head>
 3: <title>Listing 10.1 Using include()</title>
 4: </head>
 5: <body>
 6: <?php
 7: include("listing10.2.php");
 8: ?>
 9: </body>
10: </html>
```

The include() statement in Listing 10.1 incorporates the document listing10.2.php, the contents of which you can see in Listing 10.2.

LISTING 10.2   The File Included in Listing 10.1

```
1: I have been included!!
```

Put the contents of Listing 10.1 in a file named listing10.1.php, and the contents of Listing 10.2 in a file named listing10.2.php. Place both files in your Web server document root. When you access listing10.1.php through your Web browser, the output on the screen is

```
I have been included!!
```

This might seem strange to you, given that we've included plain text within a block of PHP code. In fact, the contents of an included file are displayed as text by default. If you want to execute PHP code in an included file, you must enclose it in PHP start and end tags. In Listings 10.3 and 10.4, we amend the previous example so that code is executed in the included file.

LISTING 10.3 Using the `include()` Statement to Execute PHP in Another File

```
 1: <html>
 2: <head>
 3: <title>Listing 10.3 Using include to execute PHP in another file</title>
 4: </head>
 5: <body>
 6: <?php
 7: include("listing10.4.php");
 8: ?>
 9: </body>
10: </html>
```

LISTING 10.4 An Include File Containing PHP Code

```
1: <?php
2: print "I have been included!!<BR>";
3: print "But now I can add up...  4 + 4 = ".(4 + 4);
4: ?>
```

Put the contents of Listing 10.3 in a file named `listing10.3.php`, and the contents of Listing 10.4 in a file named `listing10.4.php`. Place both these files in your Web server document root. When you access `listing10.3.php` through your Web browser, the output on the screen is

```
I have been included!!

But now I can add up... 4 + 4 = 8
```

Returning a Value from an Included Document

Included files in PHP can return a value in the same way that functions do. As in a function, using the `return` statement ends the execution of code within the included file. Additionally, no further HTML is included. In Listings 10.5 and 10.6, we include a file and assign its return value to a variable.

LISTING 10.5 Using `include()` to Execute PHP and Assign the Return Value

```
1: <html>
2: <head>
3: <title>Listing 10.5 Using include() to execute PHP and
4:     assign the return value</title>
5: </head>
6: <body>
7: <?php
```

10

LISTING 10.5   continued

```
 8: $addResult = include("listing10.6.php");
 9: print "The include file returned $addResult";
10: ?>
11: </body>
12: </html>
```

LISTING 10.6   An Include File That Returns a Value

```
1: <?php
2: $retval = ( 4 + 4 );
3: return $retval;
4: ?>
5: This HTML will never be displayed because it comes after a return statement!
```

Put the contents of Listing 10.5 in a file named `listing10.5.php`, and the contents of Listing 10.6 in a file named `listing10.6.php`. Place both of these files in your Web server document root. When you access `listing10.5.php` through your Web browser, the output is

```
The include file returned 8
```

Using `include()` Within Control Structures

You can use an `include()` statement in a conditional statement, and the referenced file is read only if the condition is met. For example, the `include()` statement in the following fragment will never be called:

```
$test = false;
if ( $test ) {
    include( "a_file.txt" ); // won't be included
}
```

If you use an `include()` statement within a loop, it's replaced with the contents of the referenced file each time the `include()` statement is called. This content is executed for every call. Listing 10.7 illustrates this concept by using an `include()` statement in a `for` loop. The `include()` statement references a different file for each iteration.

LISTING 10.7   Using include() Within a Loop

```
1: <html>
2: <head>
3: <title>Listing 10.7 Using include() within a loop</title>
```

Listing 10.7 continued

```
 4: </head>
 5: <body>
 6: <?php
 7: for ( $x = 1; $x<=3; $x++ ) {
 8:    $incfile = "incfile$x".".txt";
 9:    print "Attempting include $incfile<br>";
10:    include( "$incfile" );
11:    print "<p>";
12: }
13: ?>
14: </body>
15: </html>
```

When Listing 10.7 is run, it includes the content of three different files: "incfile1.txt", "incfile2.txt", and "incfile3.txt". Assuming that each of these files simply contains a confirmation of its own name, the output should look like Figure 10.1.

Figure 10.1

Output of Listing 10.7.

include_once()

One of the problems caused by using multiple libraries within your code is the danger of calling include() twice on the same file. This can occur in larger projects when different library files call include() on a common file. Including the same file twice often results in repeated declarations of functions and classes, thereby causing the PHP engine great unhappiness.

The situation is saved by the include_once() statement. include_once() requires the path to an include file and behaves the same way as include() the first time it's called. However, if include_once() is called again for the same file during script execution, the file is *not* included again. This makes include_once() an excellent tool for the creation of reusable code libraries!

The `include_path` Directive

Using `include()` and `include_once()` to access libraries can increase the flexibility and reusability of your projects. However, there are still headaches to overcome. Portability in particular can suffer if you hard-code the paths to included files. Imagine that you create a `lib` directory and reference it throughout your project:

```
include_once("/home/user/bob/htdocs/project4/lib/mylib.inc.php");
```

When you move your project to a new server, you might find that you have to change a hundred or more `include` paths. You can escape this fate by setting the `include_path` directive in your `php.ini` file:

```
include_path   .:/home/user/bob/htdocs/project4/lib/
```

The `include_path` can include as many directories as you want, separated by colons (semicolons in Windows). The first dot (`.`) before the first colon indicates "current directory." You can then reference your library file by only its name:

```
include_once("mylib.inc.php");
```

When you move your project, you need to change only the `include_path` directive.

> PHP has both a `require()` statement, which performs a similar function to `include()`, and a `require_once()` statement.
>
> `require()` is executed regardless of a script's flow, and therefore shouldn't be used as part of conditional or loop structures.
>
> A file included as a result of a `require()` statement cannot return a value.

Testing Files

Before you work with a file or directory, it's often a good idea to learn more about it. PHP provides many functions to help you to discover information about files on your system. This section briefly covers some of the most useful functions.

Checking for Existence with `file_exists()`

You can test for the existence of a file with the `file_exists()` function. This function requires a string representing an absolute or relative path to a file that might or might not be there. If the file is found, `file_exists()` returns `true`; otherwise, it returns `false`.

```
if (file_exists("test.txt")) {
        print "The file exists!";
}
```

A File or a Directory?

You can confirm that the entity you're testing is a file, as opposed to a directory, with the is_file() function. is_file() requires the file path and returns a Boolean value.

```
if (is_file( "test.txt" )) {
        print "test.txt is a file!";
}
```

Conversely, you might want to check that the entity you're testing is a directory. You can do this with the is_dir() function. is_dir() requires the path to the directory and returns a Boolean value.

```
if (is_dir( "/tmp" )) {
        print "/tmp is a directory";
}
```

10

Checking the Status of a File

When you know that a file exists, and it's what you expect it to be, you can find out some things that you can do with it. Typically, you might want to read, write to, or execute a file. PHP can help you with all of these operations.

is_readable() tells you whether you can read a file. On Unix systems, you might be able to see a file but still be barred from reading its contents. is_readable() accepts the file path as a string and returns a Boolean value.

```
if (is_readable("test.txt")) {
        print "test.txt is readable";
}
```

is_writable() tells you whether you can write to a file. As with is_readable(), the is_writable() function requires the file path and returns a Boolean value.

```
if (is_writable( "test.txt")) {
        print "test.txt is writable";
}
```

is_executable() tells you whether you can run a file, relying on either the file's permissions or its extension depending on your platform. It accepts the file path and returns a Boolean value.

```
if (is_executable("test.txt")) {
        print "test.txt is executable";
}
```

Determining File Size with `filesize()`

Given the path to a file, filesize() attempts to determine and return its size in bytes. It returns false if it encounters problems.

```
print "The size of test.txt is.. ";
print filesize( "test.txt" );
```

Getting Date Information About a File

Sometimes you need to know when a file was last written to or accessed. PHP provides several functions that can provide this information.

You can find out when a file was last accessed with `fileatime()`. This function requires the file path and returns the date that the file was last accessed. To *access* a file means either to read or write to it. Dates are returned from all the date information functions in Unix epoch format—that is, the number of seconds since January 1, 1970. In our examples, we use the `date()` function to translate this into human-readable form. You learn more about date functions in Hour 11, "Working with Dates and Times."

```
$atime = fileatime("test.txt");
print "test.txt was last accessed on ";
print date("D d M Y g:i A", $atime);
// Sample output: Sat 14 Sep 2002 9:54 PM
```

You can discover the modification date of a file with the function `filemtime()`, which requires the file path and returns the date in Unix epoch format. To *modify* a file means to change its contents in some way.

```
$mtime = filemtime("test.txt");
print "test.txt was last modified on ";
print date("D d M Y g:i A", $mtime);
// Sample output: Sat 14 Sep 2002 9:54 PM
```

PHP also enables you to test the change time of a document with the `filectime()` function. On Unix systems, the change time is set when a file's contents are modified or changes are made to its permissions or ownership. On other platforms, the `filectime()` returns the creation date.

```
$ctime = filectime("test.txt");
print "test.txt was last changed on ";
print date("D d M Y g:i A", $ctime);
// Sample output: Sat 14 Sep 2002 9:54 PM
```

Creating a Function That Performs Multiple File Tests

Listing 10.8 creates a function that brings together the file test functions we've looked at into one script.

LISTING 10.8 A Function to Output the Results of Multiple File Tests

```
 1: <html>
 2: <head>
 3: <title>Listing 10.8 A function to output the results of
 4:     multiple file tests</title>
 5: </head>
 6: <body>
 7: <?php
 8: $file = "test.txt";
 9: outputFileTestInfo($file);
10:
11: function outputFileTestInfo($f) {
12:     if (!file_exists( $f)) {
13:         print "$f does not exist<BR>";
14:         return;
15:     }
16:     print "$f is ".(is_file($f)?"":"not ")."a file<br>";
17:     print "$f is ".(is_dir($f)?"":"not ")."a directory<br>";
18:     print "$f is ".(is_readable($f)?"":"not ")."readable<br>";
19:     print "$f is ".(is_writable($f)?"":"not ")."writable<br>";
20:     print "$f is ".(is_executable($f)?"":"not ")."executable<br>";
21:     print "$f is ".(filesize($f))." bytes<br>";
22:     print "$f was accessed on ".date( "D d M Y g:i A",fileatime($f))."<br>";
23:     print "$f was modified on ".date( "D d M Y g:i A",filemtime($f))."<br>";
24:     print "$f was changed on ".date( "D d M Y g:i A",filectime($f) )."<br>";
25: }
26:
27: ?>
28: </body>
29: </html>
```

If this code were saved to the document root of your Web server and run through your Web browser, the output would look something like Figure 10.2.

FIGURE 10.2

Output of Listing 10.8.

Notice that we used the ternary operator as a compact way of working with some of these tests. Let's look at one such test, found in line 16, in more detail:

```
print "$f is ".(is_file($f)?"":"not ")."a file<br>";
```

We use the is_file() function as the right-side expression of the ternary operator. If it returns true, an empty string is returned. Otherwise, the string "not " is returned. The return value of the ternary expression is added to the string to be printed with concatenation operators. This statement could be made clearer, but less compact, as follows:

```
$is_it = is_file( $f )?"":"not ";
print "$f is $is_it a file";
```

We could, of course, be even clearer with an if statement, but imagine how large the function would become if we used the following:

```
if (is_file($f)) {
        print "$f is a file<br>";
} else {
        print "$f is not a file<br>";
}
```

Because the result of these three approaches is the same, the approach you take becomes a matter of preference.

Creating and Deleting Files

If a file does not yet exist, you can create it with the touch() function. Given a string representing a file path, touch() attempts to create an empty file of that name. If the file already exists, the contents aren't disturbed, but the modification date is updated to the time at which the function executed.

```
touch("myfile.txt");
```

You can remove an existing file with the unlink() function. As did the touch() function, unlink() accepts a file path:

```
unlink("myfile.txt");
```

All functions that create, delete, read, write, and modify files on Unix systems require the correct file or directory permissions to be set.

Opening a File for Writing, Reading, or Appending

Before you can work with a file, you must first open it for reading, writing, or both. PHP provides the fopen() function for doing so. fopen() requires a string that contains the file path followed by a string containing the mode in which the file is to be opened. The most common modes are read (r), write (w), and append (a). fopen() returns a file resource you'll use later to work with the open file. To open a file for reading, you use the following:

```
$fp = fopen("test.txt", 'r');
```

You use the following to open a file for writing:

```
$fp = fopen("test.txt", 'w');
```

To open a file for *appending* (that is, to add data to the end of a file), you use this:

```
$fp = fopen("test.txt", 'a');
```

fopen() returns false if the file cannot be opened for any reason. Therefore, it's a good idea to test the function's return value before proceeding to work with it. You can do so with an if statement:

```
if ($fp = fopen("test.txt", "w")) {
    // do something with $fp
}
```

Or you can use a logical operator to end execution if an essential file can't be opened:

```
($fp = fopen("test.txt", "w")) or die ("Couldn't open file, sorry");
```

If the fopen() function returns true, the rest of the expression won't be parsed, and the die() function (which writes a message to the browser and ends the script) is never reached. Otherwise, the right side of the or operator is parsed and the die() function is called.

Assuming that all is well and you go on to work with your open file, you should remember to close it when you finish. You can do so by calling fclose(), which requires the file resource returned from a successful fopen() call as its argument:

```
fclose($fp);
```

10

Reading from Files

PHP provides a number of functions for reading data from files. These enable you to read by the byte, the line, and even by the character.

Reading Lines from a File with `fgets()` and `feof()`

After you open a file for reading, you often need to access it line by line. To read a line from an open file, you can use `fgets()`, which requires the file resource returned from `fopen()` as an argument. You must also pass `fgets()` an integer as a second argument. The integer argument specifies the number of bytes that the function should read if it doesn't first encounter a line end or the end of the file. The `fgets()` function reads the file until it reaches a newline character (`"\n"`), the number of bytes specified in the length argument, or the end of the file.

```
$line = fgets($fp, 1024); // where $fp is the file resource returned by fopen()
```

Although you can read lines with `fgets()`, you need some way to tell when you reach the end of the file. The `feof()` function does this by returning `true` when the end of the file has been reached and `false` otherwise. `feof()` requires a file resource as its argument.

```
feof($fp); // where $fp is the file resource returned by fopen()
```

You now have enough information to read a file line by line, as shown in Listing 10.9.

LISTING 10.9   Opening and Reading a File Line by Line

```
 1: <html>
 2: <head>
 3: <title>Listing 10.9 Opening and reading a file line by line</title>
 4: </head>
 5: <body>
 6: <?php
 7: $filename = "test.txt";
 8: $fp = fopen($filename, "r") or die("Couldn't open $filename");
 9: while (!feof($fp)) {
10:     $line = fgets($fp, 1024);
11:     print "$line<br>";
12: }
13: ?>
14: </body>
15: </html>
```

If this code were saved to the document root of your Web server and run through your Web browser, the output would look something like Figure 10.3 (the contents of your sample text file might be different).

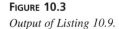

FIGURE **10.3**

Output of Listing 10.9.

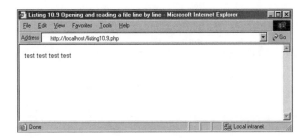

We call `fopen()` on line 8 with the name of the file that we want to read, using the `or` operator to ensure that script execution ends if the file cannot be read. This usually occurs if the file does not exist, or (on a Unix system) if the file's permissions don't allow the script read access to the file. The actual reading takes place in the `while` statement on line 9. The `while` statement's test expression calls `feof()` for each iteration, ending the loop when it returns `true`. In other words, the loop continues until the end of the file is reached. Within the code block, we use `fgets()` on line 10 to extract a line (or 1024 bytes) of the file. We assign the result to `$line` and print it to the browser on line 11, appending a `<BR>` tag for the sake of readability.

Reading Arbitrary Amounts of Data from a File with `fread()`

Rather than reading text by the line, you can choose to read a file in arbitrarily defined chunks. The `fread()` function accepts a file resource as an argument, as well as the number of bytes you want to read. `fread()` returns the amount of data you requested, unless the end of the file is reached first.

```
$chunk = fread($fp, 16);
```

Listing 10.10 amends our previous example so that it reads data in chunks of 16 bytes rather than by the line.

LISTING 10.10 Reading a File with `fread()`

```
 1: <html>
 2: <head>
 3: <title>Listing 10.10 Reading a file with fread()</title>
 4: </head>
 5: <body>
 6: <?php
 7: $filename = "test.txt";
 8: $fp = fopen($filename, "r") or die("Couldn't open $filename");
 9: while (!feof($fp)) {
```

10

LISTING 10.10   continued

```
10:     $chunk = fread($fp, 16);
11:     print "$chunk<br>";
12: }
13: ?>
14: </body>
15: </html>
```

If this code were saved to the document root of your Web server and run through your Web browser, the output could look something like Figure 10.4.

FIGURE 10.4

Output of Listing 10.10.

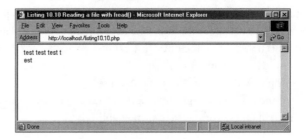

Although `fread()` enables you to define the amount of data acquired from a file, it doesn't let you decide the position from which the acquisition begins. You can set this manually with the `fseek()` function. `fseek()` enables you to change your current position within a file. It requires a file resource and an integer that represents the offset from the start of the file (in bytes) to which you want to jump:

```
fseek( $fp, 64 );
```

Listing 10.11 uses `fseek()` and `fread()` to output the second half of a file to the browser.

LISTING 10.11   Moving Around a File with `fseek()`

```
 1: <html>
 2: <head>
 3: <title>Listing 10.11 Moving around a file with fseek()</title>
 4: </head>
 5: <body>
 6: <?php
 7: $filename = "test.txt";
 8: $fp = fopen($filename, "r") or die("Couldn't open $filename");
 9: $fsize = filesize($filename);
10: $halfway = (int)($fsize / 2);
11: print "Halfway point: $halfway <BR>\n";
```

LISTING 10.11   continued

```
12: fseek($fp, $halfway);
13: $chunk = fread( $fp, ($fsize - $halfway));
14: print $chunk;
15: ?>
16: </body>
17: </html>
```

If this code were saved to the document root of your Web server and run through your
Web browser, the output could look something like Figure 10.5.

FIGURE 10.5

*Output of Listing
10.11.*

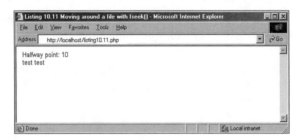

10

We calculate the halfway point of our file by dividing the return value of filesize() by
2 on line 10. We use this as the second argument to fseek() on line 12, jumping to the
halfway point. Finally, we call fread() on line 13 to extract the second half of the file
and then print the result to the browser.

Reading Characters from a File with `fgetc()`

fgetc() is similar to fgets() except that it returns only a single character from a file
every time it is called. Because a character is always one byte in size, fgetc() doesn't
require a length argument. You must simply pass it a file resource:

```
$char = fgetc( $fp );
```

Listing 10.12 creates a loop that reads the file "test.txt" one character at a time, outputting each character to the browser on its own line.

LISTING 10.12   Moving Around a File with `fseek()`

```
1: <html>
2: <head>
3: <title>Listing 10.12</title>
4: </head>
5: <body>
```

LISTING 10.12 continued

```
 6: <?php
 7: $filename = "test.txt";
 8: $fp = fopen( $filename, "r") or die("Couldn't open $filename");
 9: while (!feof($fp)) {
10:     $char = fgetc($fp);
11:     print "$char<BR>";
12: }
13: ?>
14: </body>
15: </html>
```

If this code were saved to the document root of your Web server and run through your Web browser, the output could look something like Figure 10.6.

FIGURE 10.6

Output of Listing 10.12.

Writing or Appending to a File

The processes for writing to and appending to a file are the same. The difference lies in the fopen() call. When you write to a file, you use the mode argument "w" when you call fopen():

```
$fp = fopen("test.txt", "w");
```

All subsequent writing occurs from the start of the file. If the file doesn't already exist, it is created. If the file already exists, any prior content is destroyed and replaced by the data you write.

When you append to a file, you use mode argument "a" in your fopen() call:

```
$fp = fopen("test.txt", "a");
```

Any subsequent writes to your file are added to the existing content, but if you attempt to append content to a nonexistent file, the file is first created.

Writing to a File with `fwrite()` or `fputs()`

fwrite() accepts a file resource and a string, and then writes the string to the file. fputs() works in exactly the same way.

```
fwrite($fp, "hello world");
fputs($fp, "hello world");
```

Writing to files is as straightforward as that. Listing 10.13 uses fwrite() to print to a file. We then append a further string to the same file using fputs().

10

LISTING 10.13   Writing and Appending to a File

```
 1: <html>
 2: <head>
 3: <title>Listing 10.13 Writing and appending to a file</title>
 4: </head>
 5: <body>
 6: <?php
 7: $filename = "test.txt";
 8: print "Writing to $filename<br>";
 9: $fp = fopen($filename, "w") or die("Couldn't open $filename");
10: fwrite($fp, "Hello world\n");
11: fclose($fp);
12: print "Appending to $filename<br>";
13: $fp = fopen($filename, "a") or die("Couldn't open $filename");
14: fputs($fp, "And another thing\n");
15: fclose($fp);
16: ?>
17: </body>
18: </html>
```

The screen output of this script, when run from your Web browser, is

```
Writing to test.txt
```

```
Appending to test.txt
```

If you open the test.txt file or use listing10.9.php to read its contents, you'll find the file now contains:

```
Hello world
```

```
And another thing
```

Locking Files with `flock()`

The techniques you learned for reading and amending files work fine if you're presenting your script to only a single user. In the real world, however, you'd expect many users to access your projects at more or less the same time. Imagine what would happen if two users were to execute a script that writes to one file at the same moment. The file would quickly become corrupt.

PHP provides the `flock()` function to forestall this eventuality. `flock()` locks a file to warn other processes against writing to or reading from that file while the current process is working with it. `flock()` requires a valid file resource and an integer representing the kind of lock you want to set. PHP provides predefined constants for each of the integers you're likely to need. Table 10.1 lists three kinds of locks you can apply to a file.

TABLE 10.1   Integer Arguments to the `flock()` Function

Constant	Integer	Lock Type	Description
LOCK_SH	1	Shared	Allows other processes to read the file but prevents writing (used when reading a file)
LOCK_EX	2	Exclusive	Prevents other processes from either reading from or writing to a file (used when writing to a file)
LOCK_UN	3	Release	Releases a shared or exclusive lock

You should call `flock()` directly after calling `fopen()` and call it again to release the lock before closing the file. If the lock is not released, you will not be able to read from or write to the file.

```
$fp = fopen( "test.txt", "a") or die("couldn't open");
flock($fp, LOCK_EX); // exclusive lock
// write to the file
flock($fp, LOCK_UN); // release the lock
fclose($fp);
```

> For more information on file locking, see the PHP Manual entry for the `flock()` function, at `http://www.php.net/manual/en/function.flock.php`.

Working with Directories

Now that you can test, read, and write to files, let's turn our attention to directories. PHP provides many functions for working with directories. Let's look at how to create, remove, and read them.

Creating Directories with `mkdir()`

`mkdir()` enables you to create a directory. `mkdir()` requires a string that represents the path to the directory you want to create, and an octal number integer that represents the mode you want to set for the directory. You specify an octal (base 8) number with a leading 0. The mode argument has an effect only on Unix systems. The mode should consist of three numbers between 0 and 7, representing permissions for the directory owner, group, and everyone, respectively. `mkdir()` returns `true` if it successfully creates a directory, or `false` if it doesn't. If `mkdir()` fails, it's usually because the containing directory has permissions that preclude processes with the script's user ID from writing. If you're not comfortable setting Unix directory permissions, you should find that one of the following examples fits your needs. Unless you really need your directory to be world writable, you should probably use 0755, which allows the world to read your directory but not to write to it.

```
mkdir("testdir", 0777); // global read/write/execute permissions
mkdir("testdir", 0755); // world and group: read/execute only
                        // owner: read/write/execute
```

Removing a Directory with `rmdir()`

`rmdir()` enables you to remove a directory from the file system if the process running your script has the right to do so and if the directory is empty. `rmdir()` requires only a string representing the path to the directory you want to create.

```
rmdir("testdir");
```

Opening a Directory for Reading with `opendir()`

Before you can read the contents of a directory, you must first obtain a directory resource. You can do so with the `opendir()` function. `opendir()` requires a string that represents the path to the directory you want to open. `opendir()` returns a directory handle unless the directory isn't present or readable; in that case, it returns `false`.

```
$dh = opendir("testdir");
```

10

Reading the Contents of a Directory with `readdir()`

Just as you use `gets()` to read a line from a file, you can use `readdir()` to read a file or directory name from a directory. `readdir()` requires a directory handle and returns a string containing the item name. If the end of the directory is reached, `readdir()` returns `false`. Note that `readdir()` returns only the names of its items, rather than full paths. Listing 10.14 shows the contents of a directory.

LISTING 10.14   Listing the Contents of a Directory with `readdir()`

```
 1: <html>
 2: <head>
 3: <title>Listing 10.14 Listing the contents
 4: of a directory with readdir()</title>
 5: </head>
 6: <body>
 7: <?php
 8: $dirname = ".";
 9: $dh = opendir($dirname) or die("couldn't open directory");
10:
11: while (!(($file = readdir($dh)) === false ) ) {
12:     if (is_dir("$dirname/$file")) {
13:             print "(D) ";
14:     }
15:     print "$file<br>";
16: }
17: closedir($dh);
18: ?>
19: </body>
20: </html>
```

If this code were saved to the document root of your Web server and run through your Web browser, the output could look something like Figure 10.7.

We open our directory for reading with the `opendir()` function on line 9 and use a `while` statement to loop through each of its elements on line 11. We call `readdir()` as part of the `while` statement's test expression and assign its result to the `$file` variable. Within the body of the `while` statement, we use the `$dirname` variable in conjunction with the `$file` variable to create a full file path, which we can then test on line 12. If the path leads to a directory, we print `"(D) "` to the browser on line 13. Finally, we print the filename on line 15.

FIGURE 10.7

Output of Listing 10.14.

We used a cautious construction in the test of the `while` statement. Most PHP programmers (myself included) would use something like the following:

```
while ($file = readdir($dh)) {
      print "$file<BR>\n";
}
```

The value returned by `readdir()` is tested. Because any string other than `"0"` resolves to `true`, there should be no problem. Imagine, however, a directory that contains four files: `"0"`, `"1"`, `"2"`, and `"3"`. On my system, the output from the preceding code is as follows:

```
.
..
```

When the loop reaches the file named `"0"`, the string returned by `readdir()` resolves to `false`, which causes the loop to end. The approach in Listing 10.14 uses `===` to check that the return value returned by `readdir()` is not *exactly* equivalent to false. `0` only *resolves* to false in the test, so we circumvent the problem.

If you find the ordering of items in a directory listing to be arbitrary, it's because the order is determined by the file system. If you want the items ordered in a specific fashion, you must read the contents into an array, which can then be sorted to your liking and subsequently displayed.

10

Summary

In this hour, you learned how to use `include()` to incorporate files into your documents and to execute any PHP code contained in include files. You learned how to use some of PHP's file test functions. You explored functions for reading files by the line, by the character, and in arbitrary chunks. You learned how to write to files, either replacing or appending to existing content. Finally, you learned how to create, remove, and read directories.

Now that we can work with files, we can save and access substantial amounts of data. If we need to look up data from large files, however, our scripts begin to slow down quite considerably. What we need is some kind of database.

Q&A

Q Does the `include()` statement slow down my scripts?

A Because an included file must be opened and parsed by the engine, it adds some overhead. However, the benefits of reusable code libraries often outweigh the relatively low performance overhead.

Q Should I always end script execution if a file cannot be opened for writing or reading?

A You should always allow for this possibility. If your script absolutely depends on the file you want to work with, you might want to use the `die()` function, writing an informative error message to the browser. In less critical situations, you still need to allow for the failure, perhaps by adding it to a log file.

Workshop

The workshop is designed to help you anticipate possible questions, review what you've learned, and begin putting your knowledge into practice.

Quiz

1. What functions do you use to add library code to the currently running script?
2. What function do you use to find out whether a file is present on your file system?
3. How do you determine the size of a file?
4. What function do you use to open a file for reading or writing?
5. What function do you use to read a line of data from a file?

6. How can you tell when you've reached the end of a file?

7. What function do you use to write a line of data to a file?

8. How do you open a directory for reading?

9. What function do you use to read the name of a directory item after you've opened a directory for reading?

Answers

1. You can use the `require()` or `include()` statement to incorporate PHP files into the current document. You could also use `include_once()` or `require_once()`.

2. You can test for the existence of a file with the `file_exists()` function.

3. The `filesize()` function returns a file's size in bytes.

4. The `fopen()` function opens a file. It accepts the path to a file and a character representing the mode. It returns a file resource.

5. The `fgets()` function reads data up to the buffer size you pass it, the end of the line, or the end of the document, whichever comes first.

6. The `feof()` function returns `true` when the file resource it's passed reaches the end of the file.

7. You can write data to a file with the `fputs()` function.

8. The `opendir()` function enables you to open a directory for reading.

9. The `readdir()` function returns the name of a directory item from an opened directory.

Activities

1. Create a form that accepts a user's first and second name. Create a script that saves this data to a file.

2. Create a script that reads the data file you created in activity 1. In addition to writing its contents to the browser (adding a <BR> tag to each line), print a summary that includes the number of lines in the file and the file's size.

10

HOUR 11

Working with Dates and Times

Dates are so much a part of everyday life that it becomes easy to work with them without thinking. However, the quirks of the Gregorian calendar can be difficult to work with in programs. Fortunately, PHP provides powerful tools for date arithmetic that make date manipulation an easy task. Similarly, MySQL comes with its own set of date-related functions. You learn about these in this hour as well, and find that MySQL can take a lot of the programming burden off your hands.

In this hour, you will learn

- How to acquire the current date and time
- How to get information about a date
- How to format date information
- How to test dates for validity
- How to set dates
- How to use MySQL's date and time-related functions

- How to format date and time results in MySQL
- How to find and express intervals between dates and times using MySQL

Using Date and Time Functions in PHP

The several sections that follow introduce you to the date- and time-related functions specifically in PHP. You learn about the MySQL functions later in this hour. Try each listing yourself, as you march along through this hour.

Getting the Date with `time()`

PHP's `time()` function gives you all the information that you need about the current date and time. It requires no arguments and returns an integer. For us humans, the returned number is a little hard on the eyes, but it's extremely useful nonetheless.

```
print time();
// sample output: 1127732399
```

The integer returned by `time()` represents the number of seconds elapsed since midnight GMT on January 1, 1970. This moment is known as the *Unix epoch*, and the number of seconds that have elapsed since then is referred to as a *timestamp*. PHP offers excellent tools to convert a timestamp into a form that humans are comfortable with. Even so, isn't a timestamp a needlessly convoluted way of storing a date? In fact, the opposite is true. From just one number, you can extract enormous amounts of information. Even better, a timestamp can make date arithmetic much easier than you might imagine.

Think of a homegrown date system in which you record days of the month as well as months and years. Now imagine a script that must add one day to a given date. If this date happened to be 31 December 1999, rather than adding 1 to the date, you'd have to write code to set the day of the month to 1, the month to January, and the year to 2000. Using a timestamp, you need only add a day's worth of seconds to your current figure and you're done. You can convert this new figure into something more friendly at your leisure.

Converting a Timestamp with `getdate()`

Now that you have a timestamp to work with, you must convert it before you present it to the user. `getdate()` optionally accepts a timestamp and returns an associative array containing information about the date. If you omit the timestamp, `getdate()` works with the current timestamp as returned by `time()`. Table 11.1 lists the elements contained in the array returned by `getdate()`.

TABLE 11.1 The Associative Array Returned by `getdate()`

Key	Description	Example
seconds	Seconds past the minute (0–59)	28
minutes	Minutes past the hour (0–59)	7
hours	Hours of the day (0–23)	12
mday	Day of the month (1–31)	20
wday	Day of the week (0–6)	4
mon	Month of the year (1–12)	1
year	Year (4 digits)	2000
yday	Day of year (0–365)	19
weekday	Day of the week (name)	Thursday
month	Month of the year (name)	January
0	Timestamp	948370048

Listing 11.1 uses `getdate()` (line 7) to extract information from a timestamp, employing a `foreach` statement to print each element (line 8). You can see typical output in Figure 11.1. `getdate()` returns the date according to the local time zone.

LISTING 11.1 Acquiring Date Information with `getdate()`

```
 1: <html>
 2: <head>
 3: <title>Listing 11.1 Acquiring date information with getdate()</title>
 4: </head>
 5: <body>
 6: <?php
 7: $date_array = getdate(); // no argument passed so today's date will be used
 8: foreach ($date_array as $key => $val) {
 9:     print "$key = $val<br>";
10: }
11: ?>
12: <hr>
13: <?
14: print "Today's date: ".$date_array['mday']."/".$date_array['mon']."/".
15:     $date_array['year']."<p>";
16: ?>
17: </body>
18: </html>
```

11

FIGURE **11.1**

Using getdate().

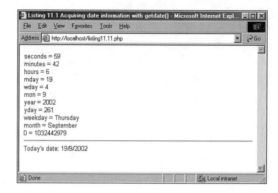

Converting a Timestamp with date()

You can use getdate() when you want to work with the elements that it outputs.
Sometimes, though, you want to display the date as a string. The date() function returns
a formatted string that represents a date. You can exercise an enormous amount of control
over the format that date() returns with a string argument that you must pass to it. In
addition to the format string, date() optionally accepts a timestamp. Table 11.2 lists the
codes that a format string can contain. Any other data you include in the format string
passed to date() is included in the return value.

TABLE 11.2 Format Codes for Use with date()

Format	Description	Example
a	am or pm (lowercase)	pm
A	AM or PM (uppercase)	PM
d	Day of month (number with leading zeroes)	20
D	Day of week (three letters)	Thu
F	Month name	January
h	Hour (12-hour format—leading zeroes)	12
H	Hour (24-hour format—leading zeroes)	12
g	Hour (12-hour format—no leading zeroes)	12
G	Hour (24-hour format—no leading zeroes)	12
i	Minutes	47
j	Day of the month (no leading zeroes)	20
l	Day of the week (name)	Thursday
L	Leap year (1 for yes, 0 for no)	1

TABLE 11.2   continued

Format	Description	Example
m	Month of year (number—leading zeroes)	01
M	Month of year (three letters)	Jan
n	Month of year (number—no leading zeroes)	1
s	Seconds of hour	24
r	Full date standardized to RFC 822 (http://www.faqs.org/rfcs/rfc822.html)	Wed, 26 Sep 2001 15:15:14 +0100
U	Timestamp	948372444
y	Year (two digits)	00
Y	Year (four digits)	2000
z	Day of year (0–365)	19
Z	Offset in seconds from GMT	0

Listing 11.2 puts a few of these format codes to the test.

LISTING 11.2   Formatting a Date with date()

```
 1: <html>
 2: <head>
 3: <title>Listing 11.2 Formatting a date with date()</title>
 4: </head>
 5: <body>
 6: <?php
 7: $time = time();
 8: print date("m/d/y G.i:s", $time);
 9: print "<br>";
10: print "Today is ";
11: print date("j of F Y, \a\\t g.i a", $time);
12: ?>
13: </body>
14: </html>
```

Listing 11.2 calls date() twice: the first time on line 8 to output an abbreviated date format, and the second time on line 11 for a longer format. Save the text of this listing in a file called listing11.2.php and open it in your Web browser. Your date will differ from the following, obviously, but here's some sample output:

```
09/16/02 8.52:06

Today is 16 of September 2002, at 8.52 am
```

11

Although the format string looks arcane, it's easy to build. If you want to add a string that contains letters that are also format codes to the format, you can escape them by placing a backslash (\) in front of them. For characters that become control characters when escaped, you must escape the backslash that precedes them. For example, \t is a format code for a tab, so to ensure that the tab prints, use \\t as in the previous example.

Also note that the date() function returns information according to your local time zone. If you want to format a date in GMT, you use the gmdate() function, which works in exactly the same way.

Creating Timestamps with mktime()

You can already get information about the current time, but you cannot yet work with arbitrary dates. mktime() returns a timestamp that you can then use with date() or getdate(). mktime() accepts up to six integer arguments in the following order:

Hour

Minute

Second

Month

Day of month

Year

Listing 11.3 uses mktime() to get a timestamp that we then use with the date() function.

LISTING 11.3   Creating a Timestamp with mktime()

```
 1: <html>
 2: <head>
 3: <title>Listing 11.3 Creating a timestamp with mktime()</title>
 4: </head>
 5: <body>
 6: <?php
 7: // make a timestamp for Aug 23 2002 at 4.15 am
 8: $ts = mktime(4, 15, 0, 8, 23, 2002);
 9: print date("m/d/y G.i:s<br>", $ts);
10: print "<br>";
11: print "The date is ";
12: print date("j of F Y, \a\\t g.i a", $ts );
13: ?>
14: </body>
15: </html>
```

We call `mktime()` on line 8 and assign the returned timestamp to the `$ts` variable. We then use `date()` on lines 9 and 12 to output formatted versions of the date using `$ts`. You can choose to omit some or all the arguments to `mktime()`, and the value appropriate to the current time is used instead. `mktime()` also adjusts for values that go beyond the relevant range, so an hour argument of 25 translates to 1:00 a.m. on the day after that specified in the month, day, and year arguments.

Save the text of this listing in a file called `listing11.2.php` and open it in your Web browser. You should see:

```
08/23/02 4.15:00
```

```
The date is 23 of August 2002, at 4.15 am
```

Testing a Date with `checkdate()`

You might need to accept date information from user input. Before you work with a user-entered date or store it in a database, you should check that the date is valid. `checkdate()` accepts three integers: month, day, and year. `checkdate()` returns `true` if the month is between 1 and 12, the day is acceptable for the given month and year (accounting for leap years), and the year is between 0 and 32767. Be careful, though: A date might be valid but not acceptable to other date functions. For example, the following line returns `true`:

```
checkdate( 4, 4, 1066 )
```

If you were to attempt to build a date with `mktime()` using these values, you'd end up with a timestamp of `-1`. As a rule of thumb, don't use `mktime()` with years before 1902, and be cautious of using date functions with any date before 1970. You learn more about using `checkdate()` in Hour 12, "Creating a Simple Calendar."

Using Date and Time Functions in MySQL

MySQL's built-in date-related functions can be used in `SELECT` statements, with or without specifying a table, to retrieve a result of the function. Or you can use the functions with any type of date field: `date`, `datetime`, `timestamp`, and `year`. Depending on the type of field in use, the results of the date-related functions are more or less useful.

Working with Days

The `DAYOFWEEK()` and `WEEKDAY()` functions do similar things with slightly different results. Both functions are used to find the weekday index of a date, but the difference lies in the starting day and position.

11

If you use `DAYOFWEEK()`, the first day of the week is Sunday, at position 1, and the last day of the week is Saturday, at position 7. For example:

```
mysql> select dayofweek('2001-11-13');
+-----------------------+
| DAYOFWEEK('2001-11-13') |
+-----------------------+
|                     3 |
+-----------------------+
1 row in set (0.00 sec)
```

The result shows that November 13, 2001 was weekday index 3, or Tuesday. Using the same date with `WEEKDAY()` gives you a different result with the same meaning:

```
mysql> select weekday('2001-11-13');
+---------------------+
| WEEKDAY('2001-11-13') |
+---------------------+
|                   1 |
+---------------------+
1 row in set (0.00 sec)
```

The result shows that November 13, 2001 was weekday index 1. Because `WEEKDAY()` uses Monday as the first day of the week at position 0 and Sunday as the last day at position 6, 1 is accurate: Tuesday.

The `DAYOFMONTH()` and `DAYOFYEAR()` functions are more straightforward, with only one result and a range that starts at 1 and ends at 31 for `DAYOFMONTH()` and 366 for `DAYOFYEAR()`. Some examples follow:

```
mysql> select dayofmonth('2001-11-13');
+------------------------+
| DAYOFMONTH('2001-11-13') |
+------------------------+
|                     13 |
+------------------------+
1 row in set (0.00 sec)
```

```
mysql> select dayofyear('2001-11-13');
+-----------------------+
| DAYOFYEAR('2001-11-13') |
+-----------------------+
|                   317 |
+-----------------------+
1 row in set (0.00 sec)
```

It might seem odd to have a function that returns the day of the month on a particular date because the day is right there in the string. But think about using these types of functions in `WHERE` clauses to perform comparisons on records. If you have a table that holds online orders with a field containing the date the order was placed, you can quickly get a count of the orders placed on any given day of the week, or see how many orders were placed during the first half of the month versus the second half.

The following two queries show how many orders were placed during the first three days of the week (throughout all months) and then the remaining days of the week:

```
mysql> select count(id) from orders where dayofweek(date_ordered) < 4;
+-----------+
| COUNT(id) |
+-----------+
|         3 |
+-----------+
1 row in set (0.00 sec)

mysql> select count(id) from orders where dayofweek(date_ordered) > 3;
+-----------+
| COUNT(id) |
+-----------+
|         5 |
+-----------+
1 row in set (0.00 sec)
```

Using DAYOFMONTH(), the following examples show the number of orders placed during the first half of any month versus the second half:

```
mysql> select count(id) from orders where dayofmonth(date_ordered) < 16;
+-----------+
| COUNT(id) |
+-----------+
|         6 |
+-----------+
1 row in set (0.00 sec)

mysql> select count(id) from orders where dayofmonth(date_ordered) > 15;
+-----------+
| COUNT(id) |
+-----------+
|         2 |
+-----------+
1 row in set (0.00 sec)
```

You can use the DAYNAME() function to add more life to your results because it returns the name of the weekday for any given date:

```
mysql> select dayname(date_ordered) from orders;
+-----------------------+
| DAYNAME(date_ordered) |
+-----------------------+
| Thursday              |
| Monday                |
| Thursday              |
| Thursday              |
```

11

```
| Wednesday              |
| Thursday               |
| Sunday                 |
| Sunday                 |
+------------------------+
8 rows in set (0.00 sec)
```

Functions aren't limited to WHERE clauses—you can use them in ORDER BY clauses as well:

```
mysql> select dayname(date_ordered) from orders
    -> order by dayofweek(date_ordered);
+------------------------+
| DAYNAME(date_ordered)  |
+------------------------+
| Sunday                 |
| Sunday                 |
| Monday                 |
| Wednesday              |
| Thursday               |
| Thursday               |
| Thursday               |
| Thursday               |
+------------------------+
8 rows in set (0.00 sec)
```

Working with Months and Years

Days of the week aren't the only parts of the calendar, and MySQL has functions specifically for months and years as well. Just like the DAYOFWEEK() and DAYNAME() functions, MONTH() and MONTHNAME() return the number of the month in a year and the name of the month for a given date. For example:

```
mysql> select month('2001-11-13'), monthname('2001-11-13');
+---------------------+-------------------------+
| MONTH('2001-11-13') | MONTHNAME('2001-11-13') |
+---------------------+-------------------------+
|                  11 | November                |
+---------------------+-------------------------+
1 row in set (0.00 sec)
```

Using MONTHNAME() on the sample orders table shows the proper results but a lot of repeated data:

```
mysql> select monthname(date_ordered) from orders;
+-------------------------+
| MONTHNAME(date_ordered) |
+-------------------------+
| November                |
| November                |
```

```
| November              |
| November              |
| November              |
| November              |
| November              |
| October               |
+-----------------------+
8 rows in set (0.00 sec)
```

You can use DISTINCT to get nonrepetitive results:

```
mysql> select distinct monthname(date_ordered) from orders;
+-----------------------+
| MONTHNAME(date_ordered) |
+-----------------------+
| November              |
| October               |
+-----------------------+
2 rows in set (0.00 sec)
```

For work with years, the YEAR() function will return the year of a given date:

```
mysql> select distinct year(date_ordered) from orders;
+--------------------+
| YEAR(date_ordered) |
+--------------------+
|               2001 |
+--------------------+
1 row in set (0.00 sec)
```

Working with Weeks

Weeks can be tricky things—there can be 53 weeks in a year if Sunday is the first day of the week and December hasn't ended. For example, December 30th of 2001 was a Sunday:

```
mysql> select dayname('2001-12-30');
+----------------------+
| DAYNAME('2001-12-30') |
+----------------------+
| Sunday               |
+----------------------+
1 row in set (0.00 sec)
```

That fact made December 30th of 2001 part of the 53rd week of the year:

```
mysql> select week('2001-12-30');
+--------------------+
| WEEK('2001-12-30') |
+--------------------+
|                 53 |
+--------------------+
```

```
1 row in set (0.00 sec)
```

The 53rd week contains December 30th and 31st, and is only two days long; the first week of 2002 begins with January 1st.

If you want your weeks to start on Mondays but still want to find the week of the year, the optional second argument enables you to change the start day. A 1 indicates a week that starts on Monday. In the following examples, a Monday start day makes December 30th part of the 52nd week of 2001, but December 31 is still part of the 53rd week of 2001.

```
mysql> select week('2001-12-30',1);
+----------------------+
| WEEK('2001-12-30',1) |
+----------------------+
|                   52 |
+----------------------+
1 row in set (0.00 sec)

mysql> select week('2001-12-31',1);
+----------------------+
| WEEK('2001-12-31',1) |
+----------------------+
|                   53 |
+----------------------+
1 row in set (0.00 sec)
```

Working with Hours, Minutes, and Seconds

If you're using a date that includes the exact time, such as datetime or timestamp, or even just a time field, there are functions to find the hours, minutes, and seconds from that string. Not surprisingly, these functions are called HOUR(), MINUTE(), and SECOND(). HOUR() returns the hour in a given time, which is between 0 and 23. The range for MINUTE() and SECOND() is 0 to 59.

Here are some examples:

```
mysql> select hour('2001-11-13 07:27:49') as hour,minute('2001-11-13 07:27:49')
    -> as minute,second('2001-11-13 07:27:49') as second;
+------+--------+--------+
| hour | minute | second |
+------+--------+--------+
|    7 |     27 |     49 |
+------+--------+--------+
1 row in set (0.00 sec)
```

That's a lot of queries to get at one time from a datetime field—you can put the hour and minute together and even use CONCAT_WS() to put the : between the results and get a representation of the time:

```
mysql> select concat_ws(':',hour('2001-11-13 07:27:49'),
    -> minute('2001-11-13 07:27:49')) as sample_time;
+-------------+
| sample_time |
+-------------+
| 7:27        |
+-------------+
1 row in set (0.00 sec)
```

If you use field names instead of strings, remember not to use quotation marks. Here's an example that uses the dateadded field from the sometable table:

```
mysql> select concat_ws(':',hour(dateadded), minute(dateadded))
    -> as sample_time from sometable;
+-------------+
| sample_time |
+-------------+
| 13:11       |
| 13:11       |
| 13:11       |
| 13:11       |
| 14:16       |
| 10:12       |
| 10:12       |
| 10:12       |
| 10:12       |
+-------------+
9 rows in set (0.00 sec)
```

This is cheating because it's not the actual time—it's just two numbers stuck together to look like a time. If you used the concatenation trick on a time such as 02:02, the result would be 2:2, as shown here:

```
mysql> select concat_ws(':',hour('02:02'), minute('02:02')) as sample_time;
+-------------+
| sample_time |
+-------------+
| 2:2         |
+-------------+
1 row in set (0.00 sec)
```

This result is obviously not the intended result. In the next section, you learn how to use the DATE_FORMAT() function to properly format dates and times.

Formatting Dates and Times with MySQL

The DATE_FORMAT() function formats a date, datetime, or timestamp field into a string by using options that tell it exactly how to display the results. The syntax of DATE_FORMAT() is

DATE_FORMAT(date,format)

There are many formatting options, as shown in Table 11.3, which should look somewhat similar to Table 11.2. It's the same concept as the PHP date() function.

TABLE 11.3 DATE_FORMAT() Format String Options

Option	Result
%M	Month name (January through December)
%b	Abbreviated month name (Jan through Dec)
%m	Month, padded digits (01 through 12)
%c	Month (1 through 12)
%W	Weekday name (Sunday through Saturday)
%a	Abbreviated weekday name (Sun through Sat)
%D	Day of the month using the English suffix, such as first, second, third, and so on
%d	Day of the month, padded digits (00 through 31)
%e	Day of the month (0 through 31)
%j	Day of the year, padded digits (001 through 366)
%Y	Year, four digits
%y	Year, two digits
%X	Four-digit year for the week where Sunday is the first day; used with %V
%x	Four-digit year for the week where Monday is the first day; used with %v
%w	Day of the week (0=Sunday...6=Saturday)
%U	Week (0 through 53) where Sunday is the first day of the week
%u	Week (0 through 53) where Monday is the first day of the week
%V	Week (1 through 53) where Sunday is the first day of the week; used with %X
%v	Week (1 through 53) where Monday is the first day of the week; used with %x
%H	Hour, padded digits (00 through 23)
%k	Hour (0 through 23)
%h	Hour, padded digits (01 through 12)
%l	Hour (1 through 12)
%i	Minutes, padded digits (00 through 59)
%S	Seconds, padded digits (00 through 59)
%s	Seconds, padded digits (00 through 59)
%r	Time, 12-hour clock (hh:mm:ss [AP]M)
%T	Time, 24-hour clock (hh:mm:ss)
%p	AM or PM

Any other characters used in the DATE_FORMAT() option string appear literally.

To display the `02:02` result that we rigged in the previous section, you'd use the `%h` and `%i` options to return the hour and minute from the date with a `:` between the two options. For example:

```
mysql> select date_format('2001-11-13 02:02:00', '%h:%i') as sample_time;
+-------------+
| sample_time |
+-------------+
| 02:02       |
+-------------+
1 row in set (0.00 sec)
```

The following are just a few more examples of the DATE_FORMAT() function in use, but this function is best understood by practicing it yourself.

```
mysql> select date_format('2001-11-13', '%W, %M %D, %Y') as sample_time;
+--------------------------+
| sample_time              |
+--------------------------+
| Tuesday, November 13th, 2001 |
+--------------------------+
1 row in set (0.00 sec)
```

 11

```
mysql> select date_format(now(),'%W the %D of %M, %Y around %l o\'clock %p')
    -> as sample_time;
+------------------------------------------------------+
| sample_time                                          |
+------------------------------------------------------+
| Tuesday the 13th of November, 2001 around 8 o'clock AM |
+------------------------------------------------------+
1 row in set (0.00 sec)
```

If you're working specifically with time fields, the TIME_FORMAT() function works just like the DATE_FORMAT() function. Only the format options for hours, minutes, and seconds are allowed:

```
mysql> select time_format('02:02:00', '%h:%i') as sample_time;
+-------------+
| sample_time |
+-------------+
| 02:02       |
+-------------+
1 row in set (0.00 sec)
```

Performing Date Arithmetic with MySQL

MySQL has several functions to help perform date arithmetic, and this is one of the areas where it might be quicker to allow MySQL to do the math than your PHP script. The `DATE_ADD()` and `DATE_SUB()` functions return a result given a starting date and an interval. The syntax for both functions is

```
DATE_ADD(date,INTERVAL value type)

DATE_SUB(date,INTERVAL value type)
```

Table 11.4 shows the possible types and their expected value format.

TABLE 11.4   Values and Types in Date Arithmetic

Value	Type
Number of seconds	SECOND
Number of minutes	MINUTE
Number of hours	HOUR
Number of days	DAY
Number of months	MONTH
Number of years	YEAR
"minutes:seconds"	MINUTE_SECOND
"hours:minutes"	HOUR_MINUTE
"days hours"	DAY_HOUR
"years-months"	YEAR_MONTH
"hours:minutes:seconds"	HOUR_SECOND
"days hours:minutes"	DAY_MINUTE
"days hours:minutes:seconds"	DAY_SECOND

For example, to find the date of the current day plus 21 days, use the following:

```
mysql> select date_add(now(), interval 21 day);
+----------------------------------+
| date_add(now(), interval 21 day) |
+----------------------------------+
| 2002-10-07 09:12:08              |
+----------------------------------+
1 row in set (0.00 sec)
```

To subtract 21 days, use

```
mysql> select date_sub(now(), interval 21 day);
+----------------------------------+
| date_sub(now(), interval 21 day) |
```

```
+----------------------------------+
| 2002-08-26 09:12:24              |
+----------------------------------+
1 row in set (0.00 sec)
```

Use the expression as it's shown in Table 11.4, despite what might be a natural tendency to use DAYS instead of DAY. Using DAYS results in an error:

```
mysql> select date_add(now(), interval 21 days);
ERROR 1064: You have an error in your SQL syntax near 'days)' at line 1
```

If you're using DATE_ADD() or DATE_SUB() with a date value instead of a datetime value, the result will be shown as a date value unless you use expressions related to hours, minutes, and seconds. In that case, your result will be a datetime result.

For example, the result of the first query remains a date field, whereas the second becomes a datetime:

```
mysql> select date_add("2001-12-31", interval 1 day);
+---------------------------------------+
| DATE_ADD("2001-12-31", INTERVAL 1 DAY) |
+---------------------------------------+
| 2002-01-01                            |
+---------------------------------------+
1 row in set (0.00 sec)

mysql> select date_add("2001-12-31", interval 12 hour);
+-----------------------------------------+
| DATE_ADD("2001-12-31", INTERVAL 12 HOUR) |
+-----------------------------------------+
| 2001-12-31 12:00:00                     |
+-----------------------------------------+
1 row in set (0.00 sec)
```

Starting with MySQL version 3.23, you can also perform date arithmetic using the + and - operators instead of DATE_ADD() and DATE_SUB() functions:

```
mysql> select "2001-12-31" + interval 1 day;
+------------------------------+
| "2001-12-31" + INTERVAL 1 DAY |
+------------------------------+
| 2002-01-01                   |
+------------------------------+
1 row in set (0.00 sec)

mysql> select "2001-12-31" - interval 14 hour;
+------------------------------+
| "2001-12-31" - INTERVAL 14 HOUR |
+------------------------------+
| 2001-12-30 10:00:00          |
+------------------------------+
1 row in set (0.00 sec)
```

11

Special Functions and Conversion Features

The MySQL NOW() function returns a current datetime result, and is useful for time-stamping login or access times, as well as numerous other tasks. MySQL has a few other functions that perform similarly.

The CURDATE() and CURRENT_DATE() functions are synonymous, and each returns the current date in YYYY-MM-DD format:

```
mysql> select curdate(), current_date();
+------------+----------------+
| curdate()  | current_date() |
+------------+----------------+
| 2002-09-16 | 2002-09-16     |
+------------+----------------+
1 row in set (0.01 sec)
```

Similarly, the CURTIME() and CURRENT_TIME() functions return the current time in HH:MM:SS format:

```
mysql> select curtime(), current_time();
+-----------+----------------+
| curtime() | current_time() |
+-----------+----------------+
| 09:14:26  | 09:14:26       |
+-----------+----------------+
1 row in set (0.00 sec)
```

The NOW(), SYSDATE(), and CURRENT_TIMESTAMP() functions return values in full date-time format (YYYY-MM-DD HH:MM:SS):

```
mysql> select now(), sysdate(), current_timestamp();
+---------------------+---------------------+---------------------+
| now()               | sysdate()           | current_timestamp() |
+---------------------+---------------------+---------------------+
| 2002-09-16 09:14:50 | 2002-09-16 09:14:50 | 2002-09-16 09:14:50 |
+---------------------+---------------------+---------------------+
1 row in set (0.00 sec)
```

The UNIX_TIMESTAMP() function returns the current date in—or converts a given date to—Unix timestamp format. Unix timestamp format is in seconds since the epoch, or seconds since midnight, January 1, 1970. For example:

```
mysql> select unix_timestamp();
+------------------+
| UNIX_TIMESTAMP() |
+------------------+
|       1032192914 |
+------------------+
1 row in set (0.00 sec)
```

```
mysql> select unix_timestamp('1973-12-30');
+-----------------------------+
| UNIX_TIMESTAMP('1973-12-30') |
+-----------------------------+
|                   126086400 |
+-----------------------------+
1 row in set (0.00 sec)
```

The FROM_UNIXTIME() function performs a conversion of a Unix timestamp to a full datetime format when used without any options:

```
mysql> select from_unixtime('1032192914');
+--------------------------+
| from_unixtime('1032192914') |
+--------------------------+
| 2002-09-16 09:15:14      |
+--------------------------+
1 row in set (0.00 sec)
```

You can use the format options from the DATE_FORMAT() functions to display a timestamp in a more appealing manner:

```
mysql> select from_unixtime(unix_timestamp(), '%D %M %Y at %h:%i:%s');
+--------------------------------------------------------+
| from_unixtime(unix_timestamp(), '%D %M %Y at %h:%i:%s') |
+--------------------------------------------------------+
| 16th September 2002 at 09:16:48                        |
+--------------------------------------------------------+
1 row in set (0.00 sec)
```

If you're working with a number of seconds and want to convert the seconds to a time-formatted result, you can use SEC_TO_TIME() and TIME_TO_SEC() to convert values back and forth.

For example, 1440 seconds is equal to 24 minutes and vice versa:

```
mysql> select sec_to_time('1440'), time_to_sec('00:24:00');
+---------------------+-------------------------+
| SEC_TO_TIME('1440') | TIME_TO_SEC('00:24:00') |
+---------------------+-------------------------+
| 00:24:00            |                    1440 |
+---------------------+-------------------------+
1 row in set (0.01 sec)
```

Summary

In this hour, you learned how to use various PHP functions to perform date- and time-related actions. The time() function gets a date stamp for the current date and time, and you can use getdate() to extract date information from a timestamp and date() to convert a timestamp into a formatted string. You learned how to create a timestamp using mktime(), and how to test a date for validity with checkdate().

Additionally, you discovered that MySQL's built-in date and time functions can definitely take some of the load off your application by internally formatting dates and times and performing the date and time arithmetic. The formatting options used for the DATE_FORMAT() function provide a simple method to produce a custom display string from any sort of date field. The DATE_ADD() and DATE_SUB() functions and their numerous available interval types help you determine dates and times in the past or future. Additionally, functions such as DAY(), WEEK(), MONTH(), and YEAR() are useful for extracting parts of dates for use in WHERE or ORDER BY clauses.

Workshop

The workshop is designed to help you anticipate possible questions, review what you've learned, and begin putting your knowledge into practice.

Quiz

1. Using PHP, how do you acquire a Unix timestamp that represents the current date and time? What about using MySQL?

2. Which PHP function accepts a timestamp and returns an associative array that represents the given date?

3. Which PHP function do you use to format date information? What about using MySQL?

4. Which PHP function could you use to check the validity of a date?

Answers

1. In PHP, use time(). In MySQL, use UNIX_TIMESTAMP().

2. The getdate() function returns an associative array whose elements contain aspects of the given date.

3. In PHP, use date(). In MySQL, use DATE_FORMAT().

4. You can check a date with the checkdate() function.

Activity

Create a birthday countdown script. Given form input of month, day, and year, output a message that tells the user how many days, hours, minutes, and seconds until the big day. Use whatever combination of PHP and MySQL functions you want.

Hour 12

Creating a Simple Calendar

This hour continues the date and time lesson from the previous hour, this time in the context of creating a small calendar.

In this hour, you will learn

- How to build a simple calendar script
- How to build a class library to generate date pull-downs in HTML forms

Building a Simple Display Calendar

Let's bring together the date and time functions you learned in the previous hour, and use them to build a calendar that can display the dates for any month between 1980 and 2010. The user will be able to select both month and year with pull-down menus, and the dates for the selected month will be organized according to the days of the week. We will be working with two variables—one for month and one for year—which the user will supply.

These pieces of information will be used to build a timestamp based on the first day of the month defined. If the user input is invalid or absent, we will default to the first day of the current month.

Checking User Input

When the user opens our calendar application for the first time, he or she will not be submitting any information. We must therefore make sure that our script can handle the fact that the variables for month and year may not be defined. We could use the isset() function for this. (isset() returns false if the variable passed to it has not been defined.) However, let's use checkdate() instead. Listing 12.1 shows the fragment of code that checks for month and year variables coming from a form, and builds a timestamp based on them.

LISTING 12.1   Checking User Input for the Calendar Script

```
 1: <?php
 2: if (!checkdate($_POST[month], 1, $_POST[year])) {
 3:     $nowArray = getdate();
 4:     $month = $nowArray['mon'];
 5:     $year = $nowArray['year'];
 6: } else {
 7:     $month = $_POST[month];
 8:     $year = $_POST[year];
 9: }
10: $start = mktime (12, 0, 0, $month, 1, $year);
11: $firstDayArray = getdate($start);
12: ?>
```

Listing 12.1 is a fragment of a larger script, so it does not produce any output itself. In the if statement on line 2, we use checkdate() to test whether the month and year have been provided by a form. If they have not been defined, checkdate() returns false because the script cannot make a valid date from undefined month and year arguments. This approach has the added bonus of ensuring that the data submitted by the user constitutes a valid date.

If the date is not valid, we use getdate() on line 3 to create an associative array based on the current time. We then set values for $month and $year ourselves, using the array's mon and year elements (lines 4 and 5). If the variables have been set from the form, we put the data into $month and $year variables so as not to touch the values in the original $_POST superglobal.

Now that we are sure that we have valid data in $month and $year, we can use mktime() to create a timestamp for the first day of the month (line 10). We will need information about this timestamp later on, so on line 11 we create a variable called $firstDayArray that will store an associative array returned by getdate() and based on this timestamp.

Building the HTML Form

We need to create an interface by which users can ask to see data for a month and year. For this, we will use SELECT elements. Although we could hard-code these in HTML, we must also ensure that the pull-downs default to the currently chosen month, so we will dynamically create these pull-downs, adding a SELECT attribute to the OPTION element where appropriate. The form is generated in Listing 12.2.

LISTING 12.2 Building the HTML Form for the Calendar Script

```
 1: <?php
 2: if (!checkdate($_POST[month], 1, $_POST[year])) {
 3:     $nowArray = getdate();
 4:     $month = $nowArray['mon'];
 5:     $year = $nowArray['year'];
 6: } else {
 7:     $month = $_POST[month];
 8:     $year = $_POST[year];
 9: }
10: $start = mktime (12, 0, 0, $month, 1, $year);
11: $firstDayArray = getdate($start);
12: ?>
13: <html>
14: <head>
15: <title><?php print "Calendar:
16:     ".$firstDayArray['month']." ".$firstDayArray['year'] ?></title>
17: <head>
18: <body>
19: <form method="post" action="<?php print "$_SERVER[PHP_SELF]"; ?>">
20: <select name="month">
21: <?php
22: $months = Array("January", "February", "March", "April", "May",
23: "June", "July", "August", "September", "October", "November", "December");
24:
25: for ($x=1; $x <= count($months); $x++) {
26:     print "\t<option value=\"$x\"";
27:     print ($x == $month)?" SELECTED":"";
28:     print ">".$months[$x-1]."\n";
29: }
```

12

LISTING 12.2 continued

```
30: ?>
31: </select>
32: <select name="year">
33: <?php
34: for ($x=1980; $x<=2010; $x++) {
35:     print "\t<option";
36:     print ($x == $year)?" SELECTED":"";
37:     print ">$x\n";
38: }
39: ?>
40: </select>
41: <input type="submit" value="Go!">
42: </form>
43: </body>
44: </html>
```

Having created the $start timestamp and the $firstDayArray date array (lines 2–11), let's write the HTML for the page. Notice that we use $firstDayArray to add the month and year to the TITLE element on lines 15 and 16.

Line 19 is the beginning of our form. To create the SELECT element for the month pull-down, we drop back into PHP mode on line 21 to write the individual OPTION tags. First, we create an array called $months on line 22 that contains the 12 month names. We then loop through this array, creating an OPTION tag for each name (lines 25–29). This would probably be an overcomplicated way of writing a simple SELECT element were it not for the fact that we are testing $x (the counter variable in the for statement) against the $month variable on line 27. If $x and $month are equivalent, we add the string SELECTED to the OPTION tag, ensuring that the correct month will be selected automatically when the page loads. We use a similar technique to write the year pull-down on lines 34–38. Finally, back in HTML mode, we create a submit button on line 41.

We now have a form that can send the month and year parameters to itself, and will default either to the current month and year, or the month and year previously chosen. If you save this listing as listing12.2.php, place it in your Web server document root, and access it with your Web browser, you should see something like Figure 12.1 (your month and year may differ).

FIGURE 12.1

The calendar form.

Creating the Calendar Table

We now need to create a table and populate it with dates for the chosen month. We do this in Listing 12.3, which represents the complete calendar script.

LISTING 12.3   The Complete Calendar Script

```
 1: <?php
 2: define("ADAY", (60*60*24));
 3: if (!checkdate($_POST[month], 1, $_POST[year])) {
 4:     $nowArray = getdate();
 5:     $month = $nowArray['mon'];
 6:     $year = $nowArray['year'];
 7: } else {
 8:     $month = $_POST[month];
 9:     $year = $_POST[year];
10: }
11: $start = mktime (12, 0, 0, $month, 1, $year);
12: $firstDayArray = getdate($start);
13: ?>
14: <html>
15: <head>
16: <title><?php print "Calendar:
17:     ".$firstDayArray['month']." ".$firstDayArray['year'] ?></title>
18: <head>
19: <body>
20: <form method="post" action="<?php print "$_SERVER[PHP_SELF]"; ?>">
21: <select name="month">
22: <?php
23: $months = Array("January", "February", "March", "April", "May",
24: "June", "July", "August", "September", "October", "November", "December");
25:
26: for ($x=1; $x <= count($months); $x++) {
27:     print "\t<option value=\"$x\"";
```

12

LISTING 12.3   continued

```
28:     print ($x == $month)?" SELECTED":"";
29:     print ">".$months[$x-1]."\n";
30: }
31: ?>
32: </select>
33: <select name="year">
34: <?php
35: for ($x=1980; $x<2010; $x++) {
36:     print "\t<option";
37:     print ($x == $year)?" SELECTED":"";
38:     print ">$x\n";
39: }
40: ?>
41: </select>
42: <input type="submit" value="Go!">
43: </form>
44: <br>
45: <?php
46: $days = Array("Sunday", "Monday", "Tuesday", "Wednesday",
47: "Thursday", "Friday", "Saturday");
48:
49: print "<TABLE BORDER = 1 CELLPADDING=5>\n";
50: foreach ($days as $day) {
51:     print "\t<td><b>$day</b></td>\n";
52: }
53: for ($count=0; $count < (6*7); $count++) {
54:     $dayArray = getdate($start);
55:     if (($count % 7) == 0) {
56:         if ($dayArray['mon'] != $month) {
57:             break;
58:         } else {
59:             print "</tr><tr>\n";
60:         }
61:     }
62:     if ($count < $firstDayArray['wday'] || $dayArray['mon'] != $month) {
63:         print "\t<td><br></td>\n";
64:     } else {
65:         print "\t<td>".$dayArray['mday']."    </td>\n";
66:         $start += ADAY;
67:     }
68: }
69: print "</tr></table>";
70: ?>
71: </body>
72: </html>
```

Because the table will be indexed by days of the week, we loop through an array of day names created on lines 50–52, printing each to its own cell on line 51. All the real magic of the script happens in the final for statement on line 53.

We initialize a variable called $count and ensure that the loop will end after 42 iterations. This is to make sure that we will have enough cells to populate with date information. Within the loop, we transform the $start variable into a date array with getdate(), assigning the result to $dayArray (line 54). Although $start is the first day of the month during the loop's initial execution, we will increment this timestamp by 24 hours for every iteration.

> Adding 24 hours to a day is not necessarily the same as adding one whole day. Since the start date and time is not midnight, this format works for introducing the concept of adding time.

On line 55, we test the $count variable against the number 7 using the modulus operator. The block of code belonging to this if statement will therefore only be run when $count is either zero or a multiple of 7. This is our way of knowing whether we should end the loop altogether or start a new row.

After we have established that we are in the first iteration or at the end of a row, we can go on to perform another test on line 56. If the mon (month number) element of the $dayArray is no longer equivalent to the $month variable, we are finished. Remember that $dayArray contains information about the $start timestamp, which is the current place in the month that we are displaying. When $start goes beyond the current month, $dayArray['mon'] will hold a different figure than the $month number provided by user input. Our modulus test demonstrated that we are at the end of a row, and the fact that we are in a new month means that we can leave the loop altogether. Assuming, however, that we are still in the month that we are displaying, we end the row and start a new one on line 59.

In the next if statement, on line 62, we determine whether to write date information to a cell. Not every month begins on a Sunday, so it's likely that we will start with an empty cell or two. Few months will finish at the end of one of our rows, so it's also likely that we will need to write a few empty cells before we close the table. We have stored information about the first day of the month in $firstDayArray; in particular, we can access the number of the day of the week in $firstDayArray['wday']. If $count is smaller

12

than this number, we know that we haven't yet reached the correct cell for writing. By the same token, if the $month variable is no longer equal to $dayArray['mon'], we know that we have reached the end of the month (but not the end of the row, as we determined in our earlier modulus test). In either case, we write an empty cell to the browser on line 63.

In the final else clause on line 64, we can do the fun stuff. We have already ascertained that we are within the month that we want to list and that the current day column matches the day number stored in $firstDayArray['wday']. Now we must use the $dayArray associative array that we established early in the loop to write the day of the month and some blank space into a cell.

Finally, on line 66, we need to increment the $start variable, which contains our date stamp. We simply add the number of seconds in a day to it (we defined this value in line 2), and we're ready to begin the loop again with a new value in $start to be tested.

If you save this listing as listing12.3.php, place it in your Web server document root, and access it with your Web browser, you should see something like Figure 12.2 (your month and year may differ).

FIGURE 12.2

The calendar form and script.

Creating a Calendar Library

Because dates are ubiquitous in Web interfaces, and because working with dates is often comparatively complicated, let's look at creating a class library to automate some of the work that dates can present. Along the way we will revisit some of the techniques we have already covered.

If the concept of classes is completely foreign to you, you can supplement your knowledge by reading through Chapter 14 of the PHP Manual. It is titled "Classes and Objects," and you can find it at http://www.php.net/manual/en/language.oop.php.

The simple date_pulldown library we will look at was born during the creation of a freelance job listing site. The project necessarily involved the presentation of multiple date pull-downs allowing employers to select both the start and end of contract periods, and for candidates to indicate periods of availability. A date pull-down, in this instance, consists of three separate select elements, one for day of the month, one for month, and one for year.

When a user submits a page, the script will check his input. If there is a problem, we will need to represent the page with the user's input still in place. This is very easy to accomplish with text boxes but is more of a chore with pull-down menus. Pages that display information pulled from a database present a similar problem. Data can be entered straight into the value attributes of text type input elements. Dates will need to be split into month, day, and year values, and then the correct option elements selected.

The date_pulldown class aims to make date pull-downs sticky (so they will remember settings from page to page) and easy to set. In order to create our class, we first need to declare it and create a constructor.

A constructor is a function that exists within a class, and which is automatically called when a new instance of the class is created.

12

We can also declare some class properties. The following snippet shows the beginning of the class:

```
 1: class date_pulldown
 2:     var $name;
 3:     var $timestamp = -1;
 4:     var $months = array("Jan", "Feb", "Mar", "Apr", "May", "Jun",
 5:         "Jul", "Aug", "Sep", "Oct", "Nov", "Dec");
 6:     var $yearstart = -1;
 7:     var $yearend = -1;
 8:
 9:  function date_pulldown($name) {
10:      $this->name = $name;
11:  }
```

We first declare the $name property. This will be used to name the HTML select elements. The $timestamp property will hold a Unix timestamp. The $months array property contains the strings we will display in our month pull-down. The $yearstart and $yearend properties are both set to –1 pending initialization. They will eventually hold the first and last years of the range that will be presented in the year pull-down.

The constructor is very simple. It accepts a string, which we assign to the $name property. Now that we have the basis of our class, we need a set of methods by which the client code can set the date. The snippet continues as follows:

```
12:     function setDate_global( ) {
13:         if (!$this->setDate_array($GLOBALS[$this->name])) {
14:             return $this->setDate_timestamp(time());
15:         }
16:
17:         return true;
18:     }
19:
20:     function setDate_timestamp($time) {
21:         $this->timestamp = $time;
22:         return true;
23:     }
24:
25:     function setDate_array($inputdate) {
26:         if (is_array($inputdate) &&
27:             isset($inputdate['mon']) &&
28:             isset($inputdate['mday']) &&
29:             isset($inputdate['year'])) {
30:
31:             $this->timestamp = mktime(11, 59, 59,
32:                 $inputdate['mon'], $inputdate['mday'], $inputdate['year']);
33:
34:             return true;
35:         }
36:
37:         return false;
38:     }
```

Of these methods, setDate_timestamp() is the simplest. It requires a Unix timestamp, which it assigns to the $timestamp property.

The setDate_array() method expects an associative array with at least three keys: 'mon', 'mday', and 'year'. These fields will contain data in the same format as in the array returned by getdate(). This means that setDate_array() will accept a hand-built array such as

```
array('mday'=> 20, 'mon'=>9, 'year' => 2002);
```

or the result of a call to getdate():

getdate(1032787181);

It is no accident that the pull-downs we will build later will be constructed to produce an array containing 'mon', 'mday', and 'year' fields. The method uses the mktime() function to construct a timestamp, which is then assigned to the $timestamp variable.

The setDate_global() method is called by default. It attempts to find a global variable with the same name as the object's $name property. This is passed to setDate_array(). If this method discovers a global variable of the right structure, it uses that variable to create the $timestamp variable. Otherwise, the current date is used.

The ranges for days and months are fixed, but years are a different matter. We create a few methods to allow the client coder to set her own range of years (although we also provide default behavior):

```
39:     function setYearStart($year) {
40:         $this->yearstart = $year;
41:     }
42:
43:     function setYearEnd($year) {
44:         $this->yearend = $year;
45:     }
46:
47:     function getYearStart() {
48:         if ($this->yearstart < 0) {
49:             $nowarray = getdate(time());
50:             $this->yearstart = $nowarray[year]-5;
51:         }
52:
53:         return $this->yearstart;
54:     }
55:
56:     function getYearEnd() {
57:         if ($this->yearend < 0) {
58:             $nowarray = getdate(time());
59:             $this->yearend = $nowarray[year]+5;
60:         }
61:         return $this->yearend;
62:     }
```

The setYearStart() and setYearEnd() methods are straightforward. A year is directly assigned to the appropriate property. The getYearStart() method tests whether or not the $yearstart property has been set. If it has not been set, getYearStart() assigns a $yearstart value five years before the current year. The getYearEnd() method performs a similar operation. We're now ready to create the business end of the class:

```
63:    function output() {
64:        if ($this->timestamp < 0) {
65:            $this->setDate_global();
66:        }
67:        $datearray = getdate($this->timestamp);
68:        $out  = $this->day_select($this->name, $datearray);
69:        $out .= $this->month_select($this->name, $datearray);
70:        $out .= $this->year_select($this->name, $datearray);
71:        return $out;
72:    }
73:
74:    function day_select($fieldname, $datearray)  {
75:        $out = "<select name=\"$fieldname"."[mday]\">\n";
76:        for ($x=1; $x<=31; $x++) {
77:            $out .= "<option value=\"$x\"".($datearray['mday']==($x)
78:                ?" SELECTED":"").">".sprintf("%02d", $x ) ."\n";
79:        }
80:        $out .= "</select>\n";
81:        return $out;
82:    }
83:
84:    function month_select($fieldname, $datearray) {
85:        $out = "<select name=\"$fieldname"."[mon]\">\n";
86:        for ($x = 1; $x <= 12; $x++) {
87:            $out .= "<option value=\"".($x)."\"".($datearray['mon']==($x)
88:                ?" SELECTED":"")."> ".$this->months[$x-1]."\n";
89:        }
90:        $out .= "</select>\n";
91:        return $out;
92:    }
93:
94:    function year_select($fieldname, $datearray) {
95:        $out = "<select name=\"$fieldname"."[year]\">";
96:        $start = $this->getYearStart();
97:        $end = $this->getYearEnd();
98:        for ($x= $start; $x < $end; $x++) {
99:            $out .= "<option value=\"$x\"".($datearray['year']==($x)
100:                ?" SELECTED":"").">$x\n";
101:        }
102:        $out .= "</select>\n";
103:        return $out;
104:    }
105: }
```

The output() method orchestrates most of this code. It first checks the $timestamp
property. Unless the client coder has called one of the setDate methods, $timestamp
will be set to –1 and setDate_global() will be called by default. The timestamp is
passed to the getdate() function to construct a date array, and a method is called for
each pull-down to be produced.

The day_select() method simply constructs an HTML select element with an option element for each of the 31 possible days in a month. The object's current date is stored in the $datearray argument variable, which is used during the construction of the element to set the selected attribute of the relevant option element. The sprintf() function formats the day number, adding a leading zero to days 1–9. The month_select() and year_select() methods use similar logic to construct the month and year pull-downs.

Why did we break down the output code into four methods, rather than simply creating one block of code? When we build a class, we have two kinds of user in mind: the client coder who will want to instantiate a date_pulldown object, and the client coder who will want to subclass the date_pulldown class to refine its functionality. For the former, we want to provide a simple and clear interface to the class's functionality. The coder can instantiate an object, set its date, and call the output() method. For the latter, we want to make it easy to change discrete elements of the class's functionality. By putting all the output code into one method, we would force a child class that needed to tweak output to reproduce a lot of code that is perfectly usable. By breaking this code into discrete methods, we allow for subclasses that can change limited aspects of functionality without disturbing the whole. If a child class needs to represent the year pull-down as two radio buttons, for example, the coder can simply override the year_select() method.

Listing 12.4 contains some code that calls the library class. Before you try to execute this code, take all the class snippets we've covered and put them into a file called date_pulldown.class.php, and place this file in the document root of your Web server. You'll be calling it in a moment, so it had better be there!

LISTING 12.4 Using the date_pulldown Class

```
 1: <html>
 2: <head>
 3: <title>Listing 12.4 Using the date_pulldown Class</title>
 4: </head>
 5: <?php
 6: include("date_pulldown.class.php");
 7: $date1 = new date_pulldown("fromdate");
 8: $date2 = new date_pulldown("todate");
 9: $date3 = new date_pulldown("foundingdate");
10: $date3->setYearStart(1972);
11: if (empty($foundingdate))
12:     $date3->setDate_array(array('mday'=>26, 'mon'=>4, 'year'=>1984));
13: ?>
14: <body>
15:
16: <form>
17: From:<br>
```

12

LISTING 12.4 continued

```
18: <?php print $date1->output(); ?><p>
19:
20: To:<br>
21: <?php print $date2->output(); ?><p>
22:
23: Company founded:<br>
24: <?php print $date3->output(); ?><p>
25:
26: <input type="submit">
27: </form>
28:
29: </body>
30: </html>
```

We include the date_pulldown.class.php on line 6 (see Figure 12.3). Once we have included the class file, we can use all of its methods. We use the class's default behavior for all the pull-downs apart from "foundingdate". For this object, we override the default year start, setting it to 1972 on line 10. On line 12, we assign this pull-down an arbitrary date that will be displayed until the form is submitted. Note that this is only the front end of a form, with no action or method; you need to supply your own action or method in order for this to actually do something!

FIGURE 12.3

The pull-downs generated by the date_pulldown *class.*

Summary

In this hour, you pulled together the PHP date-related functions you learned about in the previous hour to work within a calendar application. You learned how to test the validity of an input date using checkdate(). You worked through an example script, which applies some of the tools you have looked at, and built a class library that automates some of the more tedious aspects of working with dates in forms.

Q&A

Q **Are there any functions for converting between different calendars?**

A Yes. PHP provides an entire suite of functions that cover alternative calendars. You can read about these in the official PHP Manual at `http://www.php.net/manual/en/ref.calendar.php`.

Workshop

The workshop is designed to help you anticipate possible questions, review what you've learned, and begin learning how to put your knowledge into practice.

Quiz

1. What PHP function did we use to check the validity of a date?
2. What PHP function did we use to create a timestamp?
3. What PHP function did we use to create an associative array of date-related information?

Answers

1. `checkdate()`
2. `mktime()`
3. `getdate()`

Activity

Use your fancy new date pull-down class in the context of your own form. Create a back-end script that takes the selected dates and displays their input.

12

Hour 13

Working with Strings

The World Wide Web is very much a plain text environment. No matter how rich Web content becomes, HTML lies behind it all. It is no accident, then, that PHP provides many functions with which you can format, investigate, and manipulate strings. As you might expect, MySQL also comes with its own set of string-related functions, which you will also learn about in this hour.

In this hour, you will learn

- How to format strings
- How to determine the length of a string
- How to find a substring within a string
- How to break a string down into component parts
- How to remove whitespace from the beginning or end of a string
- How to replace substrings
- How to change the case of a string

- How to use MySQL to put strings together or extract pieces of strings
- How to use MySQL to create variations of original strings
- How to use MySQL to find alternate representations of strings, in different bases

Formatting Strings with PHP

Until now, we have simply printed any strings that we want to display directly to the browser. PHP provides two functions that allow you first to apply formatting, whether to round doubles to a given number of decimal places, define alignment within a field, or display data according to different number systems. In this section, you will look at a few of the formatting options provided by `printf()` and `sprintf()`.

Working with `printf()`

If you have any experience with C, you will be familiar with the `printf()` function. The PHP version is similar but not identical. `printf()` requires a string argument, known as a *format control string*. It also accepts additional arguments of different types. The format control string contains instructions indicating how to display these additional arguments. The following snippet, for example, uses `printf()` to output an integer as a decimal:

```
printf("This is my number: %d", 55 );
// prints "This is my number: 55"
```

NEW TERM Within the format control string (the first argument), we have included a special code, known as a *conversion specification*.

A conversion specification begins with a percent (%) symbol and defines how to treat the corresponding argument to `printf()`. You can include as many conversion specifications as you want within the format control string, as long as you send an equivalent number of arguments to `printf()`.

The following snippet outputs two numbers using `printf()`:

```
printf("First number: %d<br>\nSecond number: %d<br>\n", 55, 66 );
// Output:
// First number: 55
// Second number: 66
```

The first conversion specification corresponds to the first of the additional arguments to `printf()`, which is 55. The second conversion specification corresponds to 66. The d following the percent symbol requires that the data be treated as a decimal integer. This part of a conversion specification is a type specifier.

printf() and Type Specifiers

You have already come across one type specifier, d, which displays data in decimal format. Table 13.1 lists the other available type specifiers.

TABLE 13.1 Type Specifiers

Specifier	Description
d	Display argument as a decimal number
b	Display an integer as a binary number
c	Display an integer as ASCII equivalent
f	Display an integer as a floating-point number (double)
o	Display an integer as an octal number (base 8)
s	Display argument as a string
x	Display an integer as a lowercase hexadecimal number (base 16)
X	Display an integer as an uppercase hexadecimal number (base 16)

Listing 13.1 uses printf() to display a single number according to some of the type specifiers listed in Table 13.1.

LISTING 13.1 Demonstrating Some Type Specifiers

```
 1: <html>
 2: <head>
 3: <title>Listing 13.1 Demonstrating some type specifiers</title>
 4: </head>
 5: <body>
 6: <?php
 7: $number = 543;
 8: printf("Decimal: %d<br>", $number );
 9: printf("Binary: %b<br>", $number );
10: printf("Double: %f<br>", $number );
11: printf("Octal: %o<br>", $number );
12: printf("String: %s<br>", $number );
13: printf("Hex (lower): %x<br>", $number );
14: printf("Hex (upper): %X<br>", $number );
15: ?>
16: </body>
17: </html>
```

13

Put these lines into a text file called listing13.1.php, and place this file in your Web server document root. When you access this script through your Web browser, it should look something like Figure 13.1. As you can see, printf() is a quick way of converting data from one number system to another and outputting the result.

FIGURE **13.1**

Demonstrating conversion specifiers.

When you specify a color in HTML, you combine three hexadecimal numbers between 00 and FF, representing the values for red, green, and blue. You can use printf() to convert three decimal numbers between 0 and 255 to their hexadecimal equivalents:

```
$red = 204;
$green = 204;
$blue = 204;
printf( "#%X%X%X", $red, $green, $blue );
// prints "#CCCCCC"
```

Although you can use the type specifier to convert from decimal to hexadecimal numbers, you can't use it to determine how many characters the output for each argument should occupy. Within an HTML color code, each hexadecimal number should be padded to two characters, which would become a problem if we changed our $red, $green, and $blue variables in the preceding snippet to contain 1, for example. We would end up with the output "#111". You can force the output of leading zeros by using a padding specifier.

Padding Output with the Padding Specifier

You can require that output be padded by leading characters. The padding specifier should directly follow the percent sign that begins a conversion specification. To pad output with leading zeros, the padding specifier should consist of a zero followed by the number of characters you want the output to take up. If the output occupies fewer characters than this total, the difference will be filled with zeros:

```
printf( "%04d", 36 );
// prints "0036"
```

To pad output with leading spaces, the padding specifier should consist of a space character followed by the number of characters that the output should occupy:

```
printf( "% 4d", 36 )
// prints "  36"
```

A browser will not display multiple spaces in an HTML document. You can force the display of spaces and newlines by placing <PRE> tags around your output as follows:

```
<pre>
<?php
print "The        spaces        will be visible";
?>
</pre>
```

If you want to format an entire document as text, you can use the header() function to change the Content-Type header:

```
header("Content-Type: text/plain");
```

Remember that your script must not have sent any output to the browser for the header() function to work as desired.

You can specify any character other than a space or a zero in your padding specifier with a single quotation mark followed by the character you want to use:

```
printf ( "%'x4d", 36 );
// prints "xx36"
```

We now have the tools we need to complete our HTML code example. Until now, we could convert three numbers, but we could not pad them with leading zeros:

```
$red = 1;
$green = 1;
$blue = 1;
printf( "#%02X%02X%02X", $red, $green, $blue );
// prints "#010101"
```

Each variable is output as a hexadecimal number. If the output occupies fewer than two spaces, leading zeros will be added.

Specifying a Field Width

You can specify the number of spaces within which your output should sit. The field width specifier is an integer that should be placed after the percent sign that begins a conversion specification (assuming that no padding specifier is defined). The following

13

snippet outputs a list of four items, all of which sit within a field of 20 spaces. To make the spaces visible on the browser, we place all our output within a PRE element:

```
print "<pre>";
printf("%20s\n", "Books");
printf("%20s\n", "CDs");
printf("%20s\n", "Games");
printf("%20s\n", "Magazines");
print "</pre>";
```

Figure 13.2 shows the output of this snippet.

FIGURE 13.2

Aligning with field width specifiers.

By default, output is right-aligned within the field you specify. You can make it left-aligned by prepending a minus (–) symbol to the field width specifier:

```
printf("%-20s\n", "Left aligned");
```

Note that alignment applies to the decimal portion of any number that you output. In other words, only the portion before the decimal point of a double will sit flush to the end of the field width when right-aligned.

Specifying Precision

If you want to output data in floating-point format, you can specify the precision to which you want to round your data. This capability is particularly useful when you are dealing with currency. The precision identifier should be placed directly before the type specifier. It consists of a dot (.) followed by the number of decimal places to which you want to round. This specifier has an effect only on data that is output with the f type specifier:

```
printf( "%.2f", 5.333333 );
// prints "5.33"
```

In the C language, you can use a precision specifier with printf() to specify padding for decimal output. The precision specifier has no effect on decimal output in PHP. Use the padding specifier to add leading zeros to integers.

Conversion Specifications: A Recap

Table 13.2 lists the specifiers that can make up a conversion specification in the order that they would be included. Note that it is difficult to use both a padding specifier and a field width specifier. You should choose to use one or the other, but not both.

TABLE 13.2 Components of Conversion Specification

Name	Description	Example
Padding specifier	Determines the number of characters that output should occupy, and the characters to add otherwise	`' 4'`
Field width specifier	Determines the space within which output should be formatted	`'20'`
Precision specifier	Determines the number of decimal places to which a double should be rounded	`'.4'`
Type specifier	Determines the data type that should be output	`'d'`

Listing 13.2 uses `printf()` to output a list of products and prices.

LISTING 13.2 Using `printf()` to Format a List of Product Prices

```
 1: <html>
 2: <head>
 3: <title>Listing 13.2 Using printf() to format
 4:        a list of product prices</title>
 5: </head>
 6: <body>
 7: <?php
 8: $products = array("Green armchair"=>222.4,
 9:             "Candlestick"=>"4",
10:             "Coffee table"=>80.6
11:             );
12: print "<pre>";
13: printf("%-20s%23s\n", "Name", "Price");
14: printf("%'-43s\n", "");
15: foreach ($products as $key=>$val) {
16:     printf( "%-20s%20.2f\n", $key, $val );
17: }
18: print("</pre>");
19: ?>
20: </body>
21: </html>
```

13

We first define an associative array containing product names and prices on line 8. We open print a `PRE` element so that the browser will recognize our spaces and newlines. Our first `printf()` call on line 13 defines the following format control string:

`"%-20s%23s\n"`

The first conversion specification (`"%-20s"`) uses a field width specifier of 20 characters, with the output left-justified. We use a string type specifier. The second conversion specification (`"%23s"`) sets up a right-aligned field width. This `printf()` call will output our field headers.

Our second `printf()` function call on line 14 draws a line of - characters across a field of 43 characters. We achieve this result with a padding specifier, which adds padding to an empty string.

The final `printf()` call on line 16 is part of a `foreach` statement that loops through our product array. We use two conversion specifications. The first (`"%-20s"`) prints the product name as a string left-justified within a 20-character field. The second conversion specification (`"%20.2f"`) uses a field width specifier to ensure that output will be right-aligned within a 20-character field, and a precision specifier to ensure that the double we output is rounded to two decimal places.

Put these lines into a text file called `listing13.2.php`, and place this file in your Web server document root. When you access this script through your Web browser, it should look like Figure 13.3.

FIGURE 13.3
Products and prices formatted with
`printf()`.

Argument Swapping

As of PHP 4.0.6, it became possible to use the format control string to change the order in which the provided arguments are incorporated into output.

Imagine, for example, that you are printing dates to the browser. You have the dates in a multidimensional array and are using `printf()` to format the output:

```
<?
$dates = array(
            array( 'mon'=> 12, 'mday'=>25, 'year'=>2001 ),
            array( 'mon'=>  5, 'mday'=>23, 'year'=>2000 ),
            array( 'mon'=> 10, 'mday'=>29, 'year'=>2001 )
            );

$format = include( "local_format.php" );

foreach($dates as $date) {
    printf( "$format", $date['mon'], $date['mday'], $date['year'] );
}
?>
```

In the preceding snippet, we get our format control string from an include file called `local_format.php`. Assume that this file contains only the following:

```
<?php
return "%02d/%02d/%d<br>";
?>
```

In that case, our output will be in the format `mm/dd/yyyy`:

```
12/25/2001
05/23/2000
10/29/2001
```

Imagine now that we are installing our script for a British site. In the United Kingdom dates are commonly presented with days before months (`dd/mm/yyyy`). The core code cannot be changed, but configuration files such as `local_format.php` can. Luckily, we can now alter the order in which the arguments are presented from within the format control code:

```
return "%2\$02d/%1\$02d/%3\$d<br>";
```

We can insert the argument number we are interested in after the initial percentage character that marks each conversion specification, followed by an escaped dollar ($) character. So, in the preceding snippet, we are demanding that the second argument be presented, followed by the first, followed by the third. The result is a list of dates in British format:

```
25/12/2001
23/05/2000
29/10/2001
```

Storing a Formatted String

The `printf()` function outputs data to the browser, which means that the results are not available to your scripts. You can, however, use the function `sprintf()`, which works in exactly the same way as `printf()` except that it returns a string that you can then store in a variable for later use. The following snippet uses `sprintf()` to round a double to two decimal places, storing the result in $dosh:

```
$dosh = sprintf("%.2f", 2.334454);
print "You have $dosh dollars to spend";
```

A particular use of `sprintf()` is to write formatted data to a file. You can call `sprintf()` and assign its return value to a variable that can then be printed to a file with `fputs()`.

Investigating Strings in PHP

You do not always know everything about the data that you are working with. Strings can arrive from many sources, including user input, databases, files, and Web pages. Before you begin to work with data from an external source, you often will need to find out more about it. PHP provides many functions that enable you to acquire information about strings.

A Note About Indexing Strings

We will frequently use the word *index* in relation to strings. You will have come across the word more frequently in the context of arrays. In fact, strings and arrays are not as different as you might imagine. You can think of a string as an array of characters. So you can access individual characters of a string as if they were elements of an array:

```
$test = "scallywag";
print $test[0]; // prints "s"
print $test[2]; // prints "a"
```

It is important to remember, therefore, that when we talk about the position or index of a character within a string, characters, like array elements, are indexed from 0.

Finding the Length of a String with `strlen()`

You can use `strlen()` to determine the length of a string. `strlen()` requires a string and returns an integer representing the number of characters in the variable you have passed it. `strlen()` might typically be used to check the length of user input. The following snippet tests a membership code to ensure that it is four characters long:

```
if (strlen($membership) == 4) {
    print "Thank you!";
} else {
    print "Your membership number must have 4 digits<P>";
}
```

The user is thanked for his input only if the global variable $membership contains four characters; otherwise, an error message is generated.

Finding a Substring Within a String with `strstr()`

You can use `strstr()` to test whether a string exists embedded within another string. `strstr()` requires two arguments: a source string and the substring you want to find within it. The function returns `false` if the substring is absent. Otherwise, it returns the portion of the source string beginning with the substring. For the following example, imagine that we want to treat membership codes that contain the string `AB` differently from those that do not:

```
$membership = "pAB7";
if (strstr($membership, "AB")) {
    print "Thank you. Don't forget that your membership expires soon!";
} else {
    print "Thank you!";
}
```

Because our test variable $membership does contain the string `AB`, `strstr()` returns the string `AB7`. This resolves to `true` when tested, so we print a special message. What happens if our user enters "pab7"? Because `strstr()` is case sensitive, `AB` will not be found. The `if` statement's test will fail, and the default message will be printed to the browser. If we want to search for either `AB` or `ab` within the string, we must use `stristr()`, which works in exactly the same way but is not case sensitive.

Finding the Position of a Substring with `strpos()`

The `strpos()` function tells you both whether a string exists within a larger string and where it is to be found. `strpos()` requires two arguments: the source string and the substring you are seeking. The function also accepts an optional third argument, an integer representing the index from which you want to start searching. If the substring does not exist, `strpos()` returns `false`; otherwise, it returns the index at which the substring begins. The following snippet uses `strpos()` to ensure that a string begins with the string `mz`:

```
$membership = "mz00xyz";
if (strpos($membership, "mz") === 0) {
    print "hello mz";
}
```

Notice the trick we had to play to get expected results. `strpos()` finds `mz` in our string but finds it at the first element of the string. This means that it will return zero, which will resolve to `false` in our test. To work around this problem, we use PHP's equivalence

13

operator ===, which returns true if the left- and right-hand operands are equivalent and of the same type.

Extracting Part of a String with substr()

The substr() function returns a portion of a string based on the start index and length of the portion you are looking for. This function demands two arguments: a source string and the starting index. It returns all characters from the starting index to the end of the string you are searching. It optionally accepts a third argument, which should be an integer representing the length of the string you want returned. If this argument is present, substr() returns only the number of characters specified from the start index onward.

```
$test = "scallywag";
print substr($test,6);  // prints "wag"
print substr($test,6,2) // prints "wa"
```

If you pass substr() a negative number as its second (starting index) argument, it will count from the end rather than the beginning of the string. The following snippet writes a specific message to people who have submitted an e-mail address ending in .uk:

```
$test = "matt@corrosive.co.uk";
if ($test = substr($test, -3) == ".uk") {
    print "Don't forget our special offers for British customers";
} else {
    print "Welcome to our shop!";
}
```

Tokenizing a String with strtok()

You can parse a string word by word using strtok(). The strtok() function initially requires two arguments: the string to be tokenized and the delimiters by which to split the string. The delimiter string can include as many characters as you want, and the function will return the first token found. After strtok() has been called for the first time, the source string will be cached. For subsequent calls, you should pass strtok() only the delimiter string. The function will return the next found token every time it is called, returning false when the end of the string is reached. strtok() will usually be called repeatedly within a loop.

Listing 13.3 uses strtok() to tokenize a URL, splitting the host and path from the query string, and further dividing the name/value pairs of the query string.

LISTING 13.3   Dividing a String into Tokens with `strtok()`

```
 1: <html>
 2: <head>
 3: <title>Listing 13.3 Dividing a string into tokens with strtok()</title>
 4: </head>
 5: <body>
 6: <?php
 7: $test  = "http://www.deja.com/qs.xp?";
 8: $test .= "OP=dnquery.xp&ST=MS&DBS=2&QRY=developer+php";
 9: $delims = "?&";
10: $word = strtok($test, $delims);
11: while (is_string($word)) {
12:     if ($word) {
13:         print "$word<br>";
14:     }
15:     $word = strtok($delims);
16: }
17: ?>
18: </body>
19: </html>
```

Put these lines into a text file called listing13.3.php, and place this file in your Web server document root. When you access this script through your Web browser, it should look like Figure 13.4.

FIGURE 13.4

Output of Listing 13.3, a tokenized string.

The `strtok()` function is something of a blunt instrument, and a few tricks are required to work with it. We first store the delimiters that we want to work with in a variable, `$delims` on line 9. We call `strtok()` on line 10, passing it the URL we want to tokenize and the `$delims` string. We store the first result in `$word`. Within the conditional expression of the `while` loop on line 11, we test whether `$word` is a string. If it isn't, we know that the end of the string has been reached and no further action is required.

13

We are testing the return type because a string containing two delimiters in a row would cause `strtok()` to return an empty string when it reaches the first of these delimiters. So a more conventional test such as

```
while ($word) {
      $word = strtok($delims);
}
```

would fail if $word is an empty string, even if the end of the source string has not yet been reached.

Having established that $word contains a string, we can go on to work with it. If $word does not contain an empty string, we print it to the browser on line 13. We must then call `strtok()` again on line 15 to repopulate the $word variable for the next test. Notice that we don't pass the source string to `strtok()` a second time. If we were to do this, the first word of the source string would be returned once again, and we would find ourselves in an infinite loop.

Manipulating Strings with PHP

PHP provides many functions that will transform a string argument, subtly or radically, as you'll soon see.

Cleaning Up a String with `trim()` and `strip_tags()`

When you acquire text from the user or a file, you can't always be sure that you haven't also picked up whitespace at the beginning and end of your data. The `trim()` function shaves any whitespace characters, including newlines, tabs, and spaces, from both the start and end of a string. It accepts the string to be modified, returning the cleaned-up version:

```
$text = "\t\t\tlots of room to breathe        ";
$text = trim( $text );
print $text;
// prints "lots of room to breathe";
```

Of course, removing all the whitespace might be more work than you require. You might want to keep whitespace at the beginning of a string but remove it from the end. You can use PHP's `rtrim()` function exactly the same as you would use `trim()`. Only whitespace at the end of the string argument is removed, however:

```
$text = "\t\t\tlots of room to breathe        ";
$text = rtrim( $text );
print $test;
// prints "            lots of room to breathe";
```

PHP provides the `ltrim()` function to strip whitespace only from the beginning of a string. Once again, this is called with the string you want to transform and returns a new string, shorn of tabs, newlines, and spaces:

```
$text = "\t\t\tlots of room to breathe        ";
$text = ltrim( $text );
print $test;
// prints "lots of room to breathe        ";
```

PHP, by its nature, tends to work with markup text. It is not unusual to have to remove tags from a block to be able to present it without formatting. PHP provides the `strip_tags()` function for this purpose. The `strip_tags()` function accepts two arguments. The first is the text to transform. The second argument is optional and should be a list of HTML tags that `strip_tags()` can leave in place. The tags in the exception list should not be separated by any characters.

```
$string = "I <i>simply</i> will not have it,<br>said Mr Dean<p><b>The end</b>";
print strip_tags($string, "<br><p>");
```

In the preceding code snippet, we create an HTML-formatted string. When we call `strip_tags()`, we pass it the $string variable and a list of exceptions. The result is that the <p> and <br> tags are left in place and all other tags are stripped out.

Replacing a Portion of a String Using `substr_replace()`

The `substr_replace()` function works similarly to `substr()` except that it allows you replace the portion of a string that you extract. The function requires three arguments: the string you are transforming, the text you want to add to it, and the starting index. It also accepts an optional length argument. The `substr_replace()` function finds the portion of a string specified by the starting index and length arguments, replacing this portion with the string provided in the replace string argument and returning the entire transformed string.

In the following code snippet used to renew a user's membership code, we must change its second two characters:

```
<?
$membership = "mz01xyz";
$membership = substr_replace($membership, "02", 2, 2);
print "New membership number: $membership<p>";
// prints "New membership number: mz02xyz"
?>
```

The result of this code is that the old membership number, `"mz01xyz"`, becomes the new membership number `"mz02xyz"`.

13

Replacing Substrings Using `str_replace`

The `str_replace()` function replaces all instances of a string within another string. It requires three arguments: a search string, the replacement string, and the string on which this transformation is to be effected. The function returns the transformed string. The following example uses `str_replace()` to change all references from 2001 to 2002 within a string:

```
$string  = "Site contents copyright 2001. ";
$string .= "The 2001 Guide to All Things Good in Europe";
print str_replace("2001","2002",$string);
```

As of PHP 4.0.5, `str_replace()` has been enhanced to accept arrays as well as strings for all its arguments. This allows us to perform multiple search-and-replace operations on a subject string and even on more than one subject string. Consider the following snippet, for instance:

```
<?php
$source = array(
        "The package which is at version 4.2 was released in 2001",
        "The year 2001 was an excellent period for PointyThing4.2" );
$search  = array("4.2", "2001");
$replace = array("5.0", "2002");
$source = str_replace($search, $replace, $source);
foreach($source as $str) {
        print "$str<br>";
}
// prints:
// The package which is at version 5.0 was released in 2002
// The year 2002 was an excellent period for PointyThing5.0
?>
```

When `str_replace()` is passed an array of strings for its first and second arguments, it attempts to switch each search string with its corresponding replace string in the text to be transformed. When the third argument is an array, `str_replace()` returns an array of strings. The search-and-replace operation is executed on each string in the array.

Converting Case

PHP provides several functions that allow you to convert the case of a string. Changing case is often useful for string comparisons. To get an uppercase version of a string, use the function `strtoupper()`. This function requires only the string that you want to convert and returns the converted string:

```
$membership = "mz02xyz";
$membership = strtoupper($membership);
print "$membership<br>"; // prints "MZ02XYZ"
```

To convert a string to lowercase characters, use the function `strtolower()`. Once again, this function requires the string you want to convert and returns a converted version:

```
$membership = "MZ02XYZ";
$membership = strtolower($membership);
print "$membership<br>"; // prints "mz02xyz"
```

PHP also provides a case function that has a useful cosmetic purpose. The `ucwords()` function makes the first letter of every word in a string uppercase. In the following snippet, we make the first letter of every word in a user-submitted string uppercase:

```
$full_name = "violet elizabeth bott";
$full_name = ucwords($full_name);
print $full_name; // prints "Violet Elizabeth Bott"
```

Although this function makes the first letter of each word uppercase, it does not touch any other letters. So if the user had had problems with her Shift key in the previous example and submitted VIolEt eLIZaBeTH bOTt, our approach would not have done much to fix the string. We would have ended up with VIolEt ELIZaBeTH BOTt, which isn't much of an improvement. We can deal with this problem by making the submitted string lowercase with `strtolower()` before invoking `ucwords()`:

```
$full_name = "VIolEt eLIZaBeTH bOTt";
$full_name = ucwords(strtolower($full_name));
print $full_name; // prints "Violet Elizabeth Bott"
```

Wrapping Text with `wordwrap()` and `nl2br()`

When you present plain text within a Web page, you are often faced with the problem that newlines are not displayed, and your text runs together into a featureless blob. The `nl2br()` function is a convenience method that converts every newline into an HTML break. So

```
$string  = "one line\n";
$string .= "another line\n";
$string .= "a third for luck\n";
print nl2br($string);
```

will print

```
one line<br />
another line<br />
a third for luck<br />
```

Notice that the <br> tags are output in XHTML-compliant form. This feature was introduced in PHP 4.0.5.

13

The nl2br() function is great for honoring newlines that are already in the text you are converting. Occasionally, though, you may want to add arbitrary line breaks to format a column of text. The wordwrap() function is perfect for this task. wordwrap() requires one argument: the string to be transformed. By default, wordwrap() wraps lines every 75 characters and uses '\n' as its line break character. So the code snippet

```
$string  = "Given a long line, wordwrap() is useful as a means of ";
$string .= "breaking it into a column and thereby making it easier to read";
print wordwrap($string);
```

would output

```
Given a long line, wordwrap() is useful as a means of breaking it into a
column and thereby making it easier to read
```

Because the lines are broken with the character '\n', the formatting does not show up in HTML mode, of course. wordwrap() has two more optional arguments: a number representing the maximum number of characters per line and a string representing the end of line string you would like to use. So applying the function call

```
print wordwrap( $string, 24, "<br>\n" );
```

to our $string variable, our output would be

```
Given a long line,<br>
wordwrap() is useful as<br>
a means of breaking it<br>
into a column and<br>
thereby making it easier<br>
to read
```

The wordwrap() function doesn't automatically break at your line limit if a word has more characters than the limit. You can, however, use an optional fourth argument to enforce such a break. The argument should be a positive integer. So using wordwrap() in conjunction with the fourth argument, we can now wrap a string, even where it contains words that extend beyond the limit we are setting. This snippet

```
$string  = "As usual you will find me at http://www.witteringonaboutit.com/";
$string .= "chat/eating_green_cheese/forum.php. Hope to see you there!";
print wordwrap( $string, 24, "<br>\n", 1 );
```

will output

```
As usual you will find<br>
me at<br>
http://www.witteringonab<br>
outit.com/chat/eating_gr<br>
een_cheese/forum.php.<br>
Hope to see you there!
```

instead of

```
As usual you will find<br>
me at<br>
http://www.witteringonaboutit.com/chat/eating_green_cheese/forum.php. <br>
Hope to see you there!
```

Breaking Strings into Arrays with `explode()`

The delightfully named `explode()` function is similar in some ways to `strtok()`. But `explode()` will break up a string into an array, which you can then store, sort, or examine as you want. The `explode()` function requires two arguments: the delimiter string that you want to use to break up the source string and the source string itself. The function optionally accepts a third argument, which will determine the maximum number of pieces the string can be broken into. The delimiter string can include more than one character, all of which will form a single delimiter (unlike multiple delimiter characters passed to `strtok()`, each of which will be a delimiter in its own right). The following snippet breaks up a date and stores the result in an array:

```
$start_date = "2002-01-12";
$date_array = explode("-", $start_date);
// $date[0] == "2002"
// $date[1] == "01"
// $date[2] == "12"
```

Now that your head is filled with PHP string functions, let's move on to MySQL string functions, many of which perform the same tasks.

Frequently Used String Functions in MySQL

MySQL's built-in string-related functions can be used several ways. You can use functions in SELECT statements without specifying a table to retrieve a result of the function. Or you can use functions to enhance your SELECT results by concatenating two fields to form a new string.

Even if you never use these functions in your applications, it's good to know they exist, and, if nothing else, you'll get some good practice in this hour using the MySQL monitor's command-line interface.

13

Length and Concatenation Functions

The group of length and concatenation functions focuses on the length of strings and concatenating strings together. Length-related functions include LENGTH(),

OCTET_LENGTH(), CHAR_LENGTH(), and CHARACTER_LENGTH(), which do virtually the same thing—count characters in a string.

```
mysql> select length('This is cool!');
+------------------------+
| LENGTH('This is cool!') |
+------------------------+
|                     13 |
+------------------------+
```

1 row in set (0.00 sec)

The fun begins with the CONCAT() function, which is used to concatenate two or more strings:

```
mysql> select concat('My', 'S', 'QL');
+------------------------+
| CONCAT('My', 'S', 'QL') |
+------------------------+
| MySQL                  |
+------------------------+
```
1 row in set (0.00 sec)

Imagine using this function with a table containing names, split into firstname and lastname fields. Instead of using two strings, use two field names to concatenate the firstname and the lastname fields. By concatenating the fields, you reduce the lines of code necessary to achieve the same result in your application:

```
mysql> select concat(firstname, lastname) from table_name;
+----------------------------+
| CONCAT(firstname, lastname) |
+----------------------------+
| JohnSmith                  |
| JaneSmith                  |
| JimboJones                 |
| AndySmith                  |
| ChrisJones                 |
| AnnaBell                   |
| JimmyCarr                  |
| AlbertSmith                |
| JohnDoe                    |
+----------------------------+
9 rows in set (0.00 sec)
```

If you're using a field name and not a string in a function, don't enclose the field name within quotation marks. If you do, MySQL will interpret the string literally. In the CONCAT() example, you would get the following result:

```
mysql> select concat('firstname', 'lastname') FROM table_name;
+-------------------------------+
| CONCAT('firstname', 'lastname') |
+-------------------------------+
| firstnamelastname             |
| firstnamelastname             |
| firstnamelastname             |
| firstnamelastname             |
| firstnamelastname             |
| firstnamelastname             |
| firstnamelastname             |
| firstnamelastname             |
| firstnamelastname             |
+-------------------------------+
9 rows in set (0.00 sec)
```

The CONCAT() function would be useful if there were some sort of separator between the names, and that's where the next function comes in: CONCAT_WS().

As you may have figured out, CONTACT_WS() stands for "concatenate with separator." The separator can be anything you choose, but the following example uses whitespace:

```
mysql> select concat_ws(' ', firstname, lastname) FROM table_name;
+-----------------------------------+
| CONCAT_WS(' ', firstname, lastname) |
+-----------------------------------+
| John Smith                        |
| Jane Smith                        |
| Jimbo Jones                       |
| Andy Smith                        |
| Chris Jones                       |
| Anna Bell                         |
| Jimmy Carr                        |
| Albert Smith                      |
| John Doe                          |
+-----------------------------------+
9 rows in set (0.00 sec)
```

13

If you want to shorten the width of your result table, you can use AS to name the custom result field:

```
mysql> select concat_ws(' ', firstname, lastname) AS fullname FROM table_name;
+--------------+
| fullname     |
+--------------+
| John Smith   |
| Jane Smith   |
| Jimbo Jones  |
| Andy Smith   |
| Chris Jones  |
| Anna Bell    |
| Jimmy Carr   |
| Albert Smith |
| John Doe     |
+--------------+
9 rows in set (0.00 sec)
```

Trimming and Padding Functions

MySQL provides several functions for adding and removing extra characters (including whitespace) from strings. The RTRIM() and LTRIM() functions remove whitespace from either the right or left side of a string:

```
mysql> select rtrim('stringstring    ');
+------------------------+
| RTRIM('stringstring  ') |
+------------------------+
| stringstring           |
+------------------------+
1 row in set (0.00 sec)

mysql> select ltrim('  stringstring');
+----------------------+
| LTRIM('  stringstring') |
+----------------------+
| stringstring         |
+----------------------+
1 row in set (0.00 sec)
```

You may have padded strings to trim if the string is coming out of a fixed-width field, and either doesn't need to carry along the additional padding or is being inserted into a varchar or other non–fixed-width field. If your strings are padded with a character besides whitespace, use the TRIM() function to name the characters you want to remove. For example, to remove the leading "X" characters from the string XXXneedleXXX, use

```
mysql> select trim(leading 'X' from 'XXXneedleXXX');
+-------------------------------------+
| TRIM(LEADING 'X' from 'XXXneedleXXX') |
+-------------------------------------+
| needleXXX                           |
+-------------------------------------+
1 row in set (0.00 sec)
```

Use TRAILING to remove the characters from the end of the string:

```
mysql> select trim(trailing 'X' from 'XXXneedleXXX');
+--------------------------------------+
| TRIM(TRAILING 'X' from 'XXXneedleXXX') |
+--------------------------------------+
| XXXneedle                            |
+--------------------------------------+
1 row in set (0.00 sec)
```

If neither LEADING nor TRAILING is indicated, both are assumed:

```
mysql> select trim('X' from 'XXXneedleXXX');
+-----------------------------+
| TRIM('X' from 'XXXneedleXXX') |
+-----------------------------+
| needle                      |
+-----------------------------+
1 row in set (0.00 sec)
```

Just like RTRIM() and LTRIM() remove padding characters, RPAD() and LPAD() add characters to a string. For example, you may want to add specific identification characters to a string that is part of an order number, in a database used for sales. When you use the padding functions, the required elements are the string, the target length, and the padding character. For example, pad the string needle with the X character until the string is 10 characters long:

```
mysql> select rpad('needle', 10, 'X');
+------------------------+
| RPAD('needle', 10, 'X') |
+------------------------+
| needleXXXX             |
+------------------------+
1 row in set (0.00 sec)
```

```
mysql> select lpad('needle', 10, 'X');
+------------------------+
| LPAD('needle', 10, 'X') |
+------------------------+
| XXXXneedle             |
+------------------------+
1 row in set (0.00 sec)
```

13

Location and Position Functions

The group of location and position functions is useful for finding parts of strings within other strings. The LOCATE() function returns the position of the first occurrence of a given substring within the target string. For example, you can look for a needle in a haystack:

```
mysql> select locate('needle', 'haystackneedlehaystack');
+-------------------------------------------+
| LOCATE('needle', 'haystackneedlehaystack') |
+-------------------------------------------+
|                                         9 |
+-------------------------------------------+
1 row in set (0.00 sec)
```

The substring needle begins at position 9 in the target string. If the substring cannot be found in the target string, MySQL returns 0 as a result.

 Unlike position counting within most programming languages, which starts at 0, position counting using MySQL starts at 1.

An extension of the LOCATE() function is to use a third argument for starting position. If you start looking for needle in haystack before position 9, you'll receive a result. Otherwise, because needle starts at position 9, you'll receive a 0 result if you specify a greater starting position:

```
mysql> select locate('needle', 'haystackneedlehaystack',6);
+---------------------------------------------+
| LOCATE('needle', 'haystackneedlehaystack',9) |
+---------------------------------------------+
|                                           9 |
+---------------------------------------------+
1 row in set (0.00 sec)

mysql> select locate('needle', 'haystackneedlehaystack',12);
+----------------------------------------------+
| LOCATE('needle', 'haystackneedlehaystack',12) |
+----------------------------------------------+
|                                            0 |
+----------------------------------------------+
1 row in set (0.00 sec)
```

Substring Functions

If your goal is to extract a substring from a target string, several functions fit the bill. Given a string, starting position, and length, you can use the SUBSTRING() function. This example gets three characters from the string MySQL, starting at position 2:

```
mysql> select substring("MySQL", 2, 3);
+-------------------------+
| SUBSTRING("MySQL", 2, 3) |
+-------------------------+
| ySQ                     |
+-------------------------+
1 row in set (0.00 sec)
```

If you just want a few characters from the left or right ends of a string, use the LEFT() and RIGHT() functions:

```
mysql> select left("MySQL", 2);
+-----------------+
| LEFT("MySQL", 2) |
+-----------------+
| My              |
+-----------------+
1 row in set (0.00 sec)

mysql> select right("MySQL", 3);
+------------------+
| RIGHT("MySQL", 3) |
+------------------+
| SQL              |
+------------------+
1 row in set (0.00 sec)
```

One of the many common uses of substring functions is to extract parts of order numbers, to find out who placed the order. In some applications, the system is designed to automatically generate an order number, containing a date, customer identification, and other information. If this order number always follows a particular pattern, such as XXXX-YYYYY-ZZ, you can use substring functions to extract the individual parts of the whole. For example, if ZZ always represents the state to which the order was shipped, you can use the RIGHT() function to extract these characters and report the number of orders shipped to a particular state.

String Modification Functions

Your programming language of choice likely has functions to modify the appearance of strings, but if you can perform the task as part of the SQL statement, all the better.

13

The MySQL `LCASE()` and `UCASE()` functions transform a string into lowercase or upper-case:

```
mysql> select lcase('MYSQL');
+----------------+
| LCASE('MYSQL') |
+----------------+
| mysql          |
+----------------+
1 row in set (0.00 sec)
```

```
mysql> select ucase('mysql');
+----------------+
| UCASE('mysql') |
+----------------+
| MYSQL          |
+----------------+
1 row in set (0.00 sec)
```

Remember, if you use the functions with field names, don't use quotation marks:

```
mysql> select ucase(lastname) from table_name;
+-----------------+
| UCASE(lastname) |
+-----------------+
| BELL            |
| CARR            |
| DOE             |
| JONES           |
| JONES           |
| SMITH           |
| SMITH           |
| SMITH           |
| SMITH           |
+-----------------+
9 rows in set (0.00 sec)
```

Another fun string-manipulation function is `REPEAT()`, which does just what it sounds like—repeats a string for a given number of times:

```
mysql> select repeat("bowwow", 4);
+--------------------------+
| REPEAT("bowwow", 4)      |
+--------------------------+
| bowwowbowwowbowwowbowwow |
+--------------------------+
1 row in set (0.00 sec)
```

The REPLACE() function replaces all occurrences of a given string with another string:

```
mysql> select replace('bowwowbowwowbowwowbowwow', 'wow', 'WOW');
+---------------------------------------------------+
| REPLACE('bowwowbowwowbowwowbowwow', 'wow', 'WOW') |
+---------------------------------------------------+
| bowWOWbowWOWbowWOWbowWOW                           |
+---------------------------------------------------+
1 row in set (0.00 sec)
```

Obscure String Functions

The group of obscure string functions focuses on gathering more information about characters or converting characters to different bases—far and away the least common usage of string functions in MySQL, but important nonetheless if you're into such things. The first function is the ASCII() function, which gets the ASCII code value of a given character. This example gets the ASCII value of the ampersand (&) character:

```
mysql> select ascii('&');
+------------+
| ASCII('&') |
+------------+
|         38 |
+------------+
1 row in set (0.04 sec)
```

If a string contains multiple characters, the function gets the value of the left-most character:

```
mysql> select ascii('def');
+--------------+
| ASCII('def') |
+--------------+
|          100 |
+--------------+
1 row in set (0.00 sec)
```

In this case, "100" is the ASCII value of "d."

The next three functions return string representations of binary, octal, and hexadecimal values. Like the ASCII() function, the BIN(), OCT(), and HEX() functions do not require a table selection but return values without a specified table.

The following example gets a string representation of the binary value of the integer 56895:

13

```
mysql> select bin(56895);
+ — — — — — — — — —+
| BIN(56895)        |
+ — — — — — — — — —+
| 1101111000111111 |
+ — — — — — — — — —+
1 row in set (0.00 sec)
```

The following example gets a string representation of the octal value of the integer 56895:

```
mysql> select oct(56895);
+ — — — — — —+
| OCT(56895) |
+ — — — — — —+
| 157077     |
+ — — — — — —+
1 row in set (0.00 sec)
```

The following example gets a string representation of the hexadecimal value of the integer 56895:

```
mysql> select hex(56895);
+ — — — — — —+
| HEX(56895) |
+ — — — — — —+
| DE3F       |
+ — — — — — —+
1 row in set (0.00 sec)
```

You can also use the CONV() function to convert numbers between bases. This function has three parts: the number, the base you're converting from, and the base you're converting to.

For example, to convert the integer 56895 from base 10 to base 8 and return its value, use

```
mysql> select conv(56895,10,8);
+ — — — — — — — —+
| CONV(56895,10,8) |
+ — — — — — — — —+
| 157077           |
+ — — — — — — — —+
1 row in set (0.00 sec)
```

This result is equivalent to the OCT() function. Similarly, to convert an integer from base 10 to base 16, use

```
mysql> select conv(56895,10,16);
+-----------------+
| CONV(56895,10,16) |
+-----------------+
| DE3F            |
+-----------------+
1 row in set (0.00 sec)
```

This result is equivalent to the HEX() function.

You can also convert from base 8 to base 16:

```
mysql> select conv(157077,8,16);
+-----------------+
| CONV(157077,8,16) |
+-----------------+
| DE3F            |
+-----------------+
1 row in set (0.00 sec)
```

And so on. The minimum base is 2 and the maximum base is 36.

Another function for working with characters and ASCII codes is the CHAR() function, which takes a series of integers representing ASCII codes and returns a string made up of the results:

```
mysql> select char(84,104,105,115,32,105,115,32,99,111,111,108,33);
+-------------------------------------------------+
| CHAR(84,104,105,115,32,105,115,32,99,111,111,108,33) |
+-------------------------------------------------+
| This is cool!                                   |
+-------------------------------------------------+
1 row in set (0.00 sec)
```

Summary

In this hour, you examined some of the functions that enable you to take control of the strings in your PHP scripts. You learned how to format strings with printf() and sprint(). You should be able to use these functions both to create strings that transform data and lay it out. You learned about functions that investigate strings. You should be able to discover the length of a string with strlen(), determine the presence of a substring with strpos(), or extract a substring with substr(). You should be able to tokenize a string with strtok().

You also learned about functions that transform strings. You can now remove whitespace from the beginning or end of a string with trim(), ltrim(), or rtrim(). You can change

13

case with `strtoupper()`, `strtolower()`, or `ucwords()`. You can replace all instances of a string with `str_replace()`.

After learning the PHP methods for string manipulation, you were introduced to MySQL functions that perform actions on strings. If you have strings in MySQL you want to concatenate or for which you want to count characters, you can use functions such as `CONCAT()`, `CONCAT_WS()`, and `LENGTH()`. To pad or remove padding from strings, use `RPAD()`, `LPAD()`, `TRIM()`, `LTRIM()`, and `RRIM()` to get just the strings you want. You can also find the location of a string within another, or to return a part of a given string, using the `LOCATE()`, `SUBSTRING()`, `LEFT()`, and `RIGHT()` functions. Functions such as `LCASE()`, `UCASE()`, `REPEAT()`, and `REPLACE()` also return variations of the original strings. MySQL also has numerous functions for representing strings, such as `ASCII()`, `BIN()`, `OCT()`, `HEX()`, and `CONV()` for converting between bases.

Q&A

Q Are there any other string functions that might be useful to me?

A Yes. PHP has more than 60 string functions! You can read about them all in the PHP Manual online at `http://www.php.net/manual/ref.strings.php`.

Q Can I use multiple functions in one statement, such as making a concatenated string all uppercase?

A Sure—just be mindful of your opening and closing parentheses. This example shows how to uppercase the concatenated first and last names from the master name table:

```
mysql> SELECT UCASE(CONCAT_WS(' ', firstname, lastname)) FROM table_name;
+--------------------------------------+
| UCASE(CONCAT_WS(' ', firstname, lastname)) |
+--------------------------------------+
| JOHN SMITH                           |
| JANE SMITH                           |
| JIMBO JONES                          |
| ANDY SMITH                           |
| CHRIS JONES                          |
| ANNA BELL                            |
| JIMMY CARR                           |
| ALBERT SMITH                         |
| JOHN DOE                             |
+--------------------------------------+
9 rows in set (0.00 sec)
```

If you want to uppercase just the last name, use

```
mysql> SELECT CONCAT_WS(' ', firstname, UCASE(lastname)) FROM master_name;
+-------------------------------------+
| CONCAT_WS(' ', firstname, UCASE(lastname)) |
+-------------------------------------+
| John SMITH                          |
| Jane SMITH                          |
| Jimbo JONES                         |
| Andy SMITH                          |
| Chris JONES                         |
| Anna BELL                           |
| Jimmy CARR                          |
| Albert SMITH                        |
| John DOE                            |
+-------------------------------------+
9 rows in set (0.00 sec)
```

Workshop

The workshop is designed to help you anticipate possible questions, review what you've learned, and begin learning how to put your knowledge into practice.

Quiz

1. What conversion specifier would you use with `printf()` to format an integer as a double? Indicate the full syntax required to convert the integer 33.

2. How would you pad the conversion you effected in question 1 with zeros so that the part before the decimal point is four characters long?

3. How would you specify a precision of two decimal places for the floating-point number you have been formatting in the previous questions?

4. What function would you use to extract a substring from a string?

5. How might you remove whitespace from the beginning of a string?

6. How would you break up a delimited string into an array of substrings?

7. Write an SQL query to find the starting position of a substring `"grape"` in a string `"applepearbananagrape"`.

8. Write a query that selects the last 5 characters from the string `"applepearbananagrape"`.

13

Answers

1. You use the conversion specifier f to format an integer as a double:

   ```
   printf("%f", 33 );
   ```

2. You can pad the output from `printf()` with the padding specifier—that is, a space or a zero followed by a number representing the number of characters you want to pad by.

   ```
   printf("%04f", 33 );
   ```

3. The precision specifier consists of a dot (.) followed by a number representing the precision you want to apply. It should be placed before the conversion specifier:

   ```
   printf("%04.2f", 33 );
   ```

4. The `substr()` function extracts and returns a substring.

5. The `ltrim()` function removes whitespace from the start of a string.

6. The `explode()` function splits up a string into an array.

7. `SELECT LOCATE('grape', 'applepearbananagrape');`

8. `SELECT RIGHT("applepearbananagrape", 5);`

Activities

1. Create a feedback form that accepts a user's full name and an email address. Use case conversion functions to capitalize the first letter of each name the user submits and print the result back to the browser. Check that the user's email address contains the @ symbol and print a warning otherwise.

2. Create an array of doubles and integers. Loop through the array converting each element to a floating-point number with a precision of 2. Right-align the output within a field of 20 characters.

3. Using both PHP and MySQL, practice using functions within functions, such as making case changes on substrings and concatenating strings.

HOUR **14**

Creating a Simple Discussion Forum

Although the ultimate goal of this hour is to create a simple discussion forum, a majority of the hour is devoted to understanding the thought processes behind designing an application using a relational database.

In this hour, you will learn

- Three types of table relationships
- How to normalize your database
- How to implement a good database design process
- How to create the tables, input forms, and display of a simple discussion forum

Types of Table Relationships

Table relationships come in several forms:

- One-to-one relationships
- One-to-many relationships
- Many-to-many relationships

For example, suppose you have a table called `employees` that contains each person's Social Security number, name, and the department in which he or she works. Suppose you also have a separate table called `departments`, containing the list of all available departments, made up of a Department ID and a name. In the `employees` table, the Department ID field matches an ID found in the `departments` table. You can see this type of relationship in Figure 14.1. The "PK" next to the field named stands for *primary key*, which you'll learn about during this hour.

FIGURE 14.1
The employees *and* departments *tables are related through the DeptID.*

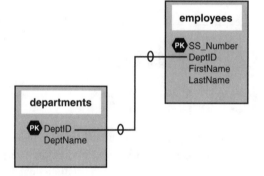

In the following sections, you will take a closer look at each of the relationship types.

One-to-One Relationships

In a one-to-one relationship, a key appears only once in a related table. The `employees` and `departments` tables do not have a one-to-one relationship because many employees undoubtedly belong to the same department. A one-to-one relationship exists, for example, if each employee is assigned one computer within a company. Figure 14.2 shows the one-to-one relationship of employees to computers.

The `employees` and `computers` tables in your database would look something like Figure 14.3, which represents a one-to-one relationship.

FIGURE 14.2
One computer is assigned to each employee.

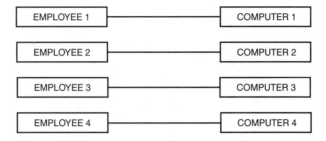

FIGURE 14.3
One-to-one relationship in the data model.

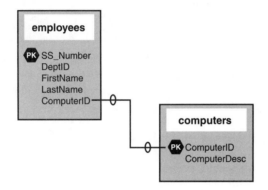

One-to-Many Relationships

In a one-to-many relationship, keys from one table appear multiple times in a related table. The example shown in Figure 14.1, indicating a connection between employees and departments, illustrates a one-to-many relationship. A real-world example would be an organizational chart of the department, as shown in Figure 14.4.

FIGURE 14.4
One department contains many employees.

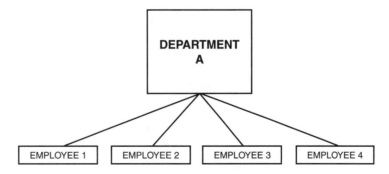

14

The one-to-many relationship is the most common type of relationship. Another practical example is the use of a state abbreviation in an address database; each state has a unique identifier (CA for California, PA for Pennsylvania, and so on), and each address in the United States has a state associated with it.

If you have eight friends in California and five in Pennsylvania, you will use only two distinct abbreviations in your table. One abbreviation represents a one-to-eight relationship (CA), and the other represents a one-to-five (PA) relationship.

Many-to-Many Relationships

The many-to-many relationship often causes problems in practical examples of normalized databases, so much so that it is common to simply break many-to-many relationships into a series of one-to-many relationships. In a many-to-many relationship, the key value of one table can appear many times in a related table. So far, it sounds like a one-to-many relationship, but here's the curveball: The opposite is also true, meaning that the primary key from that second table can also appear many times in the first table.

Think of such a relationship this way, using the example of students and classes. A student has an ID and a name. A class has an ID and a name. A student usually takes more than one class at a time, and a class always contains more than one student, as you can see in Figure 14.5.

FIGURE 14.5

Students take classes, classes contain students.

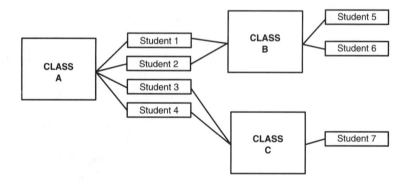

As you can see, this sort of relationship doesn't present an easy method for relating tables. Your tables could look like Figure 14.6, seemingly unrelated.

To make the theoretical many-to-many relationship, you would create an intermediate table, one that sits between the two tables and essentially maps them together. You might build one similar to the table in Figure 14.7.

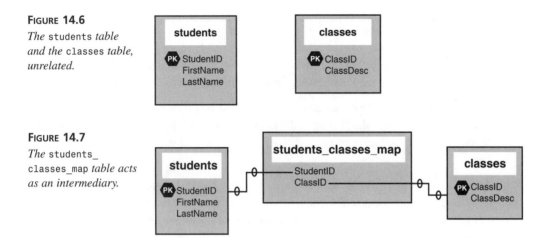

FIGURE **14.6**

The students *table and the* classes *table, unrelated.*

FIGURE **14.7**

The students_ classes_map *table acts as an intermediary.*

If you take the information in Figure 14.5 and put it into the intermediate table, you would have something like Figure 14.8.

FIGURE **14.8**

The students_ classes_map *table populated with data.*

STUDENTID	CLASSID
STUDENT 1	CLASS A
STUDENT 2	CLASS A
STUDENT 3	CLASS A
STUDENT 4	CLASS A
STUDENT 5	CLASS B
STUDENT 6	CLASS B
STUDENT 7	CLASS C
STUDENT 1	CLASS B
STUDENT 2	CLASS B
STUDENT 3	CLASS C
STUDENT 4	CLASS C

As you can see, many students and many classes happily coexist within the students_classes_map table.

With this introduction to the types of relationships, learning about normalization should be a snap.

14

Understanding Normalization

Normalization is simply a set of rules that will ultimately make your life easier when you're acting as a database administrator. It's the art of organizing your database in such a way that your tables are related where appropriate and flexible for future growth.

The sets of rules used in normalization are called *normal forms*. If your database design follows the first set of rules, it's considered in the *first normal form*. If the first three sets of rules of normalization are followed, your database is said to be in the *third normal form*.

Throughout this hour, you'll learn about each rule in the first, second, and third normal forms and, we hope, will follow them as you create your own applications. You'll be using a sample set of tables for a students and courses database and taking it to the third normal form.

Problems with the Flat Table

Before launching into the first normal form, you have to start with something that needs to be fixed. In the case of a database, it's the *flat table*. A flat table is like a spreadsheet—it has many, many columns. There are no relationships between multiple tables; all the data you could possibly want is right there in that flat table. This scenario is inefficient and consumes more physical space on your hard drive than a normalized database.

In your students and courses database, assume you have the following fields in your flat table:

- `StudentName`—The name of the student.
- `CourseID1`—The ID of the first course taken by the student.
- `CourseDescription1`—The description of the first course taken by the student.
- `CourseInstructor1`—The instructor of the first course taken by the student.
- `CourseID2`—The ID of the second course taken by the student.
- `CourseDescription2`—The description of the second course taken by the student.
- `CourseInstructor2`—The instructor of the second course taken by the student.
- Repeat `CourseID`, `CourseDescription`, and `CourseInstructor` columns many more times to account for all the classes students can take during their academic career.

With what you've learned so far, you should be able to identify the first problem area: `CourseID`, `CourseDescription`, and `CourseInstructor` columns are repeated groups.

Eliminating redundancy is the first step in normalization, so next you'll take this flat table to first normal form. If your table remained in its flat format, you could have a lot of unclaimed space, and a lot of space being used unnecessarily—not an efficient table design.

First Normal Form

The rules for the first normal form are as follows:

- Eliminate repeating information.
- Create separate tables for related data.

If you think about the flat table design, with many repeated sets of fields for the students and courses database, you can identify two distinct topics: students and courses. Taking your students and courses database to the first normal form would mean that you create two tables: one for students and one for courses, as shown in Figure 14.9.

FIGURE 14.9

Breaking the flat table into two tables.

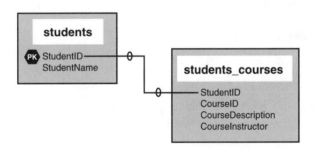

Your two tables now represent a one-to-many relationship of one student to many courses. Students can take as many courses as they want and are not limited to the number of CourseID/CourseDescription/CourseInstructor groupings that existed in the flat table.

The next step is to put the tables into second normal form.

Second Normal Form

The rule for the second normal form is

- No non-key attributes depend on a portion of the primary key.

In plain English, this means that if fields in your table are not entirely related to a primary key, you have more work to do. In the students and courses example, you need to break out the courses into their own table and modify the students_courses table.

14

CourseID, CourseDesc, and CourseInstructor can become a table called courses with a primary key of CourseID. The students_courses table should then just contain two fields: StudentID and CourseID. You can see this new design in Figure 14.10.

FIGURE 14.10

Taking your tables to second normal form.

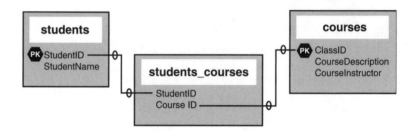

This structure should look familiar to you as a many-to-many relationship using an intermediary mapping table. The third normal form is the last form we'll look at, and you'll find it's just as simple to understand as the first two.

Third Normal Form

The rule for the third normal form is

- No attributes depend on other non-key attributes.

This rule simply means that you need to look at your tables and see whether you have more fields that can be broken down further and that aren't dependent on a key. Think about removing repeated data and you'll find your answer—instructors. Inevitably, an instructor will teach more than one class. However, CourseInstructor is not a key of any sort. So, if you break out this information and create a separate table purely for the sake of efficiency and maintenance (as shown in Figure 14.11), that's the third normal form.

FIGURE 14.11

Taking your tables to third normal form.

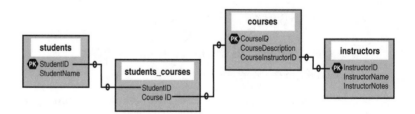

Third normal form is usually adequate for removing redundancy and allowing for flexibility and growth. The next section will give you some pointers for the thought process involved in database design and where it fits in the overall design process of your application.

Following the Design Process

The greatest problem in application design is a lack of forethought. As it applies to database-driven applications, the design process must include a thorough evaluation of your database—what it should hold, how data relates to each other, and most importantly, whether it is scalable.

The general steps in the design process are

- Define the objective.
- Design the data structures (tables, fields).
- Discern relationships.
- Define and implement business rules.
- Create the application.

Creating the application is the last step—not the first! Many developers take an idea for an application, build it, and then go back and try to make a set of database tables fit into it. This approach is completely backward, inefficient, and will cost a lot of time and money.

Before you start any application design process, sit down and talk it out. If you can't describe your application—including the objectives, audience, and target market—then you're not ready to build it, let alone model the database.

After you can describe the actions and nuances of your application to other people and have it make sense to them, you can start thinking about the tables you want to create. Start with big flat tables because, after you write them down, your newfound normalization skills will take over. You will be able to find your redundancies and visualize your relationships.

The next step is to do the normalization. Go from flat table to first normal form and so on up to the third normal form if possible. Use paper, pencils, sticky notes, or whatever helps you to visualize the tables and relationships. There's no shame in data modeling on sticky notes until you're ready to create the tables themselves. Plus, using them is a lot cheaper than buying software to do it for you; software ranges from one hundred to several thousands of dollars!

After you have a preliminary data model, look at it from the application's point of view. Or look at it from the point of view of the person using the application you're building. This is the point where you define business rules and see whether your data model will break. An example of a business rule for an online registration application is, "Each user must have one e-mail address, and it must not belong to any other user." If `EmailAddress`

14

wasn't a unique field in your data model, your model would be broken based on the business rule.

After your business rules have been applied to your data model, only then can application programming begin. You can rest assured that your data model is solid and you will not be programming yourself into a brick wall. The latter event is all too common.

Creating a Discussion Forum

In the following sections, you'll learn the design process behind a simple discussion forum. This includes developing the database tables, user input forms, and display of the results. When broken into pieces like this, such a task seems quite simple—and it is!

Designing the Database Tables

Think of the basic components of a forum: topics and posts. A forum—if properly used by its patrons—should have several topics, and each of those topics will have one or more posts by users. Knowing that, you should realize that the posts are tied to the topics through a key field. This key forms the relationship between the two tables.

Think about the requirements for the topics themselves. You definitely need a field for the title, and subsequently you may want fields to hold the creation time and the identification of the user who created the topic. Similarly, think of the requirements for the posts: You want the text of the post, the time it was created, and the person creating it. Most importantly, you need that key to tie the post to the topic.

The following two table creation statements create these tables, called forum_topics and forum_posts:

```
mysql> create table forum_topics (
    -> topic_id int not null primary key auto_increment,
    -> topic_title varchar (150),
    -> topic_create_time datetime,
    -> topic_owner varchar (150)
    -> );
Query OK, 0 rows affected (0.03 sec)

mysql> create table forum_posts (
    -> post_id int not null primary key auto_increment,
    -> topic_id int not null,
    -> post_text text,
    -> post_create_time datetime,
    -> post_owner varchar (150)
    -> );
Query OK, 0 rows affected (0.00 sec)
```

In this forum example, we will identify users by their e-mail addresses and not require any sort of login sequence. In the activity at the end of this hour, you'll be given some hints on extending this forum example to fit within an environment of registered users.

You should now have two empty tables, waiting for some input. In the next section, you'll create the input forms for adding a topic and a post.

Creating the Input Forms and Scripts

Before you can add any posts, you must add a topic to the forum. It is common practice in forum creation to add the topic and the first post in that topic at the same time. From a user's point of view, it doesn't make much sense to add a topic and then go back, select the topic, and add a reply. You want the process to be as smooth as possible.

Listing 14.1 shows the form for a new topic creation, which includes a space for the first post in the topic.

LISTING 14.1 Form for Adding a Topic

```
 1: <html>
 2: <head>
 3: <title>Add a Topic</title>
 4: </head>
 5: <body>
 6: <h1>Add a Topic</h1>
 7: <form method=post action="do_addtopic.php">
 8: <p><strong>Your E-Mail Address:</strong><br>
 9: <input type="text" name="topic_owner" size=40 maxlength=150>
10: <p><strong>Topic Title:</strong><br>
11: <input type="text" name="topic_title" size=40 maxlength=150>
12: <P><strong>Post Text:</strong><br>
13: <textarea name="post_text" rows=8 cols=40 wrap=virtual></textarea>
14: <P><input type="submit" name="submit" value="Add Topic"></p>
15: </form>
16: </body>
17: </html>
```

Seems simple enough—the three fields shown in the form, which you can see in Figure 14.12, are all you need to complete both tables; your script and database can fill in the rest. Save Listing 14.1 as something like addtopic.html and put it in your Web server document root so that you can follow along.

14

FIGURE 14.12

The topic creation form.

To create the entry in the forum_topics table, you use the topic_title and topic_owner fields from the input form. The topic_id and topic_create_time fields will be filled in automatically. Similarly, in the forum_posts table, you use the post_text and topic_owner fields from the input form, and the post_id, post_create_time, and the topic_id fields will be filled in automatically. Because you need a value for the topic_id field to be able to complete the entry in the forum_posts table, you know that query must happen after the query to insert the record in the forum_topics table.

Listing 14.2 creates the script to add these records to the table.

LISTING 14.2 Script for Adding a Topic

```
 1: <?php
 2: //check for required fields from the form
 3: if ((!$_POST[topic_owner]) || (!$_POST[topic_title])
 4:     || (!$_POST[post_text])) {
 5:     header("Location: addtopic.html");
 6:     exit;
 7: }
 8:
 9: //connect to server and select database
10: $conn = mysql_connect("localhost", "joeuser", "somepass")
11:     or die(mysql_error());
12: mysql_select_db("testDB",$conn)  or die(mysql_error());
13:
14: //create and issue the first query
15: $add_topic = "insert into forum_topics values ('', '$_POST[topic_title]',
```

LISTING **14.2** continued

```
16:      now(), '$_POST[topic_owner]')";
17: mysql_query($add_topic,$conn) or die(mysql_error());
18:
19: //get the id of the last query
20: $topic_id = mysql_insert_id();
21:
22: //create and issue the second query
23: $add_post = "insert into forum_posts values ('', '$topic_id',
24:      '$_POST[post_text]', now(), '$_POST[topic_owner]')";
25: mysql_query($add_post,$conn) or die(mysql_error());
26:
27: //create nice message for user
28: $msg = "<P>The <strong>$topic_title</strong> topic has been created.</p>";
29: ?>
30: <html>
31: <head>
32: <title>New Topic Added</title>
33: </head>
34: <body>
35: <h1>New Topic Added</h1>
36: <?php print $msg; ?>
37: </body>
38: </html>
```

Lines 3–7 check for the three required fields we need to complete both tables. If either one of these fields is not present, the user is redirected to the original form.

Lines 10–12 form the database connection, which should be familiar to you by now. Lines 15–17 create and insert the first query, which adds the topic to the forum_topics table. Note that the first field is left blank, so the automatically incrementing number is added by the system. Similarly, the now() function is used to time stamp the record with the current time. The other fields in the record are completed using values from the form.

Line 20 shows the use of a very handy function: mysql_insert_id(). This function retrieves the primary key ID of the last record inserted into the database by this script. In this case, mysql_insert_id() gets the id value from the forum_topics table, which will become the entry for the topic_id field in the forum_posts table.

Lines 23–25 create and insert the second query, again using a mixture of information known and supplied by the system. Line 28 simply creates a message for the user, and the rest of the script rounds out the display.

Save this listing as do_addtopic.php—the name of the action in the previous script—and place it in the document root of your Web server. Complete the form and then submit it,

14

and you should see the "New Topic Added" message. Figures 14.13 and 14.14 show the sequence of events.

FIGURE 14.13

Adding a topic and first post.

FIGURE 14.14

Successful addition of a topic and first post.

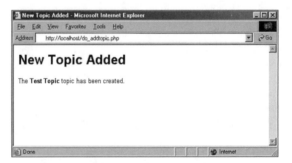

In the next section, you'll put together two more pieces of the puzzle: displaying the topics and posts, and replying to a topic.

Displaying the Topic List

Now that you have a topic and at least one post in your database, you can display this information and let people add new topics or reply to existing ones. In Listing 14.3, we take a step back and create a topic listing page. This page will show the basic information of each topic and provide the user with a link to add a new topic; you already have the form and script for that. This script would actually be an entry page for your forum.

LISTING 14.3   Topic Listing Script

```
 1: <?php
 2: //connect to server and select database
 3: $conn = mysql_connect("localhost", "joeuser", "somepass")
 4:     or die(mysql_error());
 5: mysql_select_db("testDB",$conn)  or die(mysql_error());
 6:
 7: //gather the topics
 8: $get_topics = "select topic_id, topic_title,
 9: date_format(topic_create_time,  '%b %e %Y at %r') as fmt_topic_create_time,
10: topic_owner from forum_topics order by topic_create_time desc";
11: $get_topics_res = mysql_query($get_topics,$conn) or die(mysql_error());
12: if (mysql_num_rows($get_topics_res) < 1) {
13:     //there are no topics, so say so
14:     $display_block = "<P><em>No topics exist.</em></p>";
15: } else {
16:     //create the display string
17:     $display_block = "
18:     <table cellpadding=3 cellspacing=1 border=1>
19:     <tr>
20:     <th>TOPIC TITLE</th>
21:     <th># of POSTS</th>
22:     </tr>";
23:
24:     while ($topic_info = mysql_fetch_array($get_topics_res)) {
25:         $topic_id = $topic_info['topic_id'];
26:         $topic_title = stripslashes($topic_info['topic_title']);
27:         $topic_create_time = $topic_info['fmt_topic_create_time'];
28:         $topic_owner = stripslashes($topic_info['topic_owner']);
29:
30:         //get number of posts
31:         $get_num_posts = "select count(post_id) from forum_posts
32:             where topic_id = $topic_id";
33:         $get_num_posts_res = mysql_query($get_num_posts,$conn)
34:             or die(mysql_error());
35:         $num_posts = mysql_result($get_num_posts_res,0,'count(post_id)');
36:
37:         //add to display
38:         $display_block .= "
39:         <tr>
40:         <td><a href=\"showtopic.php?topic_id=$topic_id\">
41:             <strong>$topic_title</strong></a><br>
42:         Created on $topic_create_time by $topic_owner</td>
43:         <td align=center>$num_posts</td>
44:         </tr>";
45:     }
46:
47:     //close up the table
48:     $display_block .= "</table>";
```

14

LISTING 14.3   continued

```
49: }
50: ?>
51: <html>
52: <head>
53: <title>Topics in My Forum</title>
54: </head>
55: <body>
56: <h1>Topics in My Forum</h1>
57: <?php print $display_block; ?>
58: <P>Would you like to <a href="addtopic.html">add a topic</a>?</p>
59: </body>
60: </html>
```

Although Listing 14.3 looks like a lot of code, it's actually many small, simple concepts you've already encountered. Lines 3–5 make the connection to the database, in preparation for issuing queries. Lines 8–10 show the first of these queries, and this particular one selects all the topic information, in order by descending date. In other words, display the topic that was created last (the newest topic) at the top of the list. In the query, notice the use of the `date_format()` function to create a much nicer date display than the one stored in the database.

Line 12 checks for the presence of any records returned by the query. If no records are returned, and therefore no topics are in the table, you'll want to tell the user. Line 14 creates this message. At this point, if no topics existed, the script would break out of the `if...else` construct and be over with, the next action occurring at line 51, which is the start of the static HTML. If the script ended here, the message created in line 14 would be printed in line 57, and you would see something like Figure 14.15.

FIGURE 14.15

No topics found.

If, however, you have topics in your forum_topics table, the script continues at line 15. At line 17 a block of text is started, containing the beginnings of an HTML table. Lines 18–22 set up a table with two columns: one for the title and one for the number of posts. The text block is stopped momentarily, and at line 24 we begin to loop through the results of the original query.

The while loop in line 24 says that while there are elements to be extracted from the result set, extract each row as an array called $topic_info, and use the field names as the array element to assign the value to a new variable. So, the first element we try to extract is the topic_id field, on line 25. We set the value of $topic_id to $topic_info['topic_id'], meaning that we get a local value for $topic_id from an array called $topic_info, containing a slot called topic_id. Continue doing this for the $topic_title, $topic_create_time, and $topic_owner variables in lines 26–28. The stripslashes() function removes any escape characters that were input into the table at the time of record insertion.

In lines 31–35 we issue another query, in the context of the while loop, to get the number of posts for that particular topic. In line 38 we continue the creation of the $display_block string, using the concatenation operator (.=) to make sure this string is tacked on to the end of the string we have created so far. In line 40 we create the HTML table column to display the link to the file that will show the topic (showtopic.php), and also print the topic owner and creation time. The second HTML table column, on line 43, shows the number of posts. On line 45 we break out of the while loop and in line 48 add the last bit to the $display_block string, to close the table. The remaining lines print the HTML for the page, including the value of the $display_block string.

If you save this file as topiclist.php and place it in your Web server document root, and if you have topics in your database tables, you may see something like Figure 14.16.

FIGURE 14.16

Topics are available.

14

Displaying the Posts in a Topic

As you may have guessed, the next item on the task list is to build that showtopic.php file, to show the topic's postings. Listing 14.4 does just that.

LISTING 14.4   Script to Show Topic Posts

```
 1: <?php
 2: //check for required info from the query string
 3: if (!$_GET[topic_id]) {
 4:    header("Location: topiclist.php");
 5:    exit;
 6: }
 7:
 8: //connect to server and select database
 9: $conn = mysql_connect("localhost", "joeuser", "somepass")
10:    or die(mysql_error());
11: mysql_select_db("testDB",$conn)  or die(mysql_error());
12:
13: //verify the topic exists
14: $verify_topic = "select topic_title from forum_topics where
15:    topic_id = $_GET[topic_id]";
16: $verify_topic_res = mysql_query($verify_topic, $conn)
17:    or die(mysql_error());
18:
19: if (mysql_num_rows($verify_topic_res) < 1) {
20:    //this topic does not exist
21:    $display_block = "<P><em>You have selected an invalid topic.
22:    Please <a href=\"topiclist.php\">try again</a>.</em></p>";
23: } else {
24:    //get the topic title
25:    $topic_title = stripslashes(mysql_result($verify_topic_res,0,
26:        'topic_title'));
27:
28:    //gather the posts
29:    $get_posts = "select post_id, post_text, date_format(post_create_time,
30:        '%b %e %Y at %r') as fmt_post_create_time, post_owner from
31:        forum_posts where topic_id = $_GET[topic_id]
32:        order by post_create_time asc";
33:
34:    $get_posts_res = mysql_query($get_posts,$conn) or die(mysql_error());
35:
36:    //create the display string
37:    $display_block = "
38:    <P>Showing posts for the <strong>$topic_title</strong> topic:</p>
39:
40:    <table width=100% cellpadding=3 cellspacing=1 border=1>
41:    <tr>
42:    <th>AUTHOR</th>
```

LISTING 14.4   continued

```
43:     <th>POST</th>
44:     </tr>";
45:
46:     while ($posts_info = mysql_fetch_array($get_posts_res)) {
47:         $post_id = $posts_info['post_id'];
48:         $post_text = nl2br(stripslashes($posts_info['post_text']));
49:         $post_create_time = $posts_info['fmt_post_create_time'];
50:         $post_owner = stripslashes($posts_info['post_owner']);
51:
52:         //add to display
53:         $display_block .= "
54:         <tr>
55:         <td width=35% valign=top>$post_owner<br>[$post_create_time]</td>
56:         <td width=65% valign=top>$post_text<br><br>
57:          <a href=\"replytopost.php?post_id=$post_id\"><strong>REPLY TO
58:          POST</strong></a></td>
59:         </tr>";
60:     }
61:
62:     //close up the table
63:     $display_block .= "</table>";
64: }
65: ?>
66: <html>
67: <head>
68: <title>Posts in Topic</title>
69: </head>
70: <body>
71: <h1>Posts in Topic</h1>
72: <?php print $display_block; ?>
73: </body>
74: </html>
```

In Listing 14.4, lines 3–6 check for the existence of a value for topic_id in the GET query string. Because we're showing all the posts in a selected topic, we need to know which topic, and this is the manner in which the information is given to us. If a value in $_GET[topic_id] does not exist, the user is redirected to the topic listing page.

If you made it past the check for a topic_id, Lines 9–11 make the connection to the database, in preparation for issuing queries. Lines 14–17 show the first of these queries, and this one is used to validate that the topic_id sent in the query string is actually a valid entry, by selecting the associated topic_title for the topic in question. If the validation fails the test in line 19, a message is created in lines 21–22, and the script breaks out of the if...else statement and finishes up by printing HTML. This output looks like Figure 14.17.

14

Figure 14.17

Invalid topic selected.

If, however, the topic is valid, we extract the value of `topic_title` in line 25, again using `stripslashes()` to remove any escape characters. Next, the query is issued in lines 29–32 to gather all the posts associated with that topic, in ascending order by time. In this case, newest posts are at the bottom of the list. At line 37 a block of text is started, containing the beginnings of an HTML table. Lines 40–44 set up a table with two columns: one for the author of the post and one for the post text itself. The text block is stopped momentarily and at line 46 we begin to loop through the results of the original query.

The `while` loop in line 46 says that while there are elements to be extracted from the result set, extract each row as an array called `$posts_info`, and use the field names as the array element to assign the value to a new variable. So, the first element we try to extract is the `post_id` field, on line 47. We set the value of `$post_id` to `$posts_info['post_id']`, meaning that we get a local value for `$post_id` from an array called `$posts_info`, containing a slot called `post_id`. Continue doing this for the `$post_text`, `$post_create_time`, and `$post_owner` variables in lines 48–50. The `stripslashes()` function is again used to remove any escape characters, and the `nl2br()` function is used on the value of `$posts_info[post_text]`, to replace all newline characters with HTML `<br>` characters.

In line 53 we continue the creation of the `$display_block` string, using the concatenation operator (`.=`) to make sure this string is tacked on to the end of the string we have created so far. In line 54 we create the HTML table column to display the author and creation time of the post. The second HTML table row, on line 56, shows the text of the post as well as a link to reply to the post. On line 60 we break out of the `while` loop and on line 63 add the last bit to the `$display_block` string, to close the table. The remaining lines print the HTML for the page, including the value of the `$display_block` string.

If you save this file as showtopic.php and place it in your Web server document root, and if you have posts in your database tables, you may see something like Figure 14.18.

FIGURE 14.18

Posts in a topic.

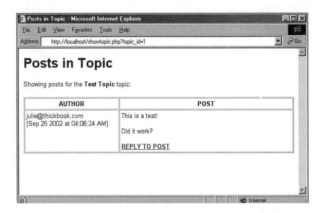

A one-post topic is boring, so let's finish up this hour by creating the script to add a post to a topic.

Adding Posts to a Topic

In this final step, you will create replytopost.php, which will look remarkably similar to the form and script used to add a topic. Listing 14.5 shows the code for this all-in-one form and script.

LISTING 14.5   Script to Add Replies to a Topic

```
 1: <?php
 2: //connect to server and select database; we'll need it soon
 3: $conn = mysql_connect("localhost", "joeuser", "somepass")
 4:     or die(mysql_error());
 5: mysql_select_db("testDB",$conn)  or die(mysql_error());
 6:
 7: //check to see if we're showing the form or adding the post
 8: if ($_POST[op] != "addpost") {
 9:    // showing the form; check for required item in query string
10:    if (!$_GET[post_id]) {
11:        header("Location: topiclist.php");
12:        exit;
13:    }
14:
15:     //still have to verify topic and post
16:    $verify = "select ft.topic_id, ft.topic_title from
17:     forum_posts as fp left join forum_topics as ft on
18:     fp.topic_id = ft.topic_id where fp.post_id = $_GET[post_id]";
```

14

LISTING 14.5   continued

```
19:
20:      $verify_res = mysql_query($verify, $conn) or die(mysql_error());
21:       if (mysql_num_rows($verify_res) < 1) {
22:          //this post or topic does not exist
23:          header("Location: topiclist.php");
24:          exit;
25:       } else {
26:          //get the topic id and title
27:          $topic_id = mysql_result($verify_res,0,'topic_id');
28:          $topic_title = stripslashes(mysql_result($verify_res,
29:           0,'topic_title'));
30:
31:          print "
32:          <html>
33:          <head>
34:          <title>Post Your Reply in $topic_title</title>
35:          </head>
36:          <body>
37:          <h1>Post Your Reply in $topic_title</h1>
38:          <form method=post action=\"$_SERVER[PHP_SELF]\">
39:
40:          <p><strong>Your E-Mail Address:</strong><br>
41:          <input type=\"text\" name=\"post_owner\" size=40 maxlength=150>
42:
43:          <P><strong>Post Text:</strong><br>
44:          <textarea name=\"post_text\" rows=8 cols=40 wrap=virtual></textarea>
45:
46:          <input type=\"hidden\" name=\"op\" value=\"addpost\">
47:          <input type=\"hidden\" name=\"topic_id\" value=\"$topic_id\">
48:
49:          <P><input type=\"submit\" name=\"submit\" value=\"Add Post\"></p>
50:
51:          </form>
52:          </body>
53:          </html>";
54:       }
55: } else if ($_POST[op] == "addpost") {
56:       //check for required items from form
57:       if ((!$_POST[topic_id]) || (!$_POST[post_text]) ||
58:        (!$_POST[post_owner])) {
59:          header("Location: topiclist.php");
60:          exit;
61:       }
62:
63:       //add the post
64:       $add_post = "insert into forum_posts values ('', '$_POST[topic_id]',
65:        '$_POST[post_text]', now(), '$_POST[post_owner]')";
66:       mysql_query($add_post,$conn) or die(mysql_error());
```

LISTING 14.5   continued

```
67:
68:     //redirect user to topic
69:     header("Location: showtopic.php?topic_id=$topic_id");
70:     exit;
71: }
72: ?>
```

Lines 3–5 make the database connection at the outset of the script. Although you're performing multiple tasks depending on the status of the form (whether it's being shown or submitted), both conditions require database interaction at some point.

Line 8 checks to see whether the form is being submitted. If the value of $_POST[op] is not "addpost", the form has not yet been submitted. Therefore, it must be shown. Before showing the form, however, you must check for that one required item; lines 10–13 check for the existence of a value for post_id in the GET query string. If a value in $_GET[post_id] does not exist, the user is redirected to the topic listing page.

If you made it past the check for a topic_id, lines 17–20 issue a complicated-looking query that gets the topic_id and topic_title from the forum_topics table, based on the only value that you know: the value of the post_id. This query both validates the existence of the post and gets information you will need later in the script. Lines 21–24 act on the results of this validity test, again redirecting the user back to the topiclist.php page.

If the post is valid, you extract the value of topic_id and topic_title in lines 27–29, again using stripslashes() to remove any escape characters. Next, the entirety of the form for adding a post is printed to the screen, and that's it for this script until the form submission button is pressed. In the form, you see that the action is $_SERVER[PHP_SELF] on line 38, indicating that this script will be recalled into action. Two hidden fields are present, in lines 46 and 47, which hold the information that needs to be passed along to the next iteration of the script.

Moving along to line 55, this block of code is executed when the script is reloaded and the value of $_POST[op] (one of the hidden fields in the form) is "addpost". This block checks for the presence of all required fields from the form (lines 57–61) and then, if they are all present, issues the query to add the post to the database (lines 64–66). After the post is added to the database, the showtopic.php page is reloaded (lines 69–70), showing the user's new post along in the line.

If you save this file as replytopost.php and place it in your Web server document root, try it out and you may see something like Figures 14.19 and 14.20.

14

FIGURE 14.19
Preparing to add a post.

FIGURE 14.20
A post was added to the list.

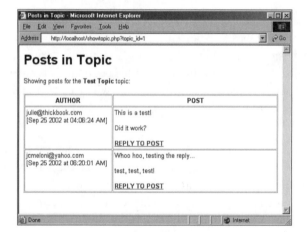

Summary

Following proper database design is the only way your application will be efficient, flexible, and easy to manage and maintain. An important aspect of database design is to use relationships between tables instead of throwing all your data into one long flat file. Types of relationships include one-to-one, one-to-many, and many-to-many.

Using relationships to properly organize your data is called normalization. There are many levels of normalization, but the primary levels are the first, second, and third normal forms. Each level has a rule or two that you must follow. Following all the rules helps ensure that your database is well organized and flexible.

To take an idea from inception through to fruition, you should follow a design process. This process essentially says "think before you act." Discuss rules, requirements, and objectives; then create the final version of your normalized tables. In this hour, you applied this knowledge to the creation of a simple discussion form, using PHP and MySQL to create input forms and display pages for topics and posts.

Q&A

Q Are there only three normal forms?

A No, there are more than three normal forms. Additional forms are the Boyce-Codd normal form, fourth normal form, and fifth normal form/Join-Projection normal form. These forms are not often followed because the benefits of doing so are outweighed by the cost in man-hours and database efficiency.

Workshop

The workshop is designed to help you anticipate possible questions, review what you've learned, and begin learning how to put your knowledge into practice.

Quiz

1. Name three types of data relationships.

2. Because many-to-many relationships are difficult to represent in an efficient database design, what should you do?

Answers

1. One-to-one, one-to-many, many-to-many.

2. Create a series of one-to-many relationships using intermediary mapping tables.

Activity

Explain each of the three normal forms to a person who works with spreadsheets and flat tables.

14

HOUR 15

Restricting Access to Your Applications

This hour explains how to use Apache to restrict access to parts of a Web site based on the identity of the user or on information about the request. On the application side, you can create your own mechanism for user validation and check the validity of your users through cookies.

In this hour, you will learn

- How to restrict access based on the user, client IP address, domain name, and browser version
- How to use the user management tools provided with Apache
- How to store and retrieve cookie information
- How to use cookies for authentication

Authentication Overview

Authorization and authentication are common requirements for many Web sites. Authentication establishes the identity of parties in a communication.

You can authenticate yourself by something you know (a password, a cookie), something you have (an ID card, a key), something you are (your fingerprint, your retina), or a combination of these elements. In the context of the Web, authentication is usually restricted to the use of passwords and certificates.

Authorization deals with protecting access to resources. You can authorize based on several factors, such as the IP address the user is coming from, the user's browser, the content the user is trying to access, or who the user is (which is previously determined via authentication).

Apache includes several modules that provide authentication and access control and that can be used to protect both dynamic and static content. You can either use one of these modules or implement your own access control at the application level and provide customized login screens, single sign-on, and other advanced functionality.

Client Authentication

Users are authenticated for tracking or authorization purposes. The HTTP specification provides two authentication mechanisms: basic and digest. In both cases, the process is the following:

1. A client tries to access restricted content in the Web server.

2. Apache checks whether the client is providing a username and password. If not, Apache returns an HTTP 401 status code, indicating user authentication is required.

3. The client reads the response and prompts the user for the required username and password (usually with a pop-up window).

4. The client retries accessing the Web page, this time transmitting the username and password as part of the HTTP request. The client remembers the username and password and transmits them in later requests to the same site, so the user does not need to retype them for every request.

5. Apache checks the validity of the credentials and grants or denies access based on the user identity and other access rules.

In the basic authentication scheme, the username and password are transmitted in clear text, as part of the HTTP request headers. This poses a security risk because an attacker could easily peek at the conversation between server and browser, learn the username and password, and reuse them freely afterward.

The digest authentication provides increased security because it transmits a digest instead of the clear text password. The digest is based on a combination of several parameters, including the username, password, and request method. The server can calculate the digest on its own and check that the client knows the password, even when the password itself is not transmitted over the network.

A *digest algorithm* is a mathematical operation that takes a text and returns another text, a digest, which uniquely identifies the original one. A good digest algorithm should make sure that, at least for practical purposes, different input texts produce different digests and that the original input text cannot be derived from the digest. MD5 is the name of a commonly used digest algorithm.

Unfortunately, although the specification has been available for quite some time, only very recent browsers support digest authentication. This means that for practical purposes, digest authentication is restricted to scenarios in which you have control over the browser software of your clients, such as in a company intranet.

In any case, for both digest and basic authentication, the requested information itself is transmitted unprotected over the network. A better choice to secure access to your Web site involves using the HTTP over SSL protocol, as described in Hour 23, "Setting Up a Secure Web Server."

User Management Methods

When the authentication module receives the username and password from the client, it needs to verify that they are valid against an existing repository of users. The usernames and passwords can be stored in a variety of back ends. Apache bundles support for file- and database-based authentication mechanisms. Third-party modules provide support for additional mechanisms such as Lightweight Directory Access Protocol (LDAP) and Network Information Services (NIS).

Apache Authentication Module Functionality

Apache provides the basic framework and directives to perform authentication and access control. The authentication modules provide support for validating passwords against a specific back end. Users can optionally be organized in groups, easing management of access control rules.

Apache provides three built-in directives related to authentication that will be used with any of the authentication modules: AuthName, AuthType, and Require.

AuthName accepts a string argument, the name for the authentication realm. A *realm* is a logical area of the Web server that you are asking the password for. It will be displayed in the browser pop-up window.

AuthType specifies the type of browser authentication: basic or digest.

`Require` enables you to specify a list of users or groups that will be allowed access. The syntax is `Require user` followed by one or more usernames, or `Require group` followed by one or more group names. For example:

```
Require user joe bob
```

or

```
Require group employee contractor
```

If you want to grant access to anyone who provides a valid username and password, you can do so with

```
Require valid-user
```

With the preceding directives, you can control who has access to specific virtual hosts, directories, files, and so on. Although authentication and authorization are separate concepts, in practice they are tied together in Apache. Access is granted based on specific user identity or group membership. Some third-party modules, such as certain LDAP-based modules, allow for clearer separation between authentication and authorization.

The authentication modules included with Apache provide

- **Back-end storage**—Provide text or database files containing the username and group information
- **User management**—Supply tools for creating and managing users and groups in the back-end storage
- **Authoritative information**—Specify whether the results of the module are authoritative

Sometimes users will not be allowed access because their information is not found in the user database provided by the module, or because no authentication rules matched their information. In that case, one of two situations will occur:

- If the module specifies its results as authoritative, a user will be denied access and Apache will return an error.
- If the module specifies its results as not authoritative, other modules can have a chance of authenticating the user.

This enables you to have a main authorization module that knows about most users, and to be able to have additional modules that can authenticate the rest of the users.

File-Based Authentication

The mod_auth Apache module provides basic authentication via text files containing usernames and passwords, similar to how traditional Unix authentication works with the /etc/passwd and /etc/groups files.

Back-End Storage

You need to specify the file containing the list of usernames and passwords and, optionally, the file containing the list of groups.

The users file is a Unix-style password file, containing names of users and encrypted passwords. The entries look like the following, on Unix, using the crypt algorithm:

```
admin:iFrlxqg0Q6RQ6
```

and on Windows, using the MD5 algorithm:

```
admin:$apr1$Ug3.....$jVTedbQWBKTfXsn5jK6UX/
```

The groups file contains a list of groups and the users that belong to each one of them, separated by spaces, such as in the following entry:

```
web: admin joe Daniel
```

The AuthUserFile and the AuthGroupFile directives take a path argument, pointing to the users file and the groups file. The groups file is optional.

User Management

Apache includes the htpasswd utility on Unix and htpasswd.exe on Windows; they are designed to help you manage user password files. Both versions are functionally identical, but the Windows version uses a different method to encrypt the password. The encryption is transparent to the user and administrator. The first time you add a user, you need to type

```
#> htpasswd -c file userid
```

where file is the password file that will contain the list of usernames and passwords, and userid is the username you want to add. You will be prompted for a password, and the file will be created. For example, on Linux/Unix, the line

```
#> htpasswd -c /usr/local/apache2/conf/htusers admin
```

will create the password file /usr/local/apache2/conf/htusers and add the admin user.

Similar functionality exists on Windows, where the command-line operation might look something like the following:

```
htpasswd -c "C:\Program Files\Apache Group\Apache2\conf\htusers" admin
```

The `-c` command-line option tells `htpasswd` that it should create the file. When you want to add users to an existing password file, do not use the `-c` option; otherwise, the file will be overwritten.

It is important that you store the password file outside the document root and thus make it inaccessible via a Web browser. Otherwise, an attacker could download the file and get a list of your usernames and passwords. Although the passwords are encrypted, when you have the file, it is possible to perform a brute-force attack to try to guess them.

Authoritative

The `AuthAuthoritative` directive takes a value of `on` or `off`. By default, it is on, meaning that the module authentication results are authoritative. That is, if the user is not found or does not match any rules, access will be denied.

Using `mod_auth`

Listing 15.1 shows a sample configuration, restricting access to the `private` directory in the document root to authenticated users present in the `htusers` password file. Note that the optional `AuthGroupFile` directive is not present.

LISTING 15.1   File-Based Authentication Example

```
1: <Directory /usr/local/apache2/htdocs/private>
2: AuthType Basic
3: AuthName "Private Area"
4: AuthUserFile /usr/local/apache2/conf/htusers
5: AuthAuthoritative on
6: Require valid-user
7: </Directory>
```

Database File-Based Access Control

Storing usernames and passwords in plain text files is convenient, but they do not scale well. Apache needs to open and read the files sequentially to look for a particular user. When the number of users grows, this operation becomes very time-consuming. The mod_auth_dbm module enables you to replace the text-based files with indexed database files, which can handle a much greater number of users without performance degradation. mod_auth_dbm is included with Apache but is not enabled by default.

15

Back-End Storage

The `mod_auth_dbm` module provides two directives, `AuthDBMUserFile` and `AuthDBMGroupFile`, that point to the database files containing the usernames and groups. Unlike plain text files, both directives can point to the same file, which combines both users and groups.

User Management

Apache provides a Perl script (`dbmmanage` on Unix and `dbmmanage.pl` on Windows) that allows you to create and manage users and groups stored in a database file. Under Unix, you might need to edit the first line of the script to point to the location of the Perl interpreter in your system. On Windows, you need to install the additional MD5 password package. If you are using ActiveState Perl, start the Perl package manager and type

```
install Crypt-PasswdMD5
```

To add a user to a database on Unix, type

```
#> ./dbmmanage dbfile adduser userid
```

On Windows, type

```
perl ./dbmmanage.pl dbfile adduser userid
```

You will be prompted for the password, and the user will be added to the existing database file or a new file will be created if one does not exist.

When adding a user, you can optionally specify the groups it belongs to as comma-separated arguments. The following command adds the user `daniel` to the database file `/usr/local/apache2/conf/dbmusers` and makes it a member of the groups `employee` and `engineering`:

```
#> dbmmanage /usr/local/apache2/conf/dbmusers adduser daniel employee,engineering
```

If you ever need to delete the user `daniel`, you can issue the following command:

```
#> dbmmanage dbfile delete daniel
```

The `dbmmanage` program supports additional options. You can find complete syntax information in the `dbmmanage` manual page or by invoking `dbmmanage` without any arguments.

> Apache 2.0 provides an additional utility, `htdbm`, that does not depend on Perl and provides all the functionality that `dbmmanage` does.

Using Apache for Access Control

The mod_access module, enabled by default, allows you to restrict access to resources based on parameters of the client request, such as the presence of a specific header or the IP address or hostname of the client.

Implementing Access Rules

You can specify access rules using the Allow and Deny directives. Each of these directives takes a list of arguments such as IP addresses, environment variables, and domain names.

Allow/Deny Access by IP Addresses

You can deny or grant access to a client based on its IP address:

```
Allow from 10.0.0.1 10.0.0.2 10.0.0.3
```

You can also specify IP address ranges, with a partial IP address or a network/mask pair. Additionally, you can specify the first one, two, or three bytes of an IP address. Any IP address containing those will match this rule. For example, the rule

```
Deny from 10.0
```

will match any address starting with 10.0, such as 10.0.1.0 and 10.0.0.1.

You can also utilize the IP address and the netmask; the IP address specifies the network and the mask specifies which bits belong to the network prefix and which ones belong to the nodes. The rule

```
Allow from 10.0.0.0/255.255.255.0
```

will match IP addresses 10.0.0.1, 10.0.0.2, and so on, to 10.0.0.254.

You can also specify the network mask via high-order bits. For example, you could write the previous rule as

```
Allow from 10.0.0.0/24
```

Allow/Deny Access by Domain Name

You can control access based on specific hostnames or partial domain names. For example, Allow from example.com will match www.example.com, foo.example.com, and so on.

Enabling access rules based on domain names forces Apache to do a reverse
DNS lookup on the client address, bypassing the settings of the
HostNameLookups directive. This has performance implications.

Allow/Deny Access Based on Environment Variables

You can specify access rules based on the presence of a certain environment variable,
prefixing the name of the variable with env=. You can use this feature to grant or deny
access to certain browsers or browser versions, to prevent specific sites from linking to
your resources, and so on. For this example to work as intended, the client needs to
transmit the User-Agent header.

For example:

```
BrowserMatch MSIE iexplorer
Deny from env=iexplorer
```

Because the client sends the User-Agent header, it could possibly be omitted or manipulated, but most users will not do so and this technique will work in most cases.

Allow/Deny Access to All Clients

The keyword all matches all clients. You can specify Allow from all or Deny from
all to grant or deny access to all clients.

Evaluating Access Rules

You can have several Allow and Deny access rules. You can choose the order in which the
rules are evaluated by using the Order directive. Rules that are evaluated later have
higher precedence. Order accepts one argument, which can be Deny,Allow, Allow,Deny,
or Mutual-Failure. Deny,Allow is the default value for the Order directive. Note that
there is no space in the value.

Deny,Allow

Deny,Allow specifies that Deny directives are evaluated before Allow directives. With
Deny,Allow, the client is granted access by default if there are no Allow or Deny directives or the client does not match any of the rules. If the client matches a Deny rule, it
will be denied access unless it also matches an Allow rule, which will take precedence
because Allow directives are evaluated last and have greater priority.

Listing 15.2 shows how to configure Apache to allow access to the /private location to clients coming from the internal network or the domain example.com and deny access to everyone else.

LISTING 15.2   Sample Deny,Allow Access Control Configuration

```
1: <Location /private>
2:   Order Deny,Allow
3:  Deny from all
4:   Allow from 10.0.0.0/255.255.255.0  example.com
5: </Location>
```

Allow,Deny

Allow,Deny specifies that Allow directives are evaluated before Deny directives. With Allow,Deny, the client is denied access by default if there are no Allow or Deny directives or if the client does not match any of the rules. If the client matches an Allow rule, it will be granted access unless it also matches a Deny rule, which will take precedence.

Note that the presence of Order Allow,Deny without any Allow or Deny rules causes all requests to the specified resource to be denied because the default behavior is to deny access.

Listing 15.3 allows access to everyone except a specific host.

LISTING 15.3   Sample Allow,Deny Access Control Configuration

```
1: <Location /some/location/>
2:   Order Allow,Deny
3:   Allow from all
4:   Deny from host.example.com
5: </Location>
```

Mutual-Failure

In the case of Mutual-Failure, the host will be granted access only if it matches an Allow directive *and* does not match any Deny directive.

Combining Apache Access Methods

In previous sections, you learned how to restrict access based on user identity or request information. The Satisfy directive enables you to determine whether both types of access restrictions must be satisfied in order to grant access. Satisfy accepts one parameter, which can be either all or any.

15

`Satisfy all` means that the client will be granted access if it provides a valid username and password *and* passes the access restrictions. `Satisfy any` means the client will be granted access if it provides a valid username and password *or* passes the access restrictions.

Why is this directive useful? For example, you might want to provide free access to your Web site to users coming from an internal, trusted address, but require users coming from the Internet to provide a valid username and password. Listing 15.4 demonstrates just that.

LISTING 15.4 Mixing Authentication and Access Control Rules

```
1: <Location /restricted>
2: Allow from 10.0.0.0/255.255.255.0
3: AuthType Basic
4: AuthName "Intranet"
5: AuthUserFile /usr/local/apache2/conf/htusers
6: AuthAuthoritative on
7: Require valid-user
8: Satisfy any
9: </Location>
```

Access control based on connection or request information is not completely secure. Although it provides an appropriate level of protection for most cases, the rules rely on the integrity of your DNS servers and your network infrastructure. If an attacker gains control of your DNS servers, or your routers or firewalls are incorrectly configured, he can easily change authorized domain name records to point to his machine or pretend he is coming from an authorized IP address.

Limiting Access Based on HTTP Methods

In general, you want your access control directives to apply to all types of client requests, and this is the default behavior. In some cases, however, you want to apply authentication and access rules to only certain HTTP methods such as GET and HEAD.

The `<Limit>` container takes a list of methods and contains the directives that apply to requests containing those methods. The complete list of methods that can be used is GET, POST, PUT, DELETE, CONNECT, OPTIONS, TRACE, PATCH, PROPFIND, PROPPATCH, MKCOL, COPY, MOVE, LOCK, and UNLOCK.

The <LimitExcept> section provides complementary functionality, containing directives that will apply to requests not containing the listed methods.

Listing 15.5 shows an example from the default Apache configuration file. The <Limit> and <LimitExcept> sections allow read-only methods but deny requests to any other methods that can modify the content of the file system, such as PUT.

LISTING 15.5   Restricting Access Based on Rule

```
 1: <Directory /home/*/public_html>
 2:     AllowOverride FileInfo AuthConfig Limit
 3:     Options MultiViews Indexes SymLinksIfOwnerMatch IncludesNoExec
 4:     <Limit GET POST OPTIONS PROPFIND>
 5:         Order Allow,Deny
 6:         Allow from all
 7:     </Limit>
 8:     <LimitExcept GET POST OPTIONS PROPFIND>
 9:         Order Deny,Allow
10:         Deny from all
11:     </LimitExcept>
12: </Directory>
```

In the next section, you'll learn about restricting access on the application side based on information found in cookies.

Introducing Cookies

On the application side, you can use cookies in your PHP scripts to control access to certain areas of your Web site. A *cookie* is a small amount of data stored by the user's browser in compliance with a request from a server or script. A host can request that up to 20 cookies be stored by a user's browser. Each cookie consists of a name, value, and expiry date, as well as host and path information. An individual cookie is limited to 4KB.

After a cookie is set, only the originating host can read the data, ensuring that the user's privacy is respected. Furthermore, the user can configure her browser to notify her of all cookies set, or even to refuse all cookie requests. For this reason, cookies should be used in moderation and should not be relied on as an essential element of an environment design without first warning the user.

The Anatomy of a Cookie

A PHP script that sets a cookie might send headers that look something like this:

```
HTTP/1.1 200 OK
Date: Tue, 02 Oct 2001 13:39:58 GMT
Server: Apache/1.3.26 (Unix) PHP/4.2.3
X-Powered-By: PHP/4.2.3
Set-Cookie: vegetable=artichoke; path=/; domain=yourdomain.com
Connection: close
Content-Type: text/html
```

As you can see, this Set-Cookie header contains a name/value pair, path, and domain. The name and value will be URL encoded. Should it be present, an expires field is an instruction to the browser to "forget" the cookie after the given time and date. The path field defines the position on a Web site below which the cookie should be sent back to the server. The domain field determines the Internet domains to which the cookie should be sent. The domain cannot be different from the domain from which the cookie was sent, but can nonetheless specify a degree of flexibility. In the preceding example, the browser will send the cookie to the server yourdomain.com and the server www.yourdomain.com.

If the browser is configured to store cookies, it will then keep this information until the expiry date. If the user points the browser at any page that matches the path and domain of the cookie, it will resend the cookie to the server. The browser's headers might look something like this:

```
GET / HTTP/1.0
Connection: Keep-Alive
User-Agent: Mozilla/4.0 (compatible; MSIE 5.5; Windows 98)
Host: www.yourdomain.com
Accept: image/gif, image/x-xbitmap, image/jpeg, image/pjpeg, image/png, */*
Accept-Encoding: gzip
Accept-Language: en,pdf
Accept-Charset: iso-8859-1,*,utf-8
Cookie: vegetable=artichoke
```

A PHP script will then have access to the cookie in the environment variable HTTP_COOKIE or as part of the $_COOKIE superglobal:

```
print "$_SERVER[HTTP_COOKIE]<BR>";      // prints "vegetable=artichoke"
print getenv("HTTP_COOKIE")."<BR>";     // prints "vegetable=artichoke"
print $_COOKIE['vegetable']."<BR>";     // prints "artichoke"
```

Setting a Cookie with PHP

You can set a cookie in a PHP script in two ways. You can use the header() function to set the Set-Cookie header. The header() function requires a string that will then be included in the header section of the server response. Because headers are sent automatically for you, header() must be called before any output at all is sent to the browser:

```
header ("Set-Cookie: vegetable=artichoke; expires=Wed, 19-Sep-02 14:39:58 GMT;
path=/; domain=yourdomain.com");
```

Although not difficult, this method of setting a cookie would require you to build a function to construct the header string. Formatting the date as in this example and URL encoding the name/value pair would not be a particularly arduous task. It would, however, be an exercise in wheel reinvention because PHP provides a function that does just that.

The setcookie() function does what the name suggests—it outputs a Set-Cookie header. For this reason, it should be called before any other content is sent to the browser. The function accepts the cookie name, cookie value, expiry date in Unix epoch format, path, domain, and integer that should be set to 1 if the cookie is only to be sent over a secure connection. All arguments to this function are optional apart from the first (cookie name) parameter.

Listing 15.6 uses setcookie() to set a cookie.

LISTING 15.6 Setting and Printing a Cookie Value

```
 1: <?php
 2: setcookie("vegetable", "artichoke", time()+3600, "/", "yourdomain.com", 0);
 3: ?>
 4: <html>
 5: <head>
 6: <title>Listing 15.6 Setting and printing a cookie value</title>
 7: </head>
 8: <body>
 9: <?php
10: if (isset($_COOKIE[vegetable])) {
11:     print "<p>Hello again, your chosen vegetable is
$_COOKIE[vegetable]</p>";
12: } else {
13:     print "<p>Hello you. This may be your first visit</p>";
14: }
15: ?>
16: </body>
17: </html>
```

Even though we set the cookie (line 2) when the script is run for the first time, the $_COOKIE[vegetable] variable will not be created at this point. A cookie is read only when the browser sends it to the server. This will not happen until the user revisits a page in your domain. We set the cookie name to "vegetable" on line 2 and the cookie value to "artichoke". We use the time() function to get the current time stamp and add 3600 to it (there are 3600 seconds in an hour). This total represents our expiry date. We define

15

a path of "/", which means that a cookie should be sent for any page within our server environment. We set the domain argument to "yourdomain.com", which means that a cookie will be sent to any server in that group. Finally, we pass 0 to setcookie(), signaling that cookies can be sent in an insecure environment.

Passing setcookie() an empty string ("") for string arguments or 0 for integer fields will cause these arguments to be skipped.

Deleting a Cookie

Officially, to delete a cookie, you should call setcookie() with the name argument only:

```
setcookie( "vegetable" );
```

This approach does not always work well, however, and should not be relied on. It is safest to set the cookie with a date that has already expired:

```
setcookie( "vegetable", "", time()-60, "/", "yourdomain.com", 0);
```

You should also ensure that you pass setcookie() the same path, domain, and secure parameters as you did when originally setting the cookie.

Restricting Access Based on Cookie Values

Now for the fun part—using your cookie skills to restrict access to parts of your Web site! Suppose you created a login form that checked for values against a database. If the user is authorized, you send a cookie that says as much. Then, for all pages you want to restrict only to authorized users, you check for the specific cookie. If the cookie is present, the user can see the page. If the cookie is not present, the user is either sent back to the login form, or a message regarding access restrictions can be printed to the screen.

We'll go through each of these steps in the next few sections.

Creating the Authorized Users Table

When you're integrating user accounts into a Web-based application, it is most common to store the user-specific information in a database table. The information in this table can then be used to authorize the user and grant access to areas of the site that are specifically for these "special" users.

The following table creation command will create a table called auth_users in your MySQL database, with fields for the ID, first name, last name, email address, username, and password:

```
create table auth_users (
        id int not null primary key auto_increment,
        f_name varchar(50),
        l_name varchar(50),
        email varchar(150),
        username varchar(25),
        password varchar (75)
);
```

The following `INSERT` command puts a record in the `auth_users` table for a user named John Doe, with an email address of john@doe.com, a username of jdoe, and a password of doepass:

```
mysql> insert into auth_users values ('', 'John', 'Doe', 'john@doe.com',
    -> 'jdoe', password('doepass'));
Query OK, 1 row affected (0.00 sec)
```

This `INSERT` command should be self-explanatory, with the exception of the use of the `password()` function. When this function is used in the `INSERT` command, what is stored in the table is in fact not the actual password, but a hash of the password.

When you view the contents of the `auth_users` table, you will see the hash in the password field, as follows:

```
mysql> select * from auth_users;
+----+--------+--------+--------------+----------+-----------------+
| id | f_name | l_name | email        | username | password        |
+----+--------+--------+--------------+----------+-----------------+
|  1 | John   | Doe    | john@doe.com | jdoe     | 2fae5c9d478ec4b1 |
+----+--------+--------+--------------+----------+-----------------+
1 row in set (0.01 sec)
```

NEW TERM　　Although it may look like it is encrypted, a *hash* is in fact not an encrypted bit of information. Instead, it is a "fingerprint" of the original information. Hashes are generally used, like fingerprints, to perform matches. In this case, when you check your user's password, you will be checking that the hash of the input matches the stored hash. Using hashes alleviates the need—and security risk—of storing actual passwords.

Creating the Login Form and Script

After you authorize users in your table, you need to give them a mechanism for proving their authenticity. In this case, a simple two-field form will do, as shown in Listing 15.7.

LISTING 15.7　User Login Form

```
1: <html>
2: <head>
3: <title>Listing 15.7 User Login Form</title>
```

LISTING 15.7 continued

```
 4: </head>
 5: <body>
 6: <H1>Login Form</H1>
 7: <FORM METHOD="POST" ACTION="listing15.8.php">
 8: <P><STRONG>Username:</STRONG><BR>
 9: <INPUT TYPE="text" NAME="username"></p>
10: <P><STRONG>Password:</STRONG><BR>
11: <INPUT TYPE="password" NAME="password"></p>
12: <P><INPUT TYPE="SUBMIT" NAME="submit" VALUE="Login"></P>
13: </FORM>
14: </body>
15: </html>
```

Put these lines into a text file called listing15.7.php, and place this file in your Web server document root. Next, you'll create the script itself, which the form expects to be called listing15.8.php.

LISTING 15.8 User Login Script

```
 1: <?php
 2: //check for required fields from the form
 3: if ((!$_POST[username]) || (!$_POST[password])) {
 4:     header("Location: listing15.7.php");
 5:     exit;
 6: }
 7:
 8: //connect to server and select database
 9: $conn = mysql_connect("localhost", "joeuser", "somepass")
10:     or die(mysql_error());
11: mysql_select_db("testDB",$conn)  or die(mysql_error());
12:
13: //create and issue the query
14: $sql = "select f_name, l_name from auth_users where username =
15:     '$_POST[username]' AND password = password('$_POST[password]')";
16: $result = mysql_query($sql,$conn) or die(mysql_error());
17:
18: //get the number of rows in the result set; should be 1 if a match
19: if (mysql_num_rows($result) == 1) {
20:
21:     //if authorized, get the values of f_name l_name
22:     $f_name = mysql_result($result, 0, 'f_name');
23:     $l_name = mysql_result($result, 0, 'l_name');
24:
25:     //set authorization cookie
26:     setcookie("auth", "1", 0, "/", "yourdomain.com", 0);
27:
```

15

LISTING 15.8   continued

```
28:    //prepare message for printing, and user menu
29:    $msg = "<P>$f_name $l_name is authorized!</p>";
30:    $msg .= "<P>Authorized Users' Menu:";
31:    $msg .= "<ul><li><a href=\"listing15.8.php\">secret page</a></ul>";
32:
33: } else {
34:
35:    //redirect back to login form if not authorized
36:    header("Location: listing15.7.php");
37:    exit;
38: }
39: ?>
40: <HTML>
41: <HEAD>
42: <TITLE>Listing 15.8 User Login</TITLE>
43: </HEAD>
44: <BODY>
45: <? print "$msg"; ?>
46: </BODY>
47: </HTML>
```

Put these lines into a text file called listing15.8.php, and place this file in your Web server document root. In a moment, you'll try it out, but first let's examine what the script is doing.

Line 3 checks for the two required fields from the form. They are the only two fields in the form: username and password. If either one of these fields is not present, the script will redirect the user back to the login form. If the two fields are present, the script moves along to lines 9–11, which connect to the database server and select the database to use, in preparation for issuing the SQL query to check the authenticity of the user. This query, and its execution, is found in lines 14–16. Note that the query checks the hash of the password input from the form against the password stored in the table. These two elements must match each other, and also belong to the username in question, in order to authorize the user.

Line 19 tests the result of the query by counting the number of rows in the resultset. The row count should be exactly 1 if the username and password pair represents a valid login. If this is the case, the mysql_result() function is used in lines 22–23 to extract the first and last names of the user. These names are used for aesthetic purposes only. Line 26 sets the authorization cookie. The name of the cookie is auth and the value is 1. If a 0 is put in the time slot, the cookie will last as long as this user's Web browser session is open. When the user closes the browser, the cookie will expire. Lines 29–31 create a message for display, including a link to a file we will create in a moment.

Finally, lines 33–38 handle a failed login attempt. In this case, the user is simply redirected back to the login form.

Go ahead and access the login form, and input the valid values for the John Doe user. When you submit the form, the result should look like Figure 15.1.

FIGURE 15.1

Successful login result.

Try to log in with an invalid username and password pair, and you should be redirected to the login form. In the next (and final) section, you will create the listing15.9.php script, which will read the authentication cookie you have just set and act accordingly.

Testing for the auth Cookie

The last piece of this puzzle is to use the value of the auth cookie to allow a user to access a private file. In this case, the file in question is shown in Listing 15.9.

LISTING 15.9 Checking for auth Cookie

```
 1: <?php
 2: if ($_COOKIE[auth] == "1") {
 3:     $msg = "<p>You are an authorized user.</p>";
 4: } else {
 5:     //redirect back to login form if not authorized
 6:     header("Location: listing15.6.php");
 7:     exit;
 8: }
 9. ?>
10: <html>
11: <head>
```

LISTING 15.9 continued

```
12: <title>Listing 15.8 Accessing a restricted page </title>
13: </head>
14: <body>
15: <?php print "$msg"; ?>
16: </body>
17: </html>
```

From the menu shown in Figure 15.1, click the secret page link. Because you are an authorized user, you should see a result like Figure 15.2.

FIGURE 15.2

Accessing the secret page as an authorized user.

Close your browser and attempt to access listing15.9.php directly. You will find that you cannot, and will be redirected to the login form because the cookie is not set.

Summary

This hour explained how to use Apache features to restrict access to your Web site based on the identity of the remote user and information from the HTTP request or network connection. It also covered some authentication modules included with Apache and additional tools that you can use to create and manage your user and group databases.

Additionally, you were introduced to using cookies and learned to use the setcookie() function to set cookies on the user's browser. You then learned to use cookie values to allow access to specific parts of your PHP application.

Q&A

Q I have a Unix system. Can I use `/etc/passwd` as my user database?

A Although using `/etc/passwd` might seem convenient, it is advisable that you do not use the existing `/etc/passwd` file for authenticating users of your Web site. Otherwise, an attacker who gains access to a user of your Web site will also gain access to the system. Keep separate databases and encourage users to choose different passwords for their system accounts and Web access. Periodically run password checkers that scan for weak passwords and accounts in which the username is also the password.

Q Why am I asked for my password twice in some Web sites?

A Your browser keeps track of your password so that you do not have to type it for every request. The stored password is based on the realm (`AuthName` directive) and the hostname of the Web site. Sometimes you can access a Web site via different names, such as `yourdomain.com` and `www.yourdomain.com`. If you are authorized to access a certain restricted area of `yourdomain.com` but are redirected or follow a link to `www.yourdomain.com`, you will be asked again to provide the username and password because your browser thinks it is a completely different Web site.

Q Are there any serious security or privacy issues raised by cookies?

A A server can access a cookie set only from its own domain. Although a cookie can be stored on the user's hard drive, there is no other access to the user's file system. It is possible, however, to set a cookie in response to a request for an image. So if many sites include images served from a third-party ad server or counter script, the third party may be able to track a user across multiple domains.

Workshop

The workshop is designed to help you anticipate possible questions, review what you've learned, and begin learning how to put your knowledge into practice.

Quiz

1. What are the advantages of database files over plain text files for storing user authentication information?

2. Can you name some disadvantages of HTTP basic authentication?

3. What function is designed to allow you to set a cookie on a visitor's browser?

Answers

1. Database files are much more scalable because they can be indexed. This means that Apache does not need to read the file sequentially until a match is found for a particular user, but rather can jump to the exact location.

2. One disadvantage is that the information is transmitted in clear text over the network. This means that unless you are using SSL, it is possible for an attacker to read the packets your browser sends to the server and steal your password. Another disadvantage is that HTTP authentication does not provide a means for customizing the login (except the realm name). It is very common for Web sites to implement custom login mechanisms using HTML forms and cookies.

3. The `setcookie()` function allows you to set a cookie (although you could also output a `Set-Cookie` header using the `header()` function).

Activity

Practice using the various types of authentication—both server-based and with PHP—on your development server. Get a feel for the differences between basic HTTP authentication and something you devise on your own.

Hour **16**

Working with User Sessions

In Hour 15, "Restricting Access to Your Applications," we looked at using cookies to store user-related values, but once again, PHP is one step ahead of us. PHP contains numerous functions for managing user sessions, which can be stored in the $_SESSION superglobal. Sessions use techniques similar to those explored in the preceding hour but build them into the language; thus, saving state is as easy as calling a function.

In this hour, you will learn

- What session variables are and how they work
- How to start or resume a session
- How to store variables in a session
- How to destroy a session
- How to unset session variables

Session Function Overview

Session functions implement a concept that you have already seen; that is, the provision to users of a unique identifier, which can then be used from access to access to acquire information linked to that ID. The difference is that most of the work is already done for you. When a user accesses a session-enabled page, the user is either allocated a new identifier or re-associated with one that was already established in a previous access. Any variables that have been associated with the session will become available to your code, through the $_SESSION superglobal.

When you use sessions, cookies are used by default to store the session identifier, but you can ensure success for all clients by encoding the session ID into all links in your session-enabled pages.

Session state is usually stored in a temporary file, though you can implement database storage using a function called session_set_save_handler(). The use of session_set_save_handler() is beyond the scope of this book, but you can find more information at http://www.php.net/session-set-save-handler.

Starting a Session

To work with a session, you need to explicitly start or resume that session *unless* you have changed your php.ini configuration file. By default, sessions do not start automatically. If you want to start a session this way, you will have to find the following line in your php.ini file and change the value from 0 to 1 (and restart the Web server):

```
session.auto_start = 0
```

By changing the value of session.auto_start to 1, you ensure that a session is initiated for every PHP document. If you don't change this setting, you need to call the session_start() function in each script.

After a session is started, you instantly have access to the user's session ID via the session_id() function. session_id() allows you to either set or get a session ID. Listing 16.1 starts a session and prints the session ID to the browser.

LISTING 16.1   Starting or Resuming a Session

```
1: <?php
2: session_start();
3: ?>
4: <html>
5: <head>
6: <title>Listing 16.1 Starting or resuming a session</title>
```

LISTING 16.1   continued

```
 7: </head>
 8: <body>
 9: <?php
10: print "<p>Your session ID is ".session_id()."</p>\n\n";
11: ?>
12: </body>
13: </html>
```

16

When this script is run for the first time from a browser, a session ID is generated by the `session_start()` function call on line 2. If the page is later reloaded or revisited, the same session ID is allocated to the user. This action assumes that the user has cookies enabled. For example, when I run this script the first time, the output is

`Your session ID is fa963e3e49186764b0218e82d050de7b`

When I reload the page, the output is still

`Your session ID is fa963e3e49186764b0218e82d050de7b`

because I have cookies enabled and the session ID still exists.

Because `start_session()` attempts to set a cookie when initiating a session for the first time, it is imperative that you call this function before you output anything else at all to the browser. If you do not follow this rule, your session will not be set, and you will likely see warnings on your page.

Sessions remain current as long as the Web browser is active. When the user restarts the browser, the cookie is no longer stored. You can change this behavior by altering the `session.cookie_lifetime` setting in your php.ini file. The default value is `0`, but you can set an expiry period in seconds.

Working with Session Variables

Accessing a unique session. identifier in each of your PHP documents is only the start of session functionality. When a session is started, you can store any number of variables in the `$_SESSION` superglobal and then access them on any session-enabled page.

If you are using a pre-4.1.x version of PHP, the `$_SESSION` superglobal is not present, and session functionality is much different. If you cannot upgrade to the current version of PHP, read the PHP manual section on sessions, which includes notes for early releases.

Listing 16.2 adds two variables into the. $_SESSION superglobal: product1 and product2 (lines 10 and 11).

LISTING 16.2 Storing Variables in a Session

```
 1: <?php
 2: session_start();
 3: ?>
 4: <html>
 5: <head>
 6: <title>Listing 16.2 Storing variables in a session</title>
 7: </head>
 8: <body>
 9: <?php
10: $_SESSION[product1] = "Sonic Screwdriver";
11: $_SESSION[product2] = "HAL 2000";
12: print "The products have been registered.";
13: ?>
14: </body>
15: </html>
```

The magic in Listing 16.2 will not become apparent until the user moves to a new page. Listing 16.3 creates. a separate PHP script that accesses the variables stored in the $_SESSION superglobal in Listing 16.2.

LISTING 16.3 Accessing Stored Session Variables

```
 1: <?php
 2: session_start();
 3: ?>
 4: <html>
 5: <head>
 6: <title>Listing 16.3 Accessing stored session variables</title>
 7: </head>
 8: <body>
 9: <?php
10: print "Your chosen products are:\n\n";
11: print "<ul><li>$_SESSION[product1]\n<li>$_SESSION[product2]\n</ul>\n";
12: ?>
13: </body>
14: </html>
```

Figure 16.1 shows the output from Listing 16.3. As you can see, we have access to the $_SESSION[product1] and $_SESSION[product2] variables in an entirely new page.

FIGURE 16.1

Accessing stored session variables.

So how does the magic work? Behind the scenes, PHP 4 writes to a temporary file. You can find out where this file is being written on your system by using the session_save_path() function. This function optionally accepts a path to a directory and then writes all session files to it. If you pass it no arguments, it returns a string representing the current directory to which session files are saved. On my system,

```
print session_save_path();
```

prints /tmp. A glance at my /tmp directory reveals a number of files with names like the following:

```
sess_fa963e3e49186764b0218e82d050de7b
sess_76cae8ac1231b11afa2c69935c11dd95
sess_bb50771a769c605ab77424d59c784ea0
```

Opening the file that matches the session ID I was allocated when I first ran Listing 16.1, I can see how the registered variables have been stored:

```
product1|s:17:"Sonic Screwdriver";product2|s:8:"HAL 2000";
```

When a value is placed in the $_SESSION superglobal, PHP writes the variable name and value to a file. This information can be read and the variables resurrected later—as you have already seen. After you add a variable to the $_SESSION superglobal, you can still change its value at any time during the execution of your script, but the altered value won't be reflected in the global setting until you reassign the variable to the $_SESSION superglobal.

The example in Listing 16.2 demonstrates the process of adding variables to the $_SESSION superglobal. This example is not very flexible, however. Ideally, you should be able to register a varying number of values. You might want to let users pick products from a list, for example. In this case, you can use the serialize() function to store an array in your session.

16

Listing 16.4 creates a form that allows a user to choose multiple products. You should then be able to use session variables to create a rudimentary shopping cart.

LISTING 16.4   Adding an Array Variable to a Session Variable

```
 1: <?php
 2: session_start();
 3: ?>
 4: <html>
 5: <head>
 6: <title>Listing 16.4 Storing an array with a session</title>
 7: </head>
 8: <body>
 9: <h1>Product Choice Page</h1>
10: <?php
11: if (isset($_POST[form_products])) {
12:     if (!empty($_SESSION[products])) {
13:         $products = array_unique(
14:         array_merge(unserialize($_SESSION[products]),
15:         $_POST[form_products]));
16:     }
17: $_SESSION[products] = serialize($products);
18: print "<p>Your products have been registered!</p>";
19: }
20: ?>
21: <form method="POST" action="<?php $_SERVER[PHP_SELF] ?>">
22: <P>Select some products:<br>
23: <select name="form_products[]" multiple size=3>
24: <option>Sonic Screwdriver</option>
25: <option>Hal 2000</option>
26: <option>Tardis</option>
27: <option>ORAC</option>
28: <option>Transporter bracelet</option>
29: </select>
30: <br><br>
31: <input type="submit" value="choose">
32: </form>
33: <br><br>
34: <a href="listing16.5.php">content page</a>
35: </body>
36: </html>
```

We start or resume a session by calling `session_start()` on line 2. This should give us access to any previously set session variables. We begin an HTML form on line 21 and, on line 23, create a SELECT element named `form_products[]`, which contains OPTION elements for a number of products. Remember that HTML form elements that allow multiple selections should have square brackets appended to the value of their NAME arguments. This makes the user's choices available in an array.

Within the block of PHP code beginning on line 10, we test for the presence of the $_POST[form_products] array (line 11). If the variable is present, we can assume that the form has been submitted and information has already been stored in the $_SESSION superglobal. We then test for an array called $_SESSION[products] on line 12. If the array exists, it was populated on a previous visit to this script, so we merge it with the $_POST[form_products] array, extract the unique elements, and assign the result back to the $products array (lines 13–15). We then add the $products array to the $_SESSION superglobal on line 17.

Line 34 contains a link to another script, which we will use to demonstrate our access to the products the user has. chosen. We create this new script in Listing 16.5.

16

LISTING 16.5 Accessing Session Variables

```
 1: <?php
 2: session_start();
 3: ?>
 4: <html>
 5: <head>
 6: <title>Listing 16.5 Accessing session variables</title>
 7: </head>
 8: <body>
 9: <h1> Content Page</h1>
10: <?php
11: if (isset($_SESSION[products])) {
12:     print "<b>Your cart:</b><ol>\n";
13:     foreach (unserialize($_SESSION[products]) as $p) {
14:         print "<li>$p";
15:     }
16:     print "</ol>";
17: }
18: ?>
19: <a href="listing16.4.php">Back to product choice page</a>
20: </body>
21: </html>
```

Once again, we use session_start() to resume the session on line 2. We test for the presence of the $_SESSION[products] variable on line 11. If it exists, we unserialize it and loop through it on lines 13–15, printing each of the user's chosen items to the browser. An example is shown in Figure 16.2.

For a real shopping cart program, of course, you would keep product details in a database and test user input, rather than blindly store and present it, but Listings 16.4 and 16.5 demonstrate the ease with which you can use session functions to access array variables set in other pages.

FIGURE 16.2

Accessing an array of session variables.

Passing Session IDs in the Query String

So far you have relied on a cookie to save the session ID between script requests. On its own, this method is not the most reliable way of saving state because you cannot be sure that the browser will accept cookies. You can build in a failsafe, however, by passing the session ID from script to script embedded in a query string. PHP makes a name/value pair available in a constant called SID if a cookie value for a session ID cannot be found. You can add this string to any HTML links in session-enabled pages:

```
<a href="anotherpage.html?<?php print SID; ?>">Another page</a>
```

It will reach the browser as

```
<a href="anotherpage.html?PHPSESSID=08ecedf79fe34561fa82591401a01da1">Another
page</a>
```

The session ID passed in this way will automatically be recognized in the target page when session_start() is called, and you will have access to session variables in the usual way.

Destroying Sessions and Unsetting Variables

You can use session_destroy() to end a session, erasing all session variables. The session_destroy() function requires no arguments. You should have an established session for this function to work as expected. The following code fragment resumes a session and abruptly destroys it:

```
session_start();
session_destroy();
```

When you move on to other pages that work with a session, the session you have destroyed will not be available to them, forcing them to initiate new sessions of their own. Any registered variables will be lost.

The session_destroy() function does not instantly destroy registered variables, however. They remain accessible to the script in which session_destroy() is called (until it is reloaded). The following code fragment resumes or initiates a session and registers a variable called test, which we set to 5. Destroying the session does not destroy the registered variable.

```
session_start();
$_SESSION[test] = 5;
session_destroy();
print $_SESSION[test]; // prints 5
```

To remove all registered variables from a session, you simply unset the variable:

```
session_start();
$_SESSION[test] = 5;
session_destroy();
unset($_SESSION[test]);
print $_SESSION[test]; // prints nothing.
```

Summary

In this hour, you looked at different ways of saving state in a stateless protocol. All methods use some combination of cookies and query strings, sometimes combined with the use of files or databases. These approaches all have their benefits and problems.

You learned that a cookie alone is not intrinsically reliable and cannot store much information. On the other hand, it can persist over a long period of time. Approaches that write information to a file or database involve some cost to speed and might become a problem on a popular site. Nonetheless, a simple ID can unlock large amounts of data stored on disk. To ensure that as many users as possible get the benefit of your session-enabled environment, you can use the SID constant to pass a session ID to the server as part of a query string.

With regards to sessions themselves, you learned how to initiate or resume a session with session_start(). When in a session, you learned how to add variables to the $_SESSION superglobal, check that they exist, unset them if you want, and destroy the entire session.

Q&A

Q Should I be aware of any pitfalls with session functions?

A The session functions are generally reliable. However, remember that cookies cannot be read across multiple domains, so if your project uses more than one domain name on the same server (perhaps as part of an e-commerce environment), you might need to consider disabling cookies for sessions by setting the

`session.use_cookies`

directive to 0 in the php.ini file.

Workshop

The workshop is designed to help you anticipate possible questions, review what you've learned, and begin learning how to put your knowledge into practice.

Quiz

1. Which function would you use to start or resume a session?
2. Which function contains the current session's ID?
3. How would you end a session and erase all traces of it for future visits?
4. What does the SID constant return?

Answers

1. You can start a session by using the `session_start()` function.
2. You can access the session's ID by using the `session_id()` function.
3. The `session_destroy()` function removes all traces of a session for future requests.
4. If cookies are not available, the SID constant contains a name/value pair that can be incorporated in a query string. It will pass the session ID from script request to script request.

Activity

Create a script that uses session functions to remember which pages in your environment the user has visited. Provide the user with a list of links on each page to make it easy for her to retrace her steps.

Hour 17

Logging and Monitoring Server Activity

This hour describes how the logging system in Apache works and how you can customize it—which information to store and where to do it. Additionally, you will learn to use PHP and MySQL to log specific items of interest to you, outside the realm of the Apache log files.

In this hour, you will learn how to

- Understand Apache log formats and logging levels
- Rotate and analyze Apache logs
- Interpret common errors that might appear in your logs
- Create scripts that log specific items to database tables
- Create custom reports based on these logging tables

Standard Apache Access Logging

Using Apache's basic logging features, you can keep track of who visits your Web sites by logging accesses to the servers hosting them. You can log every aspect of the requests and responses, including the IP address of the client, user, and resource accessed. You need to take three steps to create a request log:

1. Define **what** you want to log—your log format.
2. Define **where** you want to log it—your log files, a database, an external program.
3. Define **whether** or not to log—conditional logging rules.

Deciding What to Log

You can log nearly every aspect associated with the request. You can define how your log entries look by creating a log format. A log format is a string that contains text mixed with log formatting directives. Log formatting directives start with a % and are followed by a directive name or identifier, usually a letter indicating the piece of information to be logged. When Apache logs a request, it scans the string and substitutes the value for each directive. For example, if the log format is This is the client address %a, the log entry is something like This is the client address 10.0.0.2. That is, the logging directive %a is replaced by the IP address of the client making the request. Table 17.1 provides a comprehensive list of all formatting directives.

TABLE 17.1 Log Formatting Directives

Formatting Options	Explanation
Data from the Client	
%a	Remote IP address, from the client.
%h	Hostname or IP address of the client making the request. Whether the hostname is logged depends on two factors: The IP address of the client must be able to resolve to a hostname using a reverse DNS lookup, and Apache must be configured to do that lookup using the HostNameLookups directive, explained later in this hour. If these conditions are not met, the IP address of the client will be logged instead.
%l	Remote user, obtained via the identd protocol. This option is not very useful because this protocol is not supported on the majority of the client machines, and the results can't be trusted anyway because the client provides them.
%u	Remote user from the HTTP basic authentication protocol.
Data from the Server	
%A	Local IP address, from the server.
%D	Time it took to serve the request in microseconds.
%{env_variable}e	Value for an environment variable named env_variable.

TABLE 17.1 continued

Formatting Options	Explanation
Data from the Server	
%{time_format}t	Current time. If {time_format} is present, it will be interpreted as an argument to the Unix strftime function. See the logresolve Apache manual page for details.
%T	Time it took to serve the request, in seconds.
%v	Canonical name of the server that answered the request.
%V	Server name according to the UserCanonicalName directive.
%X	Status of the connection in the server. A value of x means the connection was aborted before the server could send the data. A + means the connection will be kept alive for further requests from the same client. A - means the connection will be closed.
Data from the Request	
%{cookie_name}C	Value for a cookie named cookie_name.
%H	Request protocol, such as HTTP or HTTPS.
%m	Request method such as GET, POST, PUT, and so on.
%{header_name}i	Value for a header named header_name in the request from the client. This information can be useful, for example, to log the names and versions of your visitors' browsers.
%r	Text of the original HTTP request.
%q	Query parameters, if any, prefixed by a ?.
%U	Requested URL, without query parameters.
%y	Username for the HTTP authentication (basic or digest).
Data from the Response	
%b, %B	Size, in bytes, of the body of the response sent back to the client (excluding headers). The only difference between the options is that if no data was sent, %b will log a - and %B will log 0.
%f	Path of the file served, if any.
%t	Time when the request was served.
%{header_name}o	Value for a header named header_name in the response to the client.
%>s	Final status code. Apache can process several times the same request (internal redirects). This is the status code of the final response.

17

The Common Log Format (CLF) is a standard log format. Most Web sites can log requests using this format, and the format is understood by many log processing and reporting tools. Its format is the following:

```
"%h %l %u %t \"%r\" %>s %b"
```

That is, it includes the hostname or IP address of the client, remote user via `identd`, remote user via HTTP authentication, time when the request was served, text of the request, status code, and size in bytes of the content served.

 You can read the Common Log Format documentation of the original W3C server at `http://www.w3.org/Daemon/User/Config/Logging.html`.

The following is a sample CLF entry:

```
10.0.0.1 - - [21/Sep/2001:11:27:56 -0800] "GET / HTTP/1.1" 200 1456
```

You are now ready to learn how to define log formats using the `LogFormat` directive. This directive takes two arguments: The first argument is a logging string, and the second is a nickname that will be associated with that logging string.

For example, the following directive from the default Apache configuration file defines the Common Log Format and assigns it the nickname `common`:

```
LogFormat "%h %l %u %t \"%r\" %>s %b" common
```

You can also use the `LogFormat` directive with only one argument, either a log format string or a nickname. This will have the effect of setting the default value for the logging format used by the `TransferLog` directive, explained in "Logging Accesses to Files" later in this hour.

The `HostNameLookups` Directive

When a client makes a request, Apache knows only the IP address of the client. Apache must perform what is called a *reverse DNS lookup* to find out the hostname associated with the IP address. This operation can be time-consuming and can introduce a notice-able lag in the request processing. The `HostNameLookups` directive allows you to control whether to perform the reverse DNS lookup.

`HostNameLookups` can take one of the following arguments: `on`, `off`, or `double`. The default is `off`. The `double` lookup argument means that Apache will find out the hostname from the IP and then will try to find the IP from the hostname. This process is necessary if you are really concerned with security, as described in `http://httpd.apache.org/docs-2.0/dns-caveats.html`. If you are using hostnames as part of your `Allow` and `Deny` rules, a double DNS lookup is performed regardless of the `HostNameLookups` settings.

If `HostNameLookups` is enabled (`on` or `double`), Apache will log the hostname. This does cause extra load on your server, which you should be aware of when making the decision to turn `HostNameLookups` on or off. If you choose to keep `HostNameLookups` off, which would be recommended for medium-to-high traffic sites, Apache will log only the associated IP address. There are plenty of tools to resolve the IP addresses in the logs later. Refer to the "Managing Apache Logs" section later in this hour. Additionally, the result will be passed to CGI scripts via the environment variable `REMOTE_HOST`.

The `IdentityCheck` Directive

At the beginning of the hour, we explained how to log the remote username via the `identd` protocol using the `%l` log formatting directive. The `IdentityCheck` directive takes a value of `on` or `off` to enable or disable checking for that value and making it available for inclusion in the logs. Because the information is not reliable and takes a long time to check, it is switched off by default and should probably never be enabled. We mentioned `%l` only because it is part of the Common Log Format.

Environment Variables

The `CustomLog` directive accepts an environment variable as a third argument. If the environment variable is present, the entry will be logged; otherwise, it will not. If the environment variable is negated by prefixing an `!` to it, the entry will be logged if the variable is *not* present.

The following example shows how to avoid logging images in GIF and JPEG format in your logs:

```
SetEnvIf Request_URI "(\.gif|\.jpg)$" image
CustomLog logs/access_log common env=!image
```

Status Code

You can specify whether to log specific elements in a log entry. At the beginning of the hour, you learned that log directives start with a `%`, followed by a directive identifier. In between, you can insert a list of status codes, separated by commas. If the request status is one of the listed codes, the parameter will be logged; otherwise, a `-` will be logged.

For example, the directive identifier `%400,501{User-agent}i` logs the browser name and version for malformed requests (status code 400) and requests with methods not implemented (status code 501). This information can be useful for tracking which clients are causing problems.

You can precede the method list with an ! to log the parameter if the methods are implemented:

```
%!400,501{User-agent}i
```

Logging Accesses to Files

Logging to files is the default way of logging requests in Apache. You can define the name of the file using the TransferLog and CustomLog directives.

The TransferLog directive takes a file argument and uses the latest log format defined by a LogFormat directive with a single argument (the nickname or the format string). If no log format is present, it defaults to the Common Log Format.

The following example shows how to use the LogFormat and TransferLog directives to define a log format that is based on the CLF but that also includes the browser name:

```
LogFormat "%h %l %u %t \"%r\" %>s %b \"%{User-agent}i\""
TransferLog logs/access_log
```

The CustomLog directive enables you to specify the logging format explicitly. It takes at least two arguments: a logging format and a destination file. The logging format can be specified as a nickname or as a logging string directly.

For example, the directives

```
LogFormat "%h %l %u %t \"%r\" %>s %b \"%{User-agent}i\"" myformat
CustomLog logs/access_log myformat
```

and

```
CustomLog logs/access_log "%h %l %u %t \"%r\" %>s %b \"%{User-agent}i\""
```

are equivalent.

The CustomLog format can take an optional environment variable as a third argument, as explained in the "Environment Variables" section earlier in the hour.

Logging Accesses to a Program

Both TransferLog and CustomLog directives can accept a program, prefixed by a pipe sign |, as an argument. Apache will write the log entries to the standard input of the program. The program will, in turn, process them by logging the entries to a database, transmitting them to another system, and so on.

If the program dies for some reason, the server makes sure that it is restarted. If the server stops, the program is stopped as well.

The `rotatelogs` utility, bundled with Apache and explained later in this hour, is an example of a logging program.

As a general rule, unless you have a specific requirement for using a particular program, it is easier and more reliable to log to a file on disk and do the processing, merging, analysis of logs, and so on, at a later time, possibly on a different machine.

> Make sure that the program you use for logging requests is secure because it runs as the user Apache was started with. On Unix, this usually means root because the external program will be started before the server changes its user ID to the value of the User directive, typically nobody.

17

Standard Apache Error Logging

Apache can be configured to log error messages and debug information. In addition to errors generated by Apache itself, CGI errors also will be logged.

Each error log entry is prefixed by the time the error occurred and the client IP address or hostname, if available. As with HTTP request logging, you can log error information to a file or program. On Unix systems, you can also log to the `syslog` daemon. Modules for Apache 1.3 allow you to log to the Windows event log and will likely be ported to Apache 2.0 over time.

You can use the `ErrorLog` directive to define where you want your logs to go. This directive takes one argument, which can be a file, a program, or the `syslog` daemon.

Logging Errors to a File

A file argument indicates the path to the error log file. If the path is relative, it is assumed to be relative to the server root. By default, the error log file will be located in the `logs` directory and will be named `error_log` on Unix and `error.log` on Windows. The following is an example:

```
ErrorLog logs/my_error_log
```

Logging Errors to a Program

You can specify the path to a program, prefixed by a pipe |. Apache will log errors to the standard input of the program, and the program will further process them. The following is an example:

```
ErrorLog "|/usr/local/bin/someprogram"
```

The `syslog` Daemon Argument

On a Unix system, if you specify `syslog` as an argument, you can log error messages to the Unix system log daemon `syslogd`. By default, log errors are logged to the `syslog` facility `local7`. The facility is the part of the system generating the error. You can specify a facility by providing `syslog:facility` as an argument. Examples of `syslog` facilities are `mail`, `uucp`, `local0`, `local1`, and so on. For a complete list, look at the documentation for `syslog` included with your system (try `man syslogd` or `man syslogd.conf` at the command line). The following is an example of logging to `syslog`:

```
ErrorLog syslog:local6
```

The `LogLevel` Directive

The error information provided by Apache has several degrees of importance. You can choose to log only important messages and disregard informational or trivial warning messages. The `LogLevel` directive takes an error-level argument. Only errors of that level of importance or higher will be logged.

Table 17.2 specifies the valid values for the `LogLevel` directive, as specified by the Apache documentation. By default, the `LogLevel` value is `warn`. That should be enough for most Apache installations. If you are trying to troubleshoot a specific configuration, you can alter the level to `debug`.

TABLE 17.2 LogLevel Options as Described in the Apache Documentation

Setting	Description	Example
emerg	Emergencies—system is unusable	`Child cannot open lock file. Exiting.`
alert	Action must be taken immediately	`getpwuid: couldn't determine user name from uid.`
crit	Critical conditions	`socket: Failed to get a socket, exiting child.`
error	Error conditions	`Premature end of script headers.`
warn	Warning conditions	`Child process 1234 did not exit, sending another SIGHUP.`

TABLE 17.2 continued

Setting	Description	Example
notice	Normal but significant conditions	`httpd: caught SIGBUS, attempting to dump core in...`
info	Informational	`Server seems busy, (You may need to increase StartServers, or Min/MaxSpareServers)...`
debug	Debug-level messages	`Opening config file...`

Managing Apache Logs

Apache provides several tools for managing your logs. Other Apache-specific third-party tools are available and are mentioned here. Because Apache can log requests in the Common Log Format, most generic log processing tools can be used with Apache as well.

Resolving Hostnames

Earlier in the hour, you learned how to use the `HostNameLookups` directive to enable or disable hostname resolution at the time the request is made. If `HostNameLookups` is set to `off` (the default), the log file will contain only IP addresses. Later, you can use the command-line `logresolve` utility on Unix or `logresolve.exe` on Windows to process the log file and convert the IP addresses to hostnames.

`logresolve` reads log entries from standard input and outputs the result to its standard output. To read to and from a file, you can use redirection, on both Unix and Windows:

```
logresolve < access.log > resolved.log
```

Log-resolving tools are efficient because they can cache results and they do not cause any delay when serving requests to clients.

Fastresolve is an alternative, freely available log-resolving utility that can be found at `http://www.pix.net/staff/djm/sw/fastresolve/`.

Log Rotation

In Web sites with high traffic, the log files can quickly grow in size. You need to have a mechanism to rotate logs periodically, archiving and compressing older logs at well-defined intervals.

Log files cannot be removed directly while Apache is running because the server is writing directly to them. The solution is to use an intermediate program to log the requests. The program will, in turn, take care of rotating the logs.

Apache provides the `rotatelogs` program on Unix and `rotatelogs.exe` on Windows for this purpose. It accepts three arguments: a filename, a rotate interval in seconds, and an optional offset in minutes against UTC (Coordinated Universal Time).

For example,

```
TransferLog "|bin/rotatelogs /var/logs/apachelog 86400"
```

will create a new log file and move the current log to the `/var/logs` directory daily. (At the end of the command, 86400 is the number of seconds in one day.)

> If the path to the program includes spaces, you might need to escape them by prefixing them with a \ (backslash)—for example, `My\ Documents`. This is especially common in the Windows platform.

If the name of the file includes % prefixed options, the name will be treated as input to the `strftime` function that converts the % options to time values. The manual page for `rotatelogs` contains a complete listing of options, but here's an example:

```
TransferLog "|bin/rotatelogs /var/logs/apachelog%m_%d_%y 86400"
```

This command will add the current month, day, and year to the log filename.

If the name does not include any %-formatted options, the current time in seconds is added to the name of the archived file.

cronolog and httplog are additional log-rotating programs. httplog adds support for additional compression of log files. You can find them at `http://www.cronolog.org/` and `http://nutbar.chemlab.org/downloads/`.

Merging and Splitting Logs

When you have a cluster of Web servers serving similar content, maybe behind a load balancer, you often need to merge the logs from all the servers in a unique log stream before passing it to analysis tools.

Similarly, if a single Apache server instance handles several virtual hosts, sometimes it is useful to split a single log file into different files, one per each virtual host.

Logtools is a collection of log-manipulation tools that can be found at
`http://www.coker.com.au/logtools/`.

Apache includes the `split-file` Perl script for splitting logs. You can find it in the `support` subdirectory of the Apache distribution.

Log Analysis

After you collect the logs, you can analyze them and gain information about traffic and visitor behavior.

Many commercial and freely available applications are available for log analysis and reporting. Two of the most popular open source applications are Webalizer (`http://www.mrunix.net/webalizer/`) and awstats (`http://awstats.sourceforge.net`).

Wusage is a nice, inexpensive commercial alternative and can be found at `http://www.boutell.com/wusage/`.

Monitoring Error Logs

If you run Apache on a Unix system, you can use the `tail` command-line utility to monitor, in real-time, log entries both to your access and error logs. The syntax is

```
tail -f logname
```

where *logname* is the path to the Apache log file. It will print onscreen the last few lines of the log file and will continue to print entries as they are added to the file.

You can find additional programs that enable you to quickly identify problems by scanning your error log files for specific errors, malformed requests, and so on, and reporting on them:

- Logscan can be found at `http://www.garandnet.net/security.php`.
- ScanErrLog can be found at `http://www.librelogiciel.com/software/`.

Logging Custom Information to a Database

Creating your own logging tables in MySQL, matched up with snippets of PHP code, can help you to capture access-related information for specific pages of your site. Using this information, you can create customized reports. This method can be much less cumbersome than wading through Apache log files, especially when you are just searching for a subset of access information.

Creating the Database Table

The first step in your custom logging method is to create the database table. The following table creation command will create a table called access_tracker in your MySQL database, with fields for an ID, page title, user agent, and date of access:

```
create table access_tracker (
       id int not null primary key auto_increment,
       page_title varchar(50),
       user_agent text,
       date_accessed date
);
```

Next, you'll create the code snippet that will write to this table.

Creating the PHP Code Snippet

As you may have gathered already, "code snippet" essentially means "a little bit of code." In other words, something that doesn't qualify as a long script, but just serves a simple purpose. In this case, the code snippet in Listing 17.1 will write some basic information to the access_tracker table.

LISTING 17.1 Code Snippet for Access Tracking

```
 1: <?
 2: //set up static variables
 3: $page_title = "sample page A";
 4: $user_agent = getenv("HTTP_USER_AGENT");
 5: $date_accessed = date("Y-m-d");
 6:
 7: //connect to server and select database
 8: $conn = mysql_connect("localhost", "joeuser", "somepass")
 9:     or die(mysql_error());
10: $db = mysql_select_db("testDB", $conn) or die(mysql_error());
11:
12: //create and issue query
13: $sql = "insert into access_tracker values
14:     ('', '$page_title', '$user_agent', '$date_accessed')";
15: mysql_query($sql,$conn);
16: ?>
```

What you'll do with this snippet is simple: Place it at the beginning of every page you want to track. For each page, change the value of $page_title in the snippet to represent the actual title of the page.

Now create a sample script called sample1.php, containing the contents of Listing 17.1 and then the content in Listing 17.2.

LISTING 17.2   Sample HTML Page

```
1: <HTML>
2: <HEAD>
3: <TITLE>Sample Page A</TITLE>
4: </HEAD>
5: <BODY>
6: <h1>Sample Page A</h1>
7: <P>Blah blah blah.</p>
8: </BODY>
9: </HTML>
```

Create a few copies of this file, with different filenames and values for $page_title.
Then access these different pages with your Web browser to fill up your logging table.

Creating Sample Reports

When you have the data in your access_tracker table, you can create a simple report
screen to disseminate this information. The code in Listing 17.3 creates a report that
issues queries to count total results as well as the breakdown of browsers in use.

LISTING 17.3   Creating an Access Report

```
 1: <?php
 2: //connect to server and select database
 3: $conn = mysql_connect("localhost", "joeuser", "somepass")
 4:     or die(mysql_error());
 5: $db = mysql_select_db("testDB", $conn) or die(mysql_error());
 6:
 7: //issue query and select results for counts
 8: $count_sql = "select count(page_title) from access_tracker ";
 9: $count_res = mysql_query($count_sql, $conn) or die(mysql_error());
10: $all_count = mysql_result($count_res, 0, "count(page_title)");
11:
12: //issue query and select results for user agents
13: $user_agent_sql = "select distinct user_agent, count(user_agent) as count
14:     from access_tracker group by user_agent order by count desc";
15: $user_agent_res = mysql_query($user_agent_sql, $conn)
16:     or die(mysql_error());
17: //start user agent display block
18: $user_agent_block = "<ul>";
19:
20: //loop through user agent results
21: while ($row_ua = mysql_fetch_array($user_agent_res)) {
22:     $user_agent = $row_ua['user_agent'];
23:     $user_agent_count = $row_ua['count'];
24:     $user_agent_block .= "
25:     <li>$user_agent
```

17

LISTING 17.3   continued

```
26:     <ul>
27:     <li><em>accesses per browser: $user_agent_count</em>
28:     </ul>";
29: }
30:
31: //finish up the user agent block
32: $user_agent_block .= "</ul>";
33:
34: //issue query and select results for pages
35: $page_title_sql = "select distinct page_title, count(page_title) as count
36:     from access_tracker group by page_title order by count desc";
37: $page_title_res = mysql_query($page_title_sql, $conn)
38:     or die(mysql_error());
39: //start page title display block
40: $page_title_block = "<ul>";
41:
42: //loop through results
43: while ($row_pt = mysql_fetch_array($page_title_res)) {
44:     $page_title = $row_pt['page_title'];
46:     $page_count = $row_pt['count'];
47:     $page_title_block .= "
48:     <li>$page_title
49:         <ul>
50:         <li><em>accesses per page: $page_count</em>
51:         </ul>";
52: }
53:
54: //finish up the page title block
55: $page_title_block .= "</ul>";
56:
57:?>
58: <HTML>
59: <HEAD>
60: <TITLE>Access Report</TITLE>
61: </HEAD>
62: <BODY>
63: <h1>Access Report</h1>
64: <P><strong>Total Accesses Tracked:</strong> <? echo "$all_count"; ?></p>
65: <P><strong>Web Browsers Used:</strong>
66: <?php print "$user_agent_block"; ?>
67: <P><strong>Individual Pages:</strong>
68: <?php print "$page_title_block"; ?>
69: </BODY>
70: </HTML>
```

Lines 3–5 connect to the database so that you can issue the queries against the access_tracker table. Lines 8–10 issue the query to select the count of all pages, and lines 13–15 count the user agent accesses. Line 18 starts an unordered list block for the results of the user agent query, while lines 21–29 loop through the results and create the list, which is closed in line 32.

Lines 35–37 create and issue the query to count the individual pages. Line 40 starts an unordered list block for the results of this query, while lines 43–52 loop through the results and create the list of accessed pages, which is closed in line 55.

Put these lines into a text file called accessreport.php, and place this file in your Web server document root. When you access this report, you will see something like Figure 17.1—your page names, counts, and browsers will be different, but you get the idea.

FIGURE 17.1

Custom access report for tracked pages.

This sort of tracking is a lot easier than wading through Apache access logs, but I wouldn't recommend completely replacing your access logs with a database-driven system. That's a bit too much database-connection overhead, even if MySQL is particularly nice on your system. Instead, target your page tracking to something particularly important.

Summary

This hour's lesson explained how to log specific information about the requests and errors generated by Apache. You can store the logs in files or databases, or pass them to external programs. You learned about the different utilities available for managing, processing, and analyzing logs, both the ones included with Apache and those available from third parties.

Finally, you saw a simple method for using PHP code snippets and a MySQL database to perform simple access tracking of specific pages. This information was then displayed in a simple access report, built with PHP.

Q&A

Q Why wouldn't I want to log images?

A In heavily loaded servers, logging can become a bottleneck. If the purpose of logging is to count the number of visitors and analyze their usage of the Web site, you can achieve this result by logging only the HTML pages, not the images contained in them. This reduces the number of hits stored in the logs and the time spent writing them.

Workshop

The workshop is designed to help you anticipate possible questions, review what you've learned, and begin learning how to put your knowledge into practice.

Quiz

1. How would you avoid logging hits from a client accessing your Web site from a particular network?

2. How can you log images to a different file?

Answers

1. In some situations, you may want to ignore requests coming from a particular network, such as your own, so that they do not skew the results. You can do this either by post-processing the logs and removing them or by using the SetEnvIf directive:

```
SetEnvIf Remote_Addr 10\.0\.0\. intranet
CustomLog logs/access_log "%h %l %u %t \"%r\" %>s %b" !intranet
```

2. Earlier in the hour, you learned how to avoid logging images. Instead of ignoring images altogether, you can easily log them to a separate file, using the same environment variable mechanism:

```
SetEnvIf Request_URI "(\.gif|\.jpeg)$" image
CustomLog logs/access_log common env=!image
CustomLog logs/images_log common env=image
```

Part IV
Simple Projects

Hour

18 Managing a Simple Mailing List

19 Creating an Online Address Book

20 Creating an Online Storefront

21 Creating a Shopping Cart Mechanism

HOUR 18

Managing a Simple Mailing List

This hour provides the first of several hands-on, small projects designed to pull together your PHP and MySQL knowledge. In this hour, you'll learn the methods for creating a managed distribution list, which can be used to send out newsletters or anything else that you want to send, to a list of email addresses in a database.

The mailing mechanism you'll use in this hour is not meant to be a replacement for mailing list software, which is specifically designed for bulk messages. The type of system you'll build in this lesson should be used for only small lists of fewer than a few hundred email addresses.

In this hour, you will learn how to

- Create a subscribe/unsubscribe form and script
- Create a front end for sending your message
- Create the script that sends your message

Developing the Subscription Mechanism

You learned in earlier lessons that planning is the most important aspect of creating any product. In this case, think of the elements you will need for your subscription mechanism:

- A table to hold email addresses
- A way for users to add or remove their email addresses
- A form and script for sending the message

The following sections will describe each item individually.

Creating the `subscribers` Table

You really need only one field in the `subscribers` table: to hold the email address of the user. However, you should have an ID field just for consistency among your tables, and also because referencing an ID is a lot simpler than referencing a long email address in `where` clauses. So, in this case, your MySQL query would look something like

```
mysql> create table subscribers (
    -> id int not null primary key auto_increment,
    -> email varchar (150) unique not null
    -> );
Query OK, 0 rows affected (0.00 sec)
```

Note the use of `unique` in the field definition for `email`. This means that although `id` is the primary key, duplicates should not be allowed in the `email` field either. The `email` field is a unique key, and `id` is the primary key.

This relationship is represented in the table information as `MUL` (or "multiple") in the `Key` field:

```
mysql> describe subscribers;
+-------+--------------+------+-----+---------+----------------+
| Field | Type         | Null | Key | Default | Extra          |
+-------+--------------+------+-----+---------+----------------+
| id    | int(11)      |      | PRI | NULL    | auto_increment |
| email | varchar(150) | YES  | MUL | NULL    |                |
+-------+--------------+------+-----+---------+----------------+
2 rows in set (0.00 sec)
```

Now that you have a table, you can create the form and script that place values in there.

Creating the Subscription Form

The subscription form will actually be an all-in-one form and script called manage.php, which will handle both subscribe and unsubscribe requests. Listing 18.1 shows the code for manage.php, which uses a few user-defined functions to eliminate repetitive code.

LISTING 18.1   Subscribe and Unsubscribe with manage.php

```php
 1: <?php
 2: //set up a couple of functions
 3: function doDB() {
 4:     global $conn;
 5:     //connect to server and select database; you may need it
 6:     $conn = mysql_connect("localhost", "joeuser", "somepass")
 7:         or die(mysql_error());
 8:     mysql_select_db("testDB",$conn)  or die(mysql_error());
 9: }
10:
11: function emailChecker($email) {
12:     global $conn, $check_result;
13:     //check that email is not already in list
14:     $check = "select id from subscribers where email = '$email'";
15:     $check_result = mysql_query($check,$conn) or die(mysql_error());
16: }
17:
18: //determine if they need to see the form or not
19: if ($_POST[op] != "ds") {
20:     //they do, so create form block
21:     $display_block = "
22:     <form method=POST action=\"$_SERVER[PHP_SELF]\">
23:
24:     <p><strong>Your E-Mail Address:</strong><br>
25:     <input type=text name=\"email\" size=40 maxlength=150>
26:
27:     <p><strong>Action:</strong><br>
28:     <input type=radio name=\"action\" value=\"sub\" checked> subscribe
29:     <input type=radio name=\"action\" value=\"unsub\"> unsubscribe
30:
31:     <input type=\"hidden\" name=\"op\" value=\"ds\">
32:
33:     <p><input type=submit name=\"submit\" value=\"Submit Form\"></p>
34:     </form>";
35:
36: } else if (($_POST[op] == "ds") && ($_POST[action] == "sub")) {
37:     //trying to subscribe; validate email address
38:     if ($_POST[email] == "") {
39:         header("Location: manage.php");
40:         exit;
41:     }
42:     //connect to database
43:     doDB();
44:     //check that email is in list
45:     emailChecker($_POST[email]);
46:
47:     //get number of results and do action
48:     if (mysql_num_rows($check_result) < 1) {
```

LISTING 18.1   continued

```
49:        //add record
50:        $sql = "insert into subscribers values('', '$_POST[email]')";
51:        $result = mysql_query($sql,$conn) or die(mysql_error());
52:        $display_block = "<P>Thanks for signing up!</P>";
53:    } else {
54:        //print failure message
55:        $display_block = "<P>You're already subscribed!</P>";
56:    }
57: } else if (($_POST[op] == "ds") && ($_POST[action] == "unsub")) {
58:    //trying to unsubscribe; validate email address
59:    if ($_POST[email] == "") {
60:    header("Location: manage.php");
61:        exit;
62:    }
63:    //connect to database
64:    doDB();
65:    //check that email is in list
66:    emailChecker($_POST[email]);
67:
68:    //get number of results and do action
69:    if (mysql_num_rows($check_result) < 1) {
70:        //print failure message
71:        $display_block = "<P>Couldn't find your address!</P>
72:        <P>No action was taken.</P>";
73:    } else {
74:        //unsubscribe the address
75:        $id = mysql_result($check_result, 0, "id");
76:        $sql = "delete from subscribers where id = '$id'";
77:        $result = mysql_query($sql,$conn) or die(mysql_error());
78:        $display_block = "<P>You're unsubscribed!</p>";
79:    }
80: }
81: ?>
82: <HTML>
83: <HEAD>
84: <TITLE>Subscribe/Unsubscribe</TITLE>
85: </HEAD>
86: <BODY>
87: <h1>Subscribe/Unsubscribe</h1>
88: <?php echo "$display_block"; ?>
89: </BODY>
90: </HTML>
```

Listing 18.1 may be long, but it's not complicated. In fact, it could be longer, were it not for the user-defined functions at the top of the script. One of the reasons for creating your own functions is that you know you will be reusing a bit of code and don't want to continually retype it. Lines 3–9 set up the first function, doDB(), which is simply the database connection you've been making in your lessons for a while now. Lines 11–16 define a function called emailChecker(), which takes an input and returns an output—like most functions do. We'll look at this one in the context of the script, as we get to it.

Line 19 starts the main logic of the script. Because this script performs several actions, we need to determine which action it is currently attempting. If the value of $_POST[op] is not "ds", we know the user has not submitted the form; therefore, we must show it to the user. Lines 21–34 create the subscribe/unsubscribe form, using $_SERVER[PHP_SELF] as the action (line 22), creating a text field called email for the user's email address, and setting up a set of radio buttons (lines 28–29) to find the desired task. At this point, the script breaks out of the if...else construct, skips down to line 82, and proceeds to print the HTML. The form is displayed as shown in Figure 18.1.

FIGURE 18.1

*The subscribe/
unsubscribe form.*

If the value of $_POST[op] is indeed "ds", however, we need to do something. We have two possibilities: subscribe and unsubscribe. We determine which action to take by looking at the value of $_POST[action]—the radio button group.

In line 36, if $_POST[op] is "ds" and $_POST[action] is "sub", we know the user is trying to subscribe. To subscribe, he will need an email address, so we check for one in lines 38–41. If no address is present, the user is sent back to the form.

If an address is present, we call the doDB() function in line 43 to connect to the database because we need to perform a query (or two). In line 45, we call the second of our user-defined functions, emailChecker(). This function takes an input ($_POST[email]) and processes it. If we look back to lines 12–15, we see that the function is checking for an id value in the subscribers table that matches the value of the input. The function then returns the resultset, $check_result, for use within the larger script.

Note the definition of global variables at the beginning of both user-defined functions in Listing 18.1. These variables need to be shared with the entire script, and so are declared global.

Jump down to line 48 to see how $check_result is used: The number of records in $check_result is counted to determine whether the email address already exists in the table. If the number of rows is less than 1, the address is not in the list, and it can be added. The record is added and the response is stored in lines 50–52, and the failure message (if the address is already in the table) is stored in line 55. At that point, the script breaks out of the if...else construct, skips down to line 82, and proceeds to print the HTML. You'll test this functionality later.

The last combination of inputs occurs if the value of $_POST[op] is "ds" and $_POST[action] is "unsub". In this case, the user is trying to unsubscribe. To unsubscribe, he will need an email address, so we check for one in lines 59–61. If no address is present, the user is sent back to the form.

If an address is present, we call the doDB() function in line 64 to connect to the database. Then, in line 66, we call emailChecker(), which again will return the resultset, $check_result. The number of records in the resultset is counted in line 69, to determine whether the email address already exists in the table. If the number of rows is less than 1, the address is not in the list, and it cannot be unsubscribed. In this case, the response message is stored in lines 71–72. The user is unsubscribed(the record deleted) and the response is stored in lines 75–77, and the failure message (if the address is already in the table) is stored in line 78. At that point, the script breaks out of the if...else construct, skips down to line 82, and proceeds to print the HTML.

Figures 18.2 through 18.5 show the various results of the script, depending on the actions selected and the status of email addresses in the database.

FIGURE 18.2

Successful subscription.

FIGURE **18.3**
Subscription failure.

FIGURE **18.4**
Successful unsubscribe action.

18

FIGURE **18.5**
Unsuccessful unsubscribe action.

Next, you'll create the form and script that sends along mail to each of your subscribers.

Developing the Mailing Mechanism

With the subscription mechanism in place, you can create a basic form interface for a script that will take the contents of your form and send it to every address in your subscribers table. This is another one of those all-in-one scripts, called sendmymail.php, and it is shown in Listing 18.2.

LISTING 18.2   Send Mail to Your List of Subscribers

```
 1: <?php
 2: if ($_POST[op] != "send") {
 3:     //haven't seen the form, so show it
 4:     print "
 5:     <HTML>
 6:     <HEAD>
 7:     <TITLE>Send a Newsletter</TITLE>
 8:     </HEAD>
 9:     <BODY>
10:     <h1>Send a Newsletter</h1>
11:     <form method=\"post\" action=\"$_SERVER[PHP_SELF]\">
12:     <P><strong>Subject:</strong><br>
13:     <input type=\"text\" name=\"subject\" size=30></p>
14:     <P><strong>Mail Body:</strong><br>
15:     <textarea name=\"message\" cols=50 rows=10 wrap=virtual></textarea>
16:     <input type=\"hidden\" name=\"op\" value=\"send\">
17:     <p><input type=\"submit\" name=\"submit\" value=\"Send It\"></p>
18:     </FORM>
19:     </BODY>
20:     </HTML>";
21:
22: } else if ($_POST[op] == "send") {
23:     //want to send form, so check for required fields
24:     if (($_POST[subject] =="") || ($_POST[message] == "")) {
25:         header("Location: sendmymail.php");
26:         exit;
27:     }
28:
29:     //connect to database
30:     $conn = mysql_connect("localhost", "joeuser", "somepass")
31:         or die(mysql_error());
32:     mysql_select_db("testDB",$conn)  or die(mysql_error());
33:
34:     //get emails from subscribers list
35:     $sql = "select email from subscribers";
36:     $result = mysql_query($sql,$conn) or die(mysql_error());
37:
38:     //create a From: mailheader
39:     $headers = "From: Your Mailing List <you@yourdomain.com>\n";
40:
41:     //loop through results and send mail
```

LISTING 18.2   continued

```
42:     while ($row = mysql_fetch_array($result)) {
43:         set_time_limit(0);
44:         $email = $row['email'];
45:         mail("$email", stripslashes($_POST[subject]),
46:             stripslashes($_POST[message]), $headers);
47:         print "newsletter sent to: $email<br>";
48:     }
49: }
50: ?>
```

The main logic of the script starts right there at line 2, where we determine whether the user has seen the form yet. If the value of $_POST[op] is not "send", we know the user has not submitted the form; therefore, we must show it to her. Lines 4–20 create the form for sending the newsletter, which uses $_SERVER[PHP_SELF] as the action (line 11), creates a text field called subject for the subject of the mail, and creates a textarea called message for the body of the mail to be sent. At this point, the script breaks out of the if...else construct and the HTML is printed. The form is displayed as in Figure 18.6.

FIGURE 18.6

Form for sending the bulk mail.

18

If the value of $_POST[op] is indeed "send", however, we have to send the form to the recipients. Before we send, we must check for the two required items: $_POST[subject] and $_POST[message]. If either of these items is not present, the user is redirected to the form again.

If the required items are present, the script moves on to lines 30–32, which connect to the database. The query is issued in line 36, which grabs all the email addresses from the subscribers table. There is no order to these results, although you could throw an order by clause in there if you want to send them out in alphabetical order.

Line 39 creates a From: mail header, which is used inside the upcoming while loop, when mail is sent. This header ensures that the mail looks like it is from a person and not a machine. The while loop, which begins on line 42, extracts the email addresses from the resultset one at a time. On line 43, we use the set_time_limit() function to set the time limit to 0, or "no limit." Doing so allows the script to run for as long as it needs to.

> Because all the script in Listing 18.2 does is execute the mail() function numerous times, it does not take into account the queuing factors in actual mailing list software, which are designed to ease the burden on your outgoing mail server. Using set_time_limit() does not ease its burden; it just allows the script to continue to run when it might have timed out before.

In line 45, the mail is sent using the mail() function, inserting the values from the form where appropriate. Line 46 prints a message to the screen for you, to show who should have received the mail. In Figures 18.7 and 18.8, you can see the outcome of the script.

FIGURE 18.7
Mail has been sent!

FIGURE 18.8
The mail arrived safely.

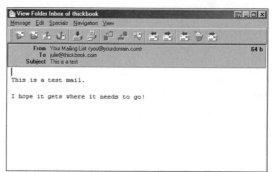

Summary

In this hands-on hour, you applied your basic PHP and MySQL knowledge to the creation of a personal mailing list. Included were the database table creation, the subscribe and unsubscribe mechanisms, and the form and script for sending the mail.

Q&A

Q How can I ease the burden on my mail server?

A Besides looking into package mailing list software, you can bypass the `mail()` function and talk directly to your SMTP server via a socket connection. Such an example is shown in the PHP Manual for the `fsockopen()` function (`http://www.php.net/manual/en/function.fsockopen.php`), as well as in other developer resource sites.

Q Where do bounced messages go?

A Bounces go to whatever address you specify in your `From:` or `Reply-to:` mail headers.

Workshop

The workshop is designed to help you anticipate possible questions, review what you've learned, and begin learning how to put your knowledge into practice.

Quiz

1. What function sends mail?
2. What function call causes the script to execute for as long as it needs to run?

Answers

1. This is not a trick question. It's the `mail()` function!
2. `set_time_limit(0)`

18

HOUR 19

Creating an Online Address Book

In this hour's hands-on lesson, the project is creating a managed, online address book. You will learn the methods for creating the relevant database tables, as well as the forms and scripts for adding, deleting, and viewing database records.

In this hour, you will learn how to

- Create relational tables for an online address book
- Create the forms and scripts for adding and deleting records in the address book
- Create the forms and scripts for viewing records

Planning and Creating the Database Tables

When you think of an address book, the obvious fields come to mind—name, address, telephone number, email address. However, if you look at your own paper-based address book, you may note that you have several entries for one person. Maybe that person has three telephone numbers, or two email addresses, and so forth. In your online address book, a set of related tables will help alleviate the redundancy and repetition of information.

Table 19.1 shows sample table and field names to use for your online address book. In a minute, you'll create the actual SQL statements, but first you should look at this information and try to see the relationships appear. Ask yourself which of the fields should be primary or unique keys.

TABLE 19.1 Address Book Table and Field Names

Table Name	Field Names
master_name	id, date_added, date_modified, f_name, 1_name
address	id, master_id, date_added, date_modified, address, city, state, zipcode, type
telephone	id, master_id, date_added, date_modified, tel_number, type
fax	id, master_id, date_added, date_modified, fax_number, type
email	id, master_id, date_added, date_modified, email, type
personal_notes	id, master_id, date_added, date_modified, note

Notice the use of date-related fields; each table has a date_added and date_modified field in it. The fields will help maintain your data; you may at some point want to issue a query that removes all records that are older than a certain number of months or years, or that removes all records that haven't been updated within a certain period of time.

As you can see in the following SQL statements, the master_name table has two fields besides the ID and date-related fields: f_name and 1_name, for first name and last name. The id field is the primary key. No other keys need to be primary or unique, unless you really want to limit your address book to one John Smith, one Mary Jones, and so forth.

> The field lengths for the text fields in the following statements are arbitrary; you can make them as long or as short as you want, within the allowable definition of the field type.

```
mysql> create table master_name (
    -> id int not null primary key auto_increment,
    -> date_added datetime,
    -> date_modified datetime,
```

```
    -> f_name varchar (75),
    -> l_name varchar (75)
    -> );
Query OK, 0 rows affected (0.01 sec)
```

The address table has the basic primary key id field and the date_added and date_modified fields. In addition, you should now see where the relationship will be made—through the use of the master_id field. The master_id will be equal to the id field in the master_name table, matching the person whose address this is. The master_id field is not a unique key because it is a perfectly valid assumption that one person may have several address entries. We see this in the type field, which is defined as an enumerated list containing three options: home, work, or other. A person may have one or more of all three types, so no other keys are present in this table besides the primary key id. Assuming this particular address book contains only United States addresses, we round out the table with address, city, state, and zipcode fields.

```
mysql> create table address (
    -> id int not null primary key auto_increment,
    -> master_id int not null,
    -> date_added datetime,
    -> date_modified datetime,
    -> address varchar (255),
    -> city varchar (30),
    -> state char (2),
    -> zipcode varchar (10),
    -> type enum ('home', 'work', 'other')
    -> );
Query OK, 0 rows affected (0.01 sec)
```

The telephone, fax, and email tables are all variations on the same theme:

```
mysql> create table telephone (
    -> id int not null primary key auto_increment,
    -> master_id int not null,
    -> date_added datetime,
    -> date_modified datetime,
    -> tel_number varchar (25),
    -> type enum ('home', 'work', 'other')
    -> );
Query OK, 0 rows affected (0.01 sec)

mysql> create table fax (
    -> id int not null primary key auto_increment,
    -> master_id int not null,
    -> date_added datetime,
    -> date_modified datetime,
    -> fax_number varchar (25),
    -> type enum ('home', 'work', 'other')
    -> );
```

19

```
Query OK, 0 rows affected (0.00 sec)

mysql> create table email (
    -> id int not null primary key auto_increment,
    -> master_id int not null,
    -> date_added datetime,
    -> date_modified datetime,
    -> email varchar (150),
    -> type enum ('home', 'work', 'other')
    -> );
Query OK, 0 rows affected (0.00 sec)
```

The personal_notes table also follows the same sort of pattern, except that master_id a unique key and allows only one notes record per person:

```
mysql> create table personal_notes (
    -> id int not null primary key auto_increment,
    -> master_id int not null unique,
    -> date_added datetime,
    -> date_modified datetime,
    -> note text
    -> );
Query OK, 0 rows affected (0.00 sec)
```

Now that your tables are created, you can work through the forms and scripts for managing and viewing your records.

Creating a Menu

Your online address book will contain several actions, so it makes sense to create a menu for your links. Listing 19.1 creates a menu for all the scripts you will create in this section, called mymenu.php.

LISTING 19.1   Address Book Menu

```
 1: <html>
 2: <head>
 3: <title>My Address Book</title>
 4: </head>
 5: <body>
 6: <h1>My Address Book</h1>
 7:
 8: <P><strong>Management</strong>
 9: <ul>
10: <li><a href="addentry.php">Add an Entry</a>
11: <li><a href="delentry.php">Delete an Entry</a>
12: </ul>
13:
```

LISTING 19.1 continued

```
14: <P><strong>Viewing</strong>
15: <ul>
16: <li><a href="selentry.php">Select a Record</a>
17: </ul>
18: </body>
19: </html>
```

Figure 19.1 shows the output of Listing 19.1. You'll tackle each of these items in order, starting with "Add an Entry" in the next section.

FIGURE 19.1

Address book menu.

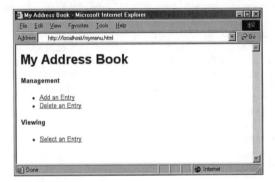

Creating the Record Addition Mechanism

Just because you'll potentially be adding information to six different tables doesn't mean your form or script will be monstrous. In fact, your scripts won't look much different from any of the ones you created in previous lessons, and with practice, you will be able to make these verbose scripts much more streamlined and efficient.

In Listing 19.2, you can see a basic record addition script, called `addentry.php`.

LISTING 19.2 Basic Record Addition Script Called addentry.php

```
1: <?php
2: if ($_POST[op] != "add") {
3:     //haven't seen the form, so show it
4:     $display_block = "<h1>Add an Entry</h1>
5:     <form method=\"post\" action=\"$_SERVER[PHP_SELF]\">
6:     <P><strong>First/Last Names:</strong><br>
7:     <input type=\"text\" name=\"f_name\" size=30 maxlength=75>
8:     <input type=\"text\" name=\"l_name\" size=30 maxlength=75>
9:
```

19

LISTING 19.2   continued

```
10:     <P><strong>Address:</strong><br>
11:     <input type=\"text\" name=\"address\" size=30>
12:
13:     <P><strong>City/State/Zip:</strong><br>
14:     <input type=\"text\" name=\"city\" size=30 maxlength=50>
15:     <input type=\"text\" name=\"state\" size=5 maxlength=2>
16:     <input type=\"text\" name=\"zipcode\" size=10 maxlength=10>
17:
18:     <P><strong>Address Type:</strong><br>
19:     <input type=\"radio\" name=\"add_type\" value=\"home\" checked> home
20:     <input type=\"radio\" name=\"add_type\" value=\"work\"> work
21:    <input type=\"radio\" name=\"add_type\" value=\"other\"> other
22:
23:     <P><strong>Telephone Number:</strong><br>
24:     <input type=\"text\" name=\"tel_number\" size=30 maxlength=25>
25:     <input type=\"radio\" name=\"tel_type\" value=\"home\" checked> home
26:     <input type=\"radio\" name=\"tel_type\" value=\"work\"> work
27:     <input type=\"radio\" name=\"tel_type\" value=\"other\"> other
28:
29:     <P><strong>Fax Number:</strong><br>
30:     <input type=\"text\" name=\"fax_number\" size=30 maxlength=25>
31:     <input type=\"radio\" name=\"fax_type\" value=\"home\" checked> home
32:     <input type=\"radio\" name=\"fax_type\" value=\"work\"> work
33:     <input type=\"radio\" name=\"fax_type\" value=\"other\"> other
34:
35:     <P><strong>Email Address:</strong><br>
36:     <input type=\"text\" name=\"email\" size=30 maxlength=150>
37:     <input type=\"radio\" name=\"email_type\" value=\"home\" checked> home
38:     <input type=\"radio\" name=\"email_type\" value=\"work\"> work
39:     <input type=\"radio\" name=\"email_type\" value=\"other\"> other
40:
41:     <P><strong>Personal Note:</strong><br>
42:     <textarea name=\"note\" cols=35 rows=5 wrap=virtual></textarea>
43:      <input type=\"hidden\" name=\"op\" value=\"add\">
44:
45:     <p><input type=\"submit\" name=\"submit\" value=\"Add Entry\"></p>
46:     </FORM>";
47:
48: } else if ($_POST[op] == "add") {
49:     //time to add to tables, so check for required fields
50:      if (($_POST[f_name] == "") || ($_POST[l_name] == "")) {
51:          header("Location: addentry.php");
52:          exit;
53:      }
54:
55:     //connect to database
56:     $conn = mysql_connect("localhost", "joeuser", "somepass")
57:         or die(mysql_error());
```

LISTING 19.2 continued

```
58:    mysql_select_db("testDB",$conn)  or die(mysql_error());
59:
60:    //add to master_name table
61:    $add_master = "insert into master_name values ('', now(), now(),
62:        '$_POST[f_name]', '$_POST[l_name]')";
63:    mysql_query($add_master) or die(mysql_error());
64:
65:    //get master_id for use with other tables
66:    $master_id = mysql_insert_id();
67:
68:    if (($_POST[address]) || ($_POST[city]) || ($_POST[state]) ||
69:        ($_POST[zipcode])) {
70:        //something relevant, so add to address table
71:        $add_address = "insert into address values ('', $master_id,
72:            now(), now(), '$_POST[address]', '$_POST[city]',
73:            '$_POST[state]', '$_POST[zipcode]', '$_POST[add_type]')";
74:        mysql_query($add_address) or die(mysql_error());
75:    }
76:
77:    if ($_POST[tel_number]) {
78:        //something relevant, so add to telephone table
79:        $add_tel = "insert into telephone values ('', $master_id,
80:         now(), now(), '$_POST[tel_number]',  '$_POST[tel_type]')";
81:        mysql_query($add_tel) or die(mysql_error());
82:    }
83:
84:    if ($_POST[fax_number]) {
85:        //something relevant, so add to fax table
86:        $add_fax = "insert into fax values ('', $master_id, now(),
87:         now(), '$_POST[fax_number]',  '$_POST[fax_type]')";
88:        mysql_query($add_fax) or die(mysql_error());
89:    }
90:
91:    if ($_POST[email]) {
92:        //something relevant, so add to email table
93:        $add_email = "insert into email values ('', $master_id,
94:            now(), now(), '$_POST[email]',  '$_POST[email_type]')";
95:        mysql_query($add_email) or die(mysql_error());
96:    }
97:
98:    if ($_POST[note]) {
99:        //something relevant, so add to notes table
100:        $add_note = "insert into personal_notes values ('', $master_id,
101:            now(), now(), '$_POST[note]')";
102:        mysql_query($add_note) or die(mysql_error());
103:    }
104:
105:    $display_block = "<h1>Entry Added</h1>";
```

19

LISTING 19.2   continued

```
106:    <P>Your entry has been added.  Would you like to
107:     <a href=\"addentry.php\">add another</a>?</p>";
108: }
109: ?>
110: <HTML>
111: <HEAD>
112: <TITLE>Add an Entry</TITLE>
113: </HEAD>
114: <BODY>
115: <? print $display_block; ?>
116: </BODY>
117: </HTML>
```

This script will perform one of two tasks at any given time: It either shows the record addition form, or it performs all the SQL queries related to adding the record. The logic that determines the task begins at line 2, with a test for the value of $_POST[op]. If the value of $_POST[op] is not "add", the user is not coming from the form and therefore needs to see the form. The HTML for the form is placed in a string called $display_block, from lines 4–55. The script then breaks out of the if...else construct and jumps down to line 110, which outputs the HTML and prints the value of $display_block, in this case the form. This outcome is shown in Figure 19.2.

FIGURE 19.2

The record addition form.

Line 48 begins the second condition if the value of $_POST[op] is "add", meaning the user has submitted the form. For the sake of argument, two fields have been designated as required fields: the first name and last name of the person. So, lines 50–53 check for values in $_POST[f_name] and $_POST[l_name] and redirect the user back to the form if either value is missing.

After making it through the check for required fields, we connect to the database in lines 56–59. Next comes the multitude of insertion statements, only one of which is required—the insertion of a record into the master_name table. This occurs on lines 61–63. After the insertion is made, the id of this record is extracted using mysql_insert_id() on line 66. We use this value, now referred to as $master_id, in our remaining SQL queries.

The SQL queries for inserting records into the remaining tables are all conditional. This means that they occur only if some condition is true. In lines 68–69, we see that the condition that must be met is that a value exists for any of the following variables: $_POST[address], $_POST[city], $_POST[state], $_POST[zipcode]. Lines 70–74 create and issue the query if the condition is met.

The same principle holds true for adding to the telephone table (lines 77–82), the fax table (lines 84–89), the email table (lines 91–96), and the personal_notes table (lines 98–103). Once through this set of conditions, the message for the user is placed in the $display_block variable, and the script exits this if...else construct and prints HTML from lines 110–117.

An output of the record addition script is shown in Figure 19.3.

19

FIGURE 19.3

Adding a record.

Add a few records using this form so that you have some values to play with in the following sections. On your own, try to modify this script in such a way that the values entered in the form are printed to the screen after successful record insertion.

Viewing Records

If you verified your work in the preceding section by issuing queries through the MySQL monitor or other interface, you probably became tired of typing SELECT * FROM... for every table. In this section, you'll create the two-part script that shows you how to select and view records in your database.

Listing 19.3 shows the select-and-view script called selentry.php.

LISTING 19.3 Script Called selentry.php for Selecting and Viewing a Record

```
 1: <?php
 2: //connect to database
 3: $conn = mysql_connect("localhost", "joeuser", "somepass")
 4:    or die(mysql_error());
 5: mysql_select_db("testDB",$conn)  or die(mysql_error());
 6:
 7: if ($_POST[op] != "view")  {
 8:    //haven't seen the form, so show it
 9:    $display_block = "<h1>Select an Entry</h1>";
10:
11:    //get parts of records
12:    $get_list = "select id, concat_ws(', ', l_name, f_name) as display_name
13:       from master_name order by l_name, f_name";
14:    $get_list_res = mysql_query($get_list) or die(mysql_error());
15:
16:    if (mysql_num_rows($get_list_res) < 1) {
17:       //no records
18:       $display_block .= "<p><em>Sorry, no records to select!</em></p>";
19:
20:    } else {
21:       //has records, so get results and print in a form
22:       $display_block .= "
23:       <form method=\"post\" action=\"$_SERVER[PHP_SELF]\">
24:       <P><strong>Select a Record to View:</strong><br>
25:       <select name=\"sel_id\">
26:       <option value=\"\">-- Select One --</option>";
27:
28:       while ($recs = mysql_fetch_array($get_list_res)) {
29:          $id = $recs['id'];
30:          $display_name = stripslashes($recs['display_name']);
31:
32:          $display_block .= "<option value=\"$id\">
33:             $display_name</option>";
34:       }
35:       $display_block .= "
36:       </select>
37:       <input type=\"hidden\" name=\"op\" value=\"view\">
```

LISTING 19.3   continued

```
38:            <p><input type=\"submit\" name=\"submit\"
39:                value=\"View Selected Entry\"></p>
40:            </FORM>";
41:    }
42:
43:} else if ($_POST[op] == "view") {
44:
45:    //check for required fields
46:     if ($_POST[sel_id] == "")  {
47:        header("Location: selentry.php");
48:        exit;
49:    }
50:
51:    //get master_info
52:    $get_master = "select concat_ws(' ', f_name, l_name) as display_name
53:        from master_name where id = $_POST[sel_id]";
54:    $get_master_res = mysql_query($get_master);
55:    $display_name = stripslashes(mysql_result($get_master_res,
56:        0,'display_name'));
57:    $display_block = "<h1>Showing Record for $display_name</h1>";
58:    //get all addresses
59:    $get_addresses = "select address, city, state, zipcode, type
60:        from address where master_id = $_POST[sel_id]";
61:    $get_addresses_res = mysql_query($get_addresses);
62:
63:    if (mysql_num_rows($get_addresses_res) > 0) {
64:
65:        $display_block .= "<P><strong>Addresses:</strong><br>
66:        <ul>";
67:
68:        while ($add_info = mysql_fetch_array($get_addresses_res)) {
69:            $address = $add_info[address];
70:            $city = $add_info[city];
71:            $state = $add_info[state];
72:            $zipcode = $add_info[zipcode];
73:            $address_type = $add_info[type];
74:
75:            $display_block .= "<li>$address $city $state $zipcode
76:                ($address_type)";
77:        }
78:
79:        $display_block .= "</ul>";
80:    }
81:
82:    //get all tel
83:    $get_tel = "select tel_number, type from telephone where
84:        master_id = $_POST[sel_id]";
```

LISTING 19.3   continued

```
85:      $get_tel_res = mysql_query($get_tel);
86:
87:      if (mysql_num_rows($get_tel_res) > 0) {
88:
89:          $display_block .= "<P><strong>Telephone:</strong><br>
90:          <ul>";
91:
92:          while ($tel_info = mysql_fetch_array($get_tel_res)) {
93:              $tel_number = $tel_info[tel_number];
94:              $tel_type = $tel_info[type];
95:
96:              $display_block .= "<li>$tel_number ($tel_type)";
97:          }
98:
99:          $display_block .= "</ul>";
100:     }
101:
102:     //get all fax
103:     $get_fax = "select fax_number, type from fax where
104:         master_id = $_POST[sel_id]";
105:     $get_fax_res = mysql_query($get_fax);
106:
107:     if (mysql_num_rows($get_fax_res) > 0) {
108:
109:         $display_block .= "<P><strong>Fax:</strong><br>
110:         <ul>";
111:
112:         while ($fax_info = mysql_fetch_array($get_fax_res)) {
113:             $fax_number = $fax_info[fax_number];
114:             $fax_type = $fax_info[type];
115:
116:             $display_block .= "<li>$fax_number ($fax_type)";
117:         }
118:
119:         $display_block .= "</ul>";
120:     }
121:
122:     //get all email
123:     $get_email = "select email, type from email where
124:         master_id = $_POST[sel_id]";
125:     $get_email_res = mysql_query($get_email);
126:
127:     if (mysql_num_rows($get_email_res) > 0) {
128:
129:         $display_block .= "<P><strong>Email:</strong><br>
130:         <ul>";
131:
132:         while ($email_info = mysql_fetch_array($get_email_res)) {
```

LISTING 19.3   continued

```
133:               $email = $email_info[email];
134:               $email_type = $email_info[type];
135:
136:               $display_block .= "<li>$email ($email_type)";
137:          }
138:
139:          $display_block .= "</ul>";
140:     }
141:
142:     //get personal note
143:     $get_notes = "select note from personal_notes where
144:          master_id = $_POST[sel_id]";
145:     $get_notes_res = mysql_query($get_notes);
146:
147:     if (mysql_num_rows($get_notes_res) == 1) {
148:          $note = nl2br(stripslashes(mysql_result($get_notes_res,0,'note')));
149:
150:          $display_block .= "<P><strong>Personal Notes:</strong><br>$note";
151:     }
152:
153:     $display_block .= "<br><br><P align=center>
154:          <a href=\"$_SERVER[PHP_SELF]\">select another</a></p>";
155: }
156: ?>
157: <HTML>
158: <HEAD>
159: <TITLE>My Records</TITLE>
160: </HEAD>
161: <BODY>
162: <? print $display_block; ?>
163: </BODY>
164: </HTML>
```

As with the addentry.php script, the selentry.php script will perform one of two tasks at any given time: it either shows the selection form, or it performs all the SQL queries related to viewing the record. No matter which of the two tasks will be performed, the database still comes into play. Given that, we connect to it in lines 3–5.

The logic that determines the task begins at line 7, with a test for the value of $_POST[op]. If the value of $_POST[op] is not "view", the user is not coming from the form and therefore needs to see the selection form. A string called $display_block is started in line 9, and this string will be added to throughout this task. We hope that it will ultimately hold a selection form.

In lines 12–14, we select part of the master_name records to build the selection option in the form. For this step, you need only the name and ID of the person whose record you want to select. Line 16 tests for results of the query. If the query has no results, you can't build a form. In this case, the value of $display_block would be filled with an error message and the script would end, printing the resulting HTML to the screen.

However, assume you have a few records in the master_name table. In this case, you have to extract the information from the query results to be able to build the form. This is done in lines 28–33, with form elements written to the $display_block string both above and below it. The script then breaks out of the if...else construct and jumps down to line 110, which outputs the HTML and prints the value of $display_block, in this case the form. This outcome is shown in Figure 19.4.

FIGURE 19.4

The record selection form.

Line 43 begins the second condition if the value of $_POST[op] is "view", meaning the user has submitted the form and wants to see a specific record. The required field in this section of the script is $_POST[sel_id], holding the ID from the master_name table of the user selected in the form. If that value does not exist, the user is redirected to the selection form. In lines 52–55, a query obtains the name of the user whose record you want to view. This information is placed in the now-familiar $display_block string, which will continue to be built as the script continues.

Lines 59–80 represent the query against the address table. If the selected individual has no records in the address table, nothing is added to the $display_block string. However, if there are one or more entries, they are placed in $display_block as unordered list elements, as shown in lines 65–79.

The same principle is followed for records in the `telephone` (lines 83–100), `fax` (lines 103–120), and `email` (lines 123–140) tables. If there are one or more entries, place the results in `$display_block`. Otherwise, the script moves on. Because there can be only one entry per individual in the `personal_notes` table, the script checks for the entry beginning in line 143, and moves on if it doesn't exist. If a note exists, it's written in `$display_block` in lines 147–151.

The final action in this part of the script is to print a link in lines 153–154, in case the user wants to return to the selection screen. After this point, the script exits from the `if...else` construct and prints the HTML to the screen. Figure 19.5 shows a record from the record selection script, with one entry in each table.

FIGURE 19.5

An individual's record.

Try this script yourself. You should see data only for individuals who have data associated with them. For example, if you have an entry for a friend, and all you have is an email address for that person, you shouldn't see any text relating to address, telephone, fax, or personal notes.

Creating the Record Deletion Mechanism

The record deletion mechanism is virtually identical to the script used to view a record. In fact, you can just take the first 42 lines of Listing 19.3 and paste them into a new file, called `delentry.php`, and make the following changes:

- In lines 7, 37, and 43, change "view" to "delete"
- In lines 24 and 39, change "View" to "Delete"

Starting with a new line 45, the remainder of the code for delentry.php is shown in Listing 19.4.

LISTING 19.4 Script Called delentry.php for Selecting and Deleting a Record

```
45:    //check for required fields
46:      if ($_POST[sel_id] == "")  {
47:        header("Location: delentry.php");
48:        exit;
49:      }
50:
51:    //issue queries
52:    $del_master = "delete from master_name where id = $_POST[sel_id]";
53:    mysql_query($del_master);
54:
55:    $del_address = "delete from address where id = $_POST[sel_id]";
56:    mysql_query($del_address);
57:
58:    $del_tel = "delete from telephone where id = $_POST[sel_id]";
59:    mysql_query($del_tel);
60:
61:    $del_fax = "delete from fax where id = $_POST[sel_id]";
62:    mysql_query($del_fax);
63:
64:    $del_email = "delete from email where id = $_POST[sel_id]";
65:    mysql_query($del_email);
66:
67:    $del_note = "delete from personal_notes where id = $_POST[sel_id]";
68:    mysql_query($del_master);
69:
70:    $display_block = "<h1>Record(s) Deleted</h1>
71:    <P>Would you like to
72:    <a href=\"$_SERVER[PHP_SELF]\">delete another</a>?</p>";
73: }
74: ?>
75: <HTML>
76: <HEAD>
77: <TITLE>My Records</TITLE>
78: </HEAD>
79: <BODY>
80: <? print $display_block; ?>
81: </BODY>
82: </HTML>
```

Picking up with Line 45, the script looks for the required field, $_POST[sel_id]. If that value does not exist, the user is redirected to the selection form. In lines 52–68, queries delete all information related to the selected individual, from all tables. Lines 70–72 place a nice message in $display_block, and the script exits and prints the HTML to the screen. An output of the record deletion script is shown in Figure 19.6.

FIGURE 19.6

Deleting a record.

Now go back to the record selection form and note that the individual you deleted is no longer in the selection menu.

Adding Subentries to a Record

At this point, you've learned to add, delete, and view records. What's missing is adding those additional entries to the related tables—entries for home versus work telephone number, for example. All you need to do is make a few changes to existing scripts.

In the selentry.php script in Listing 19.3, change lines 153–154 to read

```
$display_block .= "<P align=center>
<a href=\"addentry.php?master_id=$_POST[sel_id]\">add info</a> ...
<a href=\"$_SERVER[PHP_SELF]\">select another</a></p>";
```

This change simply adds a link to the addentry.php script and also passes it a variable called $master_id.

Now we need to modify the addentry.php script in Listing 19.2 to account for its dual purposes. Here is a summary of the changes to the original script.

Replace the first 10 lines of the original addentry.php script with the following snippet:

```
<?php
if (($_POST[op] != "add") || ($_GET[master_id] != "")) {
```

19

```
//haven't seen the form, so show it
$display_block = "
<h1>Add an Entry</h1>
<form method=\"post\" action=\"$_SERVER[PHP_SELF]\">";

if ($_GET[master_id] != "") {
    //connect to database
    $conn = mysql_connect("localhost", "joeuser", "somepass")
                or die(mysql_error());
    mysql_select_db("testDB",$conn)  or die(mysql_error());

    //get first, last names for display/tests validity
    $get_names = "select concat_ws(' ', f_name, l_name) as
                display_name from master_name where id = $_GET[master_id]";
    $get_names_res = mysql_query($get_names) or die(mysql_error());

    if (mysql_num_rows($get_names_res) == 1) {
        $display_name = mysql_result($get_names_res,0,'display_name');
    }
}

if ($display_name != "") {
    $display_block .= "<P>Adding information for
                    <strong>$display_name</strong>:</p>";
} else {
    $display_block .= "
    <P><strong>First/Last Names:</strong><br>
    <input type=\"text\" name=\"f_name\" size=30 maxlength=75>
    <input type=\"text\" name=\"l_name\" size=30 maxlength=75>";
}
$display_block .= "<P><strong>Address:</strong><br>
```

This snippet simply moves around the form elements, printing the first and last name fields only if they contain a new record. If they contain an addition to a record, the individual's name is extracted from the database for aesthetic purposes as well as for a validity check of the ID.

Next, find this line:

```
<input type=\"hidden\" name=\"op\" value=\"add\">
```

Beneath it, add the following:

```
<input type=\"hidden\" name=\"master_id\" value=\"$_GET[master_id]\">
```

This modification ensures the known value of master_id is passed along to the next task.

Identify what were lines 49–67 of the original script, beginning with the comment time to add to tables and ending with obtaining the value of $master_id. These lines should be replaced with the following:

```
//time to add to tables, so check for required fields
if ((($_POST[f_name] == "") || ($_POST[l_name] == "")) &&
        ($_POST[master_id] == "")) {
    header("Location: addentry.php");
    exit;
}

//connect to database
$conn = mysql_connect("localhost", "joeuser", "somepass")
        or die(mysql_error());
mysql_select_db("testDB",$conn)  or die(mysql_error());

if ($_POST[master_id] == "") {
    //add to master_name table
    $add_master = "insert into master_name values ('', now(),
                now(), '$_POST[f_name]', '$_POST[l_name]')";
    mysql_query($add_master) or die(mysql_error());
    //get master_id for use with other tables
    $master_id = mysql_insert_id();
} else {
    $master_id = $_POST[master_id];
}
```

These lines modify the check for required fields, allowing the script to continue without values for first and last names, but only if it has a $_POST[master_id] value. Then the script connects to the database to perform all the additions we want it to, but it skips the addition to the master_name table if a value for $_POST[master_id] exists.

Finally, in the section of the script that handles the insertion into the personal_notes table, change insert into to replace into to handle an update of the notes field.

The new script should look Listing 19.5.

LISTING 19.5 New addentry.php Script

```
1: <?php
2: if (($_POST[op] != "add") || ($_GET[master_id] != "")) {
3:      //haven't seen the form, so show it
4:      $display_block = "
5:      <h1>Add an Entry</h1>
6:      <form method=\"post\" action=\"$_SERVER[PHP_SELF]\">";
7:
8:          if ($_GET[master_id] != "") {
9:              //connect to database
10:             $conn = mysql_connect("localhost", "joeuser", "somepass")
11:                     or die(mysql_error());
12:             mysql_select_db("testDB",$conn)  or die(mysql_error());
13:
14:             //get first, last names for display/tests validity
```

19

LISTING 19.5   continued

```
15:          $get_names = "select concat_ws(' ', f_name, l_name) as
16:                  display_name from master_name where id = $_GET[master_id]";
17:          $get_names_res = mysql_query($get_names) or die(mysql_error());
18:
19:          if (mysql_num_rows($get_names_res) == 1) {
20:              $display_name = mysql_result($get_names_res,0,'display_name');
21:          }
22:      }
23:
24:      if ($display_name != "") {
25:          $display_block .= "<P>Adding information for
26:                          <strong>$display_name</strong>:</p>";
27:      } else {
28:          $display_block .= "
29:       <P><strong>First/Last Names:</strong><br>
30:       <input type=\"text\" name=\"f_name\" size=30 maxlength=75>
31:       <input type=\"text\" name=\"l_name\" size=30 maxlength=75>";
32:      }
33:  $display_block .= "<P><strong>Address:</strong><br>
34:     <input type=\"text\" name=\"address\" size=30>
35:
36:     <P><strong>City/State/Zip:</strong><br>
37:     <input type=\"text\" name=\"city\" size=30 maxlength=50>
38:     <input type=\"text\" name=\"state\" size=5 maxlength=2>
39:     <input type=\"text\" name=\"zipcode\" size=10 maxlength=10>
40:
41:     <P><strong>Address Type:</strong><br>
42:     <input type=\"radio\" name=\"add_type\" value=\"home\" checked> home
43:     <input type=\"radio\" name=\"add_type\" value=\"work\"> work
44:   <input type=\"radio\" name=\"add_type\" value=\"other\"> other
45:
46:     <P><strong>Telephone Number:</strong><br>
47:     <input type=\"text\" name=\"tel_number\" size=30 maxlength=25>
48:     <input type=\"radio\" name=\"tel_type\" value=\"home\" checked> home
49:     <input type=\"radio\" name=\"tel_type\" value=\"work\"> work
50:     <input type=\"radio\" name=\"tel_type\" value=\"other\"> other
51:
52:     <P><strong>Fax Number:</strong><br>
53:     <input type=\"text\" name=\"fax_number\" size=30 maxlength=25>
54:     <input type=\"radio\" name=\"fax_type\" value=\"home\" checked> home
55:     <input type=\"radio\" name=\"fax_type\" value=\"work\"> work
56:     <input type=\"radio\" name=\"fax_type\" value=\"other\"> other
57:
58:     <P><strong>Email Address:</strong><br>
59:     <input type=\"text\" name=\"email\" size=30 maxlength=150>
60:     <input type=\"radio\" name=\"email_type\" value=\"home\" checked> home
61:     <input type=\"radio\" name=\"email_type\" value=\"work\"> work
62:     <input type=\"radio\" name=\"email_type\" value=\"other\"> other
```

LISTING 19.5   continued

```
63:
64:    <P><strong>Personal Note:</strong><br>
65:    <textarea name=\"note\" cols=35 rows=5 wrap=virtual></textarea>
66:    <input type=\"hidden\" name=\"op\" value=\"add\">
67:    <input type=\"hidden\" name=\"master_id\" value=\"$_GET[master_id]\">
68:
69:    <p><input type=\"submit\" name=\"submit\" value=\"Add Entry\"></p>
70:    </FORM>";
71:
72: } else if ($_POST[op] == "add") {
73:    //time to add to tables, so check for required fields
74:    if ((($_POST[f_name] == "") || ($_POST[l_name] == "")) &&
75:    ($_POST[master_id] == "")) {
76:        header("Location: addentry.php");
77:        exit;
78:    }
79:
80:    //connect to database
81: $conn = mysql_connect("localhost", "joeuser", "somepass")
82: or die(mysql_error());
83: mysql_select_db("testDB",$conn)  or die(mysql_error());
84:
85:    if ($_POST[master_id] == "") {
86:        //add to master_name table
87:        $add_master = "insert into master_name values ('', now(),
88:        now(), '$_POST[f_name]', '$_POST[l_name]')";
89:        mysql_query($add_master) or die(mysql_error());
90:        //get master_id for use with other tables
91:        $master_id = mysql_insert_id();
92:    } else {
93:        $master_id = $_POST[master_id];
94:    }
95:
96:    if (($_POST[address]) || ($_POST[city]) || ($_POST[state]) ||
97:        ($_POST[zipcode])) {
98:        //something relevant, so add to address table
99:        $add_address = "insert into address values ('', $master_id,
100:           now(), now(), '$_POST[address]', '$_POST[city]',
101:           '$_POST[state]', '$_POST[zipcode]', '$_POST[add_type]')";
102:        mysql_query($add_address) or die(mysql_error());
103:    }
104:
105:    if ($_POST[tel_number]) {
106:        //something relevant, so add to telephone table
107:        $add_tel = "insert into telephone values ('', $master_id,
108:         now(), now(), '$_POST[tel_number]',  '$_POST[tel_type]')";
109:        mysql_query($add_tel) or die(mysql_error());
110:    }
```

19

LISTING 19.5   continued

```
111:
112:    if ($_POST[fax_number]) {
113:        //something relevant, so add to fax table
114:        $add_fax = "insert into fax values ('', $master_id, now(),
115:          now(), '$_POST[fax_number]',  '$_POST[fax_type]')";
116:        mysql_query($add_fax) or die(mysql_error());
117:    }
118:
119:    if ($_POST[email]) {
120:        //something relevant, so add to email table
121:        $add_email = "insert into email values ('', $master_id,
122:            now(), now(), '$_POST[email]',  '$_POST[email_type]')";
123:        mysql_query($add_email) or die(mysql_error());
124:    }
125:
126:    if ($_POST[note]) {
127:        //something relevant, so add to notes table
128:        $add_note = "replace into personal_notes values ('', $master_id,
129:            now(), now(), '$_POST[note]')";
130:        mysql_query($add_note) or die(mysql_error());
131:    }
132:
133:    $display_block = "<h1>Entry Added</h1>
134:    <P>Your entry has been added.  Would you like to
135:      <a href=\"addentry.php\">add another</a>?</p>";
136: }
137: ?>
138: <HTML>
139: <HEAD>
140: <TITLE>Add an Entry</TITLE>
141: </HEAD>
142: <BODY>
143: <? print $display_block; ?>
144: </BODY>
145: </HTML>
```

You can try out this revised script by selecting a record to view and then following the add info link. You should see a form like Figure 19.7.

After submitting this form, you can go back through the selection sequence and view the record to verify that your changes have been made.

FIGURE 19.7

Adding to a record.

Summary

In this hands-on hour, you applied your basic PHP and MySQL knowledge to the creation of a personal address book. You learned how to create the database table and scripts for record addition, deletion, and simple viewing. You also learned the process for adding multiple records attached to a single master entry.

Workshop

The workshop is designed to help you anticipate possible questions, review what you've learned, and begin learning how to put your knowledge into practice.

Quiz

1. When passing a variable through the query string, which superglobal does it belong in? (Hint: You passed a variable this way in the last section.)

2. How many records in the address, email, telephone, and fax tables can you have for each individual in your master_name table?

19

Answers

1. The $_GET superglobal.
2. As many as you want—it's relational!

Activities

1. Go through each of the administration scripts and modify the code so that a link to the menu is printed at the bottom of each screen.
2. Use the second version of the addentry.php script to add secondary contact information to records in your database. Figure 19.8 shows how a record will look, after secondary contact information is added to it.

FIGURE 19.8

An individual's record, with multiple entries in tables.

HOUR **20**

Creating an Online Storefront

In this hour's hands-on lesson, the project is creating a generic online storefront. You will learn the methods for creating the relevant database tables, as well as the scripts for displaying the information to the user. The examples used in this hour represent one of an infinite number of possibilities to complete these tasks, and are meant to provide a foundation of knowledge rather than a definitive method for completing this task.

In this hour, you will learn how to

- Create relational tables for an online store
- Create the scripts to display store categories
- Create the scripts to display individual items

Planning and Creating the Database Tables

Before you tackle the process of creating database tables for a store, think about how you shop in real life. When you walk into a store, items are ordered in some fashion: The hardware and the baby clothes aren't mixed together, the electronics and the laundry detergent aren't side by side, and so on. Applying that knowledge to database normalization, already you know that you will need a table to hold categories and a table to hold items. These items will each belong to one category.

Next, think about the items themselves. Depending on the type of store you have, your items may or may not have colors, and may or may not have sizes. But all your items will have a name, a description, and a price. Again, thinking in terms of normalization, you know that you will have one general items table and two additional tables that relate to the general items table.

Table 20.1 shows sample table and field names to use for your online storefront. In a minute, you'll create the actual SQL statements, but first you should look at this information and try to see the relationships appear. Ask yourself which of the fields should be primary or unique keys.

TABLE 20.1 Storefront Table and Field Names

Table Name	Field Names
store_categories	id, cat_title, cat_desc
store_items	id, cat_id, item_title, item_price, item_desc, item_image
store_item_size	item_id, item_size
store_item_color	item_id, item_color

As you can see in the following SQL statements, the store_categories table has two fields besides the id field: cat_title and cat_desc, for title and description. The id field is the primary key, and cat_title is a unique field because there's no reason you would have two identical categories.

```
mysql> create table store_categories (
    -> id int not null primary key auto_increment,
    -> cat_title varchar (50) unique,
    -> cat_desc text
    -> );
Query OK, 0 rows affected (0.03 sec)
```

The store_items table has five fields besides the id field, none of which are unique keys. The lengths specified in the field definitions are arbitrary; you should use whatever best fits your store. The cat_id field relates the item to a particular category in the store_categories table. This field is not unique because you will want more than one item in each category. The item_title, item_price, and item_desc (for description) fields are self-explanatory. The item_image field in this case will hold a filename—in this case, the file is assumed to be local to your server—which you will use to build an HTML <IMG> tag when it's time to display your item information.

```
mysql> create table store_items (
    -> id int  not null primary key auto_increment,
    -> cat_id int not null,
    -> item_title varchar (75),
    -> item_price float (8,2),
    -> item_desc text,
    -> item_image varchar (50)
    -> );
Query OK, 0 rows affected (0.00 sec)
```

Both the store_item_size and store_item_color tables contain optional information: If you sell books, they won't have sizes or colors, but if you sell shirts, they will. For each of these tables, no keys are involved because you can associate as many colors and sizes with a particular item as you want.

```
mysql> create table store_item_size (
    -> item_id int not null,
    -> item_size varchar (25)
    -> );
Query OK, 0 rows affected (0.00 sec)
mysql> create table store_item_color (
    -> item_id int not null,
    -> item_color varchar (25)
    -> );
Query OK, 0 rows affected (0.00 sec)
```

These are all the tables necessary for a basic storefront—that is, for displaying the items you have for sale. Hour 21, "Creating a Shopping Cart Mechanism," integrates the user experience into the mix. For now, just concentrate on your inventory.

In Hour 19, "Creating an Online Address Book," you learned how to use PHP forms and scripts to add or delete records in your tables. If you apply the same principles to this set of tables, you can easily create an administrative front end to your storefront. We won't go through that process in this book, but feel free to do it on your own. At this point, you know enough about PHP and MySQL to complete the tasks.

For now, simply issue MySQL queries via the MySQL monitor or other interface, to add information to your tables. Following are some examples, if you want to follow along with sample data.

20

Inserting Records into the `store_categories` Table

The following queries create three categories in your `store_categories` table: hats, shirts, and books.

```
mysql> insert into store_categories values
    -> ('1', 'Hats', 'Funky hats in all shapes and sizes!');
Query OK, 1 row affected (0.01 sec)

mysql> insert into store_categories values ('2', 'Shirts', 'From t-shirts to
sweatshirts to polo shirts and beyond, we have them all.');
Query OK, 1 row affected (0.00 sec)

mysql> insert into store_categories values ('3', 'Books', 'Paperback,
hardback, books for school and books for play, you name it, we have it.');
Query OK, 1 row affected (0.00 sec)
```

In the next section, we'll add some items to the categories.

Inserting Records into the `store_items` Table

The following queries add three item records to each category. Feel free to add many more.

```
mysql> insert into store_items values ('1', '1', 'Baseball Hat', '12.00',
'Fancy, low-profile baseball hat.', 'baseballhat.gif');
Query OK, 1 row affected (0.00 sec)

mysql> insert into store_items values ('2', '1', 'Cowboy Hat', '52.00',
'10 gallon variety', 'cowboyhat.gif');
Query OK, 1 row affected (0.01 sec)

mysql> insert into store_items values ('3', '1', 'Top Hat', '102.00',
'Good for costumes.', 'tophat.gif');
Query OK, 1 row affected (0.00 sec)

mysql> insert into store_items values ('4', '2', 'Short-Sleeved T-Shirt',
'12.00', '100% cotton, pre-shrunk.', 'sstshirt.gif');
Query OK, 1 row affected (0.00 sec)

mysql> insert into store_items values ('5', '2', 'Long-Sleeved T-Shirt',
'15.00', 'Just like the short-sleeved shirt, with longer sleeves.',
'lstshirt.gif');
Query OK, 1 row affected (0.00 sec)

mysql> insert into store_items values ('6', '2', 'Sweatshirt', '22.00',
'Heavy and warm.', 'sweatshirt.gif');
Query OK, 1 row affected (0.00 sec)

mysql> insert into store_items values ('7', '3', 'Jane\'s Self-Help Book',
'12.00', 'Jane gives advice.', 'selfhelpbook.gif');
Query OK, 1 row affected (0.00 sec)
```

```
mysql> insert into store_items values ('8', '3', 'Generic Academic Book',
'35.00', 'Some required reading for school, will put you to sleep.',
'boringbook.gif');
Query OK, 1 row affected (0.00 sec)

mysql> insert into store_items values ('9', '3', 'Chicago Manual of Style',
'9.99', 'Good for copywriters.', 'chicagostyle.gif');
Query OK, 1 row affected (0.00 sec)
```

Inserting Records into the `store_item_size` Table

The following queries associate sizes with one of the three items in the `shirts` category and a generic "one size fits all" size to each of the hats (assume they're strange hats). On your own, insert the same set of size associations for the remaining items in the `shirts` category.

```
mysql> insert into store_item_size values (1, 'One Size Fits All');
Query OK, 1 row affected (0.00 sec)

mysql> insert into store_item_size values (2, 'One Size Fits All');
Query OK, 1 row affected (0.00 sec)

mysql> insert into store_item_size values (3, 'One Size Fits All');
Query OK, 1 row affected (0.00 sec)

mysql> insert into store_item_size values (4, 'S');
Query OK, 1 row affected (0.00 sec)

mysql> insert into store_item_size values (4, 'M');
Query OK, 1 row affected (0.00 sec)

mysql> insert into store_item_size values (4, 'L');
Query OK, 1 row affected (0.00 sec)

mysql> insert into store_item_size values (4, 'XL');
Query OK, 1 row affected (0.00 sec)
```

Inserting Records into the `store_item_color` Table

The following queries associate colors with one of the three items in the `shirts` category. On your own, insert color records for the remaining shirts and hats.

```
mysql> insert into store_item_color values (1, 'red');
Query OK, 1 row affected (0.00 sec)

mysql> insert into store_item_color values (1, 'black');
Query OK, 1 row affected (0.00 sec)

mysql> insert into store_item_color values (1, 'blue');
Query OK, 1 row affected (0.00 sec)
```

20

Displaying Categories of Items

Believe it or not, the most difficult task in this project is finished. Compared to thinking up categories and items, creating the scripts used to display the information is easy! The first script you will make is one that lists categories and items. Obviously, you wouldn't want to list all categories and all items all at once as soon as the user walks in the door, but you do want to give the user the option of immediately picking a category, seeing its items, and then picking another category. In other words, this script will serve two purposes: It will show the categories and then show the items in that category.

Listing 20.1 shows the code for seestore.php.

LISTING 20.1   Script to View Categories

```
 1: <?php
 2: //connect to database
 3: $conn = mysql_connect("localhost", "joeuser", "somepass")
 4:     or die(mysql_error());
 5: mysql_select_db("testDB",$conn)  or die(mysql_error());
 6:
 7: $display_block = "<h1>My Categories</h1>
 8: <P>Select a category to see its items.</p>";
 9:
10: //show categories first
11: $get_cats = "select id, cat_title, cat_desc from
12:     store_categories order by cat_title";
13: $get_cats_res = mysql_query($get_cats) or die(mysql_error());
14:
15: if (mysql_num_rows($get_cats_res) < 1) {
16:     $display_block = "<P><em>Sorry, no categories to browse.</em></p>";
17: } else {
18:
19:     while ($cats = mysql_fetch_array($get_cats_res)) {
20:         $cat_id   = $cats[id];
21:         $cat_title = strtoupper(stripslashes($cats[cat_title]));
22:         $cat_desc = stripslashes($cats[cat_desc]);
23:
24:         $display_block .= "<p><strong><a
25:         href=\"$_SERVER[PHP_SELF]?cat_id=$cat_id\">$cat_title</a></strong>
26:         <br>$cat_desc</p>";
27:
28:         if ($_GET[cat_id] == $cat_id) {
29:             //get items
30:             $get_items = "select id, item_title, item_price
31:             from store_items where cat_id = $cat_id
32:              order by item_title";
33:             $get_items_res = mysql_query($get_items) or die(mysql_error());
34:
35:             if (mysql_num_rows($get_items_res) < 1) {
```

LISTING 20.1 continued

```
36:                    $display_block = "<P><em>Sorry, no items in
37:                     this category.</em></p>";
38:                } else {
39:
40:                    $display_block .= "<ul>";
41:
42:                    while ($items = mysql_fetch_array($get_items_res)) {
43:                        $item_id    = $items[id];
44:                        $item_title = stripslashes($items[item_title]);
45:                        $item_price = $items[item_price];
46:
47:                        $display_block .= "<li><a
48:                         href=\"showitem.php?item_id=$item_id\">$item_title</a>
49:                         </strong> (\$$item_price)";
50:                    }
51:
52:                    $display_block .= "</ul>";
53:                }
54:            }
55:        }
56: }
57: ?>
58: <HTML>
59: <HEAD>
60: <TITLE>My Categories</TITLE>
61: </HEAD>
62: <BODY>
63 :<? print $display_block; ?>
64: </BODY>
65: </HTML>
```

Given the length of scripts in Hour 19, these 65 fully functional lines should be a welcome change. In lines 3–5 the database connection is opened, because regardless of
which action the script is taking—showing categories or showing items in categories—
the database is necessary.

In lines 7–8, the $display_block string is started, with some basic page title informa-
tion. Lines 11–13 create and issue the query to retrieve the category information. Line 15
checks for categories; if none were in the table, a message is printed to the user and
that's all this script does. However, if categories are found, the script moves on to line
19, which begins a while loop to extract the information.

In the while loop, lines 20–22 retrieve the ID, title, and description of the category.
String operations are performed to ensure that no slashes are in the text and that the category title is in uppercase for display purposes. Lines 24–26 place the category information, including a self-referential page link, in the $display_block string. If a user clicks

20

the link, she will return to this same script, except with a category ID passed in the query string. The script checks for this value in line 28.

If a $cat_id value has been passed to the script because the user clicked on a category link in hopes of seeing listed items, the script builds and issues another query (lines 30–33) to retrieve the items in the category. Lines 42–53 check for items and then build an item string as part of $display_block. Part of the information in the string is a link to a script called showitem.php, which you'll create in the next section.

After reaching that point, the script has nothing left to do, so it prints the HTML and value of $display_block. Figure 20.1 shows the outcome of the script when accessed directly; only the category information shows.

FIGURE 20.1

Categories in the store.

In Figure 20.2, you see what happens when the user clicked on the HATS link: the script gathered all the items associated with the category and printed them on the screen. The user can still jump to another category on this same page, and it will gather the items for that category.

The last piece of the puzzle for this hour is the creation of the item display page.

FIGURE 20.2

Items within a category in the store.

Displaying Items

The item display page in this hour will simply show all the item information. In the next hour, you'll add a few lines to it to make it function with an "add to cart" button. So for now, just assume this is a paper catalog.

Listing 20.2 shows the code for showitem.php.

LISTING 20.2   Script to View Item Information

```
 1: <?php
 2: //connect to database
 3: $conn = mysql_connect("localhost", "joeuser", "somepass")
 4:    or die(mysql_error());
 5: mysql_select_db("testDB",$conn)  or die(mysql_error());
 6:
 7: $display_block = "<h1>My Store - Item Detail</h1>";
 8:
 9: //validate item
10: $get_item = "select c.cat_title, si.item_title, si.item_price,
11: si.item_desc, si.item_image from store_items as si left join
12: store_categories as c on c.id = si.cat_id where si.id = $_GET[item_id]";
13:
14: $get_item_res = mysql_query($get_item) or die (mysql_error());
15:
16: if (mysql_num_rows($get_item_res) < 1) {
17:    //invalid item
18:    $display_block .= "<P><em>Invalid item selection.</em></p>";
19: } else {
20:    //valid item, get info
```

20

LISTING **20.2**   continued

```
21:    $cat_title = strtoupper(stripslashes(
22:        mysql_result($get_item_res,0,'cat_title')));
23:    $item_title = stripslashes(mysql_result($get_item_res,0,'item_title'));
24:    $item_price = mysql_result($get_item_res,0,'item_price');
25:    $item_desc = stripslashes(mysql_result($get_item_res,0,'item_desc'));
26:    $item_image = mysql_result($get_item_res,0,'item_image');
27:
28:    //make breadcrumb trail
29:    $display_block .= "<P><strong><em>You are viewing:</em><br>
30:    <a href=\"seestore.php?cat_id=$cat_id\">$cat_title</a>
31:     &gt; $item_title</strong></p>
32:
33:    <table cellpadding=3 cellspacing=3>
34:    <tr>
35:    <td valign=middle align=center><img src=\"$item_image\"></td>
36:    <td valign=middle><P><strong>Description:</strong><br>$item_desc</p>
37:    <P><strong>Price:</strong> \$$item_price</p>";
38:
39:    //get colors
40:    $get_colors = "select item_color from store_item_color where
41:     item_id = $item_id order by item_color";
42:    $get_colors_res = mysql_query($get_colors) or die(mysql_error());
43:
44:    if (mysql_num_rows($get_colors_res) > 0) {
45:
46:        $display_block .= "<P><strong>Available Colors:</strong><br>";
47:
48:        while ($colors = mysql_fetch_array($get_colors_res)) {
49:            $item_color = $colors['item_color'];
50:
51:            $display_block .= "$item_color<br>";
52:        }
53:    }
54:
55:    //get sizes
56:    $get_sizes = "select item_size from store_item_size where
57:        item_id = $item_id order by item_size";
58:    $get_sizes_res = mysql_query($get_sizes) or die(mysql_error());
59:
60:    if (mysql_num_rows($get_sizes_res) > 0) {
61:
62:        $display_block .= "<P><strong>Available Sizes:</strong><br>";
63:
64:        while ($sizes = mysql_fetch_array($get_sizes_res)) {
65:            $item_size = $sizes['item_size'];
66:
67:            $display_block .= "$item_size<br>";
68:        }
69:    }
70:
```

LISTING 20.2 continued

```
71:    $display_block .= "
72:    </td>
73:    </tr>
74:    </table>";
75:
76: }
77: ?>
78: <HTML>
79: <HEAD>
80: <TITLE>My Store</TITLE>
81: </HEAD>
82: <BODY>
83: <? print $display_block; ?>
84: </BODY>
85: </HTML>
```

In lines 3–5 the database connection is opened, because information in the database forms all the content of this page. In line 7, the $display_block string is started, with some basic page title information.

Lines 10–14 create and issue the query to retrieve the category and item information. This particular query is a table join. Instead of selecting the item information from one table and then issuing a second query to find the name of the category, this query simply joins the table on the category ID to find the category name.

Line 16 checks for a result; if there is no matching item in the table, a message is printed to the user and that's all this script does. However, if item information is found, the script moves on and gathers the information in lines 21–26.

In lines 29–31, you create what's known as a "breadcrumb trail." This is simply a navigational device used to get back to the top-level item in the architecture. Those are fancy words that mean "print a link so you can get back to the category."

In lines 33–37, you continue to add to the $display_block, setting up a table for information about the item. You use the values gathered in lines 21–26 to create an image link, print the description, and print the price. What's missing are the colors and sizes, so lines 39–53 select and print any colors associated with this item, and lines 55–69 gather the sizes associated with the item.

Lines 71–74 wrap up the $display_block string, and because the script has nothing left to do, it prints the HTML and value of $display_block. Figure 20.3 shows the outcome of the script when selecting the cowboy hat from the hats category. Of course, your display will differ from mine, but you get the idea.

20

FIGURE 20.3

The cowboy hat item page.

That's all there is to creating a simple item display. In the next hour, you'll modify this script so that it can add the item to a shopping cart.

Summary

In this hands-on hour, you applied your basic PHP and MySQL knowledge to the creation of a storefront display. You learned how to create the database table and scripts for viewing categories, item lists, and single items.

Workshop

The workshop is designed to help you anticipate possible questions, review what you've learned, and begin learning how to put your knowledge into practice.

Quiz

1. Which PHP function was used to uppercase the category title strings?
2. Why don't the `store_item_size` and `store_item_color` tables contain any primary or unique keys?

Answers

1. `strtoupper()`
2. Presumably, you will have items with more than one color and more than one size. Therefore, `item_id` is not a primary or unique key. Also, items may have the same colors or sizes, so the `item_color` and `item_size` fields must not be primary or unique either.

HOUR 21

Creating a Shopping Cart Mechanism

In the last of the directly hands-on hours, the project is to integrate a shopping cart and checkout procedure into the storefront you created in the previous hour. You will be shown the methods for creating the relevant database tables as well as the scripts for adding and deleting cart items. Once again, the examples used in this hour represent one of an infinite number of possibilities to complete these tasks and are meant as working examples rather than the definitive guide for building an online store.

In this hour, you will learn

- How to create relational tables for the shopping cart and checkout portion of an online store
- How to create the scripts to add and remove cart items
- Some methods for processing transactions, and how to create your checkout sequence

Planning and Creating the Database Tables

Because the goal of this hour is to provide the user with a way to select and order items, you can imagine what the tables will be—first and foremost you need a cart table! In addition to the cart table, you'll need a table to store orders, along with one to store the items purchased as part of each order.

The following SQL statements were used to create the three new tables, starting with the store_shoppertrack table. This is the table used to hold items as users add them to their shopping cart.

 The field lengths used to define these tables were chosen arbitrarily to try and accommodate several possible inputs. Please feel free to modify the lengths to meet your specific needs.

```
mysql> create table store_shoppertrack (
    -> id int not null primary key auto_increment,
    -> session_id varchar (32),
    -> sel_item_id int,
    -> sel_item_qty smallint,
    -> sel_item_size varchar(25),
    -> sel_item_color varchar(25),
    -> date_added datetime
    -> );
Query OK, 0 rows affected (0.01 sec)
```

In this table, the only key is the id field for the record. The session_id cannot be unique; otherwise users could only order one item from your store, which is not a good business practice. The session_id identifies the user. The sel_* fields are the selections by the user: the selected item, the selected quantity of the item, and the selected color and size of the item. Finally, there's a date_added field. Many times, users place items in their cart and never go through the checkout process. This practice leaves straggling items in your tracking table, which you may want to clear out periodically. For example, you might want to delete all cart items more than a week old—this is where the date_added field is helpful.

The next table holds the order information:

```
mysql> create table store_orders (
    -> id int not null primary key auto_increment,
    -> order_date datetime,
    -> order_name varchar (100),
    -> order_address varchar (255),
```

```
    -> order_city varchar (50),
    -> order_state char(2),
    -> order_zip varchar(10),
    -> order_tel varchar(25),
    -> order_email varchar(100),
    -> item_total float(6,2),
    -> shipping_total float(6,2),
    -> authorization varchar (50),
    -> status enum('processed', 'pending')
    -> );
Query OK, 0 rows affected (0.00 sec)
```

The only key field in the store_orders table is the id. For the sake of brevity in this lesson, an assumption is made that the billing and shipping addresses of the user are the same, and that this store sells only to United States addresses. It's simple enough to add another block of fields for shipping address information, if you want to do so. Also, this table assumes that you are not storing credit-card information, which you shouldn't do unless you have super-encrypted the information and are positive your firewall is secure. This table is based on the idea of real-time, credit-card processing. You'll learn a few transaction options at the end of this lesson.

The final table is the table to hold the line items in each order, store_orders_items:

```
mysql> create table store_orders_itemmap (
    -> id int not null primary key auto_increment,
    -> order_id int,
    -> sel_item_id int,
    -> sel_item_qty smallint,
    -> sel_item_size varchar(25),
    -> sel_item_color varchar(25),
    -> sel_item_price float(6,2)
    -> );
Query OK, 0 rows affected (0.00 sec)
```

The sel_* fields should look familiar—with the exception of sel_item_price, they are the same fields that appear in the store_shoppertrack table! The primary key is the id field, and the order_id field is used to tie each line item to the appropriate record in store_orders. The sel_item_price field is included here, as opposed to simply relating to the item record because you might have occasion to change the pricing in your item record. If you change the price in the item record, and you relate the sold line items to the current catalog price, your line item prices won't reflect what the user actually paid.

With your tables all squared away we can move on to adding an item to the user's shopping cart.

21

Integrating the Cart with Your Storefront

In this section, you'll make modifications to the showitem.php script from Hour 20, "Creating an Online Storefront." The goal is to transform the item information page into an item information page with a form for selecting colors, sizes, and quantities.

In the original script, insert the following before Line 2:

```
session_start();
```

Because the shopping cart elements are attached to the user through a session id, the session must be started. The next changes don't occur until what was line 37 of the original script, so that's where we start Listing 21.1.

LISTING 21.1 New Lines in showitem.php

```
37:    <P><strong>Price:</strong> \$$item_price</p>
38:    <form method=post action=\"addtocart.php\">";
39:    //get colors
40:    $get_colors = "select item_color from store_item_color where
41:        item_id = $item_id order by item_color";
42:    $get_colors_res = mysql_query($get_colors) or die(mysql_error());
43:
44:    if (mysql_num_rows($get_colors_res) > 0) {
45:
46:        $display_block .= "<P><strong>Available Colors:</strong>
47:        <select name=\"sel_item_color\">";
48:
49:        while ($colors = mysql_fetch_array($get_colors_res)) {
50:            $item_color = $colors['item_color'];
51:            $display_block .=
52:            "<option value=\"$item_color\">$item_color</option>";
53:        }
54:
55:        $display_block .= "</select>";
56:    }
57:
58:    //get sizes
59:    $get_sizes = "select item_size from store_item_size where
60:        item_id = $item_id order by item_size";
61:    $get_sizes_res = mysql_query($get_sizes) or die(mysql_error());
62:
63:    if (mysql_num_rows($get_sizes_res) > 0) {
64:
65:        $display_block .= "<P><strong>Available Sizes:</strong>
66:        <select name=\"sel_item_size\">";
67:
68:        while ($sizes = mysql_fetch_array($get_sizes_res)) {
69:            $item_size = $sizes['item_size'];
```

LISTING 21.1   continued

```
70:                    $display_block .= "
71:                      <option value=\"$item_size\">$item_size</option>";
72:            }
73:
74:        $display_block .= "</select>";
75:    }
76:
77:    $display_block .= "
78:    <P><strong>Select Quantity:</strong>
79:    <select name=\"sel_item_qty\">";
80:
81:    for($i=1; $i<11; $i++) {
82:            $display_block .= "<option value=\"$i\">$i</option>";
83:    }
84:
85:    $display_block .= "
86:    </select>
87:    <input type=\"hidden\" name=\"sel_item_id\" value=\"$_GET[item_id]\">
88:    <P><input type=\"submit\" name=\"submit\" value=\"Add to Cart\"></p>
89:    </form>
90:     </td>
91:    </tr>
92:    </table>";
93: }
94: ?>
95: <HTML>
96: <HEAD>
97: <TITLE>My Store</TITLE>
98: </HEAD>
99: <BODY>
100: <? print $display_block; ?>
101: </BODY>
102: </HTML>
```

The first change is at what was line 37, where the `$display_block` string is continued to include the beginning `<form>` element. The action of the form is a script called addtocart.php, which you will create in the next section.

The next change occurs at line 47, where the `$display_block` string is continued to include the opening tag of a `<select>` element, named sel_item_color. In lines 51-52, the colors are put into `<option>` elements for the user to choose from, instead of simply printing on the screen. Line 55 closes the `<select>` element.

The same types of changes are made for item sizes. Lines 66-67 reflect the continuation of the `$display_block` string to include the `<select>` element, named sel_item_size.

21

Lines 70-71 write the colors in `<option>` elements, and line 74 closes the `<select>` element.

Lines 77-83 are additions to the script. These lines create a `<select>` element, called `sel_item_qty`, for the user to pick how many items to purchase. Line 86 closes this `<select>` element, and line 87 adds a hidden field for the `item_id`. Line 88 adds the submit button and line 89 closes the form. The remaining lines are unchanged from the original script.

When viewing the cowboy hat item using the new version of `showitem.php`, you would see Figure 21.1, reflecting the addition of the form elements.

Figure 21.1

The new cowboy hat item page.

The next step is to create the `addtocart.php` script.

Adding Items to Your Cart

The `addtocart.php` script will simply write information to the `store_shoppertrack` table, and redirect the user to the view of the shopping cart. We'll create the `addtocart.php` script first, then tackle the `showcart.php` script next.

Listing 21.2 The `addtocart.php` Script

```
1: <?php
2: session_start();
3:
```

LISTING 21.2   continued

```
 4: //connect to database
 5: $conn = mysql_connect("localhost", "joeuser", "somepass")
 6:    or die(mysql_error());
 7: mysql_select_db("testDB",$conn)  or die(mysql_error());
 8:
 9: if ($_POST[sel_item_id] != "") {
10:    //validate item and get title and price
11:    $get_iteminfo = "select item_title from store_items
12:        where id = $_POST[sel_item_id]";
13:    $get_iteminfo_res = mysql_query($get_iteminfo)
14:        or die(mysql_error());
15:
16:    if (mysql_num_rows($get_iteminfo_res) < 1) {
17:        //invalid id, send away
18:        header("Location: seestore.php");
19:        exit;
20:    } else {
21:        //get info
22:        $item_title =  mysql_result($get_iteminfo_res,0,'item_title');
24:
25:        //add info to cart table
26:        $addtocart = "insert into store_shoppertrack values
27:        ('', '$PHPSESSID', '$_POST[sel_item_id]', '$_POST[sel_item_qty]',
28:        '$_POST[sel_item_size]', '$_POST[sel_item_color]', now())";
29:
30:        mysql_query($addtocart);
31:
32:        //redirect to showcart page
33:        header("Location: showcart.php");
34:        exit;
35:
36:    }
37: } else {
38:    //send them somewhere else
39:    header("Location: seestore.php");
40:    exit;
41: }
42: ?>
```

Line 2 continues the user session, which is important because you will need to capture the user's session id, to write to the store_shoppertrack table. Lines 5-7 make the database connection, and line 9 begins the validation of the actions.

In line 9, the script verifies that a value is present in $_POST[sel_item_id], meaning the user came to this script from a form. If there is no value, the script jumps down to line 37 and sends the user away in line 39, and that's it for the script.

21

However, if there is a value in $_POST[sel_item_id], the next action is to verify that it is a valid value. Lines 11-14 create and issue an SQL query to gather the title of the selected item. Line 16 checks for a result; if there is no result, the user is again redirected away in line 18.

If the selected item is a valid item, the script continues on to line 22 and extracts the value from the result set. The script now has enough information to add the item selection to the store_shoppertrack table, which it does in lines 26-30.

After the query has been issued, the user is redirected to showcart.php, which will contain all cart items. You'll create this in the next section.

Viewing the Cart

Now that you can add items to a cart, you'll want to see them! Listing 21.3 shows the code for showcart.php.

LISTING 21.3   The showcart.php Script

```
 1: <?php
 2: session_start();
 3: //connect to database
 4: $conn = mysql_connect("localhost", "joeuser", "somepass")
 5:     or die(mysql_error());
 6: mysql_select_db("testDB",$conn)  or die(mysql_error());
 7:
 8: $display_block = "<h1>Your Shopping Cart</h1>";
 9:
10: //check for cart items based on user session id
11: $get_cart = "select st.id, si.item_title, si.item_price, st.sel_item_qty,
12: st.sel_item_size, st.sel_item_color from store_shoppertrack as st
13: left join store_items as si on si.id = st.sel_item_id where
14: session_id = '$PHPSESSID'";
15:
16: $get_cart_res = mysql_query($get_cart) or die(mysql_error());
17:
18: if (mysql_num_rows($get_cart_res) < 1) {
19:     //print message
20:     $display_block .= "<P>You have no items in your cart.
21:     Please <a href=\"seestore.php\">continue to shop</a>!</p>";
22:
23: } else {
24:     //get info and build cart display
25:     $display_block .= "
26:     <table celpadding=3 cellspacing=2 border=1 width=98%>
27:     <tr>
28:     <th>Title</th>
29:     <th>Size</th>
```

LISTING 21.3 continued

```
30:    <th>Color</th>
31:    <th>Price</th>
32:    <th>Qty</th>
33:    <th>Total Price</th>
34:    <th>Action</th>
35:    </tr>";
36:
37:    while ($cart = mysql_fetch_array($get_cart_res)) {
38:        $id = $cart['id'];
39:        $item_title = stripslashes($cart['item_title']);
40:        $item_price = $cart['item_price'];
41:        $item_qty = $cart['item_qty'];
42:        $item_color = $cart['sel_item_color'];
43:        $item_size = $cart['sel_item_size'];
44:
45:        $total_price = sprintf("%.02f", $item_price * $item_qty);
46:
47:        $display_block .= "<tr>
48:        <td align=center>$item_title <br></td>
49:        <td align=center>$item_size <br></td>
50:        <td align=center>$item_color <br></td>
51:        <td align=center>\$ $item_price <br></td>
52:        <td align=center>$item_qty <br></td>
53:        <td align=center>\$ $total_price</td>
54:        <td align=center><a href=\"removefromcart.php?id=$id\">remove</a></td>
55:        </tr>";
56:    }
57:
58:    $display_block .= "</table>";
59: }
60: ?>
61: <HTML>
62: <HEAD>
63: <TITLE>My Store</TITLE>
64: </HEAD>
65: <BODY>
66: <? print $display_block; ?>
67: </BODY>
68: </HTML>
```

Line 2 continues the user session, which is important because you need to match the user's session id with the records in the store_shoppertrack table. Lines 4-6 make the database connection, and line 8 begins the $display_block string, with a heading for the page.

21

Lines 10-14 represent a joined query, in which the user's saved items are retrieved. The id, sel_item_qty, sel_item_size, and sel_item_color fields are extracted from store_shoppertrack, and the item_title and item_price fields are retrieved from the store_items table, based on the matching information from store_shoppertrack. In other words, instead of printing 2 for the selected item, Cowboy Hat is shown as the title. Line 16 issues the query, and line 18 checks for results.

If there are no results, the user has no items in the store_shoppertrack table, and a message is written to the $display_block string and the script exits and shows the message.

If there are indeed results, the beginning of an HTML table is created in lines 25-35, with columns defined for all the information in the cart (and then some). Line 37 begins the while loop to extract each item from the store_shoppertrack, and this loop continues until line 56, printing the information in the proper table cell.

In line 54, you see a link created for a removal script, which you will create in the next section. Line 58 closes the table, and the script finishes up and prints HTML to the screen in lines 59-68.

Now, go back to an item page and add the item to your cart. After the items are written to the store_shoppertrack table, you should be redirected to the showcart.php page, and your newly selected items should be displayed. Figure 21.2, shows my cart after adding some items.

FIGURE 21.2

Items added to cart.

The next step is to create the removefromcart.php script.

Removing Items from Your Cart

The removefromcart.php script is quite short because all it does is issue a query and redirect the user to another script. Inevitably, a user will want to weed items out of his cart, and this script enables him to do just that. Listing 21.4 shows the complete script.

LISTING 21.4 The removefromcart.php Script

```
 1: <?php
 2: session_start();
 3: //connect to database
 4: $conn = mysql_connect("localhost", "joeuser", "somepass")
 5:    or die(mysql_error());
 6: mysql_select_db("testDB",$conn)  or die(mysql_error());
 7:
 8: if ($_GET[id] != "") {
 9:    $delete_item = "delete from store_shoppertrack where
10:     id = $_GET[id] and session_id = '$PHPSESSID'";
11:    mysql_query($delete_item) or die(mysql_error());
12:
13:    //redirect to showcart page
14:    header("Location: showcart.php");
15:    exit;
16:
17: } else {
18:    //send them somewhere else
19:    header("Location: seestore.php");
20:    exit;
21: }
22: ?>
```

Line 2 continues the user session because you need to match the user's session id with the records in the store_shoppertrack table. Lines 4-6 make the database connection, and line 8 checks for a value in $_GET[id]. If a value does not exist in $_GET[id], the user is not clicking the link from her cart and, thus, is sent away in line 19.

If a value exists in $_GET[id], an SQL query (lines 9-10) is issued (line 11) and the user is redirected to the showcart.php script (line 14), where the item should no longer show up. Try it and see!

21

Payment Methods and the Checkout Sequence

Several commerce methods exist when it comes time to pay for the purchases in the shopping cart. The "right" method for you depends on your business—merchant accounts through banking institutions often require you to have a business license, a reseller's permit, and other pieces of paper proving you're a legitimate business. If you're simply a person who has a few items to sell, you might not want to go through all that paperwork. However, you still have options!

Regardless of the payment method you choose, one thing is certain—if you are passing credit-card information over the Web, you must do so over an SSL connection. Obtaining an SSL certificate and installing it on your system is covered in Hour 23, "Setting Up a Secure Web Server." You do not have to use this secure connection during the user's entire shopping experience, just from the point at which sensitive information is captured, such as the checkout form.

Creating the Checkout Form

At this point in the book, you should be well versed in creating a simple form. At the beginning of this hour, the store_orders table was created with fields to be used as a guideline for your form:

- order_name
- order_address
- order_city
- order_state
- order_zip
- order_tel
- order_email

Additionally, your form will need fields for the credit-card number, expiration date, and the name on the credit card. Another nice feature is to repeat the user's shopping cart contents with an item subtotal, so the customer remembers what he's paying for and approximately how much the order will cost. Also at this point of the checkout sequence, you offer any shipping options you might have. Shipping and sales tax would be calculated in the next step of the process.

From the point of pressing the submit button on the form, the checkout sequence depends on the payment method you are using. The next section goes through the basic steps and offers suggestions on various methods of payment processing.

Performing the Checkout Actions

If you have obtained a merchant account through your bank, you can utilize real-time payment services such as Verisign's PayFlo Pro. PHP has a built-in set of functions that, when used with the PayFlo libraries from Verisign, enable you to create a simple script to handle the credit-card transaction. You can learn more about PayFlo Pro at the Verisign Web site: `http://www.verisign.com/products/payflow/pro/index.html`. The PHP manual section for PayFlo functions is at `http://www.php.net/manual/en/ref.pfpro.php`.

Verisign's product is one of several transaction-processing gateways that exist for use by merchants. Your bank will usually provide a list of merchants they prefer you to use. If you stray from their list of preferred vendors, be sure to research your selected vendor thoroughly, to avoid any delays with deposits and to ensure you're getting the best deal.

After you have selected a transaction processor, your checkout script should follow a path like the following:

1. Total the items, add tax, add shipping. This gives you the total amount to authorize from the credit card.

2. Perform credit-card authorization for the total amount.

3. You will receive either a success or failure response from your card processing routine. If the response is a failure, print a message to the user, and the transaction is over. If the response is a success, continue to Step 4.

4. Write the basic order information to a table like `store_orders`, including the authorization code you will receive upon successful authorization. Get the `id` value of this record using `mysql_insert_id()`.

5. For each item in the shopping cart that is tied to this user, insert a record into `store_orders_itemmap`. Each record will reference the `id` (as `order_id`) gathered in the previous step.

6. Delete the shopping cart items for this user.

7. Display the order with authorization code in place of the credit-card information on the screen, so the user can print it and hold it as a receipt. You can also send this information via email to the user.

21

Each of the steps listed previously—with the exception of the actual payment authorization code—are the same simple steps you have been using throughout this book, and there's no reason to make them more difficult than they need to be!

Summary

In this hands-on lesson, you applied your basic PHP and MySQL knowledge to the integration of a shopping cart into the storefront from the previous chapter. Included were the database table creation, modifications to the item detail page, and new scripts for adding and removing cart items.

Workshop

The Workshop is designed to help you anticipate possible questions, review what you've learned, and begin learning how to put your knowledge into practice.

Quiz

1. When removing an item from the cart, why do you suppose the query validates the session id of the user against the record?

2. What would be a reason not to store the price in a hidden field when adding to the cart?

Answers

1. Users should only be able to remove their own items.

2. If you stored the price in a hidden field, a rogue user could change that value before posting the form, therefore, writing whatever price they wanted into the `store_shoppertrack` table, as opposed to the actual price.

PART V

Administration and Fine-Tuning

Hour

22 Apache Performance Tuning and Virtual Hosting

23 Setting Up a Secure Web Server

24 Optimizing and Tuning MySQL

HOUR **22**

Apache Performance Tuning and Virtual Hosting

In this administration-related hour, consideration will be given to increasing the performance and scalability of your Apache installation. Additionally, you will learn about name-based and IP-based virtual hosting, and DNS and client issues. It explains different mechanisms that can be used to isolate clients from each other and the associated security tradeoffs.

In this hour, you will learn

- Which operating system and Apache-related settings can limit the server scalability or degrade performance
- About several tools for load testing Apache
- How to fine-tune Apache for optimum performance
- How to configure Apache to detect and prevent abusive behavior from clients

- How to configure name-based virtual hosts, IP-based virtual hosts, and the difference between the two
- About the dependencies virtual hosting has on DNS
- How to set up scaled-up cookie-cutter virtual hosts

Scalability Issues

This section covers scalability problems and how to prevent them. This is more of a "don't do this" list, explaining limiting factors that can degrade performance or prevent the server from scaling. We will also investigate the proactive tuning of Apache for optimal performance.

Operating System Limits

Several operating system factors can prevent Apache from scaling. These factors are related to process creation, memory limits, and maximum simultaneous number of open files or connections.

 The Unix `ulimit` command enables you to set several of the limits covered in this section on a per-process basis. Please refer to your operating system documentation for details on `ulimit`'s syntax.

Processes

Apache provides settings for preventing the number of server processes and threads from exceeding certain limits. These settings affect scalability because they limit the number of simultaneous connections to the Web server, which in turn affects the number of visitors that you can service simultaneously.

The Apache MPM settings are in turn constrained by OS settings limiting the number of processes and threads. How to change those limits varies from operating system to operating system. In Linux 2.0.x and 2.2.x kernels, it requires changing the NR_TASKS defined in `/usr/src/linux/include/linux/tasks.h` and recompiling the kernel. In the 2.4.x series, the limit can be accessed at runtime from the `/proc/sys/kernel/threads-max` file. You can read the contents of the file with

```
cat /proc/sys/kernel/threads-max
```

and write to it using

```
echo value > /proc/sys/kernel/threads-max
```

In Linux (unlike most other Unix versions), there is a mapping between threads and processes, and they are similar from the point of view of the OS.

In Solaris, those parameters can be changed in the /etc/system file. Those changes don't require rebuilding the kernel, but might require a reboot to take effect. You can change the total number of processes by changing the max_nprocs entry and the number of processes allowed for a given user with maxuproc.

File Descriptors

Whenever a process opens a file (or a socket), a structure called a *file descriptor* is assigned until the file is closed. The OS limits the number of file descriptors that a given process can open, thus limiting the number of simultaneous connections the Web server can have. How those settings are changed depends on the operating system. On Linux systems, you can read or modify /proc/sys/fs/file-max (using echo and cat, as explained in the previous section). On Solaris systems, you must edit the value for rlim_fd_max in the /etc/system file. This change will require a reboot to take effect.

You can find additional information at http://httpd.apache.org/docs/misc/descriptors.html.

Controlling External Processes

Apache provides several directives to control the amount of resources external processes use. This applies to CGI scripts spawned from the server and programs executed via Server Side Includes. Support for the following directives is available only on Unix and varies from system to system:

- **RLimitCPU**—Accepts two parameters: the soft limit and the hard limit for the amount of CPU time in seconds that a process is allowed. If the max keyword is used, it indicates the maximum setting allowed by the operating system. The hard limit is optional. The soft limit can be changed between restarts, and the hard limit specifies the maximum allowed value for that setting.

- **RlimitMem**—The syntax is identical to RLimitCPU, but this directive specifies the amount (in bytes) of memory used per process.

- **RlimitNProc**—The syntax is identical to RLimitCPU, but this directive specifies the number of processes.

These three directives are useful to prevent malicious or poorly written programs from running out of control.

Performance-Related Apache Settings

This section presents you with different Apache settings that affect performance.

File System Access

Accessing files on disk is expensive. You should try to minimize the number of disk accesses required for serving a request. Symbolic links, per-directory configuration files, and content negotiation are some of factors that affect the number of disk accesses:

- **Symbolic links**—In Unix, a *symbolic link* (or *symlink*) is a special kind of file that points to another file. It is created with the Unix ln command and is useful for making a certain file appear in different places.

  Two of the parameters that the Options directive allows are FollowSymLinks and SymLinksIfOwnerMatch.

  By default, Apache won't follow symbolic links because they can be used to bypass security settings. For example, you can create a symbolic link from a public part of the Web site to a restricted file or directory not otherwise accessible via the Web. So, also by default, Apache needs to perform a check to verify that the file isn't a symbolic link. If SymLinksIfOwnerMatch is present, it will follow a symbolic link if the same user sho created the symbolic link owns the target file. Because those tests must be performed for every path element and for every path that refers to a filesystem object, they can be expensive. If you control the content creation, you should add an Options +FollowSymLinks directive to your configuration and avoid the SymLinksIfOwnerMatch argument. In this way, the tests won't take place and performance isn't affected.

- **Per-directory configuration files**—As explained in Hour 2, "Installing and Configuring Apache," it is possible to have per-directory configuration files. These files, normally named .htaccess, provide a convenient way of configuring the server and allow for some degree of delegated administration. However, if this feature is enabled, Apache has to look for these files in each directory in the path leading to the file being requested, resulting in expensive filesystem accesses. If you don't have a need for per-directory configuration files, you can disable this feature by adding AllowOverride none to your configuration. Doing so will avoid the performance penalty associated with accessing the filesystem looking for .htaccess files.

- **Content negotiation**—Apache can serve different versions of a file depending on client language or preferences. This can be accomplished with file extensions, but for every request, Apache must access the filesystem repeatedly looking for files with appropriate extensions. If you need to use content negotiation, make sure that you at least use a type-map file, minimizing accesses to disk.

- **Scoreboard file**—This is a special file that the main Apache process uses to communicate with its children in certain older operating systems. You can specify its location with `ScoreBoardFile`, but most modern platforms do not require this directive. If this file is required, you might find improved performance if you place it on a RAM disk. A *RAM disk* is a mechanism that allows a portion of the system memory to be accessed as a filesystem. The details on creating a RAM disk vary from system to system.

Network and Status Settings

A number of network-related Apache settings can degrade performance:

- **`HostnameLookups`**—When `HostnameLookups` is set to `on` or `double`, Apache will perform a DNS lookup to capture the hostname of the client, introducing a delay. The default setting is `HostnameLookups off`. If you need to use the hostnames, you can always process the request logs with a log resolver later.

- **Accept mechanism**—Apache can use different mechanisms to control how Apache children arbitrate requests. The optimal mechanism depends on the specific platform and number of processors. You can find detailed tests and performance analysis at `http://research.covalent.net/projects/osdl1.html`. Additional information can be found at `http://httpd.apache.org/docs-2.0/misc/perf-tuning.html`.

- **`mod_status`**—This module collects statistics about the server, connections, and requests, which slows down Apache. For optimal performance, disable this module, or at least make sure that `ExtendedStatus` is set to `off`, which is the default.

Load Testing with ApacheBench

You can test the scalability and performance of your site with benchmarking and traffic generation tools. There are many commercial and open-source tools, with varying degrees of sophistication. It is difficult to accurately simulate real-world request traffic because visitors have different navigation patterns, access the Internet using connections with different speeds, stop a download if it is taking too long, press the reload button repeatedly if they get impatient, and so on. That is why some tools record actual network traffic for later replay.

The Apache server comes with a simple, but useful, load-testing tool, called ApacheBench, or `ab`. You can find it in the `/bin` directory of the Apache distribution.

This tool enables you to request a certain URL a number of times and display a summary of the result. The following command requests the main page of the `www.example.com` server 1000 times, with 10 simultaneous clients at any given time:

```
#> /usr/local/apache2/bin/ab -n 1000 -c 10 http://www.example.com/
```

If you invoke ab without any arguments, you will get a complete listing of command-line options and syntax. Additionally, the trailing slash on the target URL is required, unless a specific page is named.

The result will look similar to the following:

```
This is ApacheBench, Version 2.0.40 <$Revision: 1.87 $>
Copyright (c) 1996 Adam Twiss, Zeus Technology Ltd,
http://www.zeustech.net/org/
Copyright (c) 1998-2001 The Apache Software Foundation, http://www.apache.org/

Benchmarking www.example.com (be patient)
Completed 100 requests
Completed 200 requests
Completed 300 requests
Completed 400 requests
Completed 500 requests
Completed 600 requests
Completed 700 requests
Completed 800 requests
Completed 900 requests
Finished 1000 requests
Server Software:        Apache/2.0.40
Server Hostname:        www.example.com
Server Port:            80

Document Path:          /
Document Length:        8667 bytes

Concurrency Level:      10
Time taken for tests:   64.525026 seconds
Complete requests:      1000
Failed requests:        0
Write errors:           0
Total transferred:      8911000 bytes
HTML transferred:       8667000 bytes
Requests per second:    15.50 [#/sec] (mean)
Time per request:       0.645 - (mean)
Time per request:       0.065 - (mean, across all concurrent requests)
Transfer rate:          134.86 [Kbytes/sec] received

Connection Times (ms)
              min  mean[+/-sd] median    max
Connect:       19    62   59.7 45 727
Processing:   178   572  362.8 478 3151
Waiting:       18   114  176.9 74 1906
Total:        255   634  390.3 536 3301
```

```
Percentage of the requests served within a certain time (ms)
50%    536
66%    611
75%    662
80%    693
90%    872
95%    1436
98%    2162
99%    2461
100%   3301 (longest request)
```

These requests were made over the Internet to a sample server. You should get many more requests per second if you conduct the test against a server in the same machine or over a local network. The output of the tool is self-explanatory. Some of the relevant results are the number of requests per second and the average time it takes to service a request. You can also see how more than 90% of the requests were served in less than one second.

You can play with different settings for the number of requests and with the number of simultaneous clients to find the point at which your server slows down significantly.

Proactive Performance Tuning

Although previous sections explained which settings might prevent Apache from scaling, the following are some techniques for proactively increasing the performance of your server.

Mapping Files to Memory

As explained previously, accesses to disk affect performance significantly. Although most modern operating systems keep a cache of the most frequently accessed files, Apache also enables you to explicitly map a file into memory so that access to disk isn't necessary. The module that performs this mapping is mod_file_cache. You can specify a list of files to memory map by using the MMapFile directive, which applies to the server as a whole. An additional directive in Apache 2.0, CacheFile, takes a list of files, caches the file descriptors at startup, and keeps them around between requests, saving time and resources for frequently requested files.

Distributing the Load

Another way to increase performance is to distribute the load among several servers. This can be done in a variety of ways:

- A hardware load balancer directing network and HTTP traffic across several servers, making it look like a single server from the outside.

- A software load balancer solution using a reverse proxy with mod_rewrite.
- Separate servers providing images, large download files, and other static material. For example, you can place your images in a server called images.example.com and link to them from your main server.

Caching

The fastest way to serve content is not to serve it! This can be achieved by using appropriate HTTP headers that instruct clients and proxies of the validity in time of the requested resources. In this way, some resources that appear in multiple pages, but don't change frequently, such as logos or navigation buttons, are transmitted only once for a certain period of time.

Additionally, you can use mod_cache in Apache 2.0 to cache dynamic content so that it doesn't need to be created for every request. This is potentially a big performance boost because dynamic content usually requires accessing databases, processing templates, and so on, which can take significant resources.

 As of this writing, mod_cache is still experimental. You can read more about it at http://httpd.apache.org/docs-2.0/mod/mod_cache.html.

Reduce Transmitted Data

Another way to reduce the load on the servers is to reduce the amount of data being transferred to the client. This in turn makes your clients' Web site access faster, especially for those over slow links. You can do a number of things to achieve this:

- Reduce the number of images.
- Reduce the size of your images.
- Compress big downloadable files.
- Precompress static HTML and use content negotiation.
- Use mod_deflate to compress HTML content. This can be useful if CPU power is available and clients are connecting over slow links. The content will be delivered quicker and the process will be free sooner to answer additional requests.

Network Settings

HTTP 1.1 allows multiple requests to be served over a single connection. HTTP 1.0 enables the same thing with keep-alive extensions. The KeepAliveTimeout directive

22

enables you to specify the maximum time in seconds that the server will wait before closing an inactive connection. Increasing the timeout means that you will increase the chance of the connection being reused. On the other hand, it also ties up the connection and Apache process during the waiting time, which can prevent scalability, as discussed earlier in the hour.

Preventing Abuse

Denial of service (DoS) attacks work by swamping your server with a great number of simultaneous requests, slowing down the server or preventing access altogether to legitimate clients. DoS attacks are difficult to prevent in general, and usually the most effective way to address them is at the network or operating system level. One example is blocking specific addresses from making requests to the server; although you can block those addresses at the Web server level, it is more efficient to block them at the network firewall/router or with the operating system network filters.

Other kinds of abuse include posting extremely big requests or opening a great number of simultaneous connections. You can limit the size of requests and timeouts to minimize the effect of attacks. The default request timeout is 300 seconds, but you can change it with the `TimeOut` directive. A number of directives enable you to control the size of the request body and headers: `LimitRequestBody`, `LimitRequestFields`, `LimitRequestFieldSize`, `LimitRequestLine`, and `LimitXMLRequestBody`.

To prevent abuse, the `mod_bwshare` module enables you to limit the number of files or bytes that a given client can download from the server. You can learn more about `mod_bwshare` at `http://www.topology.org/src/bwshare/README.html`.

Robots

Robots, *Web spiders*, and *Web crawlers* are names that define a category of programs that download pages from your Web site, recursively following your site's links. Web search engines use these programs to scan the Internet for Web servers, download their content, and index it. Normal users use them to download an entire Web site or portion of a Web site for later offline browsing. Normally, these programs are well behaved, but sometimes they can be very aggressive and swamp your Web site with too many simultaneous connections or become caught in cyclic loops.

Well-behaved spiders will request a special file, called `robots.txt`, that contains instructions about how to access your Web site and which parts of the Web site won't be available to them. The syntax for the file can be found at `http://www.robotstxt.org/`. You can stop the requests at the router or operating system levels.

Implementing Virtual Hosting

Early Web servers were designed to handle the contents of a single site. The standard way of hosting several Web sites in the same machine was to install and configure different, and separate, Web server instances. As the Internet grew, so did the need for hosting multiple Web sites and a more efficient solution was developed: virtual hosting. Virtual hosting allows a single instance of Apache to serve different Web sites, identified by their domain names. *IP-based* virtual hosting means that each of the domains is assigned a different IP address; *name-based* virtual hosting means that several domains share a single IP address. As is explained later in the hour, name-based virtual hosting requires HTTP/1.1 support.

Web clients use the domain name server system (DNS) to translate hostnames into IP addresses, and vice versa. Several mappings are possible:

- **One to one**—Means that each hostname is assigned a single, unique IP address. This is the foundation for IP-based virtual hosting.

- **One to many**—Means that a single hostname is assigned to several IP addresses. This is useful for having several Apache instances serving the same Web site. If each of the servers is installed in a different machine, it is possible to balance the Web traffic among them, improving scalability.

- **Many to one**—Means that you can assign the same IP address to several hostnames. The client will specify the Web site it is accessing by using the Host: header in the request. This is the foundation for name-based virtual hosting.

When a many-to-one mapping is in place, a DNS server usually can be configured to respond with a different IP address for each DNS query, which helps to distribute the load. This is known as round robin DNS.

IP-Based Virtual Hosting

The simplest virtual host configuration is when each host is assigned a unique IP address. Each IP address maps the HTTP requests that Apache handles to separate content trees in their own VirtualHost containers, as shown in the following snippet:

```
Listen 192.168.128.10:80
Listen 192.168.129.10:80
<VirtualHost 192.168.128.10:80>
    DocumentRoot /usr/local/www-docs/host1
</VirtualHost>
<VirtualHost 192.168.129.10:80>
```

22

```
    DocumentRoot /usr/local/www-docs/host2
</VirtualHost>
```

If a DocumentRoot is not specified for a given virtual host, the global setting, specified outside any <VirtualHost> section, will be used. In the previous example, each virtual host has its own DocumentRoot. When a request arrives, Apache will use the destination IP address to direct the request to the appropriate host. For example, if a request comes for IP 192.168.128.10, Apache will return the documents from /usr/local/www-docs/host1. If the host operating system cannot resolve an IP address used as the VirtualHost container's name, and there's no ServerName directive, Apache will complain at server startup time that it can't map the IP addresses to hostnames. This complaint is not a fatal error. Apache will still run, but the error indicates that there might be some work to be done with the DNS configuration so that Web browsers can find your server. A fully qualified domain name (FQDN) can be used instead of an IP address as the VirtualHost container name and the Listen directive binding (if the domain name resolves in DNS to an IP address configured on the machine and Apache can bind to it).

Name-Based Virtual Hosts

As a way to mitigate the consumption of IP addresses for virtual hosts, the HTTP/1.1 protocol version introduced the Host: header, which enables a browser to specify the exact host for which the request is intended. This allows several hostnames to share a single IP address. Most browsers nowadays provide HTTP/1.1 support.

> Although Host: usage was standardized in the HTTP/1.1 specification, some older HTTP/1.0 browsers also provided support for this header.

A typical set of request headers from Microsoft Internet Explorer is shown in Listing 22.1. If the URL were entered with a port number, it would be part of the Host header contents as well.

LISTING 22.1 Request Headers

```
GET / HTTP/1.1
Accept: image/gif, image/x-xbitmap, image/jpeg, image/pjpeg, */*
Accept-Language: en-us
Accept-Encoding: gzip, deflate
User-Agent: Mozilla/4.0 (compatible; MSIE 5.01; Windows NT 5.0)
Host: host1.example.com
Connection: Keep-Alive
```

Apache uses the Host: header for configurations in which multiple hostnames can be shared by a single IP address—the many-to-one scenario outlined earlier this hour—thus, the description *name-based virtual hosts*.

The NameVirtualHost directive enables you to specify IP address and port combinations on which the server will receive requests for name-based virtual hosts. This is a required directive for name-based virtual hosts. Listing 22.2 has Apache dispatch all connections to 192.168.128.10 based on the Host header contents.

LISTING 22.2 Name-Based Virtual Hosts

```
NameVirtualHost 192.168.128.10
Listen 192.168.128.10:80
<VirtualHost 192.168.128.10>
    ServerName host1.example.com
    DocumentRoot /usr/local/www-docs/host1
</VirtualHost>
<VirtualHost 192.168.128.10>
    ServerName host2.example.com
    DocumentRoot /usr/local/www-docs/host2
</VirtualHost>
```

For every hostname that resolves in DNS to 192.168.128.10, Apache can support another name-based virtual host. If a request comes for that IP address for a hostname that is not included in the configuration file, say host3.example.com, Apache will simply associate the request to the first container in the configuration file; in this case, host1.example.com. The same behavior is applied to requests that are not accompanied by a Host header; whichever container is first in the configuration file is the one that gets the request.

An end user from the example.com domain might have his machine set up with example.com as his default domain. In that case, he might direct his browser to http://host1/ instead of the fully qualified http://host1.example.com/. The Host header would simply have host1 in it instead of host1.example.com. To make sure that the correct virtual host container gets the request, you can use the ServerAlias directive as shown in Listing 22.3.

LISTING 22.3 The ServerAlias Directive

```
NameVirtualHost 192.168.128.10
Listen 192.168.128.10:80
<VirtualHost 192.168.128.10>
    ServerName host1.example.com
```

22

LISTING 22.3   continued

```
        ServerAlias host1
        DocumentRoot /usr/local/www-docs/host1
</VirtualHost>
<VirtualHost 192.168.128.10>
        ServerName host2.example.com
        ServerAlias host2
        DocumentRoot /usr/local/www-docs/host2
</VirtualHost>
```

In fact, you can give ServerAlias a space-separated list of other names that might show up in the Host header so that you don't need a separate VirtualHost container with a bunch of common directives just to handle all the name variants.

HTTP 1.1 forces the use of the Host header. If the protocol version is identified as 1.1 in the HTTP request line (that is, GET / HTTP/1.1), the request *must* be accompanied by a Host header. In the early days of name-based virtual hosts, Host headers were considered a tradeoff: Fewer IP resources were required, but legacy browsers that did not send Host headers were still in use and, therefore, could not access all of the server's virtual hosts. Today, that is not a consideration; there is no statistically significant number of such legacy browsers in use.

The only reason to opt for IP-based and not use name-based virtual hosts is if there are virtual hosts that must use SSL. You can learn more about SSL and this limitation in Hour 23, "Setting Up a Secure Web Server."

Mass Virtual Hosting

In the previous listings, the DocumentRoots follow a simple pattern:

```
DocumentRoot /usr/local/www-docs/hostname
```

where *hostname* is the hostname portion of the fully qualified domain name used in the virtual host's ServerName. For just a few virtual hosts, this configuration is fine. But what if there are dozens, hundreds, or even thousands of these virtual hosts? The configuration file can become difficult to maintain. Apache provides a good solution for cookie-cutter virtual hosts with mod_vhost_alias. You can configure Apache to map the virtual host requests to separate content trees with pattern-matching rules in the VirtualDocumentRoot directive. This functionality is especially useful for ISPs that want to provide a virtual host for each one of their users. The following example provides a simple mass virtual host configuration:

```
NameVirtualHost 192.168.128.10
Listen 192.168.128.10:80
VirtualDocumentRoot /usr/local/www-docs/%1
```

The %1 token used in this example's `VirtualDocumentRoot` directive will be substituted for the first portion of the FQDN. mod_vhost_alias directives have a language for mapping FQDN components to filesystem locations. Even characters within the FQDN can be accessed.

If we eliminated all the `VirtualHost` containers and simplified our configuration to the one shown here, the server would serve requests for any subdirectories created in the `/usr/local/www-docs` directory. If the hostname portion of the FQDN is matched as a subdirectory, that's where Apache will look for content when it translates the request to a filesystem location.

Note that although virtual hosts normally inherit directives from the main server context, some of them, such as `Alias` directives, do not get propagated. For instance, the virtual hosts will not inherit this filesystem mapping:

```
Alias /icons /usr/local/apache2/icons
```

The `FollowSymLinks` flag for the `Options` directive is also disabled in this context. However, a variant of the `ScriptAlias` directive is supported.

The `VirtualScriptAlias` directive shown in the following snippet treats requests for any resources under `/cgi-bin` as containing CGI scripts:

```
NameVirtualHost 192.168.128.10
Listen 192.168.128.10:80
VirtualDocumentRoot /usr/local/vhosts/%1/docs
VirtualScriptAlias /usr/local/vhosts/%1/cgi-bin
```

Note that `cgi-bin` is a special token for that directive; calling the directory just `cgi` won't work; it must be `cgi-bin`.

For IP-based virtual hosting needs, there are variants of these directives: `VirtualDocumentRootIP` and `VirtualScriptAliasIP`. However, because the primary motivation of IP-based virtual hosts is for SSL and there's no pattern-matched path support for SSL resources such as certificates and keys, the uses are fairly limited.

Summary

This hour provided you with information on Apache and operating system settings that can affect scalability and performance. In most cases, however, the problems in Web site scalability relate to dynamic content generation and database access. Hardware-related improvements, such as high-quality network cards and drivers, increased memory, and disk arrays can also provide enhanced performance.

With regard to virtual hosting, Apache can be configured to handle virtual hosts in a variety of ways. Whether you need a large number of cookie-cutter virtual hosts, a varied set of different virtual host configurations, or the number of IP addresses you can use is limited, there's a way to configure Apache for your application. Name-based virtual hosting is a common technique for deploying virtual hosts without using up IP addresses. IP-based virtual hosting is still necessary when a virtual host is used for SSL. If you cannot change your DNS configuration, your only recourse is to use separate port numbers for your virtual hosts.

Q&A

Q How can I measure whether my site is fast enough?

A Many developers test their sites locally or over an internal network, but if you run a public Web site, chances are good that many of your users will access it over slow links. Try navigating your Web site from a dialup account and make sure that your pages load fast enough, with the rule of thumb being that pages should load in less than three seconds.

Q How can I migrate an existing name-based virtual host to its own machine while maintaining continuous service?

A If a virtual host is destined to move to a neighboring machine, which by definition cannot have the same IP address, there are some extra measures to take. A common practice is to do the following:

1. Set the time-to-live of the DNS mapping to a very low number. This increases the frequency of client lookups of the hostname.

2. Configure an IP alias on the old host with the new IP address.

3. Configure the virtual host's content to be served by both name- and IP-address-based virtual hosts.

4. After all the requests for the virtual host at the old IP address diminish (due to DNS caches expiring their old lookups), the server can be migrated.

Q Can I mix IP- and name-based virtual hosting?

A Yes. If multiple IP addresses are bound, you can allocate their usage a number of different ways. A family of name-based virtual hosts might be associated with each; just use a separate `NameVirtualHost` directive for each IP. One IP might be dedicated as an IP-based virtual host for SSL, for instance, whereas another might be dedicated to a family of name-based virtual hosts.

Workshop

The Workshop is designed to help you anticipate possible questions, review what you've learned, and begin learning how to put your knowledge into practice.

Quiz

1. Name some Apache settings that might limit scalability or affect Apache performance.

2. Name some operating system settings that might limit scalability.

3. Name some approaches to improve performance.

4. Which VirtualHost container gets a request if the connection uses NameVirtualHost, but no Host header is sent?

5. Is the ServerName directive necessary in a VirtualHost container?

Answers

1. Some of the Apache settings that might affect scalability include the FollowSymLinks, SymLinksIfOwnerMatch arguments to the Options directive, enabling per-directory configuration files, hostname lookups, having a scoreboard file, and statistics collection with mod_status.

2. Some operating system settings that might affect scalability include limits for number of processes, open file descriptors, and memory allowed per process.

3. The following are some suggestions for improving performance: load distribution via a hardware load balancer or reverse proxy, data compression, caching, mapping files to memory, and compiling modules statically.

4. Reading the configuration top-to-bottom, the first VirtualHost container is favored. The same behavior occurs if there is a Host header, but no VirtualHost container that matches it.

5. Only when name-based virtual hosts are used. The Host header contents are compared to the contents of the ServerName directive. If a match isn't satisfied, the VirtualHost containers' ServerAlias directive value(s) are checked for matches.

HOUR 23

Setting Up a Secure Web Server

This hour explains how to set up an Apache server capable of secure transactions. In this hour, you will learn

- The installation and configuration of the mod_ssl Apache module
- The SSL/TLS family of protocols and the underlying cryptography concepts
- What certificates are and how to create and manage them

The Need for Security

As the Internet became mainstream and the number of companies, individuals, and government agencies using it grew, so did the number and type of transactions that needed protection. Those included financial transactions, such as banking operations and electronic commerce, as well as exchange of sensitive information, such as medical records and corporate documents. Three requirements are necessary to carry on secure communications on the Internet: confidentiality, integrity, and authentication.

Confidentiality

Confidentiality is the most obvious requirement for secure communications. If you are transmitting or accessing sensitive information such as your credit-card number or your personal medical history, you certainly don't want a stranger to get hold of it.

Integrity

The information contained in the exchanged messages must be protected from external manipulation. That is, if you place an order online to buy 100 shares of stock, you don't want to allow anyone to intercept the message, change it to an order to buy 1000 shares, or replace the original message. Additionally, you want to prevent an attacker from performing replay attacks, which, instead of modifying the original message, simply resend it several times to achieve a cumulative effect.

Authentication

You need to decide whether to trust the organization or individual you are communicating with. To achieve this, you must authenticate the identity of the other party in the communication.

The science of cryptography studies the algorithms and methods used to securely transmit messages, ensuring the goals of confidentiality, integrity, and authenticity. Cryptanalysis is the science of breaking cryptographic systems.

The SSL Protocol

SSL stands for Secure Sockets Layer and TLS stands for Transport Layer Security. They are a family of protocols that were originally designed to provide security for HTTP transactions, but that also can be used for a variety of other Internet protocols such as IMAP and NNTP. HTTP running over SSL is referred to as *secure HTTP*.

Netscape released SSL version 2 in 1994 and SSL version 3 in 1995. TLS is an IETF standard designed to standardize SSL as an Internet protocol. It is just a modification of SSL version 3 with a small number of added features and minor cleanups. The TLS acronym is the result of arguments between Microsoft and Netscape over the naming of the protocol because each company proposed its own name. However, the name has not stuck and most people refer to these protocols simply as SSL. Unless otherwise specified, the rest of this hour refers to SSL/TLS as *SSL*.

You specify that you want to connect to a server using SSL by replacing `http` with `https` in the protocol component of a URI. The default port for HTTP over SSL is 443.

The following sections explain how SSL addresses the confidentiality, integrity, and authentication requirements outlined in the previous section. In doing so, it explains, in a simplified manner, the underlying mathematical and cryptographic principles SSL is based on.

Addressing the Need for Confidentiality

The SSL protocol protects data from eavesdropping by encrypting it. Encryption is the process of converting a message, the *plaintext*, into a new encrypted message, the *cipher-text*. Although the plaintext is readable by everyone, the ciphertext will be completely unintelligible to an eavesdropper. Decryption is the reverse process, which transforms the ciphertext into the original plaintext.

23

Usually, encryption and decryption processes involve an additional piece of information: a *key*. If both sender and receiver share the same key, the process is referred to as *symmetric* cryptography. If sender and receiver have different, complementary keys, the process is called *asymmetric* or *public key* cryptography.

Symmetric Cryptography

If the key used to both encrypt and decrypt the message is the same, the process is known as symmetric cryptography. DES, Triple-Des, RC4, and RC2 are algorithms used for symmetric key cryptography. Many of these algorithms can have different key sizes, measured in bits. In general, given an algorithm, the greater the number of bits in the key, the more secure the algorithm is and the slower it will run because of the increased computational needs of performing the algorithm.

Symmetric cryptography is relatively fast compared to public key cryptography, which is explained in the next section. Symmetric cryptography has two main drawbacks, however. One is that keys should be changed periodically to avoid providing an eavesdropper with access to large amounts of material encrypted with the same key. The other is the key distribution problem: How to get the keys to each one of the parties in a safe manner? This was one of the original limiting factors, and before the invention of public key cryptography, the problem was solved by periodically having people traveling around with suitcases full of keys.

Public Key Cryptography

Public key cryptography takes a different approach. Instead of both parties sharing the same key, there is a pair of keys: one public and the other private. The public key can be widely distributed, whereas the owner keeps the private key secret. These two keys are complementary—a message encrypted with one of the keys can be decrypted only by the other key.

Anyone wanting to transmit a secure message to you can encrypt the message using your public key, assured that only the owner of the private key—you—can decrypt it. Even if the attacker has access to the public key, he cannot decrypt the communication. In fact, you want the public key to be as widely available as possible. Public key cryptography can also be used to provide message integrity and authentication. RSA is the most popular public key algorithm.

People with public keys will place these keys on public key servers or simply send the keys to others with whom they want to have secure email exchanges. Using the appropriate tools, such as PGP or GnuPG, the sender will encrypt the outgoing message based on the recipient's public key.

The assertion that only the owner of the private key can decrypt it means that with the current knowledge of cryptography and availability of computing power, an attacker will not be able to break the encryption by brute force alone in a reasonable timeframe. If the algorithm or its implementation is flawed, realistic attacks are possible.

> Public key cryptography is similar to giving away many identical lockpads and retaining the key that opens them all. Anybody who wants to send you a message privately can do so by putting it in a safe and locking it with one of those lockpads (public keys) before sending it to you. Only you have the appropriate key (private key) to open that lockpad (decrypt the message).

The SSL protocol uses public key cryptography in an initial handshake phase to securely exchange symmetric keys that can then be used to encrypt the communication.

Addressing the Need for Integrity

Performing a special calculation on the contents of the message and storing the result with the message itself can preserve data integrity. When the message arrives at its destination, the recipient can perform the same calculation and compare the results. If the contents of the message changed, the results of the calculation will be different.

Digest algorithms perform just that process, creating message digests. A *message digest* is a method of creating a fixed-length representation of an arbitrary message that uniquely identifies it. You can think of it as the fingerprint of the message. A good message digest algorithm should be irreversible and collision resistant, at least for practical purposes. *Irreversible* means that the original message cannot be obtained from the digest and *collision resistant* means that no two different messages should have the same digest. Examples of digest algorithms are MD5 and SHA.

Message digests alone, however, do not guarantee the integrity of the message because an attacker could change the text *and* the message digest. Message authentication codes, or MACs, are similar to message digests, but incorporate a shared secret key in the process. The result of the algorithm depends both on the message and the key used. Because the attacker has no access to the key, he cannot modify both the message and the digest. HMAC is an example of a message authentication code algorithm.

The SSL protocol uses MAC codes to avoid replay attacks and to assure integrity of the transmitted information.

Addressing the Need for Authentication

SSL uses certificates to authenticate parties in a communication. Public key cryptography can be used to digitally sign messages. In fact, just by encrypting a message with your secret key, the receiver can guarantee it came from you. Other digital signature algorithms involve first calculating a digest of the message, and then signing the digest.

You can tell that the person who created that public and private key pair is the one sending the message. But, how can you tie that key to a person or organization that you can trust in the real world? Otherwise, an attacker could impersonate his identity and distribute a different public key, claiming it is the legitimate one. Trust can be achieved by using digital certificates. *Digital certificates* are electronic documents that contain a public key and information about its owner (name, address, and so on). To be useful, the certificate must be signed by a trusted third party (certification authority, or CA) who certifies that the information is correct. There are many different kinds of CAs, as described later in the hour. Some of them are commercial entities, providing certification services to companies conducting business over the Internet. Companies providing internal certification services create other CAs.

The CA guarantees that the information in the certificate is correct, and that the key belongs to that individual or organization. Certificates have a period of validity and can expire or be revoked. Certificates can be chained so that the certification process can be delegated. For example, a trusted entity can certify companies, which in turn can take care of certifying its own employees.

If this whole process is to be effective and trusted, the certificate authority must require appropriate proof of identity from individuals and organizations before it issues a certificate.

By default, browsers include a collection of root certificates for trusted certificate authorities.

SSL and Certificates

The main standard defining certificates is X.509, adapted for Internet usage. An X.509 certificate contains the following information:

- **Issuer**—The name of the signer of the certificate
- **Subject**—The person holding the key being certified
- **Subject public key**—The public key of the subject
- **Control information**—Data such as the dates in which the certificate is valid
- **Signature**—The signature that covers the previous data

You can check a real-life certificate by connecting to a secure server with your browser. If the connection has been successful, a little padlock icon or another visual clue will be added to the status bar of your browser. With Internet Explorer, you can click the locked padlock icon to open a page containing information on the SSL connection and the remote server certificate. You can access the same information by selecting Properties, and then Certificates from the File menu. Other browsers, such as Netscape, Mozilla, and Konqueror provide a similar interface.

Open the `https://www.zend.com` URL in your browser and analyze the certificate, following the steps outlined in the preceding paragraph. You can see how the issuer of the certificate is Thawte CA. The page downloaded seamlessly because Thawte is a trusted CA that has its own certificates bundled with Internet Explorer and Netscape Navigator.

To check which certificates are bundled with your Internet Explorer browser, select Tools, Internet Options, Content, Certificates, Trusted Root Certification Authorities.

You can see that both issuer and subject are provided as distinguished names (DN), a structured way of providing a unique identifier for every element on the network. In the case of the Thawte certificate, the DN is C=IL, S=Mehoz Tel Aviv, L=Ramat Gan, O=Zend Technologies, Ltd., CN=`www.zend.com`.

C stands for country, S for state, L for locality, O for organization, and CN for common name. In the case a Web site certificate, the common name identifies the fully qualified domain name of the Web site (FQDN). This is the server name part of the URL; in this case, `www.zend.com`. If this does not match what you typed in the top bar, the browser will issue an error.

SSL Protocol Summary

You have seen how SSL achieves confidentiality via encryption, integrity via message authentication codes, and authentication via certificates and digital signatures.

The process to establish an SSL connection is the following:

1. The user uses his browser to connect to the remote Apache server.

2. The handshake phase starts, and the browser and server exchange keys and certificate information.

3. The browser checks the validity of the server certificate, including that it has not expired, that it has been issued by a trusted CA, and so on.

4. Optionally, the server can require the client to present a valid certificate as well.

5. Server and client use each other's public key to securely agree on a symmetric key.

6. The handshake phase concludes and transmission continues using symmetric cryptography.

Installing SSL

Now that you've learned all about SSL, you need to install SLL support for Apache. SSL support is provided by mod_ssl, a module that is included with Apache, but is not enabled by default. mod_ssl, in turn, requires the OpenSSL library—an open-source implementation of the SSL/TLS protocols and a variety of other cryptographic algorithms. OpenSSL is based on the SSLeay library developed by Eric A. Young and Tim J. Hudson.

OpenSSL

This section explains how to download and install the OpenSSL toolkit for both Windows and Unix variants.

Windows

The required OpenSSL libraries are included with the Windows installer of Apache 2.0 and no further installation or download is necessary. openssl.exe is included in the bin/ directory of the Apache distribution. It is a utility for generating certificates, keys, certificate signing requests, and so on.

Unix

If you are running a recent Linux or FreeBSD distribution, OpenSSL might already be installed in your system. Use the package management tools bundled with your distribution to determine whether that is the case or, otherwise, to install it.

If you need to install OpenSSL from source, you can download OpenSSL from http://www.openssl.org. After you have downloaded the software, you need to uncompress it and cd into the created directory:

```
#> gunzip < openssl*.tar.gz | tar xvf -
#> cd openssl*
```

OpenSSL contains a `config` script to help you build the software. You must provide the path to which the software will install. The path used in this hour is `/usr/local/ssl/install`, and you probably need to have root privileges to install the software there. You can install the software as a regular user, but to do so, you will need to change the path. Then, you must build and install the software:

```
#> ./config --prefix=/usr/local/ssl/install \
--openssldir=/usr/local/ssl/install/openssl
#> make
#> make install
```

If everything went well, you have now successfully installed the OpenSSL toolkit. The `openssl` command-line tool will be located in `/usr/local/ssl/install/bin/`.

This tool is used to create and manipulate certificates and keys, and its usage is described in a later section on certificates.

mod_ssl

In the past, SSL extensions for Apache had to be distributed separately because of export restrictions. These restrictions no longer exist and `mod_ssl` is bundled and integrated with Apache 2.0. This section describes the steps necessary to build and install this module. `mod_ssl` depends on the OpenSSL library, so a valid OpenSSL installation is required.

Windows

You can download a binary distribution of Apache 2.0 for the Windows platform from `http://httpd.apache.org`; it includes `mod_ssl`. You might need to uncomment the following line in the configuration file:

```
LoadModule ssl_module modules/libmodssl.so
```

Unix

If you are using the Apache 2.0 server that came installed with your operating system, chances are that it already includes `mod_ssl`. Use the package management tools bundled with your distribution to install `mod_ssl` if it is not present in your system.

When you build Apache 2.0 from source, you must pass the following options to enable and build `mod_ssl` at compile time. The options are in addition to the options used in Hour 2, "Installing and Configuring Apache," to ensure that PHP was successfully installed.

```
--enable-ssl --with-ssl=/usr/local/ssl/install/openssl
```

This assumes that you installed OpenSSL in the location described in previous sections.

If you compiled mod_ssl statically into Apache, you can check whether it is present by issuing the following command, which provides a list of compiled-in modules:

```
#> /usr/local/apache2/bin/httpd -l
```

The command assumes that you installed Apache in the /usr/local/apache2 directory.

If mod_ssl was compiled as a dynamic loadable module, the following line must be added or uncommented to the configuration file:

```
LoadModule ssl_module modules/libmodssl.so
```

23

Managing Certificates

To have a working SSL server implementation, the first step is to create a server certificate. This section explains in detail how to create and manage certificates and keys by using the openssl command-line tool. For example, if you are using SSL for an e-commerce site, encryption prevents customer data from eavesdroppers, and the certificate enables customers to verify that you are who you claim to be.

> The examples refer to the Unix version of the command-line program openssl. If you are running under Windows, you need to use openssl.exe instead and change the paths of the examples to use backslashes instead of forward slashes. The examples also assume that OpenSSL was installed in the path described earlier in the OpenSSL installation section.

Creating a Key Pair

You must have a public/private key pair before you can create a certificate request. Assume that the FQDN for the certificate you want to create is www.example.com. (You will need to substitute this name for the FQDN of the machine on which you have installed Apache.) You can create the keys by issuing the following command:

```
#> ./usr/local/ssl/install/bin/openssl genrsa -des3 -rand file1:file2:file3 \
      -out www.example.com.key 1024
```

genrsa indicates to OpenSSL that you want to generate a key pair.

des3 indicates that the private key should be encrypted and protected by a pass phrase.

The rand switch is used to provide OpenSSL with random data to ensure that the generated keys are unique and unpredictable. Substitute file1, file2, and so on, for the path

to several large, relatively random files for this purpose (such as a kernel image, compressed log files, and so on). You can also use /dev/random if it exists on your system.
The rand switch is not necessary on Windows because the random data is automatically
generated by other means.

The out switch indicates where to store the results.

1024 indicates the number of bits of the generated key.

The result of invoking this command looks like this:

```
625152  semi-random bytes loaded
Generating RSA private key, 1024 bit long modulus
.....++++++
......................++++++
e is 65537 (0x10001)
Enter PEM pass phrase:
Verifying password - Enter PEM pass phrase:
```

As you can see, you will be asked to provide a pass phrase; choose a secure one. The
pass phrase is necessary to protect the private key, and you will be asked for it whenever
you want to start the server. You can choose not to protect the key. This is convenient
because you will not need to enter the pass phrase during reboots, but it is highly insecure and a compromise of the server means a compromise of the key as well. In any
case, you can choose to unprotect the key either by leaving out the -des3 switch in the
generation phase or by issuing the following command:

```
#> ./usr/local/ssl/install/bin/openssl rsa -in www.example.com.key \
        -out www.example.com.key.unsecure
```

It is a good idea to back up the www.example.com.key file. You can learn about the contents of the key file by issuing the following command:

```
#> ./usr/local/ssl/bin/openssl rsa -noout -text -in www.example.com.key
```

Creating a Certificate Signing Request

To get a certificate issued by a CA, you must submit what is called a *certificate signing
request*. To create a request, issue the following command:

```
#> ./usr/local/ssl/install/bin/openssl req -new -key www.example.com.key \
        -out www.example.com.csr
```

You will be prompted for the certificate information:

```
Using configuration from /usr/local/ssl/install/openssl/openssl.cnf
Enter PEM pass phrase:
You are about to be asked to enter information that will be incorporated
into your certificate request.
```

```
What you are about to enter is what is called a Distinguished Name or a DN.
There are quite a few fields but you can leave some blank
For some fields there will be a default value,
If you enter '.', the field will be left blank.
-----
Country Name (2 letter code) [AU]:US
State or Province Name (full name) [Some-State]:CA
Locality Name (eg, city) []: San Francisco
Organization Name (eg, company) [Internet Widgits Pty Ltd]:.
Organizational Unit Name (eg, section) []:.
Common Name (eg, YOUR name) []:www.example.com
Email Address []:administrator@example.com
Please enter the following 'extra' attributes
to be sent with your certificate request
A challenge password []:
An optional company name []:
```

It is important that the `Common Name` field entry matches the address that visitors to your Web site will type in their browsers. This is one of the checks that the browser will perform for the remote server certificate. If the names differ, a warning indicating the mismatch will be issued to the user.

The certificate is now stored in `www.example.com.csr`. You can learn about the contents of the certificate via the following command:

```
#> ./usr/local/ssl/install/bin/openssl req -noout -text \
      -in www.example.com.csr
```

You can submit the certificate signing request file to a CA for processing. VeriSign and Thawte are two of those CAs. You can learn more about their particular submission procedures at their Web sites:

- **VeriSign**—http://digitalid.verisign.com/
- **Thawte**—http://www.thawte.com/

Creating a Self-Signed Certificate

You can also create a self-signed certificate. That is, you can be both the issuer and the subject of the certificate. Although this is not very useful for a commercial Web site, it will enable you to test your installation of mod_ssl, or to have a secure Web server while you wait for the official certificate from the CA.

```
#> ./usr/local/ssl/install/bin/openssl x509 -req -days 30  \
       -in www.example.com.csr -signkey www.example.com.key \
       -out www.example.com.cert
```

23

You need to copy your certificate `www.example.com.cert` (either the one returned by the CA or your self-signed one) to `/usr/local/ssl/install/openssl/certs/` and your key to `/usr/local/ssl/install/openssl/private/`.

Protect your key file by issuing the following command:

```
#> chmod 400 www.example.com.key
```

SSL Configuration

The previous sections introduced the (not-so-basic) concepts behind SSL, and you have learned how to generate keys and certificates. Now, finally, you can configure Apache to support SSL. mod_ssl must either be compiled statically or, if you have compiled as a loadable module, the appropriate LoadModule directive must be present in the file.

If you compiled Apache yourself, a new Apache configuration file, named ssl.conf, should be present in the /conf directory. That file contains a sample Apache SSL configuration, and is referenced from the main httpd.conf file via an Include directive.

If you want to start your configuration from scratch, you can add the following configuration snippet to your Apache configuration file:

```
Listen 80
Listen 443
<VirtualHost _default_:443>
ServerName www.example.com
SSLEngine on
SSLCertificateFile \
/usr/local/ssl/install/openssl/certs/www.example.com.cert
SSLCertificateKeyFile \
/usr/loca/ssl/install/openssl/certs/www.example.com.key
</VirtualHost>
```

With the previous configuration, you set up a new virtual host that will listen to port 443 (the default port for HTTPS), and you enable SSL on that virtual host with the SSLEngine directive.

You need to indicate where to find the server's certificate and the file containing the associated key. You do so by using SSLCertificateFile and SSLCertificateKeyfile directives.

Starting the Server

Now you can stop the server if it is running, and start it again. If your key is protected by a pass phrase, you will be prompted for it. After this, Apache will start, and you should be able to connect securely to it via the `https://www.example.com/` URL.

If you compiled and installed Apache yourself, in many of the vendor configuration files, you can see that an <IFDEFINE SSL> block surrounds the SSL directives. That allows for conditional starting of the server in SSL mode. If you start the httpd server binary directly, you can pass it the -DSSL flag at startup. You can also use the apachectl script by issuing the apachectl startssl command. Finally, if you always want to start Apache with SSL support, you can just remove the <ifDefine> section and start Apache in the usual way.

If you are unable to successfully start your server, check the Apache error log for clues about what might have gone wrong. For example, if you cannot bind to the port, make sure that another Apache is not running already. You must have administrator privileges to bind to port 443.

Summary

This hour explained the fundamentals of the SSL protocol and mod_ssl, the Apache module that implements support for SSL. You learned how to install and configure mod_ssl and the OpenSSL libraries, and how to use the openssl command-line tool for certificate and key generation and management. You can access the mod_ssl reference documentation for in-depth syntax explanation and additional configuration information. Bear in mind also that SSL is just part of maintaining a secure server, which includes applying security patches, OS configuration, access control, physical security, and so on.

Q&A

Q Can I have SSL with name-based virtual hosting?

A A question that comes up frequently is how to make name-based virtual hosts work with SSL. The answer is that you can't, at least currently. Name-based virtual hosts depend on the Host header of the HTTP request, but the certificate verification happens when the SSL connection is being established and no HTTP request can be sent. There is a protocol for upgrading an existing HTTP connection to TLS, but it is mostly unsupported by current browsers (see RFC 2817).

Q Can I use SSL with other protocols?

A mod_ssl implements the SSL protocol as a filter. Other protocols using the same Apache server can easily take advantage of the SSL.

Workshop

The Workshop is designed to help you anticipate possible questions, review what you've learned, and begin learning how to put your knowledge into practice.

Quiz

1. Name three requirements to carry on secure communications on the Internet.
2. How do you start an SSL-enabled instance of Apache?

Answers

1. Confidentiality, integrity, and authentication
2. Use the `apachectl` control script and the command `apachectl startssl`.

HOUR 24

Optimizing and Tuning MySQL

Proper care and feeding of your MySQL server will keep it running happily and without incident. The optimization of your system consists of proper hardware maintenance and software tuning. In this hour, you will learn

- Basic hardware and software optimization tips for your MySQL server
- Key start-up parameters for your MySQL server
- How to use the OPTIMIZE TABLE command
- How to use the EXPLAIN command
- How to use the FLUSH command to clean up tables, caches, and log files
- How to use SHOW commands to retrieve information about databases, tables, and indexes
- How to use SHOW commands to find system status information

Building an Optimized Platform

Designing a well-structured, normalized database schema is just half of the optimization puzzle. The other half is building and fine-tuning a server to run this fine database. Think about the four main components of a server: CPU, memory, hard drive, and operating system. Each of these better be up to speed or no amount of design or programming will make your database faster!

- **CPU**—The faster the CPU, the faster MySQL will be able to process your data. There's no real secret to this, but a 750MHz processor is significantly faster than a 266MHz processor. With processor speeds now more than 1GHz and with reasonable prices all around, it's not difficult to get a good bang for your buck.
- **Memory**—Put as much RAM in your machine as you can. You can never have enough, and RAM prices will be at rock bottom for the foreseeable future. Having available RAM can help balance out sluggish CPUs.
- **Hard Drive**—The proper hard drive will be both large enough and fast enough to accommodate your database server and its traffic. An important measurement of hard-drive speed is its seek time, or the amount of time it takes for the drive to spin around and find a specific piece of information. Seek time is measured in milliseconds, and an average disk-seek time is around eight or nine milliseconds. When buying a hard drive, make sure it's big enough to accommodate all the data you'll eventually store in your database and fast enough to find it quickly.
- **Operating System**—If you use an operating system that's a resource hog, you have two choices: buy enough resources (that is, RAM) so that it doesn't matter, or use an operating system that doesn't suck away all your resources just so that you can have windows and pretty colors. Also, if you are blessed with a machine that has multiple processors, be sure your operating system can handle this condition and handle it well.

If you put the proper pieces together at the system level, you'll have taken several steps toward overall server optimization.

Using the `benchmark()` Function

A quick test of your server speed is to use the `benchmark()` MySQL function to see how long it takes to process a given expression. You can make the expression something simple, such as 10+10, or something more extravagant, such as extracting pieces of dates.

No matter the result of the expression, the result of `benchmark()` will always be 0. The purpose of `benchmark()` is not to retrieve the result of the expression, but to see how long it takes to repeat the expression for a specific number of times. For example, the following command executes the expression 10+10 one million times:

```
mysql> select benchmark(1000000,10+10);
+--------------------------+
| benchmark(1000000,10+10) |
+--------------------------+
|                        0 |
+--------------------------+
1 row in set (0.14 sec)
```

This command executes the date extraction expression, also one million times:

```
mysql> select benchmark(1000000, extract(year from now()));
+----------------------------------------------+
| benchmark(1000000, extract(year from now())) |
+----------------------------------------------+
|                                            0 |
+----------------------------------------------+
1 row in set (0.20 sec)
```

The important number is the time in seconds, which is the elapsed time for the execution of the function. You might want to run the same uses of benchmark() multiple times during different parts of day (when your server is under different loads) to get a better idea of how your server is performing.

MySQL Startup Options

MySQL AB provides a wealth of information regarding the tuning of server parameters, much of which the average user will never need to use. So, as not to completely overwhelm you with information, this section will contain a few of the more common startup options for a finely tuned MySQL server.

When you start MySQL, a configuration file called my.cnf is loaded. This file contains information ranging from port number to buffer sizes, but can be overruled by command-line startup options. At installation time, my.cnf is placed in the /etc directory, but you can also specify an alternate location for this file during start-up.

In the support-files subdirectory of your MySQL installation directory, you'll find four sample configuration files, each tuned for a specific range of installed memory:

- my-small.cnf—For systems with less than 64MB of RAM, where MySQL is used occasionally.

- my-medium.cnf—For systems with less than 64MB of RAM, where MySQL is the primary activity on the system, or for systems with up to 128MB of RAM, where MySQL shares the box with other processes. This is the most common configuration, where MySQL is installed on the same box as a Web server and receives a moderate amount of traffic.

24

- `my-large.cnf`—For a system with 128MB to 512MB of RAM, where MySQL is the primary activity.

- `my-huge.cnf`—For a system with 1GB to 2GB of RAM, where MySQL is the primary activity.

To use any of these as the base configuration file, simply copy the file of your choice to `/etc/my.cnf` (or wherever `my.cnf` is on your system) and change any system-specific information, such as port or file locations.

Key Startup Parameters

There are two primary start-up parameters that will affect your system the most: `key_buffer_size` and `table_cache`. If you get only two server parameters correctly tuned, make sure they're these two!

The value of `key_buffer_size` is the size of the buffer used with indexes. The larger the buffer, the faster the SQL command will finish and a result will be returned. Try to find the fine line between finely tuned and over-optimized; you might have a `key_buffer_size` of 256MB on a system with 512MB of RAM, but any more than 256MB could cause degraded server performance.

A simple way to check the actual performance of the buffer is to examine four additional variables: `key_read_requests`, `key_reads`, `key_write_requests`, and `key_writes`. You can find the values of these variables by issuing the SHOW STATUS command:

mysql> show status;

A long list of variables and values will be returned, listed in alphabetical order. Find the rows that look something like this (your values will differ):

```
| Key_read_requests    | 602843  |
| Key_reads            | 151     |
| Key_write_requests   | 1773    |
| Key_writes           | 805     |
```

If you divide the value of `key_read` by the value of `key_reads_requests`, the result should be less than 0.01. Also, if you divide the value of `key_write` by the value of `key_writes_requests`, the result should be less than 1. Using the previous values, we have results of 0.000250479809834401 and 0.454032712915962, respectively, well within the acceptable parameters. To try to get these numbers even smaller, more tuning could occur by increasing the value of `key_buffer_size`, but these numbers would be fine to leave as they are.

The other important server parameter is `table_cache`, which is the number of open tables for all threads. The default is 64, but you might need to adjust this number. Using the SHOW STATUS command, look for a variable called open_tables in the output. If this number is large, the value of table_cache should be increased.

The sample configuration files use various combinations of key_buffer_size and table_cache, which you can use as a baseline for any modifications you need to make. Whenever you modify your configuration, you'll be restarting your server for changes to take effect, sometimes with no knowledge of the consequences of your changes. In this case, be sure to try your modifications in a development environment before rolling the changes into production.

Optimizing Your Table Structure

An optimized table structure is different from a well-designed table. Table structure optimization has to do with reclaiming unused space after deletions and basically cleaning up the table after structural modifications have been made. The OPTIMIZE TABLE SQL command takes care of this, using the following syntax:

```
OPTIMIZE TABLE table_name[,table_name]
```

For example, if you want to optimize the grocery_inventory table in the testDB database, use

```
mysql> optimize table grocery_inventory;
+-----------------------+----------+----------+----------+
| Table                 | Op       | Msg_type | Msg_text |
+-----------------------+----------+----------+----------+
| testDB.grocery_inventory | optimize | status   | OK       |
+-----------------------+----------+----------+----------+
1 row in set (0.08 sec)
```

The output doesn't explicitly state what was fixed, but the text in the Msg_text column shows that the grocery_inventory table was indeed optimized. If you run the command again, the text will change, showing that it is a useful message:

```
mysql> optimize table grocery_inventory;
+-----------------------+----------+----------+--------------------------+
| Table                 | Op       | Msg_type | Msg_text                 |
+-----------------------+----------+----------+--------------------------+
| testDB.grocery_inventory| optimize | status   | Table is already up to date |
+-----------------------+----------+----------+--------------------------+
1 row in set (0.03 sec)
```

Be aware that the table is locked while it is optimized, so if your table is large, optimize it during scheduled downtime or when little traffic is flowing to your system.

Optimizing Your Queries

Query optimization has a lot to do with the proper use of indexes. The EXPLAIN command will examine a given SELECT statement to see whether it's optimized the best that it can be, using indexes wherever possible. This is especially useful when looking at complex queries involving JOINs. The syntax for EXPLAIN is

EXPLAIN SELECT *statement*

The output of the EXPLAIN command is a table of information containing the following columns:

- table—The name of the table.
- type—The join type, of which there are several.
- possible_keys—This column indicates which indexes MySQL could use to find the rows in this table. If the result is NULL, no indexes would help with this query. You should then take a look at your table structure and see whether there are any indexes that you could create that would increase the performance of this query.
- key—The key actually used in this query, or NULL if no index was used.
- key_len—The length of the key used, if any.
- ref—Any columns used with the key to retrieve a result.
- rows—The number of rows MySQL must examine to execute the query.
- extra—Additional information regarding how MySQL will execute the query. There are several options, such as Using index (an index was used) and Where (a WHERE clause was used).

The following EXPLAIN command output shows a nonoptimized query:

```
mysql> explain select * from grocery_inventory;
+-------------------+------+---------------+------+---------+------+------+------+
| table             | type | possible_keys | key  | key_len | ref  | rows | Extra|
+-------------------+------+---------------+------+---------+------+------+------+
| grocery_inventory | ALL  | NULL          | NULL |    NULL | NULL |    6 |      |
+-------------------+------+---------------+------+---------+------+------+------+
1 row in set (0.00 sec)
```

However, there's not much optimizing you can do with a "select all" query except add a WHERE clause with the primary key. The possible_keys column would then show PRIMARY, and the Extra column would show Where, used.

When using EXPLAIN on statements involving JOIN, a quick way to gauge the optimization of the query is to look at the values in the rows column. In the previous example, you have 2 and 1. Multiply these numbers together and you have 2 as your answer. This is the number of rows that MySQL must look at to produce the results of the query. You want to get this number as low as possible, and 2 is as low as it can go!

For a great deal more information on the EXPLAIN command, please visit the MySQL manual at http://www.mysql.com/doc/E/X/EXPLAIN.html.

Using the FLUSH Command

Users with reload privileges for a specific database can use the FLUSH command to clean up the internal caches used by MySQL. Often, only the root-level user has the appropriate permissions to issue administrative commands such as FLUSH.

The FLUSH syntax is

```
FLUSH flush_option
```

The common options for the FLUSH command are

- PRIVILEGES
- TABLES
- HOSTS
- LOGS

You've used the FLUSH PRIVILEGES command before, after adding new users. This command simply reloads the grant tables in your MySQL database, enabling the changes to take effect without stopping and restarting MySQL. When you issue a FLUSH PRIVILEGES command, the Query OK response will assure you that the cleaning process occurred without a hitch.

```
mysql> flush privileges;
Query OK, 0 rows affected (0.10 sec)
```

The FLUSH TABLES command will close all tables currently open or in use and essentially give your MySQL server a millisecond of breathing room before starting back to work. When your caches are empty, MySQL can better utilize available memory. Again, you're looking for the Query OK response:

```
mysql> flush tables;
Query OK, 0 rows affected (0.21 sec)
```

The FLUSH HOSTS command works specifically with the host cache tables. If you are unable to connect to your MySQL server, a common reason is that the maximum number of connections has been reached for a particular host, and it's throwing errors. When MySQL sees numerous errors on connection, it will assume something is amiss and

24

simply block any additional connection attempts to that host. The FLUSH HOSTS command will reset this process and again allow connections to be made:

```
mysql> flush hosts;
Query OK, 0 rows affected (0.00 sec)
```

The FLUSH LOGS command closes and reopens all log files. If your log file is getting to be a burden, and you want to start a new one, this command will create a new, empty log file. Weeding through a year's worth of log entries in one file looking for errors can be a chore, so try to flush your logs at least monthly.

```
mysql> flush logs;
Query OK, 0 rows affected (0.04 sec)
```

Using the SHOW Command

There are several different uses of the SHOW command, which will produce output displaying a great deal of useful information about your MySQL database, users, and tables. Depending on your access level, some of the SHOW commands will not be available to you or will provide only minimal information. The root-level user has the capability to use all the SHOW commands, with the most comprehensive results.

The common uses of SHOW include the following, which you'll soon learn about in more detail:

```
SHOW GRANTS FOR user
SHOW DATABASES [LIKE something]
SHOW [OPEN] TABLES [FROM database_name] [LIKE something]
SHOW CREATE TABLE table_name
SHOW [FULL] COLUMNS FROM table_name [FROM database_name] [LIKE something]
SHOW INDEX FROM table_name [FROM database_name]
SHOW TABLE STATUS [FROM db_name] [LIKE something]
SHOW STATUS [LIKE something]
SHOW VARIABLES [LIKE something]
```

The SHOW GRANTS command will display the privileges for a given user at a given host. This is any easy way to check on the current status of a user, especially if you have a request to modify a user's privileges. With SHOW GRANTS, you can check first to see that the user doesn't already have the requested privileges. For example, see the privileges available to the joeuser user:

```
mysql> show grants for joe@localhost;
+----------------------------------------------------------+
| Grants for joeuser@localhost                             |
+----------------------------------------------------------+
| GRANT USAGE ON *.* TO 'joeuser'@'localhost' \
IDENTIFIED BY PASSWORD '34f3a6996d856efd'                  |
| GRANT ALL PRIVILEGES ON testDB.* TO 'joeuser'@'localhost' |
+----------------------------------------------------------+
```

If you're not the root-level user or the joeuser user, you'll get an error. Unless you're the root-level user, you can only see the information relevant to your user. For example, the joeuser user isn't allowed to view information about the root-level user:

```
mysql> show grants for root@localhost;
ERROR 1044: Access denied for user:'joeuser@localhost' to database 'mysql'
```

Be aware of your privilege level throughout the remainder of this hour. If you are not the root-level user, some of these commands will not be available to you or will display only limited information.

Retrieving Information About Databases and Tables

You've used a few of the basic SHOW commands earlier in this book to view the list of databases and tables on your MySQL server. As a refresher, the SHOW DATABASES command does just that—it lists all the databases on the MySQL server:

```
mysql> show databases;
+-------------------+
| Database          |
+-------------------+
| testDB            |
| mysql             |
+-------------------+
2 rows in set (0.00 sec)
```

After you've selected a database to work with, you can also use SHOW to list the tables in the database. In this example, we're using testDB (your table listing may vary):

```
mysql> show tables;
+---------------------+
| Tables_in_testDB    |
+---------------------+
| grocery_inventory   |
| email               |
| master_name         |
| myTest              |
| testTable           |
+---------------------+
5 rows in set (0.01 sec)
```

If you add OPEN to your SHOW TABLES command, you will get a list of all the tables in the table cache, showing how many times they're cached and in use:

```
mysql> SHOW OPEN TABLES;
+------------------------+--------------------+
| Open_tables_in_testDB  | Comment            |
+------------------------+--------------------+
| grocery_inventory      | cached=1, in_use=0 |
| email                  | cached=1, in_use=0 |
```

24

```
| testTable                | cached=1, in_use=0 |
| master_name              | cached=1, in_use=0 |
| myTest                   | cached=1, in_use=0 |
+--------------------------+--------------------+
5 rows in set (0.00 sec)
```

Using this information in conjunction with the FLUSH TABLES command you learned earlier in this hour will help keep your database running smoothly. If SHOW OPEN TABLES shows that tables are cached numerous times, but aren't currently in use, go ahead and use FLUSH TABLES to free up that memory.

Retrieving Table Structure Information

A very helpful command is SHOW CREATE TABLE, which does what it sounds like—it shows you the SQL statement used to create a specified table:

```
mysql> show create table grocery_inventory;
+-------------------+----------------------------------------------------+
| Table             | Create Table                                       |
|+-----------------+----------------------------------------------------+
| grocery_inventory | CREATE TABLE `grocery_inventory` (                |
|                   |   `id` int(11) NOT NULL auto_increment,            |
|                   |     `item_name` varchar(50) NOT NULL default '',   |
|                   |   `item_desc` text,                                |
|                   |   `item_price` float NOT NULL default '0',         |
|                   |   `curr_qty` int(11) NOT NULL default '0',         |
|                   |   PRIMARY KEY  (`id`)                              |
|                   |     ) TYPE=MyISAM                                  |
+-------------------+----------------------------------------------------+
1 row in set (0.00 sec)
```

This is essentially the same information you'd get if you dumped the table schema, but the SHOW CREATE TABLE command can be used quickly if you're just looking for a reminder or a simple reference to a particular table-creation statement.

If you need to know the structure of the table, but don't necessarily need the SQL command to create it, you can use the SHOW COLUMNS command:

```
mysql> show columns from grocery_inventory;
+------------+-------------+------+-----+---------+----------------+
| Field      | Type        | Null | Key | Default | Extra          |
+------------+-------------+------+-----+---------+----------------+
| id         | int(11)     |      | PRI | NULL    | auto_increment |
| item_name  | varchar(50) |      |     |         |                |
| item_desc  | text        | YES  |     | NULL    |                |
| item_price | float       |      |     | 0       |                |
| curr_qty   | int(11)     |      |     | 0       |                |
+------------+-------------+------+-----+---------+----------------+
5 rows in set (0.00 sec)
```

The SHOW COLUMNS and DESCRIBE commands are aliases for one another and, therefore, do the same thing.

The SHOW INDEX command will display information about all the indexes present in a particular table. The syntax is

```
SHOW INDEX FROM table_name [FROM database_name]
```

This command produces a table full of information, ranging from the column name to cardinality of the index. The columns returned from this command are described in Table 24.1.

TABLE 24.1 Columns in the SHOW INDEX Result

Column Name	Description
Table	The name of the table.
Non_unique	1 or 0.
	1 = index can contain duplicates.
	0 = index can't contain duplicates.
Key_name	The name of the index.
Seq_in_index	The column sequence number for the
	Index; starts at 1.
Column_name	The name of the column.
Collation	The sort order of the column, either
	A (ascending) or NULL (not sorted).
Cardinality	Number of unique values in the index.
Sub_part	On a partially-indexed column, this
	shows the number of indexed characters,
	or NULL if the entire key is indexed.
Packed	The size of numeric columns.
Comment	Any additional comments.

Another command that produces a wide table full of results is the SHOW TABLE STATUS command. The syntax of this command is

```
SHOW TABLE STATUS [FROM database_name] LIKE 'something'
```

This command produces a table full of information, ranging from the size and number of rows to the next value to be used in an auto_increment field. The columns returned from this command are described in Table 24.2.

TABLE 24.2   Columns in the SHOW TABLE STATUS Result

Column Name	Description
Name	The name of the table.
Type	The table type: MyISAM, BDB, InnoDB, or Gemini.
Row_format	The row storage format: fixed, dynamic, or compressed.
Rows	The number of rows.
Avg_row_length	The average row length.
Data_length	The length of the data file.
Max_data_length	The maximum length of the data file.
Index_length	The length of the index file.
Data_free	The number of bytes allocated but not used.
Auto_increment	The next value to be used in an auto_increment field.
Create_time	The date and time when the table was created (in datetime format).
Update_time	The date and time of when the data file was last updated (in datetime format).
Check_time	The date and time of when the table was last checked (in datetime format).
Create_options	Any extra options used in the CREATE TABLE statement.
Comment	Any comments added when the table was created. Additionally, InnoDB tables will use this column to report the free space in the tablespace.

Retrieving System Status

The SHOW STATUS and SHOW VARIABLES commands will quickly provide important information about your database server. The syntax for these commands is simply SHOW STATUS or SHOW VARIABLES, nothing fancy.

There are no less than 54 status variables as the output of SHOW STATUS, but the most useful are

- Aborted_connects—The number of failed attempts to connect to the MySQL server. Anytime you see an aborted connection, you should investigate the problem. It could be related to a bad username and password in a script, or your number of simultaneous connections could be set too low.

- Connections—The aggregate number of connection attempts to the MySQL server during the current period of uptime.

- Max_used_connections—The maximum number of connections that have been in use simultaneously during the current period of uptime.

- Slow_queries—The number of queries that have taken more than long_query_time, which defaults to 10 seconds. If you have more than one, it's time to investigate your SQL syntax!

- Uptime—Total number of seconds the server has been up during the current period of uptime.

24

You can find a comprehensive list of SHOW STATUS variables and an explanation of their values in the MySQL manual, located at http://www.mysql.com/doc/S/H/SHOW_STATUS.html.

The SHOW VARIABLES command produces even more results than SHOW STATUS—approximately 82! The variables reported from SHOW VARIABLES control the general operation of MySQL and include the following useful tidbits:

- connect_timeout—Shows the number of seconds the MySQL server will wait during a connection attempt before it gives up.

- have_innodb—Will show YES if MySQL supports InnoDB tables.

- have_bdb—Will show YES if MySQL supports Berkeley DB tables.

- max_connections—The allowable number of simultaneous connections to MySQL before a connection is refused.

- port—The port on which MySQL is running.

- table_type—The default table type for MySQL, usually MyISAM.

- version—The MySQL version number.

You can find a comprehensive list of the variables returned by the SHOW VARIABLES results and an explanation of their values in the MySQL manual at http://www.mysql.com/doc/S/H/SHOW_VARIABLES.html. After you know the values you have, you can change them in your MySQL configuration file or startup command.

Summary

Running an optimized MySQL server starts with the hardware and operating system in use. Your system's CPU should be sufficiently fast, and you should have enough RAM in use to pick up the slack when your CPU struggles. This is especially true if MySQL shares resources with other processes, such as a Web server. Additionally, the hard drive in use is important because a small hard drive will limit the amount of information you can store in your database. The seek time of your hard drive is important—a slow seek time will cause the overall performance of the server to be slower. Your operating system should not overwhelm your machine and should share resources with MySQL rather than using all the resources itself.

Some key startup parameters for MySQL are the values of `key_buffer_size` and `table_cache`, among others. Baseline values can be found in sample MySQL configuration files, or you can modify the values of these variables and watch the server performance to see whether you hit on the right result for your environment.

Beyond hardware and software optimization is the optimization of tables, as well as `SELECT` queries. Table optimization, using the `OPTIMIZE` command, enables you to reclaim unused space. You can see how well (or not) optimized your queries are by using the `EXPLAIN` command. The resulting output will show if and when indexes are used, and whether you can use any indexes to speed up the given query.

Paying attention to your MySQL server will ensure that it continues to run smoothly. Basic administration commands, such as `FLUSH` and `SHOW`, will help you to recognize and quickly fix potential problems. All these commands are designed to give MySQL a millisecond of rest time and breathing room if it's under a heavy load. Numerous `SHOW` commands will display structural information about databases, tables, and indexes, as well as how the system is performing.

Q&A

Q Can MySQL take advantage of multiple CPUs in a single server?

A Absolutely, if your operating system supports multiple CPUs, MySQL will take advantage of them. However, the performance and tuning of MySQL using multiple processors varies, depending on the operating system. For more information, please see the MySQL manual section for your specific operating system:
`http://www.mysql.com/doc/0/p/Operating_System_Specific_Notes.html`

Q What permission level must I have to use the OPTIMIZE command?

A Any user with INSERT privileges for a table can perform OPTIMIZE commands. If a user has only SELECT permissions, the OPTIMIZE command will not execute.

Workshop

The Workshop is designed to help you anticipate possible questions, review what you've learned, and begin learning how to put your knowledge into practice.

Quiz

1. Which MySQL function will enable you to run an expression many times over to find the speed of the iterations?

2. Which SQL command will clean up the structure of your tables?

3. Which FLUSH command resets the MySQL log files?

4. To quickly determine if MySQL has support for InnoDB tables, would you use SHOW STATUS or SHOW VARIABLES?

5. Write a SQL statement that will enable you to see the SQL statement used to create a table called myTable.

Answers

1. The benchmark() function.

2. OPTIMIZE

3. FLUSH LOGS

4. SHOW VARIABLES

5. SHOW CREATE TABLE myTable

Activities

1. If you have root-level access to your server, change the values of key_buffer_size and table_cache, and run benchmark() functions after each change to see how the execution times differ.

2. Use OPTIMIZE on all the tables you have created in your database, to clean up any structural issues.

3. Use the SHOW STATUS command to retrieve information about your MySQL server, and then issue FLUSH commands to clean up the server. After each command, use SHOW STATUS again to see which commands affect which results in the SHOW STATUS results display.

24

INDEX

Symbols

+ (addition) operator, 73-74

& (ampersand) character, 78, 279

&& (and) operator, 78

= (assignment) operator, 67, 74

* (asterisk), 20, 74

\ (backslash), 32, 100, 222

$ (dollar sign), 66, 261

. (dot), 58, 74-75, 198, 258

/* (forward slash, followed by asterisk), 60

// (forward slashes), 60

> (greater than) operator, 77

(hash sign), 60

< (less than) operator, 77

- (minus symbol), 258

\n (newline) character, 186, 204, 270

!= (nonequivalence) operator, 77

! (not) operator, 78

|| (or) operator, 77-78

% (percent symbol), 344
  conversion specification, 254
  modulus operator, 74
  wildcard, 20

(pound sign), 32, 50

; (semicolon), 94

- (subtraction) operator, 74

\t (tab character), 100

? (ternary operator), 91-92

_ (underscore), 66

A

a (append) mode, 203

A format code (date() function), 220

%a format string option (DATE FORMAT() function), 230

%A formatting directive, 344

aborted connects status variable, 467

AbriaSoft Web site, 8

abs() function, 108-109

abuse, preventing, 433

Accept mechanism, network setting (scalability), 429

access
  control access, 318
  denied, troubleshooting, 43

file system access, settings (scalability), 428
granting, 314
limiting, HTTP methods, 321-322
methods, combining, 320
restricting
access control, 318-320
authentication, 311-317
based on cookie values, 325-329
client authentication, 313
access control
access, restricting, 318-320
rules
all clients, 319
domain names, 318
environment variables, 319
evaluating, 319-320
Access denied message, 14
access log, log file, 37
AccessFileName directive, per-directory configuration files, 36
accessing
Apache, browsers, 41
files, last date accessed information, 200
MySQL, 7-8
MySQL functions, 167
variables, 115-118
ACTION argument, 174
adding
files, documents, 193
users, database file-based access control authentication, 317

addition (+) operator, 73-74
addNums() function, 113
address book, database table example
date added field, 374
date modified field, 374
menus, creating, 376-377
record addition script, 377-381
records, adding subentries to, 389-394
records, deleting, 387-389
records, selecting and viewing, 382-387
table name fields, 374-376
addresses
IP addresses
control access rules, 318
overview, 13
reverse DNS lookups, 346
listening addresses (Listen directive), 41
alerts, LogLevel directive option, 350
algorithms
digest algorithms, 313, 444
public key cryptography, 444
symmetric cryptography, 443
all clients rule, access control, 319
ALL command, 19
Allow directives, access control rule, 318
Allow, Deny argument, Order directive, 320

AllowOverride directive, per-directory configuration files, 37
ALTER command, 19
ampersand (&), 78, 279
analyzing
digital certificates, 446
logs, 353
and (&&) operator, 78
Apache
configuration file structure, 32
installing
binary method, 26
from source, 26
methods for, selecting, 25
on Linux/Unix, 26
on Windows, 29-32
PHP on Linux/Unix with, 47-49
integrating PHP with, on windows, 51-52
Web site, 27
apache.exe, 38-39
ApacheBench, performance tool (Web site), 429, 431
apachectl tool, 35, 40
append (a) mode, 203
appending files, 208
applications. *See also* discussion forums
setup.exe, 9
winmysqladmin.exe, 12
applying directives, 34
arguments, 108
ACTION, 174
Allow, Deny argument, 320
AllowOverride directive, 37
CustomLog directive, 348

default values, 120, 122

Deny, Allow argument, 319-320

directives, 32

ENCRYPT, 188

flock() function, 210

format control strings and, 260-261

function requiring two, 121

HostNameLookups directive, 346

LogFormat directive, 346

logs, rotating, 352

Mutual-Failure argument, 320

optional example, 122

reference passing, 122

ServerRoot directive, 36

syslog daemon, errors, 350

TYPE, 188

value passing, 122-124

arithmetic operators, 74

array data type, 68

arrays

getdate() function, 218

$GLOBALS, 172

mysql fetch array() function, 166

strings, breaking into, 271

ASCII() function, 279

ASP tags, 56-57

assignment operator (=), 67, 74

asterisk (*), 74

asymmetric cryptography. *See* **public key cryptography**

attacks, preventing (performance), 433

auth cookies, 329-330

auth users table, 325-326

AuthAuthoritative directive, 316

AuthConfig directive value, 37

AuthDBMGroupFile directive, 317

AuthDBMUserFile directive, 317

authentication

access, restricting, 311-312

basic, 312

browsers, AuthType directive, 313

client authentication, 313

communications, security, 442

database file-based access control, 316-317

digest, 312

errors in, 17-18

file-based, 315-316

modules

access (restricting), 314-317

directives, 313

functions, 314

realm, 313

SSL protocols, 445-447

AuthGroupFile directive, 315

AuthName directive, 313

authoritative information, 314

AuthType directive, 313

AuthUserFile directive, 315

awstats, log analysis, 353

B

%b format string option (DATE FORMAT() function), 230

%B formatting directive, 345

b type specifier, 255

backend storage

file-based authentication, 315-317

functions, authentication modules, 314

backslash (\), 32, 100, 222

backwards compatibility, 52

basic authentication, 312

benchmark() function, 456-457

BIGINT data type, 133

BIN() function, 279

binaries

installing, 26

server binary, 38

binary distribution, installing MySQL from, 8

binary installer, 29-30

bind to port, troubleshooting, 42

BLOB data type, 135

$blue variable, 256

boolean data type, 68

boolean values, test expressions, 104

break statements

code ends, 90

loops, 96-98

breaking out of loops, 96-98

browser authentication, 313

browser output, 101-102
browsers
  access, environment
    variables, 319
  Apache, accessing, 41
  cookies
    anatomy, 322-323
    deleting, 325
    setting, 323-325
  digest authentication,
    313
browsing directives, 32
building source code, 26
built-in functions, 108
**bundled digital certifi-
  cates, 446**

C

**-c command-line option,
  316**
**%c format string option
  (DATE FORMAT()
  function), 230**
**%C formatting directive,
  345**
c type specifier, 255
**CA (certification authori-
  ty)**
  certificate signing
    requests, 451
  digital certificates, 445
CacheFile directive, 431
**caching, performance,
  432**
calendar example, 237
  HTML form, 239-240
  library, creating,
    244-250
  table, creating, 241-244
  user input, 238-239
**calling functions, 108,
  110, 113-114**

**Can't connect to server
  message, 14**
**case, strings, converting,
  268-269**
case-sensitivity, 81
casting variables, 71-72
$cat id value, 404
**certificate signing
  requests, 450-451**
certificates
  digital, 445-446
  managing
    certificate signing
      requests, creating,
      450-451
    key pairs (creating),
      449
    secure servers,
      449-452
    self-signed certifi-
      cates, 451
CGI errors, logging, 349
**chaining, digital certifi-
  cates, 445**
changing data types
  by casting, 71-72
  settype() function,
    69-70
CHAR data type, 14, 134
**CHAR LENGTH() func-
  tion, 271**
CHAR() function, 281
**$check result value,
  365-366**
**checkdate() function,
  223, 238**
**checking digital certifi-
  cates, 446**
ciphertext, 443
clauses
  else, 87-88, 244
  elseif, 88-89

    ORDER BY, 139-140,
      226
    WHERE, 141-142, 226,
      362
**CLF (Common Log
  Format), 346**
client authentication, 313
client requests, 37
clients
  all clients rule, access
    control, 319
  tracking, 348
closing files, 203
code
  adding comments to, 60
  source code
    building (installation
      methods), 26
    downloading
      (Apache installa-
      tions), 27
    uncompressing
      (Apache installa-
      tions), 27
  status code, 347
  when to comment, 61
**code block (control state-
  ments), 101-104**
**collision resistant mes-
  sage digests, 444**
columns priv table, 17
**combined assignment
  operators, 75-76**
**combining access meth-
  ods, 320**
**command-line argu-
  ments, 48**
command-line tools, 449
commands. *See also*
  **functions; methods;
  statements**
  ALL, 19
  ALTER, 19

certificates signing requests, creating, 450
compress, 27
configure, 29
control script, 40
CREATE, 19
CREATE TABLE, 135-136
CROSS JOIN, 147
DELETE, 18-19, 21-22, 152-153
DROP, 19
EVOKE, 21
EXPLAIN, 460-461
FILE, 19
FLUSH, 20, 461
FLUSH HOSTS, 461
FLUSH LOGS, 462
FLUSH PRIVILEGES, 20-21, 461
FLUSH TABLES, 461, 464
GRANT, 19-20
gunzip, 8, 27
gzip, 27
INNER JOIN, 145
INSERT, 18-19, 21, 136-138, 326
JOIN, 145
key pairs, creating, 449
kill, 39
LEFT JOIN, 146-147
LIMIT, 140-141
ln commands, 428
make, 49
make install, 29, 49
mod so, 28
NATURAL JOIN, 147
OPTIMIZE TABLE, 459
PROCESS, 19
ps, 15
REFERENCES, 19

RELOAD, 20
REPLACE, 150-151
REVOKE, 21-22
RIGHT JOIN, 147
SELECT, 18, 20, 138-140, 143-145
server binary, 38
SHOW, 462
SHOW COLUMNS, 464
SHOW CREATE TABLE, 464
SHOW DATABASES, 463
SHOW GRANTS, 462-463
SHOW INDEX, 465
SHOW OPEN TABLES, 464
SHOW STATUS, 458, 467
SHOW TABLE STATUS, 465-466
SHOW TABLES, 463
SHOW VARIABLES, 13, 467
SHUTDOWN, 20
STRAIGHT JOIN, 147
tar, 8, 27
ulimit command, 426
UPDATE, 20, 148-150
USAGE, 20
comments, 60-61
Common Log Format (CLF), 346
Common Name field, certificate signing requests, 451
communications, secure, 441-442
Compact installation option, 11

comparison operators, 77
compatibility, schemas, 33
compress utility, 27
compression
    reduced transmitted data (performance), 432
    uncompressing, 27
CONCAT WS() function, 228, 273
CONCAT() function, 272-273
concatenation function, 271-274
concatenation operator (.), 74-75
conditional containers, 35-36
conditional logging
    CustomLog directives, 347
    HostNameLookups directive, 346
    HTTP requests, 347-348
    IdentityCheck directive, 347
conditional looping, 347
conditions
    else clause with if statements, 87-88
    elseif clause with if statements, 88-89
    if statements
        else clause with, 87-88
        elseif clause with, 88-89
        example of, 86
        switch, compared, 89

loops
> breaking out of,
> > 96-98
> do, while statement,
> > 93-94
> for statement, 95-96
> iterations, skipping,
> > 98-99
> nesting, 100-101
> while statement,
> > 92-93

switch statements
> example, 90-91
> if, compared, 89
> ? (ternary operator),
> > 91-92

confidentiality
> communications, 442
> SSL protocols, 443-444
> symmetric cryptography (SSL protocols), 443

config script, 448
config.log file, 28
config.status file, 28
configuration files, 32
> Apache, starting, 40
> conditional containers, 35-36
> directive containers, 34
> directives, 33
> Listen directive, 41
> modifying, 39
> my-huge.cnf, 458
> my-large.cnf, 458
> my-medium.cnf, 457
> my-small.cnf, 457
> parameters, 40
> per-directory, 36-37, 428
> processing MPMs, 35
> ServerName directive, 41
> ServerRoot directive, 36

configure command, 29
configure scripts, 27-28, 48-49
configuring
> MySQL, 12-13
> PHP, 48-50
> software (Apache installations), 27
> SSL (secure servers), 452

connection timeout variable, 467
connections
> SSL protocols, 446-447
> to MySQL with PHP, 157
> > error messages, retrieving, 161
> > queries, executing, 159-161
> > using mysql connection() function, 158-159
> > securing, 16

connections status variable, 467
constants, case-independence, 81
constructors, 235
containers
> conditional containers, 35-36
> configuration files, 34
> defined, 32
> <Limit>, 321
> <LimitExcept>, 322
> syntax, 34
> VirtualHost container, 434

content negotiation, file system access (scalability), 428
context, schemas, 33

continue statements, 98-99
control, access control
> access, restricting, 318-320
> rules, 318-319
> rules (all clients), 319
> rules (domain names), 318
> rules (environment variables), 319
> rules (evaluating), 319-320

Control Apache command (Start menu), 41
control scripts, 40
control statements, code block, 104
CONV() function, 280
conversion specification, 254, 259-260
$ COOKIE superglobal, 173
cookies
> anatomy, 322-323
> auth cookies, 329-330
> defined, 322
> deleting, 325
> setting, 323-325
> values, restricting access based on, 325-329

$count variable, 243
CPU, MySQL optimization tips, 456
CREATE command, 19
create function() function, 124-125
CREATE TABLE command, 135-136
creating
> certificate signing requests (managing certificates), 450-451

key pairs (managing certificates), 449
request logs, 344
tables
  CREATE TABLE command, 135-136
  CROSS JOIN command, 147
  DELETE command, 152-153
  INNER JOIN command, 145
  INSERT command, 136-138
  JOIN command, 145
  LEFT JOIN command, 146-147
  LIKE operator, 143
  LIMIT command, 140-141
  NATURAL JOIN command, 147
  REPLACE command, 150-151
  RIGHT JOIN command, 147
  SELECT command, 138-140, 143-145
  STRAIGHT JOIN command, 147
  UPDATE command, 148-150
  WHERE clause, 141-142
crit, LogLevel directive option, 350
CROSS JOIN command, 147
cryptography, 443
CURDATE() function, 234
CURRENT DATE() function, 234

current date/time, 218
CURRENT TIME() function, 234
CURRENT TIME-STAMP() function, 234
CURTIME() function, 234
custom installation, Apache (Windows), 31
custom logs, database tables, 353
  code snippet, 354-355
  creating, 354
  sample reports, 355-357
CustomLog directive, 347-348
Cygwin source download, 9-10

D

-D httpd option, 39
d format code (date() function), 220
%D format string option (DATE FORMAT() function), 230
%D formatting directive, 344
d type specifier, 255
data
  inserting, 162-164
  retrieving, 165-166
  transmitted data, reducing (performance), 432
data types
  array, 68
  boolean, 68
  changing
    by casting, 71-72
    settype() function, 69-70

data and time, 133-134
defined, 132
double, 68
integer, 68-69
NULL, 68
numeric, 132-133
object, 68
resource, 68
signed, 132
special, 68
string, 68-69
strings, 134-135
testing, 68-69
unsigned, 132
database file-based access control authentication
  backend storage, 317
  mod auth dbm module, 316-317
  user management, 317
database tables, discussion forums, 294-295
databases
  selecting and connecting to, 159
  SHOW DATABASE command, 463
date
  calendar example, 237
    HTML form, 239-240
    library, creating, 244-250
    table, creating, 241-244
    user input, 238-239
  checkdate() function, 223
  CURDATE() function, 234
  CURRENT DATE() function, 234

current, retrieving, 218
DATE ADD() function,
    232-233
DATE FORMAT()
    function, 229-231,
    235
DATE SUB() function,
    232-233
DATEFORMAT() func-
    tion, 231
DAYNAME() function,
    225-226
DAYOFMONTH()
    function, 224-225
DAYOFWEEK() func-
    tion, 223-224
DAYOFYEAR() func-
    tion, 224
formatting, 220-221
FROM UNIXTIME()
    function, 235
gmdate() function, 222
information, retrieving,
    getdate(), 218
MONTH() function,
    226
testing, 223
time stamps
    converting with
        date(), 220-221
    converting with get-
        date(), 218
    creating, 222
UNIX TIMESTAMP()
    function, 234
WEEKDAY() function,
    223-224
weeks, 227-228
YEAR() function, 227
YYYY-MM-DD for-
    mat, 234
DATE ADD() function,
    232-233
date added field, 374

date and time data types,
    133-134
DATE data type, 134
DATE FORMAT() func-
    tion, 229-231, 235, 300
date modified field, 374
date pulldown library,
    245
date select() function, 249
DATE SUB() function,
    232-233
date() function, 200,
    220-221
dateadded field, 229
DATETIME data type,
    134
datetime field, 228
$dayArray variable, 243
DAYNAME() function,
    225-226
DAYOFMONTH() func-
    tion, 224-225
DAYOFWEEK() func-
    tion, 223-224
DAYOFYEAR() function,
    224
db table, 17
dbmmange.pl, user man-
    agement, 317
debug, LogLevel direc-
    tive option, 351
DECIMAL data type,
    133
declaring
    functions, 110-111
    variables, 67
decrementing integer
    variables, 75-76
default schemas, 33
define() function, 80-81
defining
    constants, 80-81
    filenames (logging),
        348

functions, 110, 112
log formats, 346
DELETE command,
    18-19, 21-22, 152-153,
    161
deleting
    cookies, 325
    directories, 211
    files, 202
    records, 387-389
    users, 317
$delims variable, 265
Denial of Service (DoS),
    433
Deny directive rule,
    access control, 318
Deny, Allow argument,
    319-320
DES, symmetric cryptog-
    raphy, 443
destroying sessions,
    340-341
digest, message digests,
    444
digest algorithm, 313,
    444
digest authentication, 312
digital certificates,
    445-446
directive containers, 34
directive identifiers, 347
directives
    AccessFileName, 36
    Allow, 318
    AllowOverride, 37
    applying, 34
    arguments, 32
    AuthAuthoritative, 316
    AuthConfig value, 37
    AuthDBMGroupFile,
        317
    AuthDBMUserFile, 317
    authentication modules,
        313

AuthGroupFile, 315
AuthName, 313
AuthType, 313
AuthUserFile, 315
browsing, 32
CacheFile, 431
configuration files, 33
CustomLog, 347-348
defined, 32
Deny, 318
ErrorLog, 349
external processes,
  operating systems
  (scalability), 427
FileInfo value, 37
flag, 53
formatting, 344-346
HostNameLookups,
  319, 346
IdentityCheck, 347
include path, 198
Indexes value, 37
KeepAliveTimeout, 432
Limit value, 37
LimitRequestBody, 433
LimitRequestFields,
  433
LimitRequestFieldSize,
  433
LimitRequestLine, 433
LimitXMLRequestBod
  y, 433
Listen, 41, 435
LoadModule, 454
log directives, 347
LogFormat, 346
LogLevel, 350-351
MmapFile, 431
mod vhost alias, 437
NameVirtualHost, 436
Options, 428, 438
Order, 319-320

processing, 35
Require, 314
Satisfy, 320
Satisfy all, 321
Satisfy any, 321
schemas, 33
ScoreBoardFile, 429
ScriptAlias, 438
ServerAlias, 436
ServerName, 33, 41
ServerRoot, 36
SSLCertificateFile, 452
SSLCertificateKeyfile,
  452
TimeOut directive, 433
TransferLog, 348
value, 53
VirtualDocumentRoot,
  437
VirtualDocument-
  RootIP, 438
VirtualScriptAlias, 438
VirtualScriptAliasIP,
  438
directories
confirming, 199
contents, reading,
  212-213
creating, 211
deleting, 211
directives, applying, 34
htdocs subdirectory, 53
lib, 52, 198
opening, 211
/tmp, 337
/usr/local/apach2, 29
/usr/local/php/lib, 52
/usr/local/src, 48
/usr/src/, 48
**disabling per-directory
configuration files, 37**

discussion forums. *See
also* **applications**
creating
  database tables,
    294-295
  input forms and
    scripts, 295-297
  topic list, displaying,
    298-301
  topics, adding posts
    to, 305-307
  topics, displaying
    posts in, 302-304
design process, 293-294
normal forms, 290
  first normal forms,
    291
  second normal
    forms, 291-292
  third normal forms,
    292
table relationships
  many-to-many,
    288-289
  one-to-many,
    287-288
  one-to-one, 286
disks, RAM disks, 429
$display block value, 407
$display value, 404
DISTINCT variable, 227
**distributing loads (per-
formance), 431**
**dividing numbers by
zero, 98**
division operator (/), 74
-DMyModule switch, 35
**DNS (domain name
sever)**
  name-based virtual
    hosting, 436
  virtual hosting, 434
**do, while statements,
93-94**

documentation,
ServerName directives,
33
DocumentRoot directive,
435
documents
files, adding, 193
HTML, spaces, view-
ing, 257
doDB() function, 364-366
dollar sign ($), 66, 261
domain name server. *See*
DNS
domain names, access
control rules, 318
DoS (Denial of Service),
433
dot (.), 198, 258
double data type, 68, 133
downloading
binary installer, 30
MySQL, 7-8
PHP distribution files,
51
source code (Apache
installations), 27
DROP command, 19
dynamic function calls,
113-114

E

%e format string option
(DATE FORMAT()
function), 230
%e formatting directive,
344
editors
accessing, 55
avoiding for PHP code,
61
HTML, 55

Edmunds Keith, 55
elements
PRE, 258
TITLE, 240
else clause, 87-88, 244
elseif clause, 88-89
email field, 362
emailChecker() function,
365-366
emerg, LogLevel direc-
tive option, 350
enabling per-directory
configuration files, 36
ENCRYPT argument,
188
encrypting passwords,
315
encryption, 443
end tags, 56-58, 61
ending block of state-
ments, 57-58
ENUM data type, 135
$ ENV superglobal, 173
environment variables
access control rules,
319
conditional logging,
347
CustomLog directive,
348
equal sign (=)
assignment operator,
67, 74
equivalence operator,
77
identical operator, 77
equivalence operator, 77
error log, 38
error messages, mysql
error() function, 161
ErrorLog directive, 349

errors
authentication process,
17-18
logging, 349-351
logs, monitoring, 353
evaluating control access
rules, 319-320
events, recording, 38
exclamation mark (!), 78
existence (files), 198
exit statement, 183
EXPLAIN command,
460-461
explode() function, 271
expressions. *See also*
operators
defined, 73
subexpressions, 73
test, boolean values,
104
external processes, oper-
ating systems, 427

F

- F format code (date()
function), 220
%f formatting directive,
345
-f httpd option, 39
f type specifier, 255
Fastresolve, hostname
resolving utility, 351
fclose() function, 203
feof() function, 204-205
Fetch, 56
fgetc() function, 207-208,
213
fgets() function, 204-205
field widths (strings),
257-258

fields
  CHAR, 14
  Common Name, 451
  dateadded, 229
  datetime, 228
  MAX FILE SIZE, 188
  TEXT, 14
  VARCHAR, 14
$file array variable, 190
file-based authentication, 315-316
FILE command, 19
file descriptors, operating systems, 427
$file dir variable, 190
$file name variable, 190
file system access, 428
file upload forms
  creating, 188-189
  global variables, 188
  overview, 188
  scripts, creating, 189-191
fileatime() function, 200
filectime() function, 200
FileInfo directive value, 37
filemtime() function, 200
files
  adding, 193
  appending, 208
  closing, 203
  config.log, 28
  config.status, 28
  configuration, 32, 37
    conditional containers, 35-36
    directive containers, 34
    directives, 33
    Listen directive, 41
    modifying, 39
    parameters, 40

processing (MPMs), 35
  ServerName directive, 41
  ServerRoot directive, 36
confirming, 199
creating, 202
date information, 200
deleting, 202
directives, applying, 34
.dll, 51
errors, logging, 349
exe.file, 10
executabilities, 199
existence of, checking, 198
fontwrap.php, 121
group files, 315
HTTP requests, logging, 348
httpd configuration, 50-51
included, 195-196
.ini, 51
INSTALL, 9
last accessed date, 200
local_format.php, 261
locking, 210
log files
  access log, 37
  error log, 38
  paths (logname), 353
  pid file, 38
  scoreboard file, 38
mapping, 431
modification date, 200
multiple test function, 200-202
names, defining (logging), 348
navigating, 206-207
opening, 203
password files, 316

per-directory configuration files, 36-37, 428
php.ini, 49, 51-53
php.ini-dist, 51
phpinfo.php, 53
pid files, 38
readability, 199
reading
  arbitrary data amounts, 205-207
  characters, 207-208, 213
  lines, 204-205
README, 9
robots.txt, 433
scoreboard files, 428
size, 199
status of, checking, 199
time, customizing, 200
users file, 315
writability, 199
writing to, 208-209
zip files, 9
$ FILES superglobal, 173
<Files> tag, 34
filesize() function, 199
file_exists() function, 198
finding
  string lengths, 262-263
  substrings position, 263-264
first normal forms, 290-291
$firstDayArray variable, 243
flag directives, 53
flat tables, 290-291
FLOAT data type, 133
flock() function, 210
FLUSH command, 20, 461
FLUSH HOSTS command, 461

FLUSH LOGS command, 462

FLUSH PRIVILEGES command, 20-21, 461

FLUSH TABLES command, 461, 464

FollowSymLinks parameter, 428

fontWrap() function, 122

fontwrap.php file, 121

fopen() function, 203

for statements, 95-96

foreach statement, 190, 260

format control strings, 254

formats, log formats, 344-346

formatted strings, storing, 261-262

formatting
  dates, 220-221
  strings
    argument swapping, 260-261
    example, 259-260
    field width specifications, 257-258
    padding specifiers, 256-257
    precision specifications, 258
    printf() function, 254
    specifiers, 259-260
    type specifiers, 255-256

formatting directives, logging (HTTP requests), 344-346

forms
  file uploads
    creating, 188-189
    global variables, 188

    overview, 188
    scripts, creating, 189-191
  HTML/PHP combination
    hidden fields, 180-181
    HTML form, calling itself, 178-179
    PHP number guessing script, 179-180
  insert form, 163
  raw headers, 182-183
  server headers, 182
  submission, sending mail on
    creating script to send, 186-187
    form creation, 185
    mail() function, 184
  users, redirecting, 182

forums. *See* discussion forum

forward slash (/), 74

forward slashes (//), 60

fputs() function, 209, 262

FQDN (fully qualified domain name), 435

fread() function, 205-207

FreeBSD, 27

Frequently Asked Questions, 54

From header, 184, 187

FROM UNIXTIME() function, 235

fseek() function, 206-207

FTP client, 56

fully qualified domain name (FQDN), 435

func table, 17

function calls, 58

function exists() function, 125-127

$function holder variable, 114

function statements, 110-112

functions. *See also* methods; statements
  abs(), 108-109
  ACSII(), 279
  addNums(), 113
  anonymous, creating, 124-125
  arguments, 108
  ASCII(), 279
  benchmark(), 456-457
  BIN(), 279
  built-in, 108
  calling, 108, 110
  CHAR LENGTH(), 271
  CHAR(), 281
  CHARACTER LENGTH(), 271
  checkdate(), 223, 238
  CONCAT WS(), 228, 273
  CONCAT(), 272-273
  concatenation, 271-274
  constructors and, 245
  CONV(), 280
  create function(), 124-125
  CURDATE(), 234
  CURRENT DATE(), 234
  CURRENT TIME(), 234
  CURRENT TIMESTAMP(), 234
  CURTIME() function, 234
  DATE ADD(), 232-233
  DATE FORMAT(), 229-231, 235, 300
  date select(), 249

DATE SUB, 232-233
date(), 200, 220-221
DAYNAME(), 225-226
DAYOFMONTH(),
224-225
DAYOFWEEK(),
223-224
DAYOFYEAR(), 224
declaring, 110
define(), 80-81
defined, 58, 108
defining, 110, 112
doDB(), 364-366
dynamic calls, 113-114
emailChecker(), 365-
366
existence of, testing,
125-127
explode(), 271
fclose(), 203
feof(), 204-205
fgetc(), 207-208, 213
fgets(), 204-205
fileatime(), 200
filectime(), 200
filemtime(), 200
filesize(), 199
file_exists(), 198
flock(), 210
fontWrap, 122
fopen(), 203, 210
fputs(), 209, 262
fread(), 205-207
FROM UNIXTIME(),
235
fseek(), 206-207
function exists(),
125-127
fwrite(), 209
getdate(), 218-219,
238-239, 243, 247
gettype(), 68-69
getYearEnd(), 247

getYearStart(), 247
gmdate(), 222
header(), 257
cookies, setting, 323
forms, 182
raw headers,
182-183
HEX(), 279-281
HOUR(), 228-229
include once(), 197
include()
example listing, 194
executing PHP in
another file, 195
executing
PHP/assign return
values, 195
files, 193
loops, 196
within control struc-
tures, 196-197
is uploaded file(),
190-191
isset(), 238
is_dir(), 199
is_executable(), 199
is_file(), 199, 202
is_readable(), 199
is_writable(), 199
LCASE(), 278
LEFT(), 277
LENGTH(), 271-274
LOCATE(), 276
location and position,
276
LTRIM(), 266-267,
274-275
mail(), 184, 370
MINUTE(), 228-229
mkdir(), 211
mktime(), 222, 239, 247
month select(), 249
MONTH(), 226

MONTHNAME(), 226
move uploaded file(),
191
multiple file tests out-
put, 200-202
mysql close(), 159
mysql connect(),
158-159
mysql error(), 161
mysql fetch array(), 166
mysql insert id(), 297,
381
mysql num rows(), 165
mysql query(), 159-161,
163
mysql result(), 328
mysql select db(), 159
MySQL, accessing list
of, 167
naming rules, 110
nl2br(), 269-270
NOW(), 234, 297
numberedHeading(),
119-120
OCT(), 279-280
OCTET LENGTH(),
271
opendir(), 211
output(), 248-249
padding, 275
password(), 326
phpinfo(), 53
print(), 58, 108-109
printBR(), 112
printf(), 254-257
readdir(), 212-213
REPEAT(), 278
REPLACE(), 279
require once(), 198
require(), 198
RIGHT(), 277
rmdir(), 211
RPAD(), 275

How can we make this index more useful? Email us at indexes@samspublishing.com

rtrim(), 266-267, 274-275
SECOND(), 228-229
SECT TO TIME(), 235
serialize(), 337
session_destroy(), 340-341
session_id(), 334
session_save_path(), 337
session_set_ save_ handler(), 334
session_start(), 334-335, 412
set time limit(), 370
setcookie(), 324-325
setDate array(), 246-248
settype(), 69-70
setYearEnd(), 247
setYearStart(), 247
sprintf(), 249, 261-262
state, saving between calls, 118-120
string modification, 277-278
strip tags(), 267
stripslashes(), 301, 304, 307
strlen(), 262-263
strpos(), 263-264
strstr(), 263
strtok(), 264-266
strtolower(), 269
strtoupper(), 268
str_replace(), 268
substr(), 264
SUBSTRING(), 277
substr_replace(), 267
tagWrap(), 126-127
test(), 115
TIME FORMAT(), 231

TIME TO SEC(), 235
time(), 218, 324
touch(), 202
TRIM(), 266-267, 274
trimming, 274-275
UCASE(), 278
ucwords(), 269
underline, 126
UNIX TIMESTAMP(), 234
unlink(), 202
user-created, 17
user-defined, 110
values, returning, 112-113
variables
    accessing, 115-118
    scope, 114-115
WEEKDAY(), 223-224
with arguments, declaring, 111
wordwrap(), 270
year select(), 249
YEAR(), 227
fwrite() function, 209

G

g format code (date() function), 220
Gemini table type, 8
$ GET superglobal, 173
getdate() function, 218-219, 238-239, 243, 247
gettype() function, 68-70
getYearEnd() function, 247
getYearStart() function, 247
GIF images, 347

global statement
    remembering function variable values between calls, 118-119
    variable access, 115-118
global variables
    defined, 172
    file upload, 188
    $GLOBALS array, 172
    superglobals, 172-173, 188
GLOBALS ($) array, 172
gmdate() function, 222
GRANT command, 19-20
granting
    access, 314
    privileges, 19-20
graphical user interface, 13
greater than operator (>), 77
$green variable, 256
group settings, troubleshooting, 43
groups file, 315
gunzip command, 8, 27
gzip command, 27

H

H format code (date() function), 220
%H format string option (DATE FORMAT() function), 230
%h formatting directive, 344-345
hard drives, MySQL optimization tips, 456
hardware load balancer (performance), 431

hash, defined, 326
hash sign (#), 60
have dbd variable, 467
have innodb variable, 467
header() function, 257
    cookies, setting, 323
    forms, 182
    raw headers, 182-183
headers
    From, 184, 187
    Host header, 437
    Host: (name-based virtual hosting), 435
    HTTP headers, 432
    Raw, 182-183
    Reply-to, 187
    request headers, 435
    server, 182
    Set-Cookie, 323
    User-Agent, 319
help, for PHP installation, 54-55
HEX() function, 279-281
HH-MM-SS time format, 234
hidden fields, forms, 180-181
Host header, 437
host table, 17
HostNameLookups directive, 319
    conditional logging, 346
    network setting (scalability), 429
hostnames, resolving (managing logs), 351
HOUR() function, 228-229
.htaccess file, 428

htdocs subdirectory, 53
HTML
    calendar example, 239-240
    documents, viewing, 257
    PHP combination, 58-60
HTML editors, 55
HTML forms
    PHP combination, 180
    user input
        accessing from multiple SELECT elements, 175-178
        receiving, 174-175
HTML/PHP combination forms
    hidden fields, 180-181
    HTML form, calling itself, 178-179
    PHP number guessing script, 179-180
    raw headers, 182-183
    server headers, 182
    users, redirecting, 182
htpasswd utility, 315
HTTP
    headers, caching (performance), 432
    methods, access (limiting), 321-322
    secure HTTP, 442
HTTP requests, logging, 347-349
httpd.conf configuration file, 32, 40, 50-51
httpd file, 38
HUP, signals, sending, 39
hyphen (-), 74

i format code (date() function), 220
%i format string option (DATE FORMAT() function), 230
%i formatting directive, 345
icons
    padlock, 446
    Service, 39
identifiers, directive identifiers, 347
IdentityCheck directive, 347
IDs (session), passing in query strings, 340
if statements, 77, 243
    else clause with, 87-88
    elseif clause with, 88-89
    example of, 86
    switch, compared, 89
images
    logging, 347
    reduced transmitted data (performance), 432
in field, 163
include() function
    example listing, 194
    executing PHP in another file, 195
    executing PHP/assign return values, 195
    files, 193
    loops, 196
    within control structures, 196-197

include once() function,
197
include path directive,
198
included files, 195-196
incrementing integer
variables, 75-76
INDEX command, 19
index strings, 262
Indexes, directive value,
37
Info, LogLevel directive
option, 351
information, digital cer-
tificates, 446
INNER JOIN command,
145
INSERT command, 18-
19, 21, 136-138, 326
insert forms, 163
Insert Record button,
164
INSERT statement, 161-
162
INSTALL file, 9
installations
custom installation,
Apache (Windows),
31
methods, selecting,
25-26
typical installation,
Apache (Windows),
31
installers, binary
installer, 29-30
installing
Apache
on Windows, 29-32
source (UNIX), 26
MySQL
on Linux/Unix, 8-9
on Windows, 9-12
troubleshooting,
14-15

Open SSL library (SSL
installations), 447-448
PHP
help for, 54-55
on Linux/Unix with
Apache, 47-49
on Windows, 51
testing, 53
SSL (Secure Sockets
Layer), 447-449
instruction terminator,
66
INT data type, 132
integer data type, 68-69
integer variables,
incrementing/
decrementing, 75-76
integrity, communica-
tions, 442
IP addresses, 13
control access rules,
318
reverse DNS lookups,
346
IP-based virtual hosting,
434
Irreversible, message
digests, 444
is_dir() function, 199
is_executable() function,
199
is_file() function, 199,
202
is_readable() function,
199
is uploaded file() func-
tion, 190-191
is_writable() function,
199
isset() function, 238
iterations, loops, 98-99

J-K

j format code (date()
function), 220
%j format string option
(DATE FORMAT()
function), 230
JOIN command, 145
JPEG images, 347

%k format string option
(DATE FORMAT()
function), 230
KeepAliveTimeout direc-
tive, 432
key buffer size parame-
ter, 458-459
key pairs, creating (man-
aging certificates), 449
key reads parameter, 458
key writes parameter,
458
keys
CA (certification
authority), 445
digital certificates, 445
encryption, 443
kill command, 39

L

l format code (date()
function), 220
%l format string option
(DATE FORMAT()
function), 230
%l formatting directive,
344
LCASE() function, 278

LDAP (Lightweight Directory Access Protocol), 313
LEFT JOIN command, 146-147
LEFT() function, 277
length, strings, 262-263
length functions, 271-274
LENGTH() function, 271
less than operator (<), 77
levels, errors, logging, 350
lib directory, 52, 198
libraries, 447-448
licenses, Apache, 30
Lightweight Directory Access Protocol (LDAP), 313
LIKE operator, 143
Limit directive value, 37
LIMIT command, 140-141
limitations, symmetric cryptography, 443
limiting access, HTTP methods, 321-322
LimitRequestBody directive, 433
LimitRequestFields directive, 433
LimitRequestFieldSize directive, 433
LimitRequestLine directive, 433
LimitXMLRequestBody directive, 433
links, Start Apache, 41
Linux
    distribution CDs, 8
    file descriptors, operating systems (scalability), 427

installing Apache on, 26
installing MySQL on, 8-9
installing PHP on, with Apache, 47-49
integrating PHP with Apache on, 50
server processes, operating systems (scalability), 427
Listen directive, 41, 435
listening addresses (Listen directive), 41
listings
    abs() function, 108-109
    access, restricting, 322
    Allow, Deny argument, 320
    arguments, passing by value, 122-124
    authentication
        access control rules and, 321
        file-based, 316
    break statement, 97
    calendar
        HTML form, 239-240
        library, creating, 245-250
        table, creating, 241-242
        user input, checking, 238
    code blocks, 102-103
    connection script, 158-159
    constants, defining, 80
    continue statement, 98
    cookies
        auth cookies, 329-330
        setting/printing, 324

data, retrieving, 165-166
databases, selecting and connecting to, 159
date formatting, 221
Deny, Allow argument, 320
directories, contents, listing, 212
do, while statement, 94
file upload forms, 189
file upload scripts, 190
files
    navigating, 206-207
    opening/reading line by line, 204
    reading by characters, 207
    reading in chunks, 205
    writing to, 209
for loop dividing 4000 by 10 incremental numbers, 96
for statement, 95
forms, insert form, 163
functions
    creating anonymous, 124-125
    declaring, 110
    dynamic calls, 113-114
    existence of, testing, 126
    multiple file tests output, 200-202
    optional arguments, 122
    requiring two arguments, 121
    return values, 112-113
    with arguments, declaring, 111

getdate() function, 219
GLOBALS ($) array, looping through, 172
HTML forms, 174
    accessing from multiple SELECT statement, 176
    reading input from, 176-177
    receiving, 174
    user input, receiving, 175
HTML/PHP combination form
    hidden fields, saving state with, 181
    HTM form calling itself, 179
    HTML form calling itself, 178-179
    PHP number guessing script, 179
if else statement, 87
if elseif else statement, 88
if statement, 86
include() function, 194-196
included file with PHP code, 195
login form, 326-327
menus, address book example, 376-377
nesting loops, 100
PHP script with HTML, 58-59
PHP scripts, simple, 56
raw headers (forms), 182-183

records
    adding subentries to, 391-394
    deleting, 388
    inserting, 162
    selecting and viewing, 382-385
request headers, 435
server headers (forms), 182
ServerAlias directive, 436
sessions
    starting and resuming, 334-335
    storing variables in, 336
    variables, accessing stored, 336
    variables, adding array variables to, 338
strings
    dividing into tokens, 265-266
    formatting, 259-260
subscription project
    mail, sending, 368-369
    subscribe and unsubscribe requests, 363-364
switch statement, 90
tables
    creating, 160-161
    storefront database table example, 402-407
    record addition script, 377-380
time stamps, creating, 222

topics
    adding, 295
    adding posts to, 305-307
    adding script for, 296-297
    displaying posts in, 302-303
    topic list, displaying, 298-301
type specifiers, 255
user login script, 327-328
variables
    access, 116-117
    casting, 71
    changing type with settype() function, 70
    defined outside functions, 115-116
    scope, 114-115
    testing type of, 68-69
    values, remembering between function calls, 118-120
virtual hosts, name-based, 436
while statement, 92
lists, user lists, 314
ln command, 428
LoadModule directive, 452
Loads, distributing (performance), 431
local_format.php file, 261
LOCATE() function, 276
locating error log files, 349
location function, 276

lock screen mechanism, 16

locking files, 210

log directives, 347

log files
    access log, 37
    error log, 38
    paths, logname, 353
    pid file, 38
    scoreboard file, 38

log formats, 344-346

LogFormat directive, 346

logging
    conditional logging
        CustomLog directive, 347
        HostNameLookups directive, 346
        HTTP requests, 347-348
        IdentityCheck directive, 347
    errors
        files, 349
        LogLevel directive, 350-351
        programs, 350
        syslog daemon (Unix), 350
    formatting directives (HTTP requests), 344-346
    HTTP requests, 343-347
        files, 348
        programs, 348-349
    images, 347

logical operators, 77-78

login form, 326-329

LogLevel directive, 350-351

logname, paths, log files, 353

logresolve.exe utility, 351

logs
    analyzing, 353
    custom, 353-357
    error logs, monitoring, 353
    managing
        analysis, 353
        error logs (monitoring), 353
        hostname resolution, 351
        log rotation, 351-352
    merging, 352
    request logs, creating, 344
    rotating, 351-352
    splitting, 352

Logscan programs, monitoring error logs, 353

Logtools, 353

LONGBLOB data type, 135

LONGTEXT data type, 135

looping, conditional looping, 347

loops
    breaking out of, 96-98
    do, while statement, 93-94
    for statement, 95-96
    iterations, skipping, 98-99
    nesting, 100-101
    while statement, 92-93

LPAD() function, 275

LTRIM() function, 266-267, 274-275

M

%m format string option (DATE FORMAT() function), 230

%m formatting directive, 345

M format code (date() function), 221

machine names, 13

MACs (message authentication codes), 445

mail
    From header, 187
    Reply-to header, 187
    sending, 368-370
    sending on form submission
        creating script to send, 186-187
        form creation, 185
        mail() function, 184

mail() function, 184, 370

mailing lists
    MySQL, 15
    PHP, 54

make command, 49

make install command, 29, 49

make utility, 29

makefiles configure script, 28

management, user management, 315-317

managing
    certificates, 449-452
    logs, 351-353

many-to-one mapping, 434

many-to-many relationships, 288-289

mapping files, 431

mappings, DNS (domain name server), 434

mass virtual hosting, 437

math operators, 74

max connections variable, 467

MAX FILE SIZE field, 188

max used connections status variable, 467

MD5, digest algorithms, 444

MEDIUMBLOB data type, 135

MEDIUMINT data type, 133

MEDIUMTEXT data type, 135

$membership variable, 263

memory
files, mapping (performance), 431
MySQL optimization tips, 456

menus, creating, 376-377

merging logs, 352

Merlin Server, 8

message authentication codes (MACs), 445

message digests, 444

messages, 14

methods. *See also* functions; statements
access, combining, 320
HTTP, access (limiting), 321-322
POST, 174

minus sign (-)
field width specifiers, 258
subtraction operator (-), 74

MINUTE() function, 228-229

mirror sites, 10

mkdir() function, 211

mktime() function, 222, 239, 247

MMapFile directive, 431

mod access module, 318-319

mod auth dbm module, 316-317

mod auth module, 315-316

mod bwshare module, 433

mod cache module, 432

mod deflate module, 432

mod file cache module, 431

mod so command, 28

mod ssl module
SSL, installing, 448-449
SSL configurations, 452
SSL installations, 447

mod status module, 429

mod vhost alias directive (mass virtual hosting), 437

modification string functions, 277-278
schemas
directives, 33

modules
Apache compiles, 27
authentication, 312
access (restricting), 314-317
directives, 313
functions, 314
mod access, 318-319
mod auth, 315-316
mod auth dbm, 316-317

mod bwshare module, 433

mod cache, 432

mod deflate, 432

mod file cache, 431

mod ssl
SSL, installing, 448-449
SSL configurations, 452
SSL installations, 447
mod status, 429
schemas, 33

modulus operator (%), 74

monitoring error logs, 353

month select() function, 249

MONTH() function, 226

MONTHNAME() functions, 226

months
DAYOFMONTH() function, 224-225
MONTH() function, 226
MONTHNAME() function, 226

move uploaded file() function, 191

MPMs
configuration files, processing, 35
server processes, 426

multiline comments, 60

multiplication operator (*), 74

Mutual-Failure argument, 320

my-huge.cnf configuration file, 458

my-large.cnf configuration file, 458

my-medium.cnf configuration file, 457

my-small.cnf configuration file, 457

MySQL

accessing, 7-8

account, creating, 12

configuration options, 12-13

connecting with PHP, 157

error messages, retrieving, 161

queries, executing, 159-161

using mysql connect() function, 158-159

connections, securing, 16

data

inserting with PHP, 162-164

retrieving with PHP, 165-166

functions, accessing list of, 167

GUI administration tool, 16

installing

on Linux/Unix, 8-9

on Windows, 9-12

troubleshooting, 14-15

mailing list, 15

manual, Problems and Common Errors, 14

optimization, improving benchmark() function, 456-457

FLUSH command, 461

FLUSH HOSTS PRIVILEGES command, 461

FLUSH LOGS PRIVILEGES command, 462

FLUSH PRIVILEGES command, 461

FLUSH TABLES command, 464

FLUSH TABLES PRIVILEGES command, 461

OPTIMIZE TABLE command, 459

queries, 460-461

SHOW COLUMNS command, 464

SHOW command, 462

SHOW CREATE TABLE command, 464

SHOW DATABASES command, 463

SHOW GRANTS command, 462-463

SHOW INDEX command, 465

SHOW OPEN TABLES command, 464

SHOW STATUS command, 467

SHOW TABLE STATUS command, 465-466

SHOW TABLES command, 463

SHOW VARIABLES command, 467

tips for, 456

privilege systems

authentication process, 17-18

columns priv table, 17

db table, 17

func table, 17

granting, 19-20

host table, 17

overview, 17

revoking, 21

tables priv table, 17

user table, 17

running as root, stopping, 22

running as root user, 15-16

server, shutting down, 14

starting, 15-16

startup options, 457

key buffer size parameter, 458-459

table cache parameter, 458-459

support contracts, 15

MySQL AB, 8

mysql close() function, 159

mysql connect() function, 158-159

mysql error() function, 161

mysql fetch array() function, 166

mysql insert id() function, 381

MySQL installation wizard, 10-12

mysql num rows() function, 165

mysql query() function, 159-161, 163

mysql result() function, 328

mysql select db() function, 159

MySQL Web site, 8

MySQL-client-VERSION.i386.rpm, 8

MySQL-Pro 4.0 download pag, 9

MySQL-VERSION.i386 rpm, 8

mysql_insert_id() function, 297

N

n format code (date() function), 221

name-based virtual hosting, 435-437

$name variable, 246

names
  defining, files (logging), 348
  domain names, access control rules, 318
  of variables, selection considerations, 66

NameVirtualHost directive, 436

naming
  error log files, 349
  functions, 110

NATURAL JOIN command, 147

navigating files, 206-207

negative terms, 53

nesting loops, 100-101

network/mask pair, control access rules, 318

networks, settings
  performance, 432
  scalability, 429

newline character (\n), 100, 186, 204, 270

$newnum variable, 109

NIS (Network Information Services), 313

nl2br() function, 269-270

non-root users, 15

nonequivalence operator (!=), 77

normal forms
  defined, 290
  first normal forms, 291
  second normal forms, 291-292
  third normal forms, 292

normalization
  defined, 290
  normal forms
    defined, 290
    first normal forms, 291
    second normal forms, 291-292
    third normal forms, 292

not operator (!), 78

notice, LogLevel directive option, 351

NOW() function, 234, 297

NULL data type, 68

numberedHeading() function, 119-120

numbers, dividing by zero, 98

numeric data types, 132-133

NuSphere Corporation Web site, 8

O

%o formatting directive, 345

o type specifier, 255

object data type, 68

OCT() function, 279-280

OCTET LENGTH() function, 271

one-to-many mapping, 434

one-to-one mapping, 434

one-to-many relationships, 287-288

one-to-one relationships, 286

opendir() function, 211

opening
  directories, 211
  files, 203

openssl command-line tool (certificates), 449

OpenSSL library, installing, 447-448

openssl.exe utility, 447

OpenSSL Web site, 447

operands, 73

operating systems, MySQL optimization tips, 456

operating systems (OS), scalability, 426-427

operators. See also expressions
  addition (+), 73
  arithmetic operators, 74
  assignment (=), 67, 74
  combined assignment operators, 75-76

comparison operators, 77

concatenation (.), 74-75

defined, 73

logical, 77-78

operands combined with, 73

post-decrement, 76

post-increment, 76

precedence, 78-80

OPTIMIZE TABLE command, 459

optional arguments, 122

Options directive, 37-38, 428, 438

or operator (||), 77-78

ORDER BY clause, 139-140, 226

Order directives

Allow, Deny argument, 320

Deny, Allow argument, 319

Mutual-Failure argument, 320

OS (operating systems), scalability, 426-427

output() function, 248-249

override, schemas, 33

ownership, verifying, 15

P

%p format string option (DATE FORMAT() function), 230

padding functions, 275

padding specifiers, 256-257

padlock icon, 446

parameters

configuration files, 40

Options directive, 428

pass phrases, 450

password files, storing (file-based authentication), 316

password() function, 326

passwords

basic authentication, 312

digest authentication, 312

encrypting, 315

storing, 313

paths, log files, 353

per-directory configuration files, 36-37, 428

percent sign (%), 344

conversion specification, 254

modulus operator (%), 74

performance

abuse, preventing, 433

caching, 432

files, mapping, 431

loads, distributing, 431

network settings, 432

reduced transmitted data, 432

Web sites, tools, 429

period (.), 58, 74-75

permissions, incorrect, 14

PHP

combining HTML with, 59-60

configuring, 48-50

connecting to MySQL with, 157

error messages, retrieving, 161

queries, executing, 159-161

using mysql connect() function, 158-159

delimiter tags, 56

inserting MySQL data with, 162-164

installing

help for, 54-55

on Linux/Unix with Apache, 47-49

on Windows, 51

testing, 53

integrating with Apache on Linux/Unix, 50

integrating with Apache on Windows, 51-52

retrieving MySQL data with, 165-166

scripts, 55-56

PHP mailing lists, 54

PHP Manual Web site, 158, 167, 245

PHP Web site, 48, 51, 54

php.ini file, 49, 51-53

php.ini-dist file, 51

phpinfo() function, 53

phpinfo.php file, 53

phyMyAdmin interface, 16

pid file, 38

plaintext, 443

plus sign (+), 74

port connections variable, 467

port values (Listen directive), 41

ports, bind to port, troubleshooting, 42

position functions, 276

positive terms, 53

POST method, 174
$ POST superglobal, 173
$ POST value, 365
post-decrement opera-
tors, 76
post-increment opera-
tors, 76
posts
    adding to topics,
    305-307
    defined, 294
    displaying in topics,
    302-304
pound sign (#), 32, 50
PRE element, 258
precedence (operators),
78-80
precision specifications
(strings), 258
predefined constants, 81
preventing abuse, 433
print() function, 58,
108-109
printBR() function, 112
printf() function, strings,
254
    padding specifiers,
    256-257
    type specifiers, 255-256
printing cookies, 324
privileges
    authentication process,
    17-18
    columns priv table, 17
    db table, 17
    func table, 17
    granting, 19-20
    host table, 17
    overview, 17
    revoking, 21
    tables priv table, 17
    user table, 17

problems, MySQL instal-
lation, 14-15
Problems and Common
Errors (MySQL manu-
al), 14
PROCESS command, 19
processes
    external processes, 427
    server processes, 426
processing
    configuration files, 35
    directives, 35
    per-directory configura-
    tion files, 36
programs
    errors, logging, 350
    HTTP requests, log-
    ging, 348-349
    rotatelogs.exe, 352
Properties, Certificates
command (File menu),
446
ps command, 15
public key cryptography,
443

Q-R

%q formatting directive,
345
queries
    executing, 159-161
    optimizing, 460-461
query strings, session
IDs, passing, 340
quotation marks (), 69

r format code (date()
function), 221
%r format string option
(DATE FORMAT()
function), 230
%r formatting directive,
345

r (read)mode, 203
RAM disks, 429
rand switch, 449
raw headers, 182-183
RC2, symmetric cryptog-
raphy, 443
RC4, symmetric cryptog-
raphy, 443
read mode, 203
readdir() function,
212-213
reading
    directory contents, 212-
    213
    files
        arbitrary data
        amounts, 205-207
        characters, 207-208,
        213
        lines, 204-205
README file, 9
realms, authentication,
313
recording events, 38
records
    address book database
    table example
        record addition
        script, 377-381
        records, adding
        subentries to,
        389-394
        records, deleting,
        387-389
        records, selecting
        and viewing,
        382-387
    inserting, 162
$red variable, 256
reducing transmitted
data (performance), 432
reference passing (argu-
ments), 122

REFERENCES command, 19
registering multiple session variables, 338-339
relationships
    many-to-many, 288-289
    one-to-many, 287-288
    one-to-one, 286
RELOAD command, 20
removing privileges, 21
REPEAT() function, 278
REPLACE command, 150-151
REPLACE() function, 279
replacing
    string portions, 267
    substrings, 268
Reply-to header, 187
request headers, 435
request logs, 344
$ REQUEST superglobal, 173
requests, client requests, 37
Require directive, 314
require once() function, 198
require() function, 198
resolving hostnames (managing logs), 351
resource data type, 68
restricting access
    authentication, 311-312
    authentication modules, 314-317
    based on cookie values, 325-329
    client authentication, 313
return statements, function values, 112-113

reverse DNS lookups, IP addresses, 346
REVOKE command, 21-22
RIGHT JOIN command, 147
RIGHT() function, 277
RLimitCPU directive, 427
RLimitMem directive, 427
RLimitNProc directive, 427
rmdir() function, 211
robots.txt file, Web spiders (preventing abuse), 433
root users
    MySQL running as, 15-16
    non-root users, 15
    running MySQL as, stopping, 22
rotatelogs utility, 349
rows, mysql num rows() function, 165
RPAD() function, 275
RPMS, installing MySQL on Linux/Unix using, 8
RSA, public key cryptography, 444
rtrim() function, 266-267, 274-275

S

s format code (date() function), 221
%s format string option (DATE FORMAT() function), 230

s type specifier, 255
Satisfy directive, 320
Satisfy all directive, 321
Satisfy any directive, 321
saving
    function state between calls, 118-120
    state, hidden fields, 180-181
scalability
    operating systems, 426-427
    settings, 427-429
ScanErrLog, 353
schemas, 33
scope, function variables, 114-115
scoreboard file, 38
scoreboard files, 428
ScoreBoardFile directive, 429
screensavers, 16
Script tags, 56
ScriptAlias directive (mass virtual hosting), 438
scripts
    apachectl, 35
    config, 448
    configure, 48-49
    configure script, 27-28
    control, commands, 40
    file upload, 189-191
    PHP, 55-56
    split-file Perl, 353
SEC TO TIME() function, 235
second normal forms, 291-292
SECOND() function, 228-229
secure HTTP, 442

secure servers
certificates, managing, 449-452
communications, 441
SSL, configuring, 452

Secure Sockets Layer.
See **SSL**

security
access control, 321
basic authentication, 312
communications, 442
digest authentication, 312
lock screen mechanism, 16
MySQL
connections, securing, 16
server startup procedures, 15-16
reverse DNS lookups, 347
SSH, 16
symbolic links (symlinks), 428

SELECT command, 18, 20, 138-140, 143-145

selecting
installation methods, 25-26
variable names, 66

self-signed certificates (managing certificates), 451

semicolons (;), 41, 58, 66, 94

sending
mail, 184-187, 368-370
signals, kill command, 39

serialize() function, 337

server binary, 38

server headers, 182

server processes, 426

ServerAlias directive (syntax), 436

ServerName directive, 33, 41

ServerRoot directive, 36

servers
loads, distributing (performance), 432
MySQL, shutting down, 14
starting (SSL configurations), 452
troubleshooting, 42
virtual servers, 34
Web servers, Apache installations (Windows), 29

Service icon, 39

services, Apache, installing, 30

session IDs, passing in query strings, 340

session set save handler() function, 334

session start() function, 412

session variables, 335-339

sessions
destroying, 340-341
overview, 334
session set save handler() function, 334
starting, 334-335

session_destroy() function, 340-341

session_id() function, 334

session_save_path() function, 337

session_start() function, 334-335

set time limit() function, 370

Set-Cookie header, 323

setcookie() function, 324-325

setDate array() function, 246-247

setDate global() function, 247-248

settings
group settings, troubleshooting, 43
network settings, performance, 432
network settings (scalability), 429
scalability, 427-429
status settings (scalability), 429

settype() function, 69-70

setup.exe file, 9-10

setYearEnd() function, 247

setYearStart() function, 247

SHA, digest algorithms, 444

shopping cart database table example
cart, adding items to, 414-416
cart, removing items from, 419
cart, viewing, 416-418
checkout actions, performing, 421-422
checkout form, creating, 420-421
field lengths, 410
field names, 410-411
integrating with storefront, 412-414
planning process, 410

short open tag switch, 57

short tags, 56-57

shortcuts, commands, apache.exe , 39

SHOW COLUMNS command, 464

SHOW command, 462

SHOW CREATE TABLE command, 464

SHOW DATABASES command, 463

SHOW GRANTS command, 462-463

SHOW INDEX command, 465

SHOW OPEN TABLES command, 464

SHOW STATUS command, 458, 467

SHOW TABLE STATUS command, 465-466

SHOW TABLES command, 463

SHOW VARIABLES command, 13, 467

shut down, MySQL server, 14

SHUTDOWN command, 20

signals, sending, kill command, 39

signed data types, 132

single quotation marks ('), 69

single-line comments, 60

size, files, 199

size attribute, 122

skipping iterations (loops), 98-99

slash (/), 74

slow queries status variable, 467

SMALLINT data type, 133

software, configuring (Apache installations), 27

software load balancer (performance), 432

Solaris, 427

source code

  Apache, installing (UNIX), 26

  building, installation methods (selecting), 26

  downloading (Apache installations), 27

  uncompressing (Apache installations), 27

spaces (HTML documents), viewing, 257

specifiers (strings), 259-260

split-file Perl script, 353

splitting logs (merging), 352

sprintf() function, 249, 261-262

SSH, 16

SSL (Secure Sockets Layer)

  configuring (secure servers), 452

  digital certificates, 446

  installing

    mod ssl module, 448-449

    mod ssl module (UNIX), 448

    mod ssl module (Windows), 448

    OpenSSL library, 447-448

  protocols

    authentication, 445-447

    encryption, 443

    confidentiality, 443-444

SSLCertificateFile directive, 452

SSLCertificateKeyfile directive, 452

standard tags, 56

Start Apache link, 41

start tags, 56-58, 61

$start variable, 243

starting

  Apache, 30, 39-41

  block of statements, 57-58

  MySQL, 15-16

  servers (SSL configurations), 452

  sessions, 334-335

startup, MySQL, 457-459

state

  functions, saving between calls, 118-120

  saving, hidden fields, 180-181

statements. See also commands; functions; methods

  block of, starting/ ending, 57-58

  break

    code ends, 90

    loops, 96-98

  continue, 98-99

  control, code block brackets, 104

  defined, 58

  DELETE, 161

  do, while, 93-94

  exit, 183

  for, 95-96

  foreach, 190, 260

  function, 110, 112

  function state, saving, 118-120

global
  remembering func-
    tion variable values
    between calls,
    118-119
  variable access,
    115-118
if, 77, 243
  else clause with,
    87-88
  elseif clause with,
    88-89
  example of, 86
  switch, compared, 89
INSERT, 161-162
return, function values,
  112-113
SELECT, 161, 175
static, 119-120
switch, 89-91
  example, 90
  if, compared, 89
UPDATE, 161
while, 77, 92-93
static statement
  function state, saving,
    118-120
  remembering function
    variable values
    between calls, 119-
    120
status
  files, checking, 199
  schemas, directives, 33
**status code, conditional
  logging, 347**
**status settings,
  scalability, 429**
stopping
  Apache, 39
  MySQL server, 14

storage, backend storage
  database file-based
    access control authen-
    tication, 317
  file-based authentica-
    tion, 315
  functions (authentica-
    tion modules), 314
**store categories field,
  storefront database
  table example, 398-400**
**store item color field,
  storefront database
  table example, 398-399,
  401**
**store item size field,
  storefront database
  table example, 398, 401**
**store items field, store-
  front database table
  example, 398-401**
**storefront database table
  example**
  add to cart button,
    405-408
  categories of items, dis-
    playing, 402-404
  planning process, 398
  store categories field,
    398-400
  store item color field,
    398-399, 401
  store item size field,
    398, 401
  store items field,
    398-401
storing
  certificate signing
    requests, 451
  formatted strings,
    261-262

password files (file-
  based authentication),
  316
passwords, user man-
  agement, 313
usernames, user man-
  agement, 313
**STRAIGHT JOIN com-
  mand, 147**
**string data types, 68-69,
  134-135**
strings
  breaking into arrays,
    271
  case, converting,
    268-269
  cleaning up, 266-267
  defined, 58
  formatted, storing,
    261-262
  formatting
    argument swapping,
      260-261
    example, 259-260
    field width specifica-
      tions, 257-258
    padding specifiers,
      256-257
    precision specifica-
      tions, 258
    printf() function, 254
    specifiers, 259-260
    type specifiers,
      255-256
  indexing, 262
  length, finding, 262-263
  log formats, 344
  modification functions,
    277-278
  portions, extracting, 264
  portions, replacing, 267

query, session IDs, passing, 340
substrings
finding, 263
position, finding, 263-264
replacing, 268
text, wrapping, 269-271
tokenizing, 264-266
strip tags() function, 267
stripslashes() function, 301, 304, 307
strlen() function, 262-263
strpos() function, 263-264
strstr() function, 263
strtok() function, 264-266
strtolower() function, 269
strtoupper() function, 268
str_replace() function, 268
subexpressions, 73
subscription project
mail, sending, 368-370
subscribe and unsubscribe requests, 362-367
subscribers table, creating, 362
substr() function, 264
SUBSTRING() function, 277
substrings
finding, 263
position, finding, 263-264
replacing, 268
substr_replace() function, 267
subtraction operator (-), 74
support contracts, MySQL, 15

support-files subdirectories, 457
switch statements, 89-91
switches
-DMyModule, 35
rand, 449
symlink (system links), 428
SymLinksIfOwnerMatch parameter, 428
symmetric cryptography, 443
syntax
container directives, 34
error log, 38
<IfDefine> conditional container, 35
<IfModule conditional container, 35
per-directory configuration files, 37
request headers, 435
schemas, 33
ServerAlias directive, 436
syslog daemon, errors, 349-350

T

%T format string option (DATE FORMAT() function), 230
%t formatting directive, 345
tab character (\t), 100
table cache parameter, 458-459
table relationships
many-to-many, 288-289
one-to-many, 287-288
one-to-one, 286

table type variable, 467
tables
address book database table example
date added field, 374
date modified field, 374
menus, creating, 376-377
record addition script, 377-381
records, adding subentries to, 389-394
records, deleting, 387-389
records, selecting and viewing, 382-387
table name fields, 374-376
auth users, 325-326
calendar example, 241-244
columns priv, 17
creating, 160-161
CREATE TABLE command, 135-136
CROSS JOIN command, 147
DELETE command, 152-153
INNER JOIN command, 145
INSERT command, 136-138
JOIN command, 145
LEFT JOIN command, 146-147
LIKE operator, 143
LIMIT command, 140-141

NATURAL JOIN command, 147
REPLACE command, 150-151
RIGHT JOIN command, 147
SELECT command, 138-140, 143-145
STRAIGHT JOIN command, 147
UPDATE command, 148-150
WHERE clause, 141-142
custom logs
code snippet, 354-355
sample reports, 355-357
db, 17
discussion forums, 294-295
FLUSH TABLES command, 461
func, 17
host, 17
OPTIMIZE TABLE command, 459
shopping cart database
table example
cart, adding items to, 414-416
cart, removing items from, 419
cart, viewing, 416-418
checkout actions, performing, 421-422
checkout form, creating, 420-421
field lengths, 410

field names, 410-411
integrating with storefront, 412-414
planning process, 410
SHOW COLUMNS, 464
SHOW CREATE TABLE command, 464
SHOW INDEX command, 465
SHOW OPEN TABLES command, 464
SHOW STATUS command, 467
SHOW TABLE STATUS command, 465-466
SHOW TABLES command, 463
SHOW VARIABLES command, 467
storefront database
table example
add to cart button, 405-408
categories of items, displaying, 402-404
planning process, 398
store categories field, 398-400
store item color field, 398-399, 401
store item size field, 398, 401
store items field, 398-401
tables priv, 17
user, 17

tables priv table, 17
tags
ASP, 56-57
end tags, 61
Script, 56
short, 56-57
short open tag switch, 57
standard, 56
start tags, 61
start/end, 57-58
tagWrap() function, 126-127
tail command-line utility, 353
tar command, 8, 27
tarball, 27
targets, configure script, 28
ternary operator (?), 91-92
test expressions, boolean values, 104
test() function, 115
testing
data types, 68-69
dates, 223
functions, existence, 125-127
PHP installation, 53
text, wrapping, 269-271
TEXT data type, 134
text editors, 40
TEXT field, 14
Thawte, 451
third normal forms, 290, 292
time
calendar example, 237
HTML form, 239-240

library, creating, 244-250

table, creating, 241-244

user input, 238-239

CURRENT TIME() function, 234

CURRENT TIME-STAMP() function, 234

current, retrieving, 218

CURTIME() function, 234

formatting, 220-221

FROM UNIXTIME() function, 235

HH-MM-SS format, 234

HOUR() function, 228-229

information, retrieving, 218

MINUTE() function, 228-229

NOW() function, 234

SEC TO TIME() function, 235

SECOND() function, 228-229

TIME FORMAT() function, 231

TIME TO SEC() function, 235

UNIX TIMESTAMP() function, 234

time data types, 133-134

TIME FORMAT() function, 231

time stamps

converting

date(), 220-221

getdate(), 218

creating, 222

TIME TO SEC() function, 235

time() function, 218, 324

TimeOut directive, 433

TIMESTAMP data type, 134

TINYBLOB data type, 135

TINYINT data type, 132

TINYTEXT data type, 135

TITLE element, 240

TLS (Transport Layer Security). *See* **SSL**

/tmp directory, 337

tokenizing, 264-266

tools

apachectl, 40

command-line, 449

performance, 429

topics

adding, 295

posts to, 305-307

script for, 296-297

defined, 294

displaying posts in, 302-304

topic list, displaying, 298-301

touch() function, 202

tracking

client requests, access log, 37

clients, troubleshooting, 348

TransferLog directive, 348

transmitted data, reducing (performance), 432

Transport Layer Security (TLS). *See* **SSL**

TRIM() function, 274

trimming functions, 274-275

Triple-Des, symmetric cryptography, 443

troubleshooting

bind to port, 42

clients, tracking, 348

denied access, 43

group settings, 43

MySQL installation, 14-15

servers, starting (SSL configurations), 453

Web servers (existing), 42

TYPE argument, 188

type specifiers, 255-256

types. *See* **data types**

typical installation, Apache (Windows), 31

U

U format code (date() function), 221

%U format string option (DATE FORMAT() function), 230

%u formatting directive, 344-345

UCASE() function, 278

ucwords() function, 269

ulimit command, operating systems, 426

uncompressing, source code (Apache installations), 27

underline() function, 126

underscore (_), 66

uninitialized variables, 68

Unix
  Apache
    installing (source), 26
    starting, 41
  apachectl tool, 40
  installing MySQL on, 8-9
  installing PHP on, with Apache, 47-49
  integrating PHP with Apache on, 50
  logresolve utility, 351
  mod ssl module, 448
  OpenSSL library, installing, 447
  rotatelogs programs, 352
  syslog daemon, errors, 349-350
  tail command-line utility, 353
Unix epoch, 218
UNIX TIMESTAMP() function, 234
unlink() function, 202
unsigned data types, 132
unsubscribe requests, 362-367
unzipper, 51
UPDATE command, 20, 148-150, 161
uptime status variable, 467
URLs, directives, 34
USAGE command, 20
User-Agent header, 319
user-created functions, 17

user-defined functions, 110-113
user input
  calendar example, 238-239
  HTML forms
    accessing from multiple SELECT elements, 175-178
    receiving, 174-175
user login form, 326-329
user management, 314-317
user table, 17
usernames
  basic authentication, 312
  storing, user management, 313
users
  adding, 19-20, 317
  deleting, database file-based access control authentication, 317
  lists, Require directive, 314
  management, client authentication, 313
  ownership, verifying, 15
  redirecting (forms), 182
  root
    MySQL running as, 15-16
    non-root users, 15
    running MySQL as, stopping, 22
users files, backend storage, 315

/usr/local/apache2 directory, 29
/usr/local/php/lib directory, 52
/usr/local/src/ directory, 48
/usr/src/ directory, 48
utilities
  gzip, 27
  htpasswd.exe, 315
  logresolve.exe utility, 351
  make, 29
  openssl.exe, 447
  rotatelogs utility, 349
  tail command-line, 353

V

%V format string option (DATE FORMAT() function), 230
%V formatting directive, 345
value directives, 53
values
  functions, returning, 112-113
  port values (Listen directive), 41
VARCHAR data type, 134
VARCHAR field, 14
variables
  $blue, 256
  casting, 71-72
  $count, 243
  data types, 67-72
  $dayArray, 243

declaring, 67
defined, 66-67
$delim, 265
DISTINCT, 227
environment variables
    access control rules,
        319
    conditional looping,
        347
    CustomLog direc-
        tive, 348
$file array, 190
$file dir, 190
$file name, 190
$firstDayArray, 243
$function holder, 114
functions
    accessing, 115-118
    scope, 114-115
global
    defined, 172
    $GLOBALS array,
        looping through,
        172
    superglobals, 172-
        173
global file upload, 188
$green, 256
integers,
    incrementing/decre-
        menting, 75-76
$membership, 263
$name, 246
names of, selection con-
    siderations, 66
$newnum, 109
$red, 256
session, 335-339
$start, 243
$tst, 112
uninitialized, 68
$word, 265

values
    given to, overview,
        66
    remembering
        between calls,
        118-120
    when to use, 66
$word, 265
    given to, overview,
        66
VeriSign, 451
version type variable, 467
viewing
    directory contents,
        212-213
    spaces, HTML docu-
        ments, 257
virtual hosting
    DNS (domain name
        server), 434
    DocumentRoot, 435
    IP-based, 434
    mass virtual hosting,
        437
    name-based, 435-437
virtual servers, specify-
    ing, 34
VirtualDocumentRoot
    directive (mass virtual
    hosting), 437
VirtualDocumentRootIP
    directive (mass virtual
    hosting), 438
VirtualHost containers,
    434
VirtualScriptAlias direc-
    tive (mass virtual host-
    ing), 438
VirtualScriptAliasIP
    directive (mass virtual
    hosting), 438

W

%w format string option
    (DATE FORMAT()
    function), 230
w (write) mode, 203
warn, LogLevel directive
    option, 350
Web crawlers, abuse,
    preventing, 433
Web servers
    Apache, installing
        (Windows), 29
    existing, troubleshoot-
        ing, 42
Web sites
    AbriaSoft, 8
    Apache, 27
    awstats, 353
    Logscan, 353
    MySQL, 8
    MySQL-Pro 4.o down-
        load page, 9
    NuSphere Corporation,
        8
    OpenSSL, 447
    performance tools, 429
    PHP, 48, 51, 54
    PHP Manual, 158, 167,
        245
    ScanErrLog, 353
    Webalizer, 353
Web spiders, abuse, pre-
    venting, 433
Webalizer, 353
WEEKDAY() function,
    223-224
WHERE clause, 141-142,
    226, 362
while statements, 77,
    92-93
whitespace, 53, 266

width, of fields, specify-ing, 257-258

wildcards, 20

Windows

Apache

controlling (com-mands), 39

starting, 41

errors, logging, 349

installing Apache on, 29-32

installing MySQL on, 9-12

installing PHP on, 51

integrating PHP with Apache on, 51-52

logresolve.exe utility, 351

mod ssl module, 448

OpenSSL library, installing, 447

rotatelogs.exe pro-grams, 352

winmysqladmin.exe application, 12

$word variable, 265

wordwrap() function, 270

wrapping text, 269-271

write (w) mode, 203

writing to files, 208-209

WS-FTP for Windows, 56

X-Y-Z

X.509, digital certificates, 446

%x format string option (DATE FORMAT() function), 230

%X formatting directive, 345

X type specifier, 255

xor operator, 78

Y format code (date() function), 221

%Y format string option (DATE FORMAT() function), 230

%y formatting directive, 345

YEAR data type, 134

year select() function, 249

YEAR() function, 227

years

DAYOFYEAR() func-tion, 224

YEAR() function, 227

YYYY-MM-DD date for-mat, 234

z format code (date() function), 221

zip file, 9

What's on the CD-ROM?

The book's companion CD-ROM contains a complete PHP, MySQL and Apache starter kit for both the Windows and Linux/Unix platforms—including full versions of PHP, MySQL, and Apache, plus files containing most of the code listings in the book.

Windows Installation Instructions

If you have not already done so, insert the CD-ROM in your CD drive. Double-click the CD drive's icon to access the CD-ROM.

The files for MySQL and PHP need to be extracted to your hard drive before you can install them. If you do not have an unarchiving program, you can install a shareware version of WinZip from the CD-ROM. The extraction instructions assume you will be using WinZip, but you may use any unarchiving program that reads the Zip file format.

> If you are using Windows XP, you can double-click the Zip file. Windows XP includes an extraction wizard to facilitate unzipping files.

Apache

Double-click the Apache folder and then double-click the binary folder.

To install Apache, simply double-click the apache_2.0.43-win32-x86-no_ssl.exe file. Follow the Apache for Windows installation instructions starting on Page 30 to finish installing and configuring Apache.

MySQL

Double-click the MySQL folder and then double-click the binary folder.

Double-click the mysql-4.0.4-beta-win.zip file. Extract the contents of the Zip file to your hard drive by clicking the Extract button on the WinZip interface. Navigate to your hard drive with WinZip's interface and create a new folder (such as MySQL Install). Select this folder (if it's not already selected) and click on the Extract button.

Once extracted, navigate to the install directory and double-click Setup.exe. Follow the MySQL for Windows installation instructions starting on Page 10 to finish installing and configuring MySQL.

PHP

Double-click the PHP folder and then double-click the binary folder.

Double-click on the php-4.2.3-Win32.zip file. Extract the contents of the Zip file to your hard drive by clicking on the Extract button on the WinZip interface. Navigate to your hard drive with WinZip's interface and create a new folder (such as PHP). Select this folder (if it's not already selected) and click the Extract button.

Follow the PHP for Windows installation instructions starting on Page 50 to finish installing and configuring PHP.

Linux/Unix

These installation instructions assume that you have a passing familiarity with Unix shell commands and the basic setup of your machine. As Unix has many flavors, only generic commands are used. If you have any problems with the commands, please consult the appropriate manual page or your system administrator.

Insert the disc into your CD-ROM drive.

If you have a volume manager, mounting of the CD-ROM will be automatic. If you don't have a volume manager, you can mount the CD-ROM by typing

```
mount -tiso9660 /dev/cdrom /mnt/cdrom
```

/mnt/cdrom is just a mount point, but it must exist when you issue the mount command. You may also use any empty directory for a mount point if you don't want to use /mnt/cdrom. The installation instructions will assume that you mounted the CD-ROM at /mnt/cdrom, so adjust the instructions accordingly if you choose another mount point.

Apache

The source code for Apache is included on the CD-ROM in the Apache/UNIX/ directory. To install the version of Apache included on the CD-ROM, you will need to extract the contents of the source code file onto your hard drive. The author recommends placing the source code for Apache in the /usr/src or /usr/local/src directory.

Change to the /usr/src or /usr/local/src directory by entering

```
cd /usr/src
```

or

```
cd /usr/local/src
```

Once there, enter

```
tar -zxvf /mnt/cdrom/Apache/UNIX/httpd-2.0.43.tar.gz
```

The rest of the installation and configuration of Apache is found on Page 27.

MySQL

MySQL for Linux is included on the CD-ROM in the MySQL/UNIX/binary directory. To install the version of MySQL that is included on the CD-ROM, substitute the command on Page 9 that looks like

```
gunzip < /path/to/mysql-VERSION-OS.tar.gz | tar xvf -
```

with

```
gunzip < /mnt/cdrom/MySQL/UNIX/binary/mysql-4.0.4-beta-pc-linux-gnu-i686.tar.gz
| tar xvf -
```

PHP

The source code for PHP is included on the CD-ROM in the PHP/UNIX/ directory. To install the version of PHP included on the CD-ROM, you will need to extract the contents of the source code file onto your hard drive. The author recommends placing the source code for Apache in the /usr/src or /usr/local/src directory.

Change to the /usr/src or /usr/local/src directory by entering

```
cd /usr/src
```

or

```
cd /usr/local/src
```

Once there, enter

```
tar -zxvf /mnt/cdrom/PHP/UNIX/php-4.2.3.tar.gz
```

The rest of the installation and configuration of PHP is found on Page 48.

24

Other Related Titles

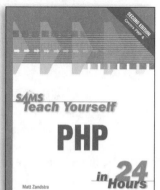

Sams Teach Yourself PHP in 24 Hours, Second Edition
Matt Zandstra
ISBN: 0-672-32311-7
$24.99 US/$38.99 CAN

Sams Teach Yourself MySQL in 21 Days, Second Edition
Anthony Butcher
ISBN: 0-672-32392-3
$39.99 US/$59.95 CAN

Sams Teach Yourself Shell Programming in 24 Hours
Sriranga Veeraraghavan
ISBN: 0-672-32358-3
$24.99 US/$38.99 CAN

PHP and MySQL Web Development
Luke Welling and Laura Thomson
ISBN: 0-672-31784-2
$49.99 US/$74.95 CAN

PHP Developer's Cookbook
Sterling Hughes and Andrei Zmievski
ISBN: 0-672-32325-7
$39.99 US/$59.95 CAN

Sams Teach Yourself Unix in 24 Hours, Third Edition
Dave Taylor
ISBN: 0-672-32127-0
$24.99 US/$38.99 CAN

SAMS
www.samspublishing.com

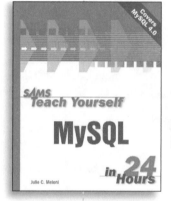

Sams Teach Yourself MySQL in 24 Hours
Julie Meloni
ISBN: 0-672-32349-4
$24.99 US/$38.99 CAN

Sams Teach Yourself Apache 2 in 24 Hours
Daniel Lopez
ISBN: 0-672-32355-9
$24.99 US/$38.99 CAN

All prices are subject to change.